Karl Dieterich Pfisterer

The Prism of Scripture:
Studies on history and historicity
in the work of Jonathan Edwards

ANGLO-AMERICAN FORUM

Herausgegeben von Professor Dr. Christoph Gutknecht

Bd./Vol. 1

Karl Dieterich Pfisterer

The Prism of Scripture:
Studies on history and historicity
in the work of Jonathan Edwards

Herbert Lang Bern
Peter Lang Frankfurt/M.
1975

Karl Dieterich Pfisterer

The Prism of Scripture:
Studies on history and historicity
in the work of Jonathan Edwards

MIDDLEBURY COLLEGE LIBRARY

Herbert Lang Bern
Peter Lang Frankfurt/M.
1975

BR
115
H5
P46

7/1979
Rel.

ISBN 3 261 00965 9

Peter Lang GmbH, Frankfurt/M. (BRD)
Herbert Lang & Cie AG, Bern (Schweiz)
1975. Alle Rechte vorbehalten.

Nachdruck oder Vervielfältigung, auch auszugsweise, in allen Formen
wie Mikrofilm, Xerographie, Mikrofiche, Mikrocard, Offset verboten.

Druck: fotokop wilhelm weihert KG, Darmstadt

MEINEN ELTERN

ZUM DANK und ZUM DENKEN

ACKNOWLEDGMENTS

At the end of any major research project, the number of people who deserve special thanks and mention is huge. I wish I could include all my friends, colleagues, teachers, library workers, research librarians, etc., who have contributed to this work.

My most special thanks must go to Dr. Robert T. Handy. He has not only supervised and directed this dissertation, but has guided my studies throughout the doctoral program. The insights which he has given me in my area of specialization and in American Studies as a whole have been invaluable. In addition, he has taken a personal interest in me that goes far beyond his duties as a teacher. He has been an advisor, a friend, and a spiritual guide. I have also been very fortunate to meet Dr. Glenn T. Miller, whose unfailing friendship has contributed in many formal and informal ways to my initiation into American culture and civilization.

I would like to thank Dr. Hans Joachim Lang of the University of Erlangen, West Germany. He has taken a continual interest in my academic development and has given me the benefit of his abilities and knowledge. In addition, he has encouraged my studies in the United States at a crucial point from the beginning.

Dr. Sacvan Bercovitch has been unusually generous in both his time and effort. My conversations with him have given me direction and substance. Dr. Joseph L. Blau has provided both administrative and scholarly help.

The Union Theological Seminary Library and its director, Professor Robert Beach, have proven invaluable. The Union Collection, with its resources in English and American Puritanism, is one of the finest in the world. The staff are a delight to work with and have an excellent grasp of the needs of a professional scholar. They have been more than tolerant of my personal idiosyncrasies and forgetfulness.

Dr. and Mrs. Roger Shinn have aided this project in more ways than they know. They have provided me with an atmosphere conducive to study and at the same time friendly and warm. My uncle and my aunt, Mr. and Mrs. Schnaufer, have contributed not only to this dissertation, but to my entire stay in New York. They have been more than willing to give generously to my support.

Only another unskilled typist can appreciate the debt which I owe to Mrs. Peggy Danley who translated my hieroglyphics into a clear first draft. Miss Gladys Burkhart, my academic typist, has put the whole into final form. Her work has been fast and, even more important, accurate.

Research, unfortunately, is expensive. The very generous grant of the Friedrich-Ebert-Foundation, Bonn, West Germany, has made possible the work on this dissertation.

Last, but by no means least I want to thank Dr. Christoph Gutknecht of the University of Hamburg whose courageous openmindedness and competent judgment have made it possible for this foreign language dissertation to be published with a Swiss publisher.

Of course, any problems in the dissertation are mine alone.

Erlangen, 1975   Karl Dieterich Pfisterer

TABLE OF CONTENTS

Chapter   Page

    INTRODUCTION   1

I   FRANCIS BACON'S CLASSIFICATION OF HISTORY: THE POINT OF
    VIEW OF FRANCIS BACON   19

    History: Fact and Fiction   22

       History as Fact   23
       Facts and the Forms of History Writing   25

    Form and Frame: History and Interpretation   30

       Alternate Contexts of Providence and Prophecy   35
       History and Interpretation: The History of Providence   37
       History and Interpretation: The History of Prophecy .   39

    Summary   49

II   HISTORIANS AND THE HISTORIOGRAPHY OF NEW ENGLAND   51

    William Hubbard: A General History of New England . . .   56
    Edward Johnson: Wonder Working Providence of
      Sions Savior   67
    Review of Scholarship   77
    Summary   85

III EXEGESIS AND HISTORY: THOMAS SHEPARD   87

    The Scope of History and the Differentiation of
      Ecclesiology and Eschatology   98
    The Sixfold Coming and the Double Coming of Christ . . . 104
    Summary 118

IV   SCRIPTURE AND HISTORY 121

    Chronology 124
    Coherence 132
    Exegesis 147
    Summary 163

V   SCRIPTURE AND REVIVAL: JONATHAN EDWARDS' DEFENSE OF
        HISTORY 165

        Virtue and History: Prejudice, Pride, Prudence 165
        Facts, Observations, and Experience 176
        Observation, Observance, and the Rules of Scripture . . . 197
        Summary 222

VI   SCRIPTURE AND METAPHYSICS: THE EMERGENCE OF A HISTORICAL
        SYSTEM 225

        Principles and Forms of Systematic Theology 225
        The Place of Doctrine 238
        The View of the End 251
        End and Exegesis 263
        End and Trend 280
        Communication 293
        Summary and Conclusions 307

VII   SCRIPTURE AND NATURE: THE EXAMPLE OF SHAFTESBURY 318

        Church History 321
        Scripture 327

            Style 329
            Miracles 338

            Summary 362

        BIBLIOGRAPHY 365

        ABSTRACT 379

INTRODUCTION

The following study is an attempt to explicate Jonathan Edwards'
view of history and to point to some of its implications. In his reply to
the invitation to become the next president of the College of New Jersey
at Princeton, Edwards told the trustees about his previous publications
and future projects. He also provided details for two of these projects,
one of which was devoted to a programmatic statement on history.[1] This
program thus far has elicited quite diverse responses by scholars, but it
has not yet been studied as a subject in its own right. A consideration
of his project and reactions to it will serve as a means to introduce the
subject of this inquiry.

In this letter, between allusions to his past achievements and his
ongoing concerns in polemical divinity[2] and the delineation of his exegetical program, Edwards in somewhat elliptical language spelled out the idea
for a systematic theology in the form of a history. Because of the claims

---

[1]Samuel Hopkins, "Memoirs of the Life, Experience and Character of
The Late Rev. Jonathan Edwards," in The Works of President Edwards (Rpt.
New York: Burt Franklin, 1968), I, p. 80 -- Volumes I-VIII and Volumes
IX-X for this reprint were taken from the London edition of 1817 and the
Edinburgh Edition of 1847 respectively. Subsequent references to Edwards'
writings will be based on this edition and will appear in the footnotes
abbreviated as "Edwards, Works." The exceptions to this rule are those
cases where Edwards' writings are available in the modern critical editions
of The Works of Jonathan Edwards, ed. John E. Smith (New Haven: Yale
University Press, 1957ff.). Individual volumes of this edition will in
the following be identified separately by title and editor.

[2]Edwards, Works, I, p. 80.

he made for this plan and because of its importance as a point of departure

for this investigation, I shall quote his proposal in its entirety:

> I have had on my mind and heart (which I long ago began, not with
> any view to publication), a great work which I call a History of the
> Work of Redemption, a body of divinity in an entire new method, being
> thrown into the form of a history; considering the affair of Christian
> theology, as the whole of it, in each part, stands in reference to the
> great work of redemption by Jesus Christ; which I suppose to be, of
> all others, the grand design of God, and the summum and ultimum of all
> the divine operations and decrees, particularly considering all parts
> of the grand scheme in their historical order. -- The order of their
> existence, or their being brought forth to view, in the course of
> divine dispensations, or the wonderful series of successive acts and
> events, beginning from eternity, and descending from thence to the
> great work and successive dispensations of the infinitely wise God, in
> time, considering the chief events coming to pass in the church of God,
> and revolutions in the world of mankind, affecting the state of the
> church and the affair of redemption, which we have an account of in
> history or prophecy; till at last, we come to the general resurrection,
> last judgment and consummation of all things; when it shall be said,
> It is done. I am Alpha and Omega, the Beginning and the End. -- Con-
> cluding my work, with the consideration of that perfect state of
> things, which shall be finally settled to last for eternity. -- This
> history will be carried on with regard to all three worlds, heaven,
> earth and hell, considering the connected, successive events and
> alterations in each, so far as the scriptures give any light; intro-
> ducing all parts of divinity in that order which is most scriptural
> and most natural; a method which appears to me the most beautiful and
> entertaining. Wherein every doctrine will appear to the greatest
> advantage, in the brightest light, in the most striking manner, shew-
> ing the admirable contexture and harmony of the whole.[1]

Edwards set out to consider the "affair of Christian theology" as a

whole and in its parts. The meaning of this intention will become clearer

as we attend to the whole and the parts of the statement in which he set

forth his intention and program. Edwards' thesis was that the work of

redemption is the referent of all theological statements. The work of

redemption was consequently more than the individual experience of conver-

sion. Insofar as conversion or religious experience became a subject of

theological meditation and reflection, it was one of those parts which must

---

[1] Edwards, Works, I, p. 80.

be referred to the work of redemption as a whole. This work of redemption was, according to Edwards, of all divine works the greatest work, design, or scheme. In it decrees as well as operations found their highest and ultimate end. The greatness and its union of decrees and operations became clearer when they were considered in "historical order." In other words, there was an affinity between the work of redemption and a "historical order" or "a history."

To students of chemistry it is well known that the best and optimal display of a combination often depends largely on whether the right solution can be found in which to exhibit it. Some solutions are better than others, some solutions do not work at all, and just one solution might provide the optimum of intelligibility and applicability in making transparent and useful the whole of its parts, aspects, and relations. When Edwards therefore maintained that the work of redemption was the center and the circumference of Christian theology and when he furthermore saw an affinity between the work of redemption and "historical order," then he said in effect that of all possible forms of systematic Christian theology a "historical order" was the best as a means of exhibiting the center, circumference, and connection of the work of redemption.

In the case of each part of Christian theology this "historical order" was to describe the order of existence of things as well as of the origin of things and at the same time this "historical order" was to describe the order of existence and origin within the course of divine dispensations as well as within the series of acts and events. The "historical order" therefore included being and act in the course of periods and events.

This historical order commenced with eternity, descended into time, and included the series of events that took place in the church and in man kind. It showed how the church was affected through the events with regar to redemption. The "historical order" finally ended with the judgment and concluded with a particular consideration of the perfect state of those things which will last for eternity. The source for this "historical orde was given in the account of both history and prophecy. It is important to point out that in this program the description of eternity came at the end rather than at the beginning. It was a goal rather than a speculation on origins. It was not so much a speculation about the logos as a vision of the end in accordance with Scripture. Moreover the goal of the "historica: order" was by no means the "general judgment" but something even beyond it This point bears emphasizing because the conjunction of judgment and elec- tion has focused interest and offense so much on the former that the end o the judgment is usually not seen in its positive side.

After Edwards had thus stated his thesis of "a history" or "histor- ical order" and after he had sketched the basic elements and the scope of it, he then touched upon the manner in which this history was to be carriec out and what use it will have. At this point he actually introduced three histories, each of which was a connected whole and which took place in the three-story universe of heaven, earth, and hell. Within the context of these histories the individual parts of theology or doctrines were to be elaborated. Both the elaboration of the histories and of the doctrines mus follow the order of Scripture in order to stay within what was natural. If Christian theology followed the path of this "historical order" then it wil not only bring beauty and joy to its task for Edwards, but it will generall make all parts of theology intellectually and affectively convincing and show the structure as well as the harmony of the whole work of redemption.

The "historical order" as the new method had thus several aspects. It was first introduced in doctrinal and speculative language. Then the movement of this "historical order" was delineated, its implementation (within what we would call a mythological universe) was described, and the resultant constructive effect of this historical order for theology was spelled out. Throughout these programmatic statements the relation of this "historical order" to Scripture was repeatedly stressed. Thus this "historical order" was based on history as well as on prophecy. But it was not just a simple repetition of Scripture which here was presented in terms of its main elements of history and prophecy.

In the implementation of the historical order it was pointed out that the elaboration of the parts of heaven, earth, and hell must follow the Scriptural order. An essay, therefore, which sets out to investigate the view of history in Edwards must do so by coming to terms with the tendency on his part to conceptualize a comprehensive historical order in close interdependence with his view and exegesis of the Scriptures. The focus on the conceptualization of history will mean that a collection of data on the extent and variety of Edwards' historical learning will receive attention only insofar as it bears on the illumination of his view of history.[1]

---

[1] In his book on The Loss of Mastery, Puritan Historians in Colonial America (1966; ppb. New York: Vintage Books, 1968), p. 155), Peter Gay mentioned a letter to him by Thomas Schafer in which Schafer suggested that a further study of Edwards' historical notebooks would repay close attention. Such an investigation would, however, at this point extend the limits set for our interpretation on Edwards' view of history.

In his programmatic statement Edwards also referred to an unpublished work on the subject which was then published posthumously under the
title History of the Work of Redemption. In his statement he said that he
had this great work on his heart and mind for a long time and thus we find
indications of his thinking about it in miscellaneous observations on
Scripture and philosophy and in treatises and sermons throughout the corpus
of his works. Each of these sources raises problems of method with which
an interpretation must deal. The observations, for example, contained
notes on the Chinese,[1] extensive thoughts on Islam,[2] and on heaven.[3]
According to the programmatic statement, the two first items belonged to
the history of the earth and mankind, the latter kind of notes belonged in
the history of heaven. Neither of these items was included in the posthumous publication of the History of the Work of Redemption. From this we
can see that the programmatic statement remained an outline, that the first
sustained attempt towards this history was an unfinished draft of the history of the earth, that the observations were thoughts without a context
and thus easily subject to arbitrary manipulations, and, finally, that the
thoughts on history which occurred in treatises and sermons appear already
built into an interpretative context where they must be found and assessed
as to their function within that context and as to their significance for
the subject of this investigation. We shall therefore use examples from
all these sources without a claim to completeness. Those thoughts that
occurred in key passages within a context were the most valuable as well

---

[1] Edwards, Works, VIII, p. 142.

[2] Ibid., pp. 236-241.

[3] Edwards, Works, X, p. 320ff.

as the most difficult for the interpreter, because, as it were, they also appeared within a story that showed them to best advantage.

The reaction of scholars to Edwards' program has been diverse. In both negative and positive ways, these appraisals are indicative of their own situations and positions, as brought to light by encounters with Edwards' draft of the History of the Work of Redemption. These attitudes are thus not based on detailed and sustained examinations of Edwards' view of history, but, rather, are personal responses, ranging from expressions of critical rejection, thoughts of sober self-criticism and hopes for a modern emulation, to panegyrical acceptance. In this way they represent first of all a random cross-section of opinion on the history and state of historiography in the United States.

In his essay on A Loss of Mastery, Puritan Historians in Colonial America, Peter Gay characterized Jonathan Edwards as a tragic genius who, however honest he was in his undertaking, wasted the powers of a superb mind upon an outmoded Augustinian view of history. Gay's own concept of history was predicated on the dichotomy of the mythic and the critical with its complementary separation of the sacred and the secular sphere. The sacred may range from the superstitious to the "sublimated," but it stays within the mythic sphere throughout and can not become the subject of historical inquiry other than by dissolving it.[1] Gay therefore ruled out a limine the desirability of any sustained investigation into Edwards' view of history, since on the basis of the existing draft he was led to doubt that any secular history, which alone would justify such research, could be produced.[2] Gay's observation on the mythic quality of Edwards'

---

[1] Edwards, Works, X, p. 121.

[2] Ibid., p. 155.

history was helpful, though, for it pointed up the difficulties for the historian who must learn a different language before he can interpret the thought contained in this language. Gay eschewed such a learning process and thus his interpretation of Jonathan Edwards remained an unsuccessful foray into an uncongenial territory.

Perry Miller called the draft of the History of the Work of Redemption a "pioneer work in American historiography,"[1] even though he was fully aware of the "peculiar mythology in which Edwards embodied his narratives."[2] As a historian of literature he looked at mythology differently from the way in which historians of western culture perceived it. Miller saw in historians not only the critics of a mythological tradition, but he also recognized them as mythmakers in their own right. Thus a historian could criticize mythology, replace it by a myth of his own and in this way miss the particular story that was intended in such a traditional mythology. Miller found such mythmakers particularly in the movement of the "new history."[3] Their reaction against a mere collection of facts in favor of the interpretation of facts was accomplished by an "arranging of the facts so as to interest the modern mind." If, according to Miller, Jonathan Edwards' own interest had consisted primarily in interpreting history in the light of contemporary interest in the Old Testament, then his view of history would have become dated as quickly as those schemes of the "new historians" who interpret history in terms of economics, class warfare, or the frontier. Miller, therefore, with the aid of Jonathan

---

[1]Perry Miller, Jonathan Edwards (Cleveland: Meridian Books, 1965), p. 311.

[2]Ibid., p. 315.   [3]Ibid., p. 410.

Edwards criticized a presentist critical history like that of Peter Gay.
Miller pointed away from the imaginary and ideological side to the imaginative aspect in mythology and thereby discovered the "real significance" in
the narrative of the History of the Work of Redemption: Edwards was concerned with the unity of history. Neither in his own method of interpreting Edwards nor in his characterization of Edwards' view of history did
Miller follow up on this insight. Miller treated Edwards' view of history
towards the end of his book and therefore this special pleading for the
"real significance" of Edwards' uncompleted draft sounded like another
turn in his overall argument to establish a cryptogram in Edwards' thought.
For the major part of his monograph he had argued that the "real" Edwards
was an empiricist and now he went on to demonstrate that Edwards was a
philosopher of history and not a biblicistic fundamentalist. If Miller
had taken seriously this historical cryptogram and the unity of history it
expressed, then he would have had to ask himself also whether in the light
of this unity of history his empiricist cryptogram for Edwards was adequate
and whether his description of Edwards' view of history as a "cosmic rationalization of the revival" was not at least guilty of loose language when
held against such a view of the unity of history. Or is the unity of history just a rationalization? For Edwards, the subject of his draft of the
History of the Work of Redemption was not only to account for what had happened but also to search out the new dimension of reality that had been
added to man's experience in religion. In the end, Miller has the perceptive insight, but remains a "new historian" himself: he makes over Edwards
in the image of the empiricist and has Edwards make over history in the
image of the revival.

Metaphysically speaking, the modern interpreter may think that the unity

of history is an impossibility, but the description and analysis of this

premise within Edwards' work is not part of such an impossibility. On the

contrary, such an approach is a way to find out about Edwards' identity as

a thinker, and a means to guard against half-truths about the

characteristics of his thought.

In his preface to the Kingdom of God in America, H. Richard Niebuhr

went several steps further toward a positive evaluation of Edwards' view

of history.[1] He expressed the hope that his account of the kingdom of God

might serve even "as a stepping-stone" to the work of some American

Augustine or Jonathan Edwards redivivus who would bring the History of the

Work of Redemption down to the present. The debt[2] to Edwards which Niebuhr

here acknowledged had to do with the dilemma he had incurred in his earlier

book on The Social Sources of Denominationalism.[3] Here Niebuhr described

both historically and sociologically the progressive disintegration of the

medieval ideal of the Corpus Christianum. At the conclusion of this inves-

tigation he met with an impasse. On the one hand all religious movements

toward a renewed integration of this ideal had become repressive as soon as

they had succeeded and, moreover, by the time of the establishment of

Methodism in England the Christian and religious resources for such move-

ments of integration had been depleted. On the other hand, Marxism as a

---

[1]H. Richard Niebuhr, The Kingdom of God in America (1937; ppb. New York: Harper, 1959), p. xvi.

[2]The phrase "apart from God the whole thing is meaningless and might as well not have been" (p. xvi) is strongly reminiscent of the famous state- ment on the "beauty of holiness" in Religious Affections, John E. Smith, Ed. (New Haven: Yale University Press, 1959), p. 274.

[3]1929; ppb. Cleveland: Maridian Books, 1957.

secular replacement began to emerge as the only viable possibility for the reconstitution of unity. What led Niebuhr out of this impasse was the discovery of the United States themselves as the third way.

Whereas in the Social Sources of Denominationalism he had applied a European philosophy of history to the comprehension of an indigenous American history, he now recognized and articulated in the Kingdom of God in America the identity of American history in its own independent and creative descent as well as in its own effective and dynamic, if not flawless, realization of the ideal of the Corpus Christianum. Jonathan Edwards' History of the Work of Redemption provided vision and unity for this ideal, which Niebuhr found as being fulfilled in the course of American history, well beyond the above mentioned European point of exhaustion. Even so, the hoped for Edwards redivivus has not yet appeared, but the frank admission on Niebuhr's part that he was engaged in this book in doing theology in the form of history shows how intimate an influence Edwards could become, but still we learn next to nothing about the ingredients of Edwards view of history.

Niebuhr's attitude might also raise some doubts as to his reliability as a historian. Miller had only pointed to the pioneering character of Edwards' work for the question of the unity of history. Niebuhr actually applied this vision of unity to the course and corpus of American history in a theological way. What remained an abstract historiographical question in Miller became a concrete story in Niebuhr. It is therefore all the more imperative that we find out from Edwards himself what this source of inspiration and provocation in his view of history actually consisted of.[1]

---

[1] That this ideal of The Corpus Christianum in its American form is not simply a figment of imagination in theologically-minded historians or in literary historians addicted to the history of the mind has been shown

12

    In an essay on the subject of history it is especially appropriate
to take into account the professional context in which such an inquiry
proceeds. It is also necessary to make explicit those cultural presuppositions which can facilitate as well as obstruct the analysis or which can
at least represent difficulties that are not easily overcome because they
have been confirmed by socialization and internationalization within a
tradition.

    The professional community of historians whose speciality is the
study of American history has witnessed in recent years an increasing concern with its own principles of inquiry and has produced a still growing
body of historiographical literature. One of the reasons for this development has certainly to do with the natural desire to keep track of and to
account for all the changes in an expanding field of research and to assimi-
late the consequences of closer interdisciplinary communication and cooperation. There is, however, also a question as to the purpose and goal of
American history itself. A good example for this aspect of the historiographical inquiry is an article by historian John Higham which was published in 1970[1] and in which he presented some "anxious afterthoughts"[2] to
his own authoritative survey of the history of American historiography which

---

in Puritan plain style as it were by R. T. Handy in his book on A Christian
America, Protestant Hopes and Historical Realities (New York: Oxford
University Press, 1971), where he traced the ecclesiastical, institutional,
and social dimensions, depths, developments as well as deviations of
"Protestant hopes and historical realities" of this Edwardsean and Niebuhrian
vision of the unity of history.

    [1]John Higham, "American Historiogrphy in the 1960's" in John Higham,
Writing American History, Essays on Modern Scholarship (Bloomington:
Indiana University Press, 1970), pp. 157-174.

    [2]Ibid., p. 158.

had been published in 1965.[1] While the historical survey had made pro-

jections for the decade of the sixties, the article now wanted to evaluate

these projections post eventum. His three projections for institutional

history, comparative studies, and moral criticism had been "consistently

and indeed determinedly cheerful"[2] and had anticipated obstacles mainly in

the area of the "conceptual." The big surprise, however, came when he

found that despite the advent of radical history "moral criticism founders

while institutional and comparative studies gather momentum."[3] Higham was

puzzled why "so few of today's professional historians operate with little

distinction in this third dimension."[4] He explored as possible explana-

tions the demise of intellectual history and biography and he paralleled

the situation to that in analytic philosophy[5] and asked whether both enter-

prises do not relieve the students of the "burden of a more or less compre-

hensive view" because too many scholars find such a burden too heavy to

bear. Higham himself finds as the cause for this moral silence the erosion

of purpose; since "a general framework for understanding American history

has collapsed . . . we have today no unifying theme which assigns a direc-

tion to American history."[6] Higham has no specific suggestions to make but

he describes the task for the future in the following terms:

---

[1]John Higham, et al., History, The Development of Historical Studies in the United States (Englewood Cliffs, N. J.: Prentice-Hall, Inc., 1965), pp. 1-232.

[2]Higham, Writing American History, p. 158.

[3]Ibid., p. 168.   [4]Ibid., p. 169.

[5]For an assessment of this question from a philosopher's point of view see also Haskell Fain, Between Philosophy and History: The Resurrection of Speculative Philosophy of History Within the Analytic Tradition (Princeton: Princeton University Press, 1970), p. 215ff.

[6]Higham, op. cit., p. 173.

> To order our historical knowledge in the years ahead we have to depend increasingly on a wider view of the nature and destiny of modern society. That some general scheme of historical meaning will emerge from the present confusion can scarcely be doubted; however, we may also be confident that an effective scheme will transcend the limits of a scientific hypothesis. It will partake as well of myth and ideology.[1]

Higham's appraisal of the state of scholarship in American history in the

sixties thus arrived at a concern with the foundations rather than the

forms of history. Without "a goal for the future and a synthesizing per-

spective on the past . . . a fully human life is impossible."[2] In order

to find both synthesis and goal he suggested an adventure in myth and idea,

in the area of the artistic and the moral. While some of the questions

that Higham raised will also occur in Edwards' own concern about history,

yet this affinity is not the argument of the subsequent essay. It was

only introduced here in order to show that our investigation may indeed

proceed in a sympathetic and responsive professional environment.

One final consideration of these introductory remarks concerns the

particular difficulty which implicit cultural assumptions put in the way

of an essay on Edwards' view of history. We see an indication of this

aspect in an American historian of the nineteenth century whose response

to and acceptance of the History of the Work of Redemption was as positive

as it was elusive. According to George Bancroft, Jonathan Edwards, Sr.,

---

[1] Higham, Writing American History, pp. 173-174. Higham uses "ideology" in a positive sense as a body of ideas that informs man's moral behavior. This must be pointed out in order to avoid confusion with my earlier negative use of ideology as a body of ideas which consciously or unconsciously misinform man's moral behavior.

[2] Ibid., p. 174.

was the first thinker who in ways "still cramped and perverted by theological forms not derived from observation" articulated "the history of the
influence of all moral truth in the regeneration of humanity."[1] Bancroft
also reserved a distinguished place for Edwards in the group of forerunners
to a philosophy of history of the nineteenth century. In many pervasive
and subtle ways such a view of the nineteenth century and its distinctive
achievements in the philosophy of history persisted even where its viability
has been questioned. In his book, The Idea of History,[2] R. G. Collingwood
gave an epitome of the course of western civilization which summed up quite
well the way in which many scholars as part of this civilization conceive
it. According to Collingwood, Greek philosophy in the sixth century before
Christ discussed knowledge in terms of mathematics; in the middle ages the
central problems of thought arose out of theology. From the sixteenth
through the nineteenth centuries the main effort of thought was concerned
with laying the foundations of natural science. Sometime in the eighteenth
century history began to emerge as a special form of knowledge which was
quite unlike either mathematics, theology, or science. Approximately at
the beginning of the nineteenth century attempts were made to establish a
theory of knowledge that would also include history. Collingwood pointed
out that all along men were also thinking historically, but it was a
simple historical thought that created no problems and which was never
forced into self-reflection. Just as Gay reserved critical history as the

---

[1]George Bancroft, History of the United States from the Discovery,
III (Boston: Charles C. Little, 1842), p. 399.

[2]R. G. Collingwood, The Idea of History (Oxford: Clarendon Press,
1946), pp. 4-5.

achievement of the European Enlightenment of the eighteenth century, so
Collingwood placed the philosophy of history in the nineteenth century.
It is not our task to assess the extent of the adequacy of these generalizations. What becomes clear, however, is that if we look at Jonathan
Edwards from the former point of view he becomes an antique survival that
showed the tenacity of outdated beliefs. If we look at him from the latter
point of view, he might belong either among the simple historical thinkers
or be a forerunner of the nineteenth century. But neither approach provides
help in undertaking an investigation into Edwards' view of history.

The following dissertation will explore Edwards' understanding of
history as a subject in its own right. In a series of studies we shall
describe the background of this understanding of history, demonstrate and
define the thesis of the argument for this dissertation, and move from there
to a proof of the thesis. In conclusion we shall demonstrate the importance
of the thesis e contrario through the explication of an argument in which
it plays only a minor role.

Chapter I will, through an interpretation of Francis Bacon, delineate
the wide spectrum of historiographical possibilities which were available in
the general climate of the seventeenth century. Chapter II will then narrow down the focus of this survey to a description of New England as Edwards
most immediate background and to the presentation of illustrative case
studies of the Massachusetts historians William Hubbard and Edward Johnson.
In Bacon's classification of the variety of historical facts and the ways of
their interpretation, Scripture appears as one historiographical mode and
is defined in terms of a concept of prophecy which is said to pay attention
to the unity of history as well as to those unique exegetical details which
are necessary facts for the shaping of such a view of unity. Hubbard and

Johnson as practicing historians help to exemplify the polyhistoric, providential, and prophetic trends of the historiography of the time. We shall see that in Johnson the providential interpretation of history receives a consistent prophetic orientation which makes possible a better appreciation of the shades and subtleties of providence itself and which leads us to a formulation and pursuit of this comprehensive historiographical tradition in terms of the interpretative thesis of Scripture and exegesis.

Scripture is the identifiable focus for a significant and flexible tradition in historiography. For this dissertation, Scripture and exegesis will be as important as the configuration of ideas which A. O. Lovejoy comprehended under the term "chain of being" and which he has traced through the history of the mind of the West. Both interpretative theses, the chain of being and Scripture, serve as frames of reference within which the problematic relation between the one and the many, between unity and variety is reviewed and resolved. Scripture in particular claims to be both the one and the many, not only in terms of a simple juxtaposition, but in terms of a synthesis in which the vision and variety of history were fused while each retained its own focus. Scripture is, as it were, a prism, for Scripture as a literary document and the prism as a technological apparatus display a structure which makes possible a substantial coexistence of simplicity and variety. According to Jonathan Edwards, holiness in Scripture is often compared to light and comprehends the moral virtues. In nature also "there is a variety of light. One and the same white light, though it seems to be an exceeding simple thing, yet contains a very great variety of rays, all of so many different lovely appearance."[1]

---

[1] Jonathan Edwards, _Images and Shadows of Divine Things_, ed. P. Miller (New Haven: Yale University Press, 1948), pp. 62-63.

This particular function of Scripture has been overlooked for the crucial time of transition and modernization in the seventeenth century because of scholarly neglect and ignorance of the hermeneutics of the exegetical process. The analysis of Thomas Shepard's interpretation of Scripture in Chapter III is designed to illustrate the importance of a detailed exegesis for a comprehensive view of history. Edwards himself used the idea if not the term *prism*. In one of his early experiments he demonstrated that if a piece of glass were held against the sun at a particular angle, then its light would be refracted into the many diverse colors of the rainbow. Chapter IV will utilize Thomas S. Kuhn's concept of the paradigm in order to define the chronology of Scripture and the coherence of Scripture in Edwards in such a way that Scripture appears at that angle where through its prismatic structure the coherence of vision and variety becomes perceptible in a view of history. Chapter V will focus on Edwards as the historian of the revival and prove how on the historiographical level Scripture as a prism integrates the uses of the past and suggests a historical model of community. Chapter VI will concentrate on Edwards' prolegomena to a historical system of theology and prove that on the metaphysical level Scripture as a prism leads to a theory of communication which conceptualizes the vision and variety of history ontologically as well as historically. Chapter VII will show in an interpretation of Shaftesbury's Characteristics that the elimination of Scripture leads to a restriction of vision and variety which in turn results in an abandonment of the world of history.

CHAPTER I

FRANCIS BACON'S CLASSIFICATION OF HISTORY:

THE POINT OF VIEW OF FRANCIS BACON

The contributions of Francis Bacon to western civilization cover
the fields of literature, of science, of politics, and law as expressed
in his mastery of the English essay, his advocacy of empiricism, his
political career, and his legal thinking. His achievements in these fields
do not concern us here. Bacon had projected a four-part Instauratio Magna,
which was to effect a complete revision and reorganization of learning.
In order to move toward that goal, the first part of his Magnum Opus, which
he did complete, was a "Classification and Codification of Existent
Learning, with gaps indicated."[1] This introductory section to his larger
undertaking was published in an English edition as The Advancement of
Learning in 1605 and in an expanded Latin edition for European distribution
as De Augmentis in 1623. In his attempt to collect different contemporary
trends and traditions, Bacon also dealt extensively with the subject of
history, which for him in his view made up one of three branches of human
knowledge. The others were poesy and reason.[2] The straightforward character

---

[1]John Herman Randall, Jr., The Career of Philosophy, Vol. I (New
York: Columbia University Press, 1962), p. 246.

[2]Francis Bacon, Works, Ed., James Spedding, et al., VI (Boston:
Taggard and Thompson, 1863), pp. 182-183. All subsequent references to
Bacon's writings will follow this edition and will be abbreviated as
Bacon, Works.

of this understanding, its purpose to classify rather than to conceptual-

ize along with Bacon's immersion in the thought of his own time, made The

Advancement of Learning into a chronicle of intellectual culture which is

a valuable tool and an authoritative source for the historian who tries to

find his way into the state of this question of history in the seventeenth

century. Bacon himself explained that "In a writing of this nature, I

avoid all subtility."[1] We shall, therefore, in the following survey of

history in the general climate of the seventeenth century consider its role

and significance in Bacon's classifications.[2] From this stance we shall

then also look beyond Bacon insofar as it can help to cast light on the

subject of this essay and to the extent that the present state of research

on history in the seventeenth century permits.[3] Bacon's classifications

---

[1] Bacon, Works, VI, 209.

[2] There were other classifications of the different varieties of
history at Bacon's time and before. A consideration of the merits of
these different attempts would lead beyond the limits set for this study
(E. Menke-Glückert, Die Geschichtschreibung der Reformation und Gegenreformation, Bodin und Die Begründung der Geschichtsmethodologie durch
Bartholomäus Keckermann (Leipzig: Hinrichs, 1912), pp. 106-132.

[3] One example may illustrate this point. Bacon mentioned one type
of ecclesiastical history that dealt with the "Church Militant" and its
different states:

> Whether fluctuant, as the ark of Noah; or moveable, as the ark in
> the wilderness; or at rest, as the ark in the Temple; that is, the
> state of the Church in persecution, in remove, and in peace. In this
> part I find no deficiency, but rather superfluities; only I would that
> the virtue and sincerity of the relations were in accordance with the
> mass and quantity of the matter. (Bacon, Works, VIII, 435-436.)

Beyond this brief statement he provided no hints besides the fact that it
was a very well-established form that needed some pruning and more sincerity
My attempt to check out these hints ran into difficulties, because the history of Protestant church historiography for a period that covered more than
a century is a much-neglected area on the map of historical learning, but my
own research turned up enough interesting suggestions to warrant a more

resembled a chart set to words and therefore frequently contained distinc-

tions which were included simply in order to maintain an orderly pattern

rather than in order to introduce something new. In the following we

shall present the state of the question of history as it appeared in Bacon

by considering, first, history as fiction and as fact, and, second, his-

tory as coherent form and as a genre, and, third, history and its frames

of reference.

---

comprehensive investigation of this period. Of the standard histories of
historiography on the subject (Ferdinand Christian Baur, Epochen der
kirchlichen Geschichtsschreibung, 1852; Walter Nigg, Die Kirchengeschicht-
schreibung, Grundzüge ihrer historischen Entwicklung, München: Beck'sche
Verlagsbuchhandlung, 1934), both consider the great Reformation achievement and collaborative effort that produced the Madgeburg Centuries (see
also Heinz Scheible, Die Entstehung der Madgeburger Zenturien, Schriften
des Vereins für Reformationsgeschichte, No. 183, Volume 72, Gütersloh:
Verlagshaus Gerd Mohn, 1966) and then move on to consider the "father of
church history," Johan Lorenz Mosheim. Both events were separated by more
than a century. (The first history of church historiography by Karl
Friedrich Städlin, Geschichte und Literatur der Kirchengeschichte, 1827,
was not available for consultation.) Monographs that bring up the story
from the Magdeburg Centuries to the beginning of the seventeenth century
(Emil Menke-Glückert, Die Geschichtsschreibung der Reformation und
Gegenreformation, Leipzig: J. C. Hinrichs'sche Buchhandlung, 1912) and a
monograph on church history that traced its place at Heidelberg University
(Gustav Adolf Benrath, Reformierte Kirchengeschichtsschreibung an der
Universität Heidelberg im 16. und 17. Jahrhundert, Veröffentlichungen des
Vereins für Pfälzische Kirchengeschichte, Vol. 9, 1963) provide a general
orientation, but since both of them are focused on the continent, the
situation with regard to the peculiar features of church historiography in
England are outside of their scope.

History: Fact[1] and Fiction

In Francis Bacon's works the word "story" could designate fictitious as well as factual accounts,[2] but he could also use the opposition of story and history as a means to express the contrast between the fictitious and the factual. In his remarks on the "Idols of the Theatre, or of Systems," he compared the systems of philosophy to the theater where "stories invente for the stage are much more compact and elegant and more as one would wish them to be, than true stories out of history."[3] In this aphorism Bacon ridiculed philosophy by identifying its logic of "invention" with the playful and fanciful inventions of the playwrights.[4] Both philosophical system and so-called historical drama are exercises of wit which can lead only to imaginary views of the whole. Over against such "stories" he insisted that history alone, though not by itself, can be the basis of "true stories." While he therefore rejected the elegant stories of the theater, he did not identify the "true stories" with history either. The aphorism on the idols of the theater led Bacon therefore to a three-way distinction which he conceived of in terms of a pyramid:

> To those which refer all things to the glory of God they are as the three acclamations, _Sancte_, _Sancte_, _Sancte_; holy in the description or dilatation of his works, holy in the connexion and concatenation of them, and holy in the union of them in a perpetual and uniform law.[5]

---

[1]K. Keuck's Study on "Historia, Geschichte des Wortes un seine Bedeutung," Diss. Münster, 1934, was not available for consultation.

[2]Bacon, _Works_, VI, p. 189.

[3]Bacon, _Works_, VIII, p. 90.

[4]Bacon, _Works_, VIII, p. 50.

[5]Bacon, _Works_, VI, 221-222; see also p. 218.

Bacon rejected the fanciful stories and chose another route of
travel to the level of truth that those fanciful stories aimed at. In
the particular statement just quoted he suggested that the description of
the facts, their connection by means of causes, and their union in a
metaphysical frame hung together in the praise of glory.

History as Fact

Bacon's classifications of history did convey a sense of the power
of facts on his part. According to him they were the foundation of the
pyramid of knowledge,and they were called upon as the critical element in
order to broaden the base of philosophical systems. What he meant by this
positive function of history was best expressed in the contrast he made
between ecclesiastical history and theological systems. A good bishop
will only be that man who did not simply master the intricacies of thought
which were set forth in the works of St. Ambrose or St. Augustine, but someone who went beyond the elaborations of those few books who labored to
obtain a knowledge of the vicissitudes of the times and of the variety of
facts in them. The former habit had led to a succession of commentators
who formed a tradition that finally had to be summarized in epitomes and
put those men at several removes from variety and vicissitude. The latter
approach will help a bishop not simply to exercise his wit, but will
enable him to serve and to administer. Since the three contemporary
schools of natural philosophy were in Bacon's mind also based on facts
only in an insufficient way, he demanded that the Aristotelian as well as
the Empirical schools broaden their base and that the Superstitious school
separate tradition from fact.[1]

---

[1] Bacon, Works, VIII, pp. 90-91.

Bacon compared tradition to a river in which whatever was light,
popular, and puffed-up rose to the surface, whereas all the weighty and
solid matter sank to the ground and had to be recovered.[1] At least part of
the reason why Bacon assigned to fact such a power was that, at the time
he wrote The Advancement of Learning, the recovery process in the field of
civil history, ecclesiastical history, and history of learning had led to a
veritable explosion of the knowledge of facts while at the same time naviga-
tion and commerce were promising to add many more unknown facts. The seventeenth century was therefore in the history of historiography also known as
the age of polyhistory.[2] A reaction to one of the undesirable effects of
this explosion was reflected in Bacon's complaint that mere "epitomes" of
"many excellent histories" had become so popular. These abridgments and
selections in his mind had proved to be a more popular systematization and
exclusion of fact than the scholastic philosophical systems had ever been.[3]
The diffusion of factual historical knowledge as well as an interest in it
had thus become part of the general culture for all groups of society well
before the emigration of the Puritans to the American colonies. The various
expressions that this diffusion assumed have been increasingly recognized by
scholars.[4] One great influence in the initiation into and the international
zation of a concern for facts was John Foxe's Acts and Monuments. He not on

---

[1]Bacon, Works, VIII, 29.

[2]Karl Heussi, Kompendium der Kirchengeschichte, 12th ed. (Tübingen:
Mohr-Siebeck, 1960), p. 2.

[3]Bacon, Works, VIII, p. 424. This particular observation on the
deficiency and corruption of history occurred in De Augmentis, 1623.

[4]F. J. Levy, Tudor Historical Thought (San Marino: The Huntington
Library, 1967), p. 77; C. Hill, Intellectual Origins of the English
Revolution (Oxford: Clarendon Press, 1965), pp. 174ff.

helped to shape a distinctive view of history, but he sought out, discovered, evaluated, and included a large amount of sources in order to
document his view.[1]

Facts and the Forms of History Writing

For Bacon, the discovery of the variety of things within the tradition and the anticipation of more variety to come in an age of exploration
put restrictions on the writing of such history which comprised larger time
spans. According to him, it had now to be assumed that in "such a wide
field of matter" not all the factual returns had come in yet. As long as
facts were missing, however, there could be conjecture, but not history,
and conjecture in turn was a characteristic of the wit which Bacon associated with metaphysicians. The obligation to attend to so many facts
would also put a serious strain upon the stamina of the historian who was
likely to tire out, omit the good, and become less diligent in his choices.[2]
Bacon demonstrated his case both for universal and for particular history.
While Bacon conceded that a world-wide and universal treatment of one particular age was a noble enterprise and had led to considerable results,
he nevertheless insisted that such a subject matter was too unwieldy.[3]
Similarly the great traditions of particular history in the form of

---

[1]Foxe insisted that "records must be sought, the registers must be
turned over, letters also and ancient instruments ought to be perused, and
authors with the same compared; finally, the writers amongst themselves
one to be conferred with another; and so with judgment matters are to be
weighed; with diligence to be laboured; and with simplicity, pure from all
addition and partiality, to be uttered." Quoted according to Glanmore
Williams, Reformation View of Church History, Ecumenical Studies in
History, II (Richmond, Va.: Knox Press, 1970), pp. 53ff.

[2]Bacon, Works, VIII, p. 431.

[3]Ibid.

chronicles were subject to the same reservations. Even though by the time of Bacon chronicles had been arranged in such a way as to follow the reigns of English kings,[1] he still thought that the time spans covered by them were too large. In the Advancement of Learning Bacon could still call the chronicle the "most complete and absolute kind of history."[2] By the time he wrote De Augmentis the incongruity between this statement and his simultaneous contention that the chronicles try to cover too much ground led to the deletion of this assertion about the absolute character of the chronicles. Such concern about the gap in the record and about the abundance of material made Bacon recommend that only subjects be taken up which would represent an argument of manageable size. As possible models he mentioned those classical histories which had dealt with the expedition of the Persian King Cyrus and the treatment of the Peleponnesian Wars.[3] While such histories in turn may have certain disadvantages because of their partisan bias, yet since each party usually wrote on the same subject, they could be compared, the truth could be found out, and if such histories were done in sufficient quantities, even the chronicles as a general history can be revived. Until such a time when this would happen, Bacon's drive for factual completeness, however, suggested a reduction of the temporal scope of history writing from a coverage of all times through the interest in one age to the kind of narration that is most reliable because it only dealt with years. There was a kind of universal history which began with the

---

[1] Levy, Tudor Historical Thought, pp. 200ff.

[2] Bacon, Works, VI, 190.

[3] Ibid.

creation of the world and brought the account down to the present time.
It was only consistent then that this universal history was reclassified
under the rubric of imperfect history, because it could only provide a
collation of facts rather than a historical account.[1]

In addition, Bacon's use of the distinction between perfect and
imperfect history made it possible for him to differentiate between history
as fact and history that had form. His criterion for such form was that
a history possessed more than a "bare" continuance of actions and that its
several parts had to be woven into each other by considering "causes and
pretexts," "commencements and occasions," "counsels and occasions," and
"other passages of action." While the mention of causes pointed in the
direction of scientific history, the other criteria such as "orations" were
more in line with a classical model of historiography. The application of
these criteria drew not only a line between the facts and the form of history, but it also put chronologies, accounts of participant observers, and
the activities of antiquarian scholarship into a less reputable class of
history writing. The accounts of participant observers and chronologies
became simple "memorials" for something better, which several historians had
to prepare. Such a classification was interesting for two reasons:
memoirs and autobiographies which were so much on the increase in the seventeenth century were recognized by Bacon as a kind of historical literature,
even though only as an imperfect part of it. Chronologies on the other
hand were for him simply bureaucratic instruments in the office of the
registrar. They were not used as a means to order history, but as a way

---

[1]Bacon, _Works_, VIII, 430.

to avoid disputes over legal titles to property. Even though we had seen
Bacon's concern about the proliferation of facts, he did not seem to have
been aware of the problems that might arise if the facts are not known in
the order in which they occurred. The kind of embarrassment that such a
lack of chronological knowledge could lead to in the writing of history was
brought home very vividly to the New England historian Thomas Prince later
on at the beginning of the eighteenth century. When he came to England he
found out that English historians of New England had the order of the facts
about the history of New England wrong and misrepresented its history
because a reliable chronological order of the facts was not available.[1]

We had seen before that Bacon severely criticized universal history
for its factual inadequacies and suggested ways to rebuild it through the
preparation of small but factually reliable histories. His strong inclination towards the factual principle was also in evidence in the category of
history of cosmography. The name cosmography referred to a combined treatment of nature, society, and the heavens of a particular part of the world.
But Bacon also seemed to look upon it as a kind of universal geography. It
included a description of the physical properties of a region, an account
of its colonization, its government, and the manners of the people. A good
example for such a history can be found in William Hubbard's General History
of New England where chapters two through seven were reserved for a natural
history of New England and a civil history of the Indians. Hubbard
described first the physical geography of New England; he then dealt with
the climate of the region and with the fertility of the soil. His civil

---

[1] Thomas Prince, A Chronological History of New England (Boston: Antiquarian Book Store, 1852), p. xiii.

history of the Indians included a description of their character, theories
about their origin, as well as a "touch upon their laws, government and
successions."[1]

Bacon also included in his classification of history the outlines
for a history of learning which he set forth as a proposal of his own. His
discussion of its argument, of its manner of execution, and of its use were
of such scope that his description of the project as "a complete and universal History of Learning"[2] fits the design of this ambitious project quite
accurately. His reserved attitude toward universal history and its philosophy of history contrasted with a program for a universal history of
ideas and institutions.

Bacon was very much aware of learning as a third force besides the
state and the church. Since both civil history and ecclesiastical history
had made such great advances in his own time, he now suggested a history
of its own for Learning and the Arts as a means to improve education. In
the case of both Increase Mather and Cotton Mather we find evidence that
they had read widely in this field. Both of them used this considerable
knowledge in their endeavor to define the role of Harvard as an identifiable force of its own within the context of the culture of New England,[3]

---

[1] William Hubbard, A General History of New England (Cambridge:
Hilliard and Metcalf, 1815), pp. 14-34.

[2] Bacon, Works, VIII, 419-421.

[3] George Huntston Williams, "Translated Study: The Puritans'
Conception of their First University in New England, 1636," Archiv
fuer Reformationsgeschichte, 57 (1966), pp. 152-180.

and Cotton Mather included a history of the college into his "ecclesiastical history of New England."[1]

Form and Frame: History and Interpretation

Features that are generally associated with the concept of scientific story include a pronounced interest in facts, the insistence on the possibility and desirability for an objective causal connection of those facts and a concomitant aversion to all interpretations which try to generalize before all the facts are in. These characteristics have been emphasized in Bacon by interpreters who were interested to show that scientific history arose in the seventeenth century along with the sciences.[2]

We have already noted that Bacon objected to the confusion that arose when tradition and facts, theology and philosophy were indiscriminately mixed in systems of natural philosophy. He repeated the same charge when he denounced the interruption of the historical narrative by means of "political reflexions." According to Bacon a perfect or "continuous history" which considered the "causes, and the pretexts" of the action was "pregnant as it were" with many political conclusions, but the historian ought not to be the "midwife" for such conclusions.[3] The observation that this division of labor followed the Machiavellian ideal of a scientific

---

[1]Cotton Mather, Magnalia Christi Americana, or The Ecclesiastical History of New England (2 vols.; 1702; Hartford: Silas Andrus and Son, 1855), II, pp. 8-177.

[2]Christopher Hill, Intellectual Origins of the English Revolution p. 175; G. Wylie Sypher, "Similarities between the Scientific and the Historical Revolutions at the End of the Renaissance," Journal of the History of Ideas, 26 (1965), 353ff.

[3]Bacon, Works, VIII, 433.

history[1] should not overlook that both versions of Bacon's Advancement

of Learning were written at a time when in England at least history writ-

ing was politics. In addition, Bacon had addressed his book to the king,

who was none too pleased by the way in which Walter Raleigh, Robert

Cotton, and Edward Coke mixed history and politics more or less openly

against him. In this kind of history it was dangerous "to follow truth

too near the heels" as Walter Raleigh put it.[2] Even antiquarianism itself

was dangerous and it was significant that the only mention of antiquarians

in Bacon's classification occurred under imperfect history and referred to

them as a small coterie of devoted though conceited men who carry no

authority because there are only a few of them.[3]

For a loyal supporter of the throne such a doctrine of the separa-

tion of history and interpretation was very convenient. But if we now

change our perspective and look again at Bacon's view of history and what

he meant by his statement that a continuous history is pregnant with mean-

ing, then we shall be able to see the question of history and interpreta-

tion in still another perspective. We shall now not look at the facts,

nor at the forms into which they were collected, but we shall move one

step further and consider the frame into which the forms were being put.

---

[1] Levy, Tudor Historical Thought, p. 289.

[2] Quoted in C. Hill, Intellectual Origins, p. 177.

[3] Bacon, Works, VIII, p. 424. Bacon expressed concern, however, over
the possibility that a dissociation of history and interpretation might
have an adverse pedagogical impact for the young and an unsettling effect
on adults. In the case of natural history he therefore took up a compro-
mise position in order to avoid a distraction by "experience and history."
He declared his intention to at least subjoin "glances of history towards
philosophy." The adults would in this way not be kept "forever tossing on
the waves of experience" and the young people would have some provisional
generalizations up to such a time when the maturing of their intellectual
abilities would let them allow to go it on their own. (Bacon, Works, VIII,
p. 50; also p. 108.)

Or to use the process of blood circulation for an illustration; we shall now not look at the quantity of the blood that was being circulated, nor at the vessels that contained it, but at the way in which the arteries related to the whole organism. For this purpose it was necessary to look at the principles of Bacon's system of classification itself. These principles were best exemplified by the three genres of Chronicles, Lives, and Narrations in the area of perfect history.

The focus of the Chronicles[1] was on the magnitude and solemnity of public actions. Their stress on grandeur often invested more gravity and prudence in human life than could actually be found in it. By the same token the Chronicles excluded the consideration of the inward springs and motivations of actions which in turn provided the center of concern for the well-written Lives of kings and aristocrats. In such a life both the trifling and the important, the great and the small, the public and the private aspects of the actions were "mingled and united." Finally, the Narrations or Relations contained perfect knowledge, perfect certainty, and full information on actions and events. Each of these genres was in existence at Bacon's time. The Chronicles had evolved out of the medieval tradition and the Lives and Narratives were patterned after classical models. Each of these genres also had a particular "excellence." The Chronicles aimed at "estimation and glory," the Lives expressed "profit and example," and the Narrations excelled in "verity and sincerity."

We must therefore distinguish between the form of a perfect history in which the facts were connected and the genres which were differentiations

---

[1]The summary of the following paragraph is based on Bacon, _Works_, VIII, pp. 424-425.

of the form of perfect history. The characteristics of these three genres
constituted the frame or union of the third _Sancte_ of the praise of glory
which we quoted at the beginning of this chapter. If we go one step further, however, and raise the question as to the unity between these three
excellencies themselves, then the answer is: _tertium non datur._

The reason the form of perfect history ended in such a tri-unity was
directly related to the principle that motivated Bacon's system of classification. The way in which Bacon proceeded in the classification of the
genres of history is to the student of literature reminiscent of the way
in which Aristotle approached the task of classifying the genres of Greek
poetry.[1] It is true that the attitudes of the two men with regard to history and poetry were at opposite ends from each other, but their desire to
classify the subject of their choice led them along methodological lines
which were similar: both set out to find the differentiating essence or
excellency through which each genre could be set apart from the others.
John Hermann Randall has pointed out that Bacon's classifications of natural history were oriented toward the finding out of essences and qualities
of natural facts and not toward a determination of their relationships
amongst each other. The latter goal was the main interest of empirical

---

[1]David Daiches, _Critical Approaches to Literature_ (London:
Longmans, 1965), p. 25. According to Aristotle, Epic poetry dealt with
men on a heroic scale. These men were better in terms of their impres-
siveness, but not in terms of their simple moral sense. Satirical poetry,
on the other hand, dealt with men as they were in everyday life, portrayed
their more trivial aspects and represented them as worse than they really
were. Again, this representation was to be taken not in a simple moral
sense. When Bacon in turn criticized the grandeur of the Chronicles he
asserted that "a truer picture of human life may be found in a satire
then in some histories of this kind." (_Works_, VIII, p. 425.)

science at Bacon's time. Consequently, he had reached his goal of classification of the genre as soon as he could name the essences of which these
genres were the particular instances. If we now compare the _Sancte_ of the
praise of glory on the level of the union of knowledge with an example from
the field of music, then we could say that, for Bacon, this union consisted
in the ability to tabulate all the elements of a harmony without hearing
that harmony. Bacon's view of the unity of perfect history was therefore a
"synopsis" or "summary law."[1] These terms Bacon understood quite literally
in the sense that the "synopsis" of the essences of glory, example, and
truth is a "summary" of logically but not substantially related items on
a classification chart.

This logic behind Bacon's classification is not unfamiliar, for in
its identification of one essence with one genre, it described quite well
that division of labor which assigned glory to general history, examples
and morality to biography, and reserved the truth for the monograph. One
of the problems that Edwards faced in his historiography of the revival was
that its opponent looked upon history in terms of the morality of Lives;
the proponents were in the danger of defining it as a great public advance
to glory and Edwards, while he set out to narrate the truth, had to find a
means to talk about all three of them at once.[2] This, of course, presupposed a view which made it possible to transcend each of these essences

---

[1]Randall, _The Career of Philosophy_, I, p. 249.

[2]Edwards, _The Great Awakening_, Ed., C. C. Goen (New Haven: Yale
University Press, 1972), p. 293. In his rejection of _a priori_ judgments,
Edwards pointed out that the comprehension of historical events goes
beyond the desire to abstract certain features as essentials and reject
everything else that does not fit the definition.

and it is interesting to see that Edwards used typology for that purpose.
In his draft for the History of the Work of Redemption he distinguished
between real types and providential types. The former referred to persons
and the latter to events, but both were defined as types and not as
essences because they relate to one antitype.[1]

Alternate Contexts of Providence and Prophecy

Bacon knew of two different ways to classify church history. The
first way involved a simple extension of the genres of civil history to
the field of church history. The chronicles reappeared as the chronicles
of the church. The lives of kings were paralleled by the lives of the
Fathers and of the bishops, and the relations of military action corresponded to the relations of the transactions of synods. Church history
therefore also shared those aspects of glory, example, and truth as the
essential interpretative means by which it was to be understood. The
second way of classification added to that three more interpretative
themes: the church militant essentially went through three phases in its
history -- persecution, migration, and rest.[2] The history of the church
was essentially a "History of Providence" and it was also essentially a
"History of Prophecy." We have already pointed out the serious implications that such an essentialist view has for the unity of history, but in
the following we shall try to inquire into the significance of these individual themes of interpretation themselves and not into their relation to
the principles of classification.

---

[1] Edwards, Works, V, 73.

[2] See footnote 3, p. 20.

The general climate of the seventeenth century was larger than the
small segment that has been considered thus far in the explication of civil
history. The historians of ideas like to look upon the seventeenth century
as a transitional period in which many indications and anticipations of a
new Weltanschauung to come can be discovered. On the other hand, if we
also take seriously the insights of social anthropologists which they have
gained in the study of religion in places such as Africa, then we can more
easily perceive how the widespread popularity in the seventeenth century of
beliefs in witchcraft, astrology, magic, providence, and prophecies led
Christianity to a confrontation with ideas and systems of ideas which
appeared either as rivals or parasites of its own beliefs.[1] In addition
to an emerging conflict of religion and science, we must therefore also be
aware of an ongoing collision between religion and religion. If we look
at providence and prophecy in Bacon also from this standpoint then we shall
see more clearly that the question that must be answered was not so much
why he still held on to quickly fading beliefs, but how he defined these
beliefs in the context of a general mental climate in which beliefs in such
things as astrology were generally accepted and even intellectually respectable. This question was not what are providence and prophecy, but what
kind of providence and prophecy was Bacon talking about over against those
other rivalling beliefs or systems of belief. From such a point of view
the widespread interest amongst many intellectuals in questions of providence and of Scripture prophecies assumes a new dimension.

---

[1]Keith Thomas, Religion and the Decline of Magic (New York:
Scribner's, 1971), p. ix.

History and Interpretation: The History of Providence

Within the context of competing religious beliefs, providence as a
scheme for the explanation of the self, of the world, and of society was
persuasive and pervasive, but also elusive. In its positive as well as in
its negative manifestations it covered a wide range of emotional, rational,
and spiritual concerns which still had to be correlated to an ultimate
concern.[1] The nature of the diffusion as well as of the diffuseness of
these beliefs associated with providence can best be characterized by comparing it to a contemporary phenomenon. In an opinion poll the vague question as to whether a person has a religious attitude over against life will
usually receive a favorable response. Any further more focused questions,
however, easily lead to such a variety of diverse patterns of belief that
the religious attitude itself in its ambiguity can be exploited for any
virtue and vice.

The emergence and articulation of a view of divine providence within
the Christian community to which the rising Puritan movement also belonged
should therefore be considered and can be appreciated against this background of diffuseness. The theologians within the Protestant scholastic
traditions of the sixteenth and seventeenth centuries responded in kind to
this challenge and worked out a series of distinctions which were aimed at
the comprehension of such a diffuse intellectual and spiritual picture.[2]

---

[1]Thomas, Religion and the Decline of Magic, pp. 78-112.

[2]Carl Heinz Ratschow, "Das Heilshandeln und das Welthandeln Gottes,"
Neue Zeitschrift Fur Systematische Theologie, I (1959), p. 30f.

Francis Bacon's statement on the "History of providence" in the Advancement

of Learning and in De Augmentis represented a summary description and defi-

nition of the "labors of many" that had gone into the elaboration of one

aspect of such a theological concept of providence as a means to understand

history:

> The History of Providence, has indeed been handled by the pens of
> some pious writers, but not without partiality. Its business is to
> observe that divine correspondence which sometimes exists between God's
> revealed and secret will. For though the judgments and counsels of
> God are so obscure that to the natural man they are altogether inscrut-
> able, yea, and many times hidden from the eyes of those that behold
> them from the tabernacle, yet at some times it pleases the Divine
> Wisdom, for the better establishment of his people and the confusion
> of those who are as without God in the world, to write it and report
> it to view in such capital letters that (as the Prophet saith) "He that
> runneth by may read it"; that is, that mere sensual persons and volup-
> tuaries, who hasten by God's judgments, and never bend or fix their
> thoughts upon them, are nevertheless, though running fast and busy
> about other things, forced to discern them. Such are late and unlooked
> for judgments; deliverances suddenly and unexpectedly vouchsafed;
> divine counsels, through tortuous labyrinths and by vast circuits, at
> length manifestly accomplishing themselves; and the like; all which
> things serve not only to console the minds of the faithful, but to
> strike and convince the consciences of the wicked.[1]

In terms of the scholastic definition of providence, Bacon here did

not refer to providence in general which dealt with God's work in creation,

nor did he think of the providence in particular which was used to describe

God's work with mankind. The position which he reported as the labor of

many was the most special providence which affected the relationship of God

and the believer, as well as the relationship of God and the community of

believers. Both creation and mankind, nature and history at large entered

into the picture only insofar as they provided the concrete means by which

the existence of the believer was kept on the move into or within the

redemptive process. The emphasis on the dialectic of secret and revealed

---

[1]Bacon, Works, VIII, 436-437.

will, the focus of this purpose by means of natural and historical accidents did remove this view of providence from notions of fortune and fate
and turn it into an active quest for the authenticity of existence by means
of a realizing eschatology.

When Bacon thus referred to "History of Providence" he had in mind
the existence of a sufficient collection of examples of such providences
or accounts which showed how nature and history at particular points concurred to interpret individual and corporate life. Collections such as
those referred to by Bacon multiplied at the end of the sixteenth century
and in the seventeenth century so that Increase Mather's Essay for the
Recording of Illustrious Providences was both late[1] and chiefly to be understood as an effort to provide New England with its own indigenous collection
of such providence. In the preface to the same essay Mather also suggested
another such effort when he "wished that the Natural History of New England
might be written and published to the world."[2] This distinction between
natural history and the history of providence corresponded to the same
differentiation that was made by Bacon in his classification chart of
learning.[3]

History and Interpretation: The History of Prophecy

The words prophecy and prophet have not retained the full range of
their meanings down to our day. Unlike the term providence, the word

---

[1] Thomas, Religion and the Decline of Magic, p. 32.

[2] Increase Mather, An Essay for the Recording of Illustrious
Providence (London: G. Calvert, 1684), n.p.

[3] Bacon, Works, VIII, 409, 436.

prophecy as it appeared in Bacon's use of the phrase "History of Prophecy" has largely sunk below the horizon of the educated liberal segment of Western civilization, be it secular or religious. Standard theological dictionaries of today are a good indicator for what we mean when we refer to a prophet or a prophecy. Within the Western tradition, the mention of prophets and prophecy as intellectually respectable subjects are generally restricted to the Hebrew prophets and to the revival of prophecy in the early church. The extent of our own indebtedness to a particular periodization of history becomes apparent when we call members of prophetic movements beyond that time enthusiasts. After centuries of abuse the term enthusiasm in turn began to assume positive aspects in Shaftebury's discussion of the French prophets. Here, however, enthusiasm has as an ideal lost its connection with eschatology as well as with history and entered the field of imagination where it had a distinguished career and provided many an artist with the mantle of a prophet. In recent years we have come full circle in Puritan studies where literary scholars have increasingly used the concept of imagination or creative imagination as an interpretative concept. Voltaire had once remarked: "To understand the prophets is the endeavor of the human mind. That is why I shall say no more on that subject."[1] In an attempt to understand the less accessible aspects of this human mind in an intellectually satisfying and respectable manner, the idea of imagination has come back to an area from which it emigrated and which had left the idea of prophecy and prophet to mean only social criticism, teacher of doctrine, and which had introduced it as an interpretative

---

[1]Voltaire, Philosophical Dictionary, trans., Peter Gay (New York: Harcourt, Brace and World, 1962), p. 434.

concept mostly in the fields of social history, be it in the history of the oppressed or the history of fundamentalism. The term prophecy at the time of Jonathan Edwards and in the general climate out of which he came could indeed mean the teacher of doctrine, but this did not exhaust the circumference of its meaning.

It is once more in Bacon that we can see how the attempt was made to fit prophecy into the system of learning. Human learning according to Bacon was organized according to the three areas of human understanding: history-poesy-reason. Since divinity was also considered to be an area of human learning it also needed organization. The transposition of this organizational scheme and its application to the field of divinity elicited a definition of prophecy from him, because in this scheme prophecy appeared "supernumerary."[1] The classification of divinity that emerged embraced church history, or "sacred history, parables, doctrine, and precept." Then followed the description of prophecy as a "kind of history" and the definition according to which such a "divine history had this prerogative over the human, that the narration may be before the event as well as after."[2] Bacon linked in somewhat nominalistic fashion this prophecy with church history or "sacred history"[3] as a "kind of history," but he did so on second thought and still distinguished between them as different kinds. The outcome of this inclusion of prophecy was that the scheme of learning now received two focal points: prophecy on the one hand and doctrine and

---

[1] Bacon, Works, VI, 182-183; VIII, 408-409.

[2] Ibid., VI, 183; VIII, 409.

[3] "Sacred history" at the time was but another name for the Scriptures of the Old and New Testaments.

precept on the other. The latter was described as a "perennial philosophy," whereas the former had been defined as a transcendent divine history.
The former was perennial, the latter was both past and future.

Bacon did not always simply report on the situation of learning and
as soon as he set out to describe also deficiencies in the state of learning, he took the side of doctrine and precept. Scripture indeed had a
prophetic sense and contained all things that would ever happen to the
church. Within this frame the literal sense was "the main stream or river"
from which sprang the moral sense as well as the allegorical or typical
sense. The moral sense was the chief sense and both it and the typical
sense were of most use for the church. The prophetic sense in this way
became a historical introduction to the church by means of affirming its
continuity, but the moral sense which was freely and allegorically derived
from the literal sense provided the basis for doctrine and precept. The
church was the place where the order of doctrine and the doctrine of order
were located and prophecy was subordinated to ascertain this claim.

When Bacon moved back into the role of the reporter on the state of
learning the outline of prophecy as a "divine history" appeared in sharper
relief, even though its subordinate function to the confirmation of faith
as doctrine was still in evidence:

> The History of Prophecy, consists of two relatives, the Prophecy
> and the Accomplishment; and therefore the plan of such a work ought
> to be, that every prophecy of Scripture be sorted with the event ful-
> filling the same, throughout all ages of the world; both for the better
> confirmation of faith, and for better instruction and skill in the
> interpretation of those arts of prophecies which are yet unfulfilled;
> allowing nevertheless that latitude which is agreeable and familiar to
> divine prophecies, that the fulfilments of them are taking place con-
> tinually, and not at the particular time only. For they are of the
> nature of their Author, "to whom a thousand years are but as one day,
> and one day as a thousand years"; and though the height or fulness of

them is commonly referred to some one age or particular period, yet
they have at the same time certain gradations and processes of accom-
plishment through divers ages of the world. This is a work which I
find deficient, but it is one that is to be done with great wisdom,
sobriety, and reverence or not at all.[1]

With regard to all the concepts of history that we have reviewed
before, prophecy then was different, for it was more comprehensive. In it
was articulated the unity of history and the means to find it out. By
definition such a unity did not exclude the facts and there was a succession of men throughout the seventeenth and eighteenth centuries who sought
out the facts because of their prophetic drive for the unity of history.
Such unity was different from any one particular genre and superseded them
all. Such unity had more latitude than the context of providence to which
it gave perspective and purpose. Prophecy as Bacon understood it comprised
"continued" presence in which "processes" and "gradations" lead through
diverse ages to a "height" of "fulness."

Such an interest in prophecy also turned the historian into an
interpreter. He did not simply explore facts and explain connections, but
his collation of prophecies with the corresponding events also involved
him in the explication and interpretation of a frame of reference. The
particular type of interpretation mentioned in the definition of the History
of Prophecy consisted in the exegetical skills that were to be acquired for
the prophecies which were as yet not fulfilled. One assumption behind this
approach was that if all the prophecies and the events have been compared,
then whatever prophecy remained without a corresponding event must belong
to that period of time which intervenes between now and the end of history.

---

[1]Bacon, _Works_, VIII, 436.

Such a "sorting" of prophecy and event raised several hermeneutical questions. One of these questions was comparable to that which concerned the priority of either reason or revelation in the ongoing debate on this subject of revelation and reason. Similar questions must also be asked with regard to the relation of prophecies and events. As William Haller has pointed out in his discussion of John Bale's commentary on Revelations, the suspicion on the part of the modern historian is very often justified that the event selected the prophecy rather than that the prophecy fulfilled the event.[1] On the other hand, the insistence on the relation between prophecies and events as a means to ascertain the unity of history was so important in Bacon's definition of the History of Prophecy that a better understanding of the hermeneutics of such a correlation was desirable. One way to approach this subject certainly is that the protestations of contemporary interpreters of prophecies be taken seriously when they insisted that prophecies must also be related to those parts of Scripture which are non-prophetical. The unity of history would therefore depend on the unity of the prophecies with the non-prophetical parts and this in turn would require a view of Scripture that took seriously its unity, coherence, and story. An exegesis of Scripture that could achieve this must depart from the proof-texting approach of interpretation. There were examples of interpreters of prophecies who insisted on the integrity of the given story and complained about random allegorizing in the prophetical texts. One of those men was Joseph Mede whose commentaries and opinions

---

[1]William Haller, Foxe's Book of Martyrs and the Elect Nation (London: J. Cape, 1963), p. 64.

came to be widely accepted and who was also known to Jonathan Edwards.[1]
Furthermore, a reading of John Cotton's and Isaac Newton's commentaries
showed that the exegesis of prophecies was done in the awareness of a
chain of interpreters against which all individual work was weighed and
evaluated. All this suggests the existence of a tradition of interpretation or a "Science of Prophecy"[2] which moved with great caution and circumspection in its attempts to correlate prophecies and events. All this
would seem to indicate that the application of prophecies was not as
random a matter as it often appears to have been.[3]

---

[1]Edwards, Works, IX, 67. Joseph Mede insisted at one point that
"If the order, method, and connexion of the visions be framed and grounded
upon supposed interpretation, then must all Proofs out of that book
[Revelations] needs be founded begged principles and humane conjectures:
But on the contrary, if the order be first fixed and settled out of the
indubitate Characters of the letter of the Text, and afterward the
Interpretation guided, framed and directed by that Order; then will the
variety of Expositions be drawn into a very narrow compass, and proofs
taken from this book be evident and infallible, and able to convince the
Gain-sayers." (Quoted according to A.J.B. Gilsdorf, "The Puritan
Apocalypse: New England Eschatology in the Seventeenth Century," Diss.,
Yale University, 1965, p. 67.) Likewise Patrick Forbes (1564-1635) pro-
tested against those who dissolved the "series, trumpets and vials to the
confusion of all order, and light of story, which in this prophecie is
most orderly set down, with special relation to distinct events." (Ibid.,
p. 39.) The orderly character of this book was also expressed by classifying it as a piece of dramatic literature: Thomas Goodwin (1600-1680)
defined the book of revelation as a "tragi-comical vision of the occurrences of the world through all times and ages." (Ibid., p. 13.)

[2]Christopher Hill, The World Turned Upside Down, Radical Ideas
During the English Revolution (New York: Viking Press, 1972), p. 74.

[3]In Increase Mather's Mystery of Israel's Salvation
Explained and Applyed (London, 1669), we do find such an instance in
which the prophecy was connected with the witness of the non-prophetical
parts of Scripture. On the one hand he said: "The truth is, that there
is not any one prophetical book (the book Jonah is rather an Historie
than a Prophesie) in all of Scripture, be it in Old Testament or in New
Testament, which does not speak something concerning the salvation of
Israel. Therefore, this must needs be brought to pass" [p. 51]. The
reason which he, Mather, gave was that the "Covenant of God is everlasting" and that "If we observe the Scripture, we shall find, that the

The respectable character of this particular pursuit of prophecy can best be evaluated when the phenomenon is again seen in the context of the mental climate of the seventeenth century. In his essay Of Prophecies[1] Bacon distinguished between "divine prophecies," "heathen oracles," and "natural predictions" on the one hand and certain well-known prophecies in his own age which were of anonymous origin. To these latter prophecies he also added astrological predictions. It was only of these latter prophecies that he disapproved. Bacon did not give them any particular name, but Keith Thomas, who has made an extensive study in this area, called them "political prophecies."[2] All of them were sayings attributed

---

salvation of Israel is still grounded upon God's covenant" [p. 51]. For Mather himself the application of this insight was twofold: he used it to bolster his view of adherence to the covenant theology of the founders of New England, but -- and that was why he devoted a whole treatise to it -- the unity of prophecies and the rest of Scripture were the two elements in his argument. Judaism was still Israel and belonged into the unity of an ongoing history that was to be consummated. Prophecy and non-prophetical parts of Scripture were here viewed as a hermeneutical circle and the result of this particular application of it amounted to no less than a considerable change for a Christian attitude toward the Jews. (See on this subject Martin Buber, Der Jude und Sein Judentum, Köln, 1963, p. 558f., as well as others in Rudolf Pfisterer, Von A Bis Z, Quellen zu Fragen um Juden und Christen, Gladbeck: Schriftenmissionsverlag, 1971, pp. 79-83.) A recognition of the relation of prophecy to the whole of Scripture is especially important in order to avoid that the current increase of scholarly interest in millenial thought moves onto a wrong track. Thus, for example, Stephen J. Stein in a recent article ("A Note on the Apocalypse by Jonathan Edwards," William and Mary Quarterly, 29, October 1972, p. 634f.) came to the conclusion that the forthcoming publication of Edwards' notebook on the book of Revelation in the New Testament should bring "some realism to the abundance of adulatory writing about Edwards." Stein had found in Edwards' notes on the apocalypse the rampant anticatholicism of the time and not the kind of creative theological thinking that had made him famous. These observations on Edwards' prejudices were adequate, but they could unwittingly lead to the false conclusion that they represented the whole of his exegetical effort.

[1]Bacon, Essays Civil and Moral, The Harvard Classics, ed., Charles W. Eliot (New York, 1909), pp. 95-98.

[2]Thomas, Religion and the Decline, pp. 397-409.

to old and famous sources or men which were shown to predict certain
political events taking place at the present time. These prophecies constituted an actual political threat so that governments had to make laws
to suppress them. Keith Thomas saw in these prophecies also the attempt
to provide a continuity with the past in light of the rapid change in the
present through the reassuring knowledge that someone long ago had foreseen
this change. The main characteristic of this literature was its unstable
character and the ad hoc application and reinterpretation in order to suit
the occasion as it arose. Thomas Hobbes therefore remarked that these
prophecies were "many times the principle cause of the events foretold."[1]
In view of this particular popular inclination to prophecies it becomes
clearer why men from John Foxe[2] through Jonathan Edwards would always
insist on Scripture prophecy in particular and condemn all the others
precisely for the reason that they did not provide a view of history.

Such an insistence on Scripture prophecy was therefore part of that
manifold process of rationalization that has been going on in the civilization of the West for several centuries. Max Weber has shown[3] that at different times different attitudes and different institutions became part
of this particular process. It worked slowly and worked partial effects
at given times. Instances of this process of rationalization were present
in the case of prophecy and providence within the context of the seventeenth

---

[1] Thomas, Religion and the Decline, p. 422.

[2] John Foxe set Scripture-Prophecy against Astrology (Acts and
Monuments, edition of 1684, I, pp. 815-817).

[3] M. Weber, The Protestant Ethic and the Rise of Capitalism, 1904-1905
(E. T.; New York: Scribner's, 1958), p. 26.

century. In our review of Bacon's notes on the state of learning, we
have also seen how many different and even contradictory trends are
reflected in his classification of history. For example, the kind of
rationalizing process that appeared in the case of providence and prophecy
was quite different from the concept of reason that underlay the views of
civil history as they were put forward in Bacon and yet they seem to co-
exist, for Bacon's classification applied both of them to the area of
ecclesiastical history. Such a situation of flexibility can easily be mistaken for crisis, but even a crisis as different from a catastrophe was
drawn out over time and involves complex processes. They were not unlike
what happens in the process of refining crude oil. Processing in an oil
refinery will induce crises in the otherwise slow to react raw materials
and shake loose combinations of molecules which in turn at different
points and times throughout the process will form and reform new and existing molecular structures. The several finished products that come out of
this refinery are diverse enough to make one wonder how they could have
come from the same source and through the same process and yet it is
apparent upon closer observation that they still share common elements.
The sixteenth and seventeenth centuries can be looked upon as a process
of crisis in this sense. At a particular time in this process a group of
congregationalist persuasion in church government moved to Plymouth Colony
and Massachusetts Bay. We would like to inquire in our next chapter how
several of the elements that we have portrayed in this chapter combined
into a view of history that provided Jonathan Edwards with his indigenous
background.

Summary

Bacon's time was a watershed in Western thought insofar as it displayed an unprecedented proliferation of historical knowledge. Bacon's
attempt to classify and to evaluate that knowledge reflected trends of his
time and expressed perspectives of his own. In accordance with Bacon's
pyramidal organization of knowledge, the argument of this chapter proceeded
on an ascending scale and dealt with history in its relation to fiction, to
fact, to form, and to frames of reference. This survey helped to provide a
sense of the general climate of opinion against which Edwards' own background
as well as his view of history can be seen adequately.

Bacon was not interested in universal history, but in polyhistory.
He, unlike his contemporary Walter Ralegh and unlike the later Jonathan
Edwards, excluded the aesthetic side of history as fictitious and fanciful,
even though he did not introduce a consistent terminological differentiation
between story and history in order to express this point. Because of his
concern for factual diligence, Bacon criticized philosophical systems as
well as traditional world histories, and demanded that their claims be based
on adequate factual foundations and that they be revised accordingly. On the
other hand, Bacon approved of the project of a cosmography and suggested
work toward a universal history of learning, because the recent accumulation
of factual material met his standards of diligence. In William Hubbard we
found elements of cosmography and in both Increase and Cotton Mather we saw
considerable acquaintance with the history of learning and its ideas. Among
the then already available forms of history, Bacon distinguished according
to the criteria of imperfect and perfect form. He described the latter in
terms of continuance and coherence. This perfect form in turn was the base

for the three genres of chronicle, life, and narration. Not unlike
Aristotle in his definition of poetic forms, Bacon in his classification of
histories assigned specific functions to specific genres only. The consequent exclusive association of glory with chronicles, or morality with live
and of narration with truth took that dynamic quality away from history
which Edwards was later on to secure in a view of typology that allowed
equally for the solemity, sobriety, and sincerity of history.

The theory of the conformity of state and church meant for Bacon tha
secular and sacred historiography shared the same genres. Nevertheless,
church history by itself had providence and prophecy as two distinctive but
as yet insufficiently developed historiographical modes. Both of these
approaches to the facts of history must be seen in the context of the vola-
tile religious climate of the seventeenth century where the appeal to follo
Scripture-providences and Scripture-prophecies represented a process of
"rationalization" (M. Weber) that opened up contemporary fatalistic attitudes in the direction of a view of history and made possible the orientation toward life in a historical world. Bacon also made a distinction betwe
fact and interpretation. Bacon's twofold classification of church history
led to a generic and a prophetic definition of this relationship. In the
former case, the result was an essentialist synopsis of several separate gen
while in the latter case the unity of history itself was the subject. The
coexistence of both views in Bacon's classification provide a good illustration for that open and competitive crisis which characterized the intellectually pluralistic situation of the seventeenth century and of which the
Massachusetts historians and New England historiography were a part.

CHAPTER II

HISTORIANS AND THE HISTORIOGRAPHY OF NEW ENGLAND

In his survey of the intellectual culture of New England in the

seventeenth century, S. E. Morison pointed out that historical literature

was next to the sermon and theology the only other native prose at the

time.[1] This literature had its sources in a wide range of human activities

and human learning and helped either to support an argument, report a

series of events, or simply to relate facts. In an age of discovery and

colonization, promotion and propaganda[2] were necessary in order to attract

settlers, defend the new settlements, and launch new projects in different

fields. This age of exploration was also a time of political and religious

upheaval which made polemics[3] and pamphlets on church polity and on politics

in general a common staple of reading for almost everyone. The Indian wars

of New England in particular became the occasion of history-writing and saw

the rise of an identifiable captivity narrative that lasted well into the

---

[1]Samuel Eliot Morison, The Intellectual Life of Colonial New
England (1936, Rpt. Ithaca: Great Seal Books), p. 177. Josephine Piercy,
in her Studies in Literary Types in Seventeenth Century America 1607-1710
(New Haven: Yale University Press, 1939), p. 210, did not include histories
as a separate type into her study.

[2]David D. Van Tassel, Recording America's Past, An Interpretation
of the Development of Historical Studies in America, 1607-1887 (Chicago:
University of Chicago Press, 1960), pp. 1-9.

[3]Edward Johnson, Wonder Working Providence of Sions Savior, Ed.,
J. Franklin Jameson, Original Narratives of Early American History. New
York: Scribner's, 1910.

eighteenth century.[1] The civil education of the gentleman relied mostly
on histories for the inculcation of morality and the acquisition of literary skills. The concern for posterity dominated both learning and piety.
Institutions of learning were an important means by which to remain within
the realms of history and civilization in the surrounding of a "howling
wilderness" and neighboring barbarism. Learning, if nothing else, was to
show that New England was neither obsolete, barbaric, nor utopian. Diaries
and autobiographies of parents became one of the means by which to keep
the children within a particular history and the church. Piety with its
twofold emphasis on self-examination and on the meditation of sermons further contributed to the interest of recording history and added to a rich
variety of printed and manuscript materials for public distribution as well
as semi-private circulation. C. K. Shipton in part referred to this phenomenon when he mentioned that New England has become the "richest area in
the world in printed and manuscript materials including the unrivalled
archives of towns, churches, and courts."[2] Shipton's own work in the history of New England has covered by now more than one hundred years and
represents an impressive testimony to the truth of this observation.

---

[1]Morison, Intellectual Life, p. 191.

[2]C. K. Shipton, New England Life in the Eighteenth Century
(Cambridge: Belknap Press, 1963), p. xvi. Such an awareness of and interes
in history should not be confused with history as a subject of formal education which did not exist at Harvard College in the seventeenth and early
eighteenth centuries. Neither the College Laws of 1655, nor the program of
1723 did include history (S. E. Morison, Harvard in the Seventeenth Century
[Cambridge: Harvard University Press, 1936], p. 265f.), even though
Jonathan Mitchell had proposed quite early the establishment of several pro-
fessorships that would have also included history (S. E. Morison, The
Intellectual Life of New England, p. 32). It is not before Cotton Mather
(Manuductio ad Ministerium, Directions for a Candidate of the Ministry,
Boston, printed for Thomas Hancock, 1726), that we get an outline of study
that included a detailed syllabus for both civil and ecclesiastical history

What strikes the modern observer therefore most of all is not so much that in seventeenth century Massachusetts there were attempts toward a combination of sources, imperfect histories, and small histories into major histories, but that the public impact of these attempts was mostly marginal at the time. William Bradford's Of Plymouth Plantation 1620-1647[1] and John Winthrop's History of New England from 1630-1649[2] were published only in the nineteenth century. Of the other major histories, which came later, only Nathaniel Morton's New England's Memorial[3] and Cotton Mather's Magnalia Christi Americana sold when they were published, and Cotton Mather's history was originally published in England first. Morton's achievement as a historian actually consisted chiefly in editing Bradford's manuscript for his purposes. Cotton Mather searched out and added sources of his own, but was nevertheless very dependent on William Hubbard's General History of New England, which in turn took over verbatim materials from John Winthrop and Nathaniel Morton. Hubbard's account existed only in manuscript at the time. He was also published in the nineteenth century and enjoyed there a good reputation until his dependence on Winthrop was found out. Finally, we must also be careful not to assign too much influence to either Edward Johnson's Wonder-Working Providence of Sions Saviour in New England, or to Thomas Prince's Chronological History of New England. Johnson had been published in London, but his book proved a "bad-seller," and since it was therefore issued under another name, Thomas Prince had to

---

[1] William Bradford, Of Plymouth Plantation 1620-1647, Ed., S. E. Morison (New York: Knopf, 1970), p. xxviiff.

[2] John Winthrop, The History of New England from 1630-1649, Ed., James Savage. Boston: Phelps and Farnham, 1825-1826.

[3] Cambridge: printed by S. Green for A. Johnson, 1669.

make an extra effort to re-establish Johnson's authorship as a "thing
familiarly known among the Fathers of the Massachusetts Colony."[1] Thomas
Prince himself had a great reputation as a scholar and a historian. His
history of New England was eagerly awaited, but its publication disappointed these expectations. Prince had collected more sources than all
New England historians before him, but he began his account with the creation of the world and carried it down only to the beginnings of New England.

Against this colonial background of great possibilities and limited
achievement, we shall inquire more closely into the work of William Hubbard
and Edward Johnson in order to find out what these Massachusetts historians
of New England in the seventeenth and early eighteenth centuries can contribute toward an understanding of the indigenous background of Jonathan
Edwards' view of history. To be sure, Hubbard and Johnson were different
in many ways. They belonged to different generations: Johnson's history
was published in 1653 and displayed a polemic spirit throughout in its
defense of the purpose of New England. Hubbard submitted the manuscript
of his history to the General Court of Massachusetts in 1680 after Urian
Oakes had called for the "Lord's Remembrancers" to record New England's
past.[3] Furthermore, Johnson was unique because he did not belong to the
chain of tradition that was dependent in one way or another on John
Winthrop or William Bradford.

---

[1]Prince, A Chronological History of New England, p. xii.

[2]Sibley's Harvard Graduates, 5, pp. 354ff.

[3]Urian Oakes, New England Pleaded With (Cambridge, Mass.: Printed
by S. Green, 1673), p. 23.

Neither Johnson nor Hubbard was a giant in his field. The historical thought of both Cotton Mather and Jonathan Edwards was much more complex. A comparison of the various components that went into the making of the position of either would provide a comprehensive introduction to the native background of Edwards' view of history. On the other hand, works like the Magnalia Christi Americana and the draft of the History of the Work of Redemption were different enough in form, in the subjects they covered and in the reasons for which they were written, that a comparison which at this point could only be brief would lead into false analogies. Therefore, a review of two minor figures is both adequate and expedient in the context of this study. Hubbard and Johnson, despite their difference, have one thing in common: whatever they try to do, they do thoroughly. They can be best treated for our purposes in a typological manner rather than in a chronological order.

The extended consideration of these two different types of historians will be followed by a review of some scholarly contributions to an understanding of the Massachusetts historians of New England in the seventeenth century and the early eighteenth century. The methodological observations of this review will end our survey of the place of history in Edwards' native background and suggest the interpretative framework within which he himself and most of his native predecessors explicated and discussed their views of history.

William Hubbard: *A General History of New England*[1]

More than forty-five years had intervened between the time when
John Winthrop's group of settlers had arrived in Massachusetts Bay in 1630
and the time when William Hubbard began work on a history of New England.
In order to make these years intelligible even if not alive, he no longer
simply resorted to John Winthrop's journal approach nor to Nathaniel
Morton's annalistic division of history. He had to come to terms with an
amount of material that no one else before him had tried to deal with. In
a preface that is usually not included in editions of his General History,
he referred to himself as a "compiler."[2] This definition of his own task
gave to his work a factual tone which was noteworthy, but which was not
indicative of a loss of faith, and represented a genuine effort on his
part to find a principle of mastery for the historical material of New
England's past.

Scholarly reactions to Hubbard's historiography have moved in two
different directions. He has either been accused of plagiarism[3] ever since
John Winthrop's history became known or he has been represented as surpris-
ingly modern in his shift toward an emphasis on second causes in the interpretation of providence over against Nathaniel Morton's history on which he

---

[1]The title is not the addition of the editor, for in the first
chapter, which is only partially preserved, Hubbard said that "for the
satisfaction of those who may be studious to inquire into the real truth
of former transactions the General History of New England is now taken in
hand" (Hubbard, op. cit., p. 8).

[2]Sibley's Harvard Graduates, 1, p. 55.

[3]For a collection of all the negative comments, see Cecilia Tichi,
"The Art of the Lords Remembrancers, A Study of New England Puritan
History," Diss., University of California (Davis), 1971, p. 157.

was also dependent.[1] Both of these explanations must be superseded by a
historically adequate assessment of the particular tools which Hubbard's
education or study gave him in order to attack this new task of formalizing
and organizing the New England past. Ever since P. Miller pointed to the
importance of Ramist logic and dialectic in the intellectual climate of the
seventeenth century in general, and to its use at Harvard College in particular, the rediscovery of this way of thinking has become a standard for
a more balanced appreciation of the intellectual character of New England
Puritanism at the time. Theology as a discipline and as a practical pursuit depended on this tradition for method and coherence. The Ramist movement, however, had its origin not in theology, but in the arts faculty where
its overriding pedagogical interest led to widespread efforts to collect all
branches of knowledge including history into arts.[2] It has escaped notice
thus far that Hubbard's organization of New England history is an application of the approach of this tradition to history. The dullness and
pedantry that has been blamed on Hubbard's historiography was based on the
same principles that led to a serious re-evaluation of the intellectual
character of New England religious thought in recent scholarship.

Within the range of the tools that were available to him, Hubbard's
formalization was professional in its intention and led to an organization
of history that consisted in the inclusion of logically differentiated kinds
of history within a sequence of chronological units that reached all the
way from the arrival of the Mayflower down to his own time.

---

[1] Kenneth B. Murdock, "William Hubbard and the Providential
Interpretation of History," Proceedings of the American Antiquarian
Society, 52 (1942), pp. 22ff.

[2] Lawrence A. Cremin, American Education, The Colonial Experience
1607-1783 (New York: Harper, 1970), p. 103.

The way in which Hubbard arranged the different kinds of history showed a similarity with Bacon's system of classification which we shall therefore use as the basis of comparison. The term similarity rather than affinity is employed because there is no circumstantial evidence that would point to an actual knowledge of Bacon by Hubbard. In the following we shall present a summary of Hubbard's historiography by considering the questions of chronology, classification, and providence.

Throughout his great work on New England, Hubbard divided time into equal segments of five years. Each of these segments he called a "lustre." The word lustre in its anglicized form existed since 1387 and the term itself was used both at Hubbard's time and later either in the sense of glory or in reference to time.[1] Hubbard, however, used it also in the strictly technical sense in which it was ultimately derived from the classical historians. Originally a "lustre" referred to an expiatory sacrifice performed every five years. From there it assumed the function of a basic chronological unit by means of which to order history.[2]

The crucial question in an evaluation of Hubbard's adoption of that particular chronological unit is not whether his choice of such a unit was arbitrary, but whether relative to his own situation he made an adequate selection in terms of the available options and in terms of his own particular project. He did not use the annalistic pattern which he had met in

---

[1]The Compact Edition of the Oxford English Dictionary (Oxford: Oxford University Press, 1971), p. 1682.

[2]Charlton T. Lewis, Charles Short, A Latin Dictionary (Oxford: Oxford University Press, 1966), p. 1087. Richard M. Gummere, The American Colonial Mind and the Classical Tradition (Cambridge: Harvard University Press, 1963), does not mention this subject.

Morton and which Morton had taken over from Bradford. On the other hand,
Hubbard could not -- for obvious reasons -- organize New England history in
terms of "centuries," which as a chronological division was still popular
with Protestant church historians at his time and which had been introduced
after careful deliberations[1] more than a century earlier by the Magdeburg
Centuries. Bacon himself in his program for a History of Learning had suggested a flexible use of the "century" as a chronological unit and had
recommended that smaller units may be used where this was required by the
"Literary Spirit of each age."[2] In Hubbard, there are indeed indications
that he did not rigidly impose the idea of "lustres" upon his material.
Thus, for example, his description at the end of the second and the beginning of the third lustre coincided with the economic crisis of Massachusetts
in 1641[3] which was caused by the sudden stop of emigration from Old England
to New England and which threatened the continued existence of the colony.
According to Hubbard, it was only through the "special providence" of God
that the colony escaped the possibly disastrous consequences of this sudden
end of the "golden age" of New England. In this particular instance
Hubbard's method was not simply one of compiling materials, but his chronological ordering agreed with a providential view and involved also a
periodization of two lustres in terms of a "golden age."[4]

---

[1] Heinz Scheible, Die Entstehung der Magdeburger Zenturien (Gütersloh:
Mohn, 1966), pp. 48, 73ff.

[2] Bacon, Works, VIII, p. 420.

[3] Bernard Bailyn, The New England Merchants in the Seventeenth Century
(1955, ppb.; New York: Harper Torchbook, 1964), pp. 46ff.

[4] The relation of chronology, periodization, and subject matter as
they appeared in Hubbard would repay an investigation of its own that
cannot be conducted here (see Scheible, Die Entstehung, p. 73f.).

What was, however, more apparent in Hubbard's handling of his chronological device was that it served primarily logical rather than historical purposes. It provided the basic unit into which different kinds of histories could be arranged topologically. A brief look at the lustre from 1636 through 1641 can illustrate this point.[1] The basic division within that lustre is between civil and ecclesiastical affairs. Since both were conceived of along similar lines they both proceed from the general toward the particular. In the case of civil history Hubbard first chronicled the "general affairs" for the period, then he went on to describe "various occurrences" within it; this was followed by a narration of the war with the Pequods. The subsequent two chapters dealt with the one year under the governorship of Henry Vane and the protracted "troublesome occurrences" that concerned the Massachusetts charter. The discussion of ecclesiastical affairs in turn began with a general survey of the lustre, then moved into the subject of the antinomian crisis and finally concluded with a relation of the "occasion and success" of the synod at Cambridge. This pattern was the same throughout all lustres, even though the subjects may increase, decrease, or change in accordance with the material available. The only exception to this pattern were the five chapters on "Memorable Accidents" which occurred in different lustres and were inserted at the end of either the civil or the ecclesiastical parts.[2] These chapters on "Memorable Accidents" especially recall Bacon's description of the "History

---

[1] Hubbard, General History, pp. 233-304.

[2] Of the five chapters, three concluded sections on church history (pp. 194ff., pp. 419ff., pp. 627ff.). One chapter concluded a section on civil history (pp. 524ff.), and one chapter toward the end extended beyond the customary five-year period (pp. 640ff.).

of Providence," but the peculiar differentiation and correlation of civil

and ecclesiastical history and the distinction between general chronicle

and particular narration were also in evidence as well as the "history of

cosmography"[1] which preceded all the lustres and made possible the

integration of natural history into a general history of New England.

The subordination of the chronological under the topological gave

Hubbard's history the appearance of a historical dictionary. As such, this

history was indeed a General History not only in name but also in fact.

Almost all those classifications that were simply listed in Bacon were here

fleshed out with facts. Hubbard "had won his spurs as a historian in the

Indian Wars," as S. E. Morison put it. It will remain speculative[2] whether

---

[1]Compare Chapter I, p. 37ff.

[2]The text of the General History as we have it was based on a manuscript that was not Hubbard's and that was incomplete with regard to both
its first and last chapters (William Hubbard, A General History of New
England, Ed., A. Holmes and Joseph McKean, Massachusetts Historical Society,
Hilliard and Metcalf, Cambridge, Massachusetts, 1815, pp. 7-8; 672-676).
Thomas Prince (A Chronological History of New England, pp. vii-viii)
reported that Hubbard's history of the Indian War was examined and approved
by a committee of the General Court in 1677. When Hubbard therefore also
submitted the manuscript of his General History he followed a precedent.
The General Court resolved that "it hath binn thought necessary, a duty
incumbent upon us, to take due notice of all occurrences and passages of
God's providence towards the people of this jurisdiction since their first
arrival in these parts, which may remain to posterity." The Court acknowledged that Hubbard had "taken paines to compile a history of this nature"
and voted him £50 upon "transcribing it fairly into a book, that it may be
the more easily perused, in order to the satisfaction of this Court." When
Hubbard did present a copy in 1683 the treasurer received orders to pay
half that sum. (Sibley's Harvard Graduates, I, 55-56.) K. B. Murdock (see
p. 57) advanced the thesis that Hubbard's attention to second causes may
have been too advanced for the General Court and therefore the General
History was not adopted as an official history. Morison,(Intellectual Life,
p. 181) suggested that the manuscript was never readable enough for an
examination, and Alan B. Howard ("The Web in the Loom: An Introduction to
the Puritan Historians of New England," Diss., Stanford, 1968) concluded
that Hubbard's positive description of the opportunities to settle in New
York in the last chapter did not go over well with the General Court. This
ending also induced Howard to say that the "open end of New England history

Hubbard lost this reputation again when he presented such a manuscript to

the General Court. Within the history of ideas, Hubbard's General History

was significant because it reflected that hybrid of the chronological and

the topological that had begun with the Magdeburg Centuries, had been rein-

forced by the Ramist tradition and by the encyclopedic trend in the learning

of the seventeenth century. This particular historiographical tradition

became also a part of Peter van Mastricht's[1] theological encyclopedia which

was also known to Jonathan Edwards. This encyclopedic ideal in history, as

---

is spatial rather than temporal" (p. 59). Morison's suggestion seemed the
most adequate interpretation of the three. In the case of Howard we have a
theory that makes too much out of its text. For Hubbard the land around the
Hudson River was simply "the most fertile and desirable tract of land in
all the southerly part of New England" (p. 666). Furthermore, the return of
this land to the English was providential since the Dutch had cheated the
New Plymouth settlers out of it by hiring a pilot who had steered them to
Cape Cod instead (p. 667). Finally, parts of Long Island had already been
colonized and "most of them are molded, as to their ecclesiastical concern-
ments, after the manner of the rest of the New English plantations, and are
of their persuasion generally in matters of religion" (p. 668). In their
ecclesiastical state they enjoyed -- what was so important to Hubbard --
peace and quiet even after the colony came back to the English. While Howard'
interpretation is suggestive, the basis for its verification here is not
sufficient.

[1]Petrus van Mastricht (1630-1706), theologian, was born at Cologne
and studied at the universities of Utrecht, Leiden, and Heidelberg. According to the funeral eulogy on van Mastricht, his first academic appointment
at Frankfurt/Oder also made him the first theologian to hold a chair that
specialized in practical theology or ethics. In 1677 he became one of the
three men who had been chosen to succeed Gisbert Voetius. Van Mastricht's
main work was the Theoretico-Practica Theologia (Ernst Bizer, ed., Die
Dogmatik der Evangelische-Reformierten Kirche Dargestellt und aus den Quellen
Belegt von H. Heppe [rev. ed.; Neukirchen: Neukirchener Verlag, 1958], pp.
lxxx-lxxi). The edition which we have used comprised 1236 quarto pages
complete with index and included much material beyond what can be found in
the original edition. Van Mastricht himself recorded these additions on the
title page: "Theoretico-Practica Theologia, qua, per singula capita
Theologica, pars exegetica, dogmatica, elenchtica and practicia, perpena
successione conjugantur. EDITIO NOVA, priori multo emendatior, and plus
quam tertia parte auctior. ACCEDUNT: Historical Ecclesiastica, Plena
Quidem; Sed Compendiosa: Idea Theologiae Moralis: Hypotyposis Theologiae
Asceticae and Prion opus quasi novum auctore Petro van Mastricht, Trajecti,
ad Rhenum: Ex Officina Thomae Appels, 1699." See also p. 272.

well as in theology, could be an obstacle to the flow of history and Jonathan Edwards had to find a different principle of organization for both in order to realize the program of a "divinity in the new form of a history." The historico-logical ideas to which both Bacon and Hubbard adhered were too much indebted to the age of erudition and polyhistory for the task he envisioned.

Hubbard had to respond to a challenge to his interpretation of providences[1] and in the course of it he provided a summary definition of the relationship between event and meaning or between event and providence. The definition of this relationship was essentially negative because the two sides to the dispute agreed on the basic presupposition of the sovereignty of God, but they disagreed about its application in a particular case. Consequently, Hubbard set out to enumerate those characteristics which did not constitute a providential event. He insisted that the providence of an event or the interpretation of a fact could not depend upon certain intrinsic qualities of a particular event. Thus, meaning could not depend on whether an event belonged to certain classes or kinds of events. Moreover, events did not have to occur at particular times in order to carry meaning, nor did events have to take place in a certain way or answer to a particular prescription in order for them to communicate meaning. Thus, for example, death was not the only kind of event in which the meaning of someone's history became apparent, nor could it be said that death carried more meaning because it occurred earlier or later in someone's life, and, finally, the suddenness of someone's death may arouse other people, but it need not say anything about the meaning of the life of the

---

[1] Hubbard, General History, p. 640.

particular person who died a sudden death. According to Hubbard, all such attempts to restrict the sovereignty of God exclusively to any of these definitions of an event were dictated by the desire to pry into the secret counsels of the "Almighty" and rationalize them. But the Almighty was, as Hubbard pointed out, not confined "to one and the same harbinger having always his arrow upon the string to shoot in the darkness and at noon day." As proof of his position, Hubbard insisted here and elsewhere on Scripture.[1] As the criterion, he pointed out that in the New Testament Christ acquitted rather than judged those on whom the tower of Siloam had fallen.[2] In other words, neither the type of event nor its spectacular character predetermined a particular meaning besides which there could be no other meaning.

The challenge for Hubbard had come from the Quakers. They had apparently claimed that the sudden death of John Norton was a divine judgment upon his participation in the persecution of the Quakers in New England. The meaning of Norton's death, according to the Quakers, was that it sprang from a mind that had failed its spiritual purpose and had thus come to an end of its earthly life. Hubbard, however, turned the argument around and reminded the Quakers that, according to the rules of historiography, the meaning of an event could not be deduced from its inherent qualities such as suddenness. Since the Quakers in this case ignored this vital distinction, their criticism was formally invalid. In his defense of Norton, who was a conspicuous member of the establishment, Hubbard therefore deflected the argument from the sovereignty of God into an apology for the standing order. An event and its providence became the subject of charges and

---

[1] Hubbard, General History, p. 378.

[2] Luke 13, 4.

countercharges, but it did not lead to the kind of self-criticism that was so prominent a feature of the providences in spiritual autobiographies at the time.

Order was also the principle toward which the several definitions of providence in the General History converged. Thus, God maintained a bounty in nature that helped New England to survive the 1640 crisis and by a "special providence" these resources suddenly became the basis of trade with the West Indies. Not only did God maintain nature and arrange[1] for a dramatic turnaround, but also the "general providence"[2] of God so ordered the Massachusetts government that the question whether it ought to be changed was more apparent than real. The benevolence of providence in nature, history, and government was a strong argument to maintain the present order. The "individual beautiful providences" were thus enjoyed in the "peaceable and quiet enjoyment of the purity of God's worship" and the "backside of the cloud that overshadows New England"[3] dealt mainly with those who ran into afflictions because they deviated from that order.[4] Providences, in other words, had become a means of internalizing an existent order. In this respect, Hubbard's view of New England history corresponded to the description of that view of ecclesiastical historiography which Bacon had characterized as the movement through the stages of persecution, migration to rest and peace.[5] Whereas Hubbard used dynamic metaphors of construction in the early parts of his General History, they disappeared in the later parts.[6]

---

[1] Hubbard, General History, p. 239.

[2] Ibid., p. 387.   [3] Ibid., p. 202.   [4] Ibid., pp. 194ff.

[5] Bacon, Works, VIII, p. 436.

[6] Cecilia Tichi, "The Puritan Historians and Their New Jerusalem," Early American Literature, 6, No. 2 (Fall 1971), p. 148f.

Every historian is bound by the limits imposed upon him by the subject matter he has chosen to deal with, and it would be dangerous therefore
to assume that what is available in print or manuscript represented all the
opinions to which Hubbard held. What can bear special emphasis, however,
is that Hubbard was quite specifically the historian of New England, and
when he addressed himself to larger questions that go beyond its confines,
his tone was reluctant and the views that he expressed differed somewhat
from the views of the sovereignty of God and order to which he held otherwise. In a comment upon the unsuccessful settlement in the West Indies by
a group of New Englanders who had left disappointed in the early 1640s and
did not want to come back, Hubbard withheld judgment and concluded his narration of this episode by saying that "the affairs of the world are carried
in a moveable wheel, wherein it is often found that what is highest in one
season is laid quite underneath soon after."[1] In a funeral sermon for one
of the pillars of his Ipswich church, Hubbard selected from universal history such examples which fitted with the idea of the vanity of history and
the declension in it. He said of the time of the judges in the Old
Testament that "each generation brought in fresh examples of Sin and
Judgment, their glory and lustre was never permanent and lasting above one
age." For the time of King Solomon he remarked that people then "obtained
their greatest glory so in this time was laid the first foundation of their
following ruin."[2] The fact that these latter two statements occurred in a

---

[1] Hubbard, General History, p. 379.

[2] William Hubbard, A Funeral Meditation, from those words of the
prophet Isaiah, Chapter 3: 1, 2, 3 occasioned by the interment of Major
Daniel Denison on September 22, 1682 (Samuel Green, Boston, 1684), p. 123.

highly conventionalized setting also showed their use: universal history
has no interest of its own. It became an arsenal of moral admonitions
which were dictated by the concern to warn his parishioners how well and
happy they were within the New England order.

Edward Johnson: *Wonder Working Providence of Sions Savior*

Hubbard as well as Johnson included in their histories a report on
the departure of the first settlers of Massachusetts from England. The way
in which they handled this emotion-laden farewell of friends and relatives
showed significant differences in history-writing between the two men. In
Johnson the doctrinal proposition of Christ the king coalesced with the
metaphor of the captain and his soldiers into an elaborate narration of
dramatic scenes, which made his readers recall other similar experiences
that they might have had of bidding farewell to those who were going off
to a war. The spontaneity, warmth, and vividness which were portrayed in
this opening of Johnson's history have not been appreciated until quite
recently,[2] but they do point to his ability to re-enact and convey past
events imaginatively in a way that was absent from Hubbard. This dramatic
quality corresponded to a sense of rhythm in Johnson's use of verse throughout the history[3] and created the impression that things were really on the
move. Hubbard's approach, on the other hand, was brief, learned, and other-
worldly. Johnson did not leave out the mention that a trip of this magnitude

[1]See for contrast Edwards, Works, V, 130.

[2]Ursula Brumm, "Edward Johnson's Wonder-Working Providence and the
Puritan Conception of History," Jahrbuch Fuer Amerika-Studien, 14-15 (1969-
70), pp. 148-149.

[3]Harold Jantz, The First Century of New England Verse (1944; rpt.
New York: Russell and Russell, 1962), pp. 23ff.

could be the last trip for some of the emigrants. But, in addition to this concern, he lets us see how the friends and relatives will miss each other simply because they like each other. On the other hand, in Hubbard, Governor Winthrop could weep because "religion never makes men stoics." The departure also resembled so very much that into another world that a manifestation of the "deepest sense of sorrow" amongst "natural relations" was in order.[1] While it is apparent that Hubbard comes across as a learned writer, Johnson is by no means simply a boisterous mythically inclined dogmatic representative of the military.

While Hubbard had made the first attempt to write a history of New England along professional principles, Edward Johnson's history provided New England with its first example of a philosopher of history in the garb of a historian. Both of them must be considered minor historians if compared to William Bradford, John Winthrop, or Cotton Mather, but in different ways they nevertheless reflected two tendencies of the age: polyhistory with its sense of professional comprehensiveness and a philosophy of history that could include a sense of the imagination. While the moral improvements on selected pieces of universal history were expressive of Hubbard's provincial cast of mind, Edward Johnson built such references into a context from which he could launch the first interpretation of the American experience in its relation to universal history.

Sacvan Bercovitch has described the technique through which Johnson achieved this purpose as the "fusion of direct narrative and Scriptural allusion." When New England Puritans related their voyage across the Atlant in terms of the crossing of the Red Sea, they could do this in such a way as

---

[1] Hubbard, General History, p. 125.

to "both participate in and surpass the miraculous biblical event and re-
enact the Israelites' sea passage in a way which points forward to their
larger purpose."[1] Johnson's narrative therefore possessed a self-
transcending character and was carried on at two mutually related levels.
Thus the first book included the departure from England, the arrival in
New England, and the formation of the civil government. A second book
dealt with the political, ecclesiastical, economic, and military progress
of the settlers. In a last book Johnson reviewed the achievement and the
implications of the emigration. Within this straightforward narrative
Johnson continually enlarged toward the past and the future in a "typological design."[2] In order to illustrate the aesthetic dimension of this
design we might mention T. S. Eliot's advice to his reader that an understanding of his Waste Land was dependent on a knowledge of James Fraser's
Golden Bough, since otherwise appreciation of the allusions and enjoyment
of the design of this work of art would be impeded. Similarly, Johnson's
reliance upon a typological design presupposed a thorough knowledge of the
whole Bible, a proficiency for which he did not have to ask, but one which
he could presuppose amongst his readers. The structure of the twofold narrative itself can best be understood against the background of the traditional doctrine of the fourfold sense of Scripture. In its application this
theory had a tendency to deal with the literal or historical sense of
Scripture only in order to find a more edifying meaning beyond it. We have
seen that Francis Bacon for his part also played the typical sense of

---

[1] Sacvan Bercovitch, "The Historiography of Johnson's Wonder-Working
Providence," EHIC, 104 (1968), 147.

[2] Ibid., p. 149.

Scripture off against the literal unedifying meaning of it.[1] The consequence of such a view of Scripture was an approach to history that included
a positive view of eternity, but a negative understanding of time. In
Johnson's case, however, the line of differentiation ran between particular and universal history rather than between a deceptive time and a
changeless eternity or morality.

The design by means of which the typological transparency was prevented from becoming an allegorical tautology was the periodization of history. The idea of the period provided that sense of anachronism[2] which held
the crossing of the Red Sea and the crossing of the Atlantic to be two distinct events. In his definition of prophecy, Bacon had pointed out[3] that,
while fulfillment took place continually throughout the ages, there were
and are nevertheless particular ages in which certain processes come to a
height. While typology made possible the expression and comprehension of
continual fulfillments of what was common to all times,[4] the gradations of
the processes point to the periods of universal history in their particular
contributions to the whole. Johnson expressed this awareness when he introduced The Wonder Working Providence of Sions Savior with the statement:

---

[1] Bacon, Works, VIII, p. 407.

[2] F. J. Levy (Tudor Historical Thought, pp. ix-x) defined anachronism
as the sense that "the past was different from the present." According to
him the idea was introduced by Italian humanism and was one of the most
important that underlay the Reformation. We use it here as a means to distinguish between the typological and the anachronistic aspects of prophecy
since, as Bercovitch pointed out, not every use of type also implies a
"typological design." There were New Englanders before Johnson who had
referred to the crossing of the Atlantic in terms of a crossing of the Red
Sea. Johnson was the first to put that into a "design."

[3] See p. 43.

[4] Samuel Mather, The Figures and the Types of the Old Testament,
Dublin, 1683, p. 28.

> Christ Jesus intending to manifest his Kingly Office towards his
> churches more fully than ever yet the Sons of men saw, even to the
> uniting of Jew and Gentile Churches in one Faith, begins with our
> English Nation (whose former Reformation being vere imperfect) doth
> now resolve to cast down their false foundation of prelacy, even in
> the hight of their domineering dignity.[1]

The period of fulfillment with which Johnson was about to deal had

significance because it was to lead to unity. This unity was a completion

of the Reformation, and was brought about by the kingly office of Christ.

We have pointed out before how the metaphor of the captain and his

troops about to embark upon a campaign had helped toward the imaginative

re-enactment on the part of the reader of the events which Johnson related.

This metaphor in addition served Johnson as a means by which to visualize,

dramatize, and clarify the integration of the dimensions and of the drive

of divine presence in history. For Johnson the able captain was a man who

had a goal, who could give the orders that will attain the goal, who would

go into battle with his troops and lead them through vicissitudes to vic-

tory. God was therefore not just an Almighty being which in its eternal

presence had "always his arrow upon the string" in order to "shoot" into

history "in the darkness and at noon day."[2] God was rather a leader who

led through history. Critics of Johnson have always recognized and

rejected, but not analyzed or assessed this predominantly militant charac-

ter of this historiographical conception which provided his historical nar-

ratives with a beginning, a middle, and an end, and through which he made

comprehensible to himself and his audience that the kingly office of Christ

was the application of the work of redemption. This interpretation was quite

different from the one that appeared in John Davenport's Creed where the

---

[1] Johnson, <u>Wonder-Working Providence</u>, p. 24.

[2] See p. 64.

church was already the one church and could have as its goal no further advancement to more glorious times, but only perfection as the glorious church triumphant in heaven.[1]

Within the period that was the subject of Johnson's history, we do find a pervasive emphasis on the end, goal, or purpose of history as the unity of the churches. This end was stated in the beginning, it was repeated with emphasis at the end, and it punctuated like so many exclamation marks his whole narrative throughout.[2] It was toward this unity that the imperfect Reformation must move. For Johnson, therefore, the goal of New England was not confined toward a restoration of the Church of England to purity in a more perfect reformation, but its purpose had become the unity of all churches throughout the world of which England was a prominent member, but by no means the only part. Did England, therefore, now at the beginning of Cromwell's reign, not adopt the New England polity which had proven so successful at the inauguration of this new age, then this constituted no threat to the mission of New England, but was simply a failure on the part of the mother country to join in with the advancement of the kingdom toward unity.[3] Reformation for Johnson was not a Reformation of

---

[1]H. Shelton Smith, Robert T. Handy, and Lefferts A. Loetscher, American Christianity: An Historical Interpretation with Representative Documents (New York: Scribner's, 1960), I, 110f.

[2]Johnson, Wonder-Working Providence, pp. 24, 30, 34, 60, 117, 138, 142, 255.

[3]Ibid., pp. 155, 160. - In his contribution to History, The Development of Historical Studies in the United States, ed. John Higham with Leonard Krieger and Felix Gilbert, L. Krieger dealt with the study of "European history in America" (233-313). He reviewed the colonial historian William Bradford, Cotton Mather, and Thomas Prince and came to the conclusion that in their case European history was simply a backdrop. In the case of Thomas Hutchinson, he observed that even the backdrop had disappeared. On the other hand, nineteenth century nationalism in American historiography

doctrine, nor a Reformation of discipline, but Reformation was in addition
the movement of all churches toward the kingdom. He pointed out that the
devil let Christians have their Reformation of doctrine as long as he was
still in charge of discipline and polity and that when the New Englanders had
finally introduced also the Reformation of discipline with such great success, he made one last assault upon doctrine itself.[1] After this
Reformation of discipline and the defense of doctrine had been completed,
the road was free for the movement toward unity.

The distinction between a Reformation of doctrine and a Reformation
of discipline reflected an accepted opinion of the age. Martin Luther was
looked upon as the reformer of doctrine and Calvin in addition to that also
as the reformer of discipline. These terms should not be understood in too
narrow a sense historically, for the understanding of discipline within
such "second reformation"[2] movements varied. William Ames' call for a
reformation of discipline arose within the context of Puritanism in England
and Precisianism in Holland, whereas another movement in some parts of

---

either led to the manifestation of a great awareness of Europe or it provided the basis for the writing of European history. This nationalism
defined America not in terms of parochialism, but as the focus within a
universal historical destiny (p. 241). It provided thus a religious motif
for the American historians of Europe which served as a "constant principle
of identity in terms of which the changing modes of Western culture
acquired meaning and coherence for Americans" (p. 245). Krieger guessed
that this attitude may be "either a residue of Enlightenment cosmopolitan-
ism or the synthetic habit of mind native to the nineteenth century" (p. 241).
Actually the "synthetic habit" appeared already in Edward Johnson's historiography. Krieger pointed out that this principle outlasted the changes of
the nineteenth century. The same could be said with regard to the Enlightenment, for George Bancroft's description of Jonathan Edwards clearly combined
the religious principle with an enlightenment of the progress of mankind.

[1] Johnson, Wonder-Working Providence, pp. 121-122ff., 136, 269.

[2] For use of the name, see Jürgen Moltmann, Christoph Pezel 1539-
1604 und der Calvinismus in Bremen (Bremen: 1958), p. 146.

Germany earlier on had proceeded along the lines of a non-pietistic
Christian humanism. It was within this latter group that we find a very
striking example of the change from the second to what we could call a
third Reformation.

Christoph Pezel, the reformer of the church of Bremen in the north-
ern part of Germany, was strongly influenced by Philip Melanchthon's view
of church history which saw in the coincidence of the revival of true learning and of the Reformation of the pure gospel the restoration of the golden
age of the unity of antiquity and of the apostolic age. In order to
secure this goal more thoroughly, a reform of polity and education was
undertaken and the idolatrous practices removed that had remained after the
reformation of doctrine.[1] In his old age, Pezel set out to write a world
history beginning with the creation and stretching down to the present.
Before he could work on the third volume that was to deal with the age of
the Reformation, he died in 1604. Another theologian of Bremen, Johannes
Lampadius, completed the work and published it in 1626 under the name of
Mellificium historicum Integrum. While Pezel had led up to the Reformation
as an age of restoration, Lampadius introduced, as Moltmann pointed out,
the different view in his completion which made the Reformation the way
to the fulfillment of the kingdom.[2] In other words, history was now as
Edward Johnson put it, "the furthering of this great worke of the
Reformation, and advancement of the kingdom of Christ."[3]

[1] Moltmann, Christoph Pezel, pp. 84-86.

[2] Moltmann, "Jacob Brocard als Vorläufer der Reich-Gottes-Theologie
und der symbolisch-prophetischen Schriftauslegung des Johann Coccejus,"
Zeitschrift fuer Kirchengeschichte, 71, No. 1 and No. 2 (1960), p. 124.

[3] Johnson, Wonder-Working Providence, p. 89.

Recent Puritan studies have not provided much interpretative help for
an understanding of this view of the kingdom. Their interest in finding a
unifying theme in seventeenth-century New England Puritanism has been
mainly confined to the tracing and defining of the concept of the covenant.
Perry Miller in particular was concerned to show how this term secured a
workable basis for revelation so that the opposite dangers of antinomianism
and Arminianism which arose out of a then dominant appeal to predestination
could be avoided. In this way he was able to show how New England
Puritanism could be established theologically, ecclesiastically, and spiritually. Discussions of the covenant consequently tended to move along the
line of its relation to the logic of the schools, of its affinity to legal
and contractual theories and of its place in the psychological analysis of
the conversion process. The place of the covenant in relation to a view
of history played no role in these discussions. In this connection another
observation by Moltmann is very helpful. He showed that the Dutch theologian Johannes Cocceius, who had also studied under William Ames, enlarged
his theology of the covenant through the inclusion of the topos of the
gradual advancement of the kingdom through history, and turned the covenant
into a historical concept in the process.[1] This dynamic view of the covenant as something new in covenant theology is usually acknowledged.
Moltmann emphasized that this change was derived from the prophetic exegesis
of the kingdom in the apocalyptic literature of Scripture.[2] When we view
Edward Johnson against this contemporary background, then we can see more

---

[1]Gottlob Schrenk, Gottesreich und Bund im Aelteren Protestantismus
vornehmlich bei Johannes Coccejus, 2nd Ed. (1923; rpt. Darmstadt:
Wissenschaftliche Buchgesellschaft, 1967), pp. 209ff.

[2]Moltmann, "Jacob Brocard als Vorläufer," p. 126.

clearly that it is the notion of the kingdom in Johnson's history which for him turned the Cambridge Platform with its covenant-inspired view of the church into dynamic action. The covenanted churches became the mobile units of the campaign that was to lead toward the unity of the churches.

Moltmann also pointed to two sources which effected these exemplary changes in historiography and in theology. For the latter case he found strong Joachimite influence[1] and in the former he could point to an acknowledged debt to John Napier's and Thomas Brightman's commentaries on the apocalypse as well as to the praise of King James I of England's prophetic exegesis.[2] The great influence of Brightman in early Massachusetts is best illustrated by John Cotton in his lecture sermons on the apocalypse. Here he was at pains to explain when he diverged from the latter's interpretation.[3] Edward Johnson was familiar with John Cotton's exegesis and also quoted him on the forthcoming arrival of the kingdom.[4] Johnson also mentioned that "the ministers many of them" were ready to use their exegetical expertise in order to see in the great earthquake of 1638 a sign that "suddenly there would follow great alterations in the kingdoms of Europe."[5] The particular examples which illustrated the import of Johnson's historiography were chosen for their demonstrative value. Beyond a sheer quantification of evidence of the revolution in historical thinking in the seventeenth century they helped us to evaluate the changed and redirected focus

---

[1] Moltmann, "Jacob Brocard als Vorläufer," p. 129.

[2] Ibid., p. 125.

[3] John Cotton, An Exposition Upon the Thirteenth Chapter of the Revelation (London: printed by M. S. for Chapman, 1655), p. 89.

[4] Edward Johnson, Wonder-Working Providence, p. 268.

[5] Ibid., p. 185.

in the interpretation of such traditional subjects as the covenant, the
Reformation, and the kingly office of Christ.

In his emphasis on the kingly office of Christ as the explicit
principle for organization and integration, Edward Johnson's history
anticipated in a surprising way the draft of the History of the Work of
Redemption by Jonathan Edwards. Both combined an interest in the universal
and in the particular and thus stand apart from a historiography that is
represented in William Hubbard's General History and Cotton Mather's
Magnalia Christi Americana.[1] Both of the latter looked backward. In his
introduction, Cotton Mather viewed the history of New England simply as
the moral improvement upon the second Reformation achieved by the Fathers
of the Colony. Hubbard for his part looked back upon the first ten years
as to the golden age. Both Edward Johnson and Jonathan Edwards looked
forward to the glorious and imminent times of the Kingdom to come.

Review of Scholarship

While our considerations of the historiography of Hubbard and
Johnson have led to a recognition of the variety of approaches that were
adopted by the Massachusetts historians of New England, we must now also
pay attention to the complexity that it showed. Hubbard and Johnson were a
good preliminary illustration of this particular issue. Both of them use
the concept of providences throughout their respective works as a means of
interpreting events. While for Hubbard providences were ultimately rooted
in the pretemporal secret will of the sovereign God, Johnson throughout
looked upon providences as part of the Sovereignty of Christ which worked

---

[1]Cotton Mather, Magnalia, p. 26.

toward the full and final arrival of the kingdom throughout history.
Providences were consequently not related to something pretemporal that
was difficult to know, but to something supertemporal that was known and
expected to come and which already moved things to prepare for its coming.
While within the framework of providences Hubbard talked about a predestination that tended toward determinism and a contained church and social
order, Johnson wrote in the awareness of a postdestination[1] and the destiny
of a communicative church and social order. In a major departure from
previous scholarship Bercovitch has set out to describe the union of these
elements in the colonial imagination by pointing to the afflictions of
daily existence as the mark of the provisional and as the promise of a
glorious future that has already been predetermined.[2] The afflictions
pointed therefore to a movement that included the moments of the
pretemporal, the supertemporal, and the posttemporal.

Shifts of emphasis like these within a view of divine sovereignty
were an indication that an interpretation of the historiography of seventeenth-century New England must move carefully in order not to end up in
avoidable interpretative dilemmas. Alan Howard has shown that William
Bradford's historiography, which also presupposed the inscrutable sovereignty of God and the limitations of man, did nevertheless relate these
two poles in such a way as to provide man positive support and help him to
see an unfolding providential design in a "howling wilderness."[3] Recent

---

[1]This term I owe to Jürgen Moltmann, Praedestination und
Perseveranz, p. 34.

[2]Sacvan Bercovitch, Horologicals and Chronometricals: The Rhetoric
of the Jeremiads, Literary Monographs, 3 (Madison: University of Wisconsin
Press, 1970), pp. 11, 15, 25.

[3]Alan B. Howard, "Art and History in Bradford's of Plymouth Plantation," William and Mary Quarterly, 28 (April 1971), pp. 243, 266.

research in the fields of preparationism[1] and of the origins of evangelical
Calvinism[2] has proven that from the beginning of the Massachusetts settlement there were "many strands in the founders rhetoric."[3] This fact illustrated clearly our earlier characterization of the seventeenth century as a
climate where several ideas or clusters of ideas compete and fuse in a way
where it is not a limine possible to pinpoint crises in the way in which we
have come to understand this word in the aftermath of the rise of a specific
concept of critical history. Thus, for example, it is ironic to dismiss
Edward Johnson as militant and at the same time criticize the Puritans for
their otherworldliness while Johnson's historiography expressed within the
context of other available options such a move toward thisworldliness.

The increasing interest in the historiography of the seventeenth-
and early eighteenth-century Massachusetts historians of New England has
led to many new insights, but a general picture of this historiography
begins to emerge only slowly because there is as yet no conceptualization
of a general framework that would explain how these Massachusetts historians operated. In a pioneering article on the providential interpretation of history,[4] K. B. Murdock observed and documented a trend in
Hubbard's Narrative of the Troubles with the Indians in New England which
pointed to a greater emphasis on second rather than primary causes in his

[1]Norman Pettit, The Heart Prepared, Grace and Conversion in Puritan
Spiritual Life (New Haven: Yale University Press, 1966), p. 86f.

[2]Glenn T. Miller, "The Rise of Evangelical Calvinism: A Study in
Jonathan Edwards and the Puritan Tradition," Diss., Union Theological
Seminary, New York, 1971.

[3]Alden T. Vaughn, Rev. of The Mathers: Three Generations of Puritan
Intellectuals 1596-1728 by Robert Middlekauf, American Historical Review,
78 (February 1973), p. 141.

[4]K. B. Murdock, "William Hubbard and the Providential Interpretation
of History." See also p. 57, footnote 1.

view of providence in history. According to Murdock, material causes were
put by Hubbard on the same level with the supernatural. Murdock supported
this observation with examples from the General History which he had
checked out against Hubbard's sources.

Murdock wanted to be understood as merely probing a question of
interpretation and therefore he offered two possible ways of understanding
this trend. The first possibility was that Hubbard moved toward modernity
and a mechanistic universe. Murdock himself was inclined toward this view
of Hubbard. He supported it by reference to the biographical fact that
Hubbard had studied medicine before he became a minister. Murdock nevertheless conceded that this trend may also have to do with the fact that Hubbard
was an "ardent believer in the theory of 'order' in society, established by
God." Insofar as Murdock provided evidence for the two possibilities, the
historian must give more credence to this latter version, since in the case
of the former, Murdock did not indicate in what way or to what extent
Hubbard had discussed the relation of primary and secondary causes and it
might therefore have been useful to probe this traditional frame of reference and its relation to Hubbard's work before an even tentative commitment
to far-reaching conclusions was made.[1] Hubbard's emphasis on second causes
looked therefore less than a discovery of modern rationality and more like
a case of routinization of charisma that occurred in the conservation of
the establishment.

[1]Murdock, "William Hubbard and the Providential Interpretation of
History," p. 34, 35n. The contemporary Quaestiones for commencement dispu-
tations at Harvard dealt with the relation of primary and secondary causation (Morison, Harvard in the Seventeenth Century, p. 611), and the well-
known reformed theologian J. Wolleb quite simply said in his exposition of
providence that "providentia dei causas non tollit, sed ponit." (Heppe,
Reformed Dogmatics, p. 209.)

In addition, Murdock's examples from the General History represented spot checks on Hubbard's relation to his sources, but the interpretation which he based on it had been extended in order to show that the
inclusion of natural history in the General History indicated a growing
awareness on the part of Hubbard of the natural environment of history.
Neither of these opinions took seriously the process of formalization that
was observable in Hubbard's history of New England and which followed a
contemporary ideal of comprehensive classification. Until a full-scale
investigation into the relation of the General History to its sources is
undertaken and until the process of the formation of tradition for the
historical and literary genre of providences is analyzed, such far-reaching
conclusions are based on methodologically insufficient grounds, and the
Baconian skepticism to wait until all the facts are in is in order.

The relation between primary and secondary causes in providence
could also be discussed less in a philosophical and more in aesthetic
terms in order to bring out the particular spiritual quest in which the
historiography of these historians was engaged. The application of the
tools of the literary imagination has the advantage of focusing more
clearly on the redemptive character of the providences over against a
technical philosophical discussion of the nature of providence in general.
Cecilia Tichi has therefore undertaken to describe this historiography in
terms of what she called a largely unconscious transposition of the spiritual
biography into the tribal context of New England society and has illustrated this tradition by an analysis of several of its unifying images
such as the journey, the sea voyage,[1] and building.[2] Especially as far as

---

[1]Tichi, "Spiritual Biography and the Lords Remembrancers," pp. 74-81.

[2]Tichi, "The Puritan Historians," p. 148f.

the analysis of images is concerned, we can see the different aspects of
the redemptive history which were stressed by the several historians: in
Bradford the pilgrim is the theme; in Johnson it was the captain and the
soldiers; and in Hubbard it was more implicitly assumed than explicitly
stated that the good churchman was the ideal. The shortcomings of this
approach are the opposite from those that occurred in the philosophical
discussion of providence. Alan B. Howard has pointed out that William
Haller's interpretation of English Puritanism was so weighted on the
spiritual side that the respect for both the spiritual and the factual in
William Bradford was taken to be a development in the direction of the
"Yankee spirit."[1] Tichi's interpretation of New England historiography
included the same "fallacy of extrapolation."[2] Thus the deliberate decision on the part of Nathaniel Morton to spiritualize in his New England
Memorial was taken to be the beginning of a tradition and Thomas Prince's
New England Chronology its abrupt end. The fallacy which is involved here
is that of an overemphasis on the spiritual in Puritan historiography. It
is indeed true that Prince set out to compile a "naked Register, comprising
only facts in a Chronological Epitome." Such chronological research, however, was a flourishing branch of the study of universal history in orthodo:
circles at the turn of the eighteenth century in Europe, and Prince's marke
antiquarian interests might have been directed in this direction during his
long stay in England.[3] In a way, his desire to include New England in the

[1]Howard, "Art and History," p. 239.

[2]David Hackett Fischer, Historians' Fallacies (New York: Harper
Torchbook, 1970), pp. 120ff.

[3]Frank E. Manuel, Isaac Newton, Historian (Cambridge: Belknap
Press, 1963), p. 38.

chronology of world history recalled Increase Mather's proposal for a

native collection of providences and a native natural history. A suspicion

of the disavowal of the spiritual side of providence on Prince's part would

probably have caused more than a simple disappointment over the esoteric

character of a long-expected history by a man whose abilities were held in

great esteem throughout Massachusetts.

Bacon had defined tradition as an authority that was taken for

granted and improved and not advanced or enlarged.[1] Such a tradition

allowed for variety but it also imposed limitations. As long as the

tradition-forming process in these individual Massachusetts historians is

not placed more in the center of a thorough research of them, the freedom

of movement within this tradition will always appear as so many furtive

departures from traditionalism and bypass the yet unexploited possibilities

for an understanding of New England historiography through the medium of

the Massachusetts historians of New England in the seventeenth and early

eighteenth centuries.

Our discussion of the New England historians proper had to be exten-

sive because they have loomed so large in the investigation into New England

historiography. At the same time, the differences that became visible in

our typological approach to its study raised points for inquiry that lead

beyond these mostly unpublished works toward the larger questions of the

---

[1] Bacon, Works, VIII, p. 30. "Men of this kind, therefore, amend some things, but advance little; and improve the condition of knowledge, but do not extend its range." There is a real change of meaning for the word "improve" between Bacon's time and our own. If we think of "internal improvements," etc., the common understanding is that of a qualitative change for the better. When Bacon addresses himself to qualitative change he speaks of De Augmentis ("enlargement") which in its English original is known as The Advancement of Knowledge. "Improve," for Bacon, retains its logical meaning of "proof" as the elaboration of a syllogism that cannot move beyond its premises.

intellectual and institutional place and focus which helped to construct,
internalize, socialize, and adapt the several aspects of a historical world
view that these historians articulated in part, but did not formulate in
its entirety. On the one hand we need an "interpretative thesis"[1] that
will help explain and comprehend a series of otherwise diverse elements,
statements, or actions without making the claim of explaining everything
or of comprehending every detail. On the other hand, the investigation of
many details will give the interpretative thesis itself viability and
explanatory force. The relation between thesis and investigation therefore constitutes a hermeneutical circle where one side helps to explicate
the other, but where neither can explain away the other in the interest of
either simplifying the thesis or the investigation. In Jonathan Edwards
and in his time there was one interpretative thesis which was concerned
with both research and interpretation of history. The exegesis of scriptur
was concerned with the pursuit of the detail and its relation to the whole.
Bacon's description of prophecy as we had seen presupposed this approach.
Edward Johnson provided a glimpse of its operation in history writing; in
Jonathan Edwards the variety and complexity as well as comprehension of
this interpretative thesis for a historical world-view will find full conceptualization. Our next step will therefore be to inquire more closely
into the view of Scripture that made possible such a view of history.

---

[1] Robert T. Handy, The Protestant Quest for a Christian America,
1830-1930, Ed., Richard C. Wolf, Facet Books, Historical Series 15
(Philadelphia: Fortress Press, 1967), pp. 1ff.

Summary

The literature of Massachusetts in the seventeenth and early eighteenth centuries was pervaded by a many-sided historical knowledge which the settlers had brought with them or which they had acquired in their new environment. This knowledge was cultivated carefully, whether it served a polemic purpose or whether it helped with the more pragmatic task of survival. Nevertheless, many of the Massachusetts historians of New England in that era were published only posthumously or with difficulty. A comparison of the two minor and neglected historians, William Hubbard and Edward Johnson, provided the point of departure for an analysis of the breadth of New England historiography at that time. Both writers availed themselves in their interpretations of the New England experience of those contemporary models which we found in Francis Bacon and both of them faced a formidable new task. William Hubbard combined cosmography, chronicles, narration, and providences, and employed them as a means to bring together the growing past of the New England experience into a general history. While Hubbard found no successor or continuator, his achievement rested on the same intellectually respectable principles which P. Miller had established for seventeenth century New England religious thought as a whole. Over against Hubbard's polyhistoric organization, Edward Johnson in a sustained way placed the New England experience in the context of a future universal history. Johnson was one of the representatives of an eschatological interpretation of providences through Scripture-prophecy which marked a decisive shift from the second Reformation toward the third Reformation and which anticipated formally as well as materially views on history held by Jonathan Edwards.

A survey of past research on the seventeenth-century Massachusetts historians of New England showed a failure to find a well-defined and

comprehensive interpretative thesis which could have aided in the pursuit
of an illuminating inquiry into New England historiography. This criticism
is true also of the pioneering work of K. B. Murdock. Such lack of conceptualization led to the erroneous assumptions that emphases on secondary
causation or on aesthetic values in the sources could be only a departure
from traditionalism and not the display of variety within tradition. The
comparative interpretation of even Hubbard and Johnson showed that New
England historiography was more sensitive to the facts of history and more
sophisticated in their articulation. Thus it has been hardly noticed that
providences within the same tradition referred to predestination and postdestination, to beginning as well as to end. The role that historians playe
in their own time and the pitfalls which their investigation entailed for
modern interpreters led us to the decision not to treat Massachusetts historians qua historians or to focus on individual themes only. Instead, we
introduced as a sociologically adequate and intellectually satisfactory
interpretative thesis the exploration of the hermeneutical circle of Scriptu
and exegesis in its significance for a view of history in New England in
general and for Edwards' attitude to history in particular.

CHAPTER III

EXEGESIS AND HISTORY: THOMAS SHEPARD

In his critical edition of Edwards' Religious Affections, John E.
Smith reviewed the evidence of the great influence of Shepard's Parable of
the Ten Virgins on Edwards' own description of the relation of understanding and will as well as on his view of holiness.[1] This comparison showed
that Shepard not only belonged to Edwards' background, but must be considered one of his teachers. The argument for the relation of exegesis and
history as one part of our interpretative thesis will therefore take as its
appropriate point of departure the Parable of the Ten Virgins.

New Englanders of the seventeenth century were besides other things
also students of Scripture, readers and writers of commentaries on Scripture
as well as preachers of and listeners to sermons based on Scripture. This
importance of both Scripture and sermon has been described unwittingly by
Thomas Shepard. In his Magnalia Christi Americana, Cotton Mather had styled
Shepard as the "Pastor Evangelicus,"[2] and indeed Shepard's reputation rested
on his two books called The Sincere Convert and The Sound Believer, both of
which became long-time favorites on conversion. In the preface to his

---

[1] Jonathan Edwards, Religious Affections, ed., John E. Smith (New
Haven: Yale University Press, 1959), pp. 53f.

[2] Cotton Mather, Magnalia Christi Americana, 2 vols. (Hartford: Silas
Andrus and Son, 1855), Vol. I, pp. 380ff.

<u>Theses Sabbaticae</u> on the other hand,[1] he confessed to be "ashamed therefore
to be seen in this garment" of polemical divinity and he set out to describe
the various structural, sociological, and substantial metamorphoses that his
sermons underwent on the way to a divinity text and treatise.

Shepard had originally "opened" the ten commandments from Scripture
in his series of sabbath sermons. As he proceeded in this homiletic effort
he had to go beyond his own plan and meet the desires of "some students in
the college" as well as resolve the doubts of "more popular capacities"
through the inclusion of an extended discussion of controversial issues
related to these commandments. Sermons by definition could not deal with
such issues in a systematic way and Shepard therefore complied with the
further request of the students and "reduced" what he had said on the
sabbath in particular into a compend. Through these students the word went
out to the elders of some churches who in turn asked Shepard to expand the
compend for the sake of removing the obscurity that was occasioned by its
brevity and littleness, but also for the sake of further and fuller doctrinal "explication." At a meeting of all the elders of the colony, Shepard
was requested to publish his extended compend. When he finally acceded to
these demands, he was aware that the publication would leave out those parts
that had been "more useful to plain people" in their public delivery. While
on the other hand he was not certain what a book like this, coming as it did
from "remote places," could achieve, and while he also thought that for a
well-stocked European market "any thing of this nature is to cast water

[1] The Works of Thomas Shepard, 3 vols. (Boston: Doctrinal Tract and
Book Society, 1853), Vol. III, p. 22. For the interpretation in the following paragraph, see <u>ibid.</u>, pp. 224-24 -- all subsequent references to and
quotations from Shepard's writings are based on this edition and will appear
as "Shepard, <u>Works.</u>"

into the sea," he was nevertheless convinced that English errors on the subject of the sabbath justified his endeavor.

Shepard's prefatorial remarks on the prehistory of this work showed a clear shift away from the dynamic, sociologically and casuistically comprehensive concern of the preaching and pastoral situation that included devotional edification as well as doctrinal education through the explication of Scripture. The finished product was rather a doctrinal treatise and a position paper for a specialized audience with primarily polemic and controversial intent. When we turn from here to Shepard's other lecture series on the Parable of the Ten Virgins, we move very close to this dynamic preaching situation, for Shepard had transcribed only one sheet of these sermon notes for publication.[1] While the notes themselves therefore were plentiful, if not discursive and extensive though not complete, we can nevertheless gain a knowledge through them of his exegesis.

Shepard with great circumspection took the whole of the Matthean apocalypse[2] and then carefully step by step led toward the reason for selection of one parable in it as the basic text of his lecture series. According to Shepard this apocalypse contained two prophecies; one on the destruction of Jerusalem (24:4-23) and one on the end of the world (24:23-25). In answer to two questions (24:36) by the disciples which in turn had arisen out of two remarks by Christ on these subjects (24:2, 23:39), the predictions on the end of the world were in turn divided into a series of different parables. The first group which contained amongst others the parable of

---

[1]Shepard, Works, II, p. 8.

[2]Chapters 24 and 25 of the gospel according to Matthew contained prophecies and warnings and are therefore referred to as Matthean apocalypse.

the unfaithful servant also compared the last days to the "sensual and degenerate" days of Noah before the flood. The second group consisted only of the parable of the ten virgins and referred to the state of "security" within the churches at the end. The third group with the parable of the man who buried his talent referred to those who had willfully neglected their first awakening. Shepard's ecclesiological typology was not without a basis in the text, for the parable of the ten virgins stood out as the most balanced description of the end. "Sensuality" and "security" respectively were eschatological signs in different "places of the world." The following notes made it clear that these signs were identified geographically as separate states rather than temporally as progressive phases. The third type of the willful backsliders left an option of apostasy in either case as it was neither put with the "sensuality" of Europe nor with the "security" of New England.[1]

The survey of the context of the Matthean apocalypse was followed by an analysis of the structure[2] of the parable of the ten virgins (25:1-13) as the pericope of his choice within that context. According to Shepard, part one of the parable (1-5) described the "church's preparation to meet with Christ, called here the bridegroom" and part two (5-12) dealt with "the bridegroom's coming forth to meet them." Both parts were oriented toward the "scope"[3] which contained a "persuasion" that did not simply

---

[1]Shepard, Works, I, pp. 13-14.

[2]This term is used in the English translation of John Calvin's commentary on a Harmony of the Evangelists, Matthew Mark and Luke, trans., William Pringle, Calvin's Commentaries, 3 (Grand Rapids: Eerdmans, 1949), p. 17.

[3]The original meaning of the term in Greek was that of "something aimed at." The word became part of the technical language of exegesis where it referred to the finding out of the goal or message of a text by means of

direct to watchfulness, but to continuance and perseverance in it from

prudent foresight of the coming of Christ (verse 13). This meticulous

analysis of context and structure in general and the focus on the scope in

particular clarified his attitude towards exegesis itself, towards the rela-

tion of ecclesiology and eschatology, towards tradition and the themes of

historiography, as well as to the concept of preparation in the light of

the scope of coming.

What made the difference for Shepard's exegesis in this particular

instance was the recognition of the importance of "Jewish customs and his-

tories" of the wedding as a background for a proper understanding of the

parable:

> The parable itself is set down agreeable to the custom of those
> times wherein our Saviour lived, wherein their marriages were usually
> celebrated in the night time; she that was the bride was attended
> with sundry virgins to meet the bridegrooms; these virgins, it being
> the night season, took therefore their lamps with them; those that were
> ready, and met the bridegroom, were admitted to the marriage room and
> supper; those that came after that time, if once the doors were shut,
> were surely kept out though they knocked hard to come in. All this,
> those who are acquainted with Jewish histories and customs know to be
> true, which we are to attend, because it gives not a little light to
> the true and genuine explication of this parable.[1]

Awareness of the integrity of a story derived from such histories exerted

an interpretative restraint which became apparent in his treatment of

particulars within the text itself.

---

grammatical, logical, and background analysis. Scope was therefore not
identical with the idea of a merely intended meaning of a passage which
purported to be something other than its literal scope. Differences and
disputes did occur over the question as to how broad or comprehensive the
scope itself was in any given case. In modern English usage the notion of
scope as "range of one's perceptions" expressed more adequately the idea of
breadth than that of objective purpose which was part of its original meaning
and of its use in exegesis.

[1]Shepard, _Works_, II, pp. 14-15.

The fact that the Parable of the Ten Virgins had been delivered over a number of years[1] makes possible a better understanding of Shepard's exegetical procedure because in this sequence of sermon lectures he had to "open" his text several times at different points.[2] Insofar as these several openings are still recognizable they show a connection with the overall scope and dispel the impression based on the reading of individual sermons as though sermon texts were only dicta probantia. A clear example of this occurred at the beginning of his sermon on verse 2 of the parable: "They that were foolish took their lamps and took no oil with them. But the wise took oil in their vessels with their lamps."[3] "Popish interpreters, as Shepard called them, would understand by oil the good works and by light the merit of faith which was answerable to their dogma that works saved rather than faith. On the other hand, "some of our own divines" and the "Rhemists"[4] as the more recent "popish" interpreters would reverse the meaning of this allegory and take oil to be the "good intention" while the lighted lamps were the good works. In both cases, the understanding of the text was centered around the doctrinal issue of justification by faith or works that was at the heart of the theological controversies of Reformation and Counter-Reformation. What the contemporary Jewish background as the

---

[1] June 1636 through May 1640, Shepard, Works, II, pp. 8-9.

[2] Ibid., pp. 14-15, 68, 183, 487, 409-410, etc.

[3] Ibid., p. 68.

[4] Rhemists referred to Roman Catholic fugitives who established their own college at Douay in France and brought out their own translation of the Bible (New Testament, Reims 1582 and the Old Testament at Douay, in 1609-1610) with annotations in order to combat Protestant corruptions of Scripture (The New Schaff - Herzog Encyclopaedia of Religious Knowledge, ed. S. Macauly Jackson, II [New York: Funk and Wagnall, 1908, pp. 138-139].)

origin of the parable suggested to Shepard was that the light pointed not
only to a general watchfulness, as Thomas Cartwright[1] had suggested, but
such a light was the means to maintain a watchful "perseverance" and an
eschatological readiness, for the scope is the coming of the bridegroom.

Another example of such interpretative restraint occurred in Shepard's
explanation of the reason why there should be five foolish and five wise
virgins. He suggested that this division into five sincere and five false
virgins "seems to carry the face of truth," but he refused to be drawn into
any discussion beyond that, for "I am fearful to rack and torment parables,
wherein I chiefly look into the scope and that is this, that not one or two,
but a great part of them were sincere, and a great part of them false."[2]
Shepard commented even more specifically on why there should be just ten
virgins. The explanations he gave were that "because it was a perfect number, and so signified the estate of all virgin churches, or because it was
the custom not to exceed the number of ten, to honour them at their marriage."[3] In either case, the emphasis that he bestowed on these different
explanations makes clear that he viewed "ten" in its allegorical and historical sense from the point of view of the scope. The idea of the perfect
number had played a crucial role in transferring the expectation of a concrete future millenium on this earth into an ecclesiastical millennium.
Augustine, for example, had taken the number one thousand to stand for
perfection which then in turn he associated with the perfection of the
church so that the church itself became the perfect reign. In this way

[1]1535-1603.

[2]Shepard, Works, II, p. 183.

[3]Ibid.

all prophetic calculations with years were eliminated and the year 1000
A.D. did not cause a debate as to whether the millennium had arrived or
not.[1] The combination of the perfect number of the virgin churches of
New England and the rejection of an earthly millennium in Shepard pointed
therefore to a strong Augustinian ecclesiastical emphasis. On the other
hand, the inclusion of the historical sense seemed to have no particular
reason for the mention of the number ten except that so many maids of
honour were customarily needed for the sake of the ceremony. The very fact,
however, that they were needed for the honour of the ceremony pointed in
and through the number ten itself toward the scope of the story. While
Shepard did therefore not relinquish the allegorical sense and gave preference to the historical sense in his interpretation because it pointed
toward the scope, he restricted at the same time the allegorical speculation as well as a solely antiquarian interest in the investigation of the
Jewish background itself. This concern with the scope as the pivotal principle of Scripture and therefore of its exegesis was something that Shepard
shared with the hermeneutics of the Reformers.[2]

Jonathan Mitchell, the successor of Thomas Shepard to the pulpit at
the church in Cambridge had supplied the preface to the posthumous publication of the lecture series. In this preface he anticipated criticism and
defended Shepard's prophetic "accommodation" of the parable "to the times

---

[1] Wilhelm Kamlah, Apokalypse und Geschichtstheologie, die Mittelalterliche Auslegung der Apokalypse vor Joachim von Fiore, Historische
Studien, 285 (Berlin: Verlag Dr. Emil Ebering, 1935), pp. 11-12.

[2] Gerhard Ebeling, Evangelische Evangelienauslegung, Eine Untersuchung
zu Luthers Hermeneutik (1942; Rpr. Darmstadt: Wissenschaftliche Buchgesellschaft
1962), pp. 225ff; 410ff; T.H.L. Parker, Calvin's New Testament Commentaries
(London: SCM Press, 1971), p. 39ff.

of the expected calling of the Jews."[1] Mitchell gave no particular reasons

for such objections, but insofar as they concern context and text of the

Matthean apocalypse they were not surprising because the traditional under-

standing of them ran in the direction that the prediction of the end of

Jerusalem included the terminus of Jewish history and that the prediction

of the end of the world which was also contained in this apocalypse referred

to the church as the end of history.[2] Mitchell, on the other hand, took up

a different line of defense which dealt not with the exegetical issues:

> The substance of the work may be accounted for in a more ordinary
> manner proper and seasonable for these times, but thereih every man
> is left free to his own further disquisitions. Neither is it for the
> sake of the bare exposition, much less chronical accommodation of the
> text, so much, that we publishe these things (in that kind of labors
> of others do abound), but for the spiritual, practical, lively soul
> searching truths and applications thereof that are therein contained;
> the substance of which truths the impartial reader will easily acknowl-
> edge to be clear, both from this and from other scriptures.[3]

According to Mitchell's description there were three kinds of exegesis:

"bare exposition," "chronical accommodation," and "spiritual applications."

As far as the former two were concerned everyone was at liberty to pursue

such "disquisitions," but such approaches did not really describe what

Shepard had in mind in his lecture series. Mitchell in other words raised

the old Puritan concern: what was more important than doctrine was its

application, and what Shepard here was after was not exposition or prophetic

accommodation, but spiritual application.

Shepard indeed deflated prophetical speculations as much as he

restricted allegorical theorizing. There was a school of thought which had

---

[1] Shepard, Works, II, pp. 5-10.

[2] John Calvin, Commentary on a Harmony, pp. 134, 136, 139.

[3] Shepard, Works, II, p. 8.

equated each day of creation with a thousand years and had applied this
generalization in such a way that the time before and under the law, as
well as the time under Christ, amounted to two thousand years each which
then in turn would be followed by the eternal millennium of the "great
Sabbath." Unfortunately for the theory, Shepard pointed out, it did not
agree with the known facts of history and "is already proved to be false
in the second two thousand years."[1] Nevertheless, Shepard did defend the
prophecies of the New Testament[2] against Cardinal Baronius,[3] the famous
church historian of the sixteenth century and Catholic counterpart of the
Protestant Magdeburg Centuries, a defense which was significant since his
own lecture series on the parable of the ten virgins was taken from the
Matthean apocalypse. The resolution to Shepard's criticism and his defense
must be seen in his admission that "I have no skill in prophecies, nor do I
believe every man's interpretation of such Scripture."[4] Shepard therefore
moved within a tradition of prophetical exegesis, but he himself did not lay
any claim to the kind of professionalism that Bacon had demanded in his
brief characterization of the history of prophecy. On the other hand, he
was confident to know enough in this field to judge for himself the work of
an interpreter of Thomas Brightman's reputation.

---

[1]Shepard, Works, II, p. 508.

[2]Ibid.

[3]Caesar Baronius (1538-1607), church historian, cardinal. He was
born in the Kingdom of Naples. Upon completion of his studies in theology
and law he joined the Congregation of the Oratory where he began extensive
studies in church history by using the original sources of the Vatican.
Because of his knowledge he was later called upon to defend the Roman church
against the attack of the anticatholic interpretation of church history by
the Magdeburg Centuries. As a result, he published the Annales Ecclesiasti
12 vols, 1588-1607 (New Schaff-Herzog Encyclopaedia, I, 489-490).

[4]Shepard, Works, III, p. 481

The kind of exegesis that Jonathan Mitchell could have had in mind
was John Cotton's A Brief Exposition of the Whole Book of Canticles.[1] This
was a commentary where Cotton had applied the allegorical method of finding
for every word in the text another prophetic meaning to the point where he
could accommodate to this book the main events of church history from the
time of Solomon through the calling of the Jews and the second coming.
John Cotton described his intentions in the following way:

> This song admitteth more variety of interpretation than any other,
> and also of singular use. Some have applied it to express the mutual
> affection and fellowship between Christ and every Christian soul; Some
> between Christ and the Catholic church; Some to particular churches,
> from Solomon's time to the last judgment. And there is a holy and use-
> ful truth in each one of these interpretations; but the last doth
> exceedingly magnify the wonderful excellency of this song, making it a
> divine abridgement of the acts and monuments of the church. . . . This
> book was chiefly penned to be such a historical prophecy or prophetical
> history. . . .[2]

Cotton here did not primarily pursue the application of soul-searching
truths, but he followed a model of traditional explanatory and expository
interpretation which allowed him to choose as his subject matter prophetical
history without excluding the individual and ecclesiological aspects of the
image of the church as the spouse of Christ.[3] The methods of exegesis in

---

[1] The edition which was available to me and which I have used was
John Cotton, A Brief Exposition of the Whole Book of Canticles; On Song of
Solomon (Edinburgh: James Nichol, 1868).

[2] Ibid., p. 3.

[4] F. W. Farrar (History of Interpretation, 1886; rpt., Grand Rapids,
Michigan: Baker Book House, 1961, pp. 32-33) found nineteen different interpretations of Canticles in Jewish and Christian exegesis. For the purposes
of Cotton's own background this multiplicity can be narrowed down to the
prevalent medieval options of the ecclesiological, individual, mariological,
and prophetico-historical interpretation, all of which could and did occur
in combination (Friedrich Ohly, Hohelied-Studien, Grundzüge einer Geschichte
der Hoheliedauslegung des Abendlandes bis um 1200, Wiesbaden: Fritz Steiner
Verlag, 1958, pp. 304f, 311) and each of which could within itself leave
room for variety so that Cotton's own exposition assumed the character of a
literary or poetic genre that poets at the time would use as the ready-made
vehicles for their own creative expressions or mere imitations.

the case of Cotton and Shepard were quite different, for while Cotton had to resort to an allegorical approach, Shepard could follow a literal approach in order to bring out the prophetic scope of their respective texts. Cotton also displayed those prophetic skills in exegesis over against which Shepard had reserved his own judgment. Because of his text Shepard emphasized much more the individual and ecclesiological aspects of the image of the church as the spouse of Christ, but for Mitchell to construe an opposition out of these different emphases in order to be able to dismiss summarily an embarrassing objection for the sake of an easy defense was a distortion of Shepard's position. For Cotton as well as for Shepard prophecy did not belong in the realm of the so-called adiaphora that could be shoved aside for the sake of concentrating on self-examination and soul-searching truths. Such pietism without prophecy was well on the road to quietism. We must therefore take exception to Mitchell's defense of his mentor Thomas Shepard, for this answer still leaves us with the question of how the calling of the Jews fitted into Shepard's exegesis. In terms of contemporary hermeneutics we could say that, while it was not contained in his text directly, it was there "by consequence"[1] as the further explication of Shepard's exegetical argument will show.

The Scope of History and the Differentiation
of Ecclesiology and Eschatology

In Shepard's understanding of it, the scope of the parable was not simply present fulfillment in the church, but the future consummation of the church. For Shepard there were several christological titles and

---

[1] See for example Jonathan Edwards, Religious Affections, p. 294.

images. Christ was the "king" for the church in oppression. Christ was the "head" for the church that needed wisdom, light, and life. Christ was the "Lord" for the church in its obedience. But "at last he appears more fully to her as a husband or as a bridegroom with whom she is to have her nearest and everlasting fellowship and communion."[1] This image of the bridegroom which was so central to the parable brought out in ecclesiology the eschatological rather than the polity aspect, for the covenant led to the consummation of the covenant: preparation was the "divorce" from the law as husband, assurance was the "espousal" of a virgin to Christ, and the coming of the bridegroom was the "consummation" of the virgin. We have seen how in Shepard's hermeneutics the scope led to a reclassification of allegory; now we can see how that same prophetic scope implied a redefinition of eschatology and ecclesiology.[2] Shepard himself was quite aware of the consequence of this scope since he first discussed the church as the place for preparation and then proceeded to eschatology as the time of preparation.

The common and received definition of eschatology was that of the "doctrine of the last things."[3] Part of these "last things" were the "last days." Since the parable was for Shepard Christ's own description of the

---

[1] Shepard, Works, II, p. 111.

[2] E. Johnson spoke of the church in terms of the Kingdom of Christ. Shepard spoke of the church as the spouse of Christ. We have seen how in the first case this inclusion of the Kingdom led to a view of history. We see here how the consistent focus on the sovereignty of the bridegroom redirected the view of the church away from itself toward a goal. The images of the church which Johnson and Shepard used are nevertheless not commensurate. Shepard talked of the goal in terms of the eternal communion with the bridegroom after the judgment; E. Johnson confined himself to the Kingdom which Christ at the judgment yielded up to the father.

[3] Moltmann, Theologie der Hoffnung, p. 11.

end of the world rather than the fulfillment of the Old Testament, one would

expect that what was meant by "last days" were the days before the end of

the world, but this was precisely the meaning that Shepard had to argue for

over against a tradition that saw it differently. Such a different view

was put forward at the time by Shepard's contemporary, John Davenport, in

the latter's Knowledge of Christ:

> This their generall expectation was grounded upon the prophesie of
> the angel Gabriel to Daniel, Dan. 9:24, 26, 27. All which we see to
> be accomplished by this Jesus, who is Christ the Lord. But the reli-
> gion now established by Jesus Christ, in the scripture of the New
> Testament shall never be altered. Hence the time from Christ and his
> apostles unto the end of the world is called the last dayes, Acts 2:17,
> Heb. 1; I Pet. 1:20 and the end of the world, I Cor. 10, not so much
> in respect of time (for above one thousand six hundred years are passed
> since these things were spoken) as in respect of the last revelation of
> God's will concerning religion which is so perfectly settled in the
> church thereby, as it shall stand firm and inviolable, without
> alteration, by any word of God, whilst the world standeth.[1]

Davenport's views were here not unlike what we have seen in Bacon's

view of prophecy, for here also the church was the "end of the world." The

history of the work of redemption now became identical with the history of

the church and the church administered the finality of the fulfillment of

the Old Testament that had occurred in Christ. When Tyconius and Augustine

made the church into the state where the devil was bound and where the

millennium meant that he was bound perfectly, they did by no means forget

that there was to be a judgment.[2] On the other hand, such ecclesiastic

millennialism began to show signs that reappear in what has been called in

modern times postmillennialism where the reality of the end as judgment

---

[1]John Davenport, The Knowledge of Christ (London: For L. Chapman, 1653), p. 85.

[2]Peter Toon "The Latter-Day Glory," in Puritans, the Millennium and the Future of Israel: Puritan Eschatology 1600-1660, ed. P. Toon (London: James Clarke & Co. Ltd., 1970), pp. 13f.

retreated progressively and led to an identification of religion and civilization. Nor is this surprising in the case of the influence of Augustine's De Civitate Dei. It was written at a time when the church had become the end of the Mediterranean world both spiritually and politically. The knowledge of the church's eschatological penultimacy was kept alive in the popular underworld[1] and in the elitist world of monasticism. While monasticism by and large lived in a division of labor with the church and provided it with reform impulses, the Joachimite eschatology of the age of the Spirit in fact led to revolts. Insofar as Joachimism was an intellectual movement, however, a man like Peter Aureoli[2] did absorb and neutralize in his commentary on Revelations the "disquieting" concerns of the Augustinian as well as of the Joachimite traditions under a juridic concept of the church, and passed this view of church history on to the later Middle Ages. From the point of view of the work of redemption, history became de-eschatologized, for if the end of the work of redemption is the "day of redemption," then the church as an ecclesiastical millennium fell short both of the goal and of the history toward it. The extreme case of such a foreshortened vision was the identification of the day of judgment with the jurisdiction of the church. The work of Redemption was replaced by a redemptive institution. We can therefore see that Shepard's dissociation of the last days from the days of the church provided a frame and function which cannot simply be brushed aside in favor of the spiritual application of soul-searching truths.

---

[1] Norman Cohn, The Pursuit of the Millennium: Revolutionary Millennarians and Mystical Anarchists of the Middle Ages, rev. and expanded edition (New York: Oxford University Press, 1970), pp. 30, 283.

[2] Ernst Benz, Ecclesia Spiritualis, Kirchenidee und Geschichts Theologie der Franziskanischen Reformation (Stuttgart: W. Kohlhammer, 1934), pp. 419ff.

Shepard had shared with Davenport the Augustinian tradition that
conceived of the "last days" as those days which extended from the ascension
of Christ through his second coming, but then also quite some time before
Davenport's own change of mind[1] must have occurred, Shepard went on to call
these last days the "large sense" of the conception and distinguished within
it "more particularly" "the latter days of those last days."[2] While Shepard
still held on to the "estate" of the virgin churches in New England as a
perfect one -- for they were societates perfectatae -- he had in fact
relocated this Augustinian view in changing the meaning of the last days by
shifting the emphasis to the latter days within them. On the other hand,
the character of this particular logical differentiation of the last and
the latter days indicated that Shepard had not intended it as a means of
discontinuity between his own exegesis and the tradition. The scope of his
exegesis functioned therefore in a comprehensive manner, for it was both
critical and constructive. It differentiated church and eschatology, it
curbed allegorical speculation and at the same time did not absolutize
exegesis itself, because the scope was also seen in interaction with tradition in order to bring out all the elements of the tradition. The principle

---

[1] Davenport in a preface to Increase Mather's Mystery of the Salvation
of Israel had left behind such exclusive Augustinian views and had become a
strong advocate of a millennial position which presupposed that church and
eschatology had to be differentiated. In the Magnalia Christi Americana
Cotton Mather even portrayed him as a pioneer in this field, for "so many
years ago when in both Englands the true notion of the Chiliad was hardly
apprehended by as many divines of note as there are mouths of Nilus,"
Davenport both preached and wrote on these things. While Mather observed
that such millennial notions "do now of late years get more ground against
the opposition of the otherwise-minded" (Vol. I, p. 331), we should add that
as far as the basic requirements for such a new view was concerned Davenport
himself had to undergo a conversion. The only treatise by Davenport on this
subject that we could find was his preface to Increase Mather's book.

[2] Shepard, Works, II, p. 24.

of comprehension which thus operated behind, beneath, and beyond Shepard's

exegesis can be best expressed in a comparison of our own: this comprehen-

sion behaved like a crystal where the complex molecular structure made for

the beauty, the cutting edges and the inability on the part of the viewer

to locate anything in one single place or to isolate any one single point.

Calvin's own exegesis was a good example for such a moving back and

forth between a larger sense and a more particular sense. His interpreta-

tion of 2 Thess. 2:1ff. has been described by interpreters as contradictory

and confusing whether they dealt with his view of history or his doctrine

of the last things:[1]

> There is obviously confusion between a purely eschatological inter-
> pretation of Antichrist and one which is based on a reading of church
> history. On the one hand, he is to emerge only after the preaching of
> the gospel is completed; on the other he is already incarnate in the
> papacy, and subjection to his dominion is shown precisely in a hardening
> of heart against the preaching of the gospel, the essence of which has
> been newly clarified by the reformers.[2]

A partial explanation of this seemingly confused way of thinking has

been given by T.H.L. Parker who recently undertook the sketch of a history

of exegesis in the sixteenth century which led to Calvin. He described

very well how Calvin could move back and forth, between the sixteenth and

the first century, with an ease that indeed confuses us:

> For Calvin, the historical document is of prime importance; it can-
> not be dispensed with, it cannot be left aside in favour of the sub-
> stance that is extracted from it. In brief, it must never cease to be
> a historical document. But then, this document is seen as addressed
> to all men of every age, to be for every age God's message, meaning

---

[1]Heinrich Berger, Calvin's Geschichtsauffassung (Zürich: Zwingli
Verlag, 1955), pp. 73-92; Heinrich Quistorp, Calvin's Doctrine of the Last
Things (ET. London: Lutterworth Press), pp. 112-122.

[2]Quistorp, op. cit., p. 121.

life or death for every man. Nothing, therefore, could be of more concern than this document. It is not right to treat it as history
unrelated to every generation. The unrelieved tension between history
and contemporaneity is reflected in Calvin's commentaries in the way that
the scene continually shifts from the first to the sixteenth century,
from the third person to the first person plural, and back again. We
almost forget which century we are in; we hardly know whether the partic-
pants are they or we. . . . St. John is speaking: but as we listen, hi
Greek strangely becomes the sort of Latin or French with which we are
familiar and we find to our surprise that he knows about our modern problems and says the definitive thing about them. In Calvin's commentaries
the first and sixteenth centuries are so intertwined that it is often
quite impossible to separate them.[1]

Such familiarity and empathy with Scripture was the focal point of

a dynamic imagination of a complexity which modern conceptualizations such

as "futurist eschatology," "realized eschatology," or even "realizing escha-

tology," in their one-dimensional selectivity cannot describe when confronte

with Calvin's exegesis.

The Sixfold Coming and the Double Coming of Christ

In Shepard himself such differentiation and comprehension worked in

two different ways which he described under the headings of a "sixfold com-

ing" and a "double coming" of Christ respectively. In the first instance

particular judgments occurred throughout the last days in the large sense,

and the general judgment will occur in the latter days of those last days

in the particular sense, but both judgments are intertwined in that they

both are a coming and not just terminal points. The comings in the last

days must be seen in terms of the second coming in the latter days and the

coming in the latter days cannot be absorbed into other comings so that the

large or general sense of the last days included in and through the church

particular things while the particular sense of the last days determined

---

[1]Parker, op. cit., p. 91.

the general purpose. Such floating comprehension could thus lead to an

equally insistent emphasis on either side:

> This coming is meant either of his coming to the last judgment, or
> of his coming to particular judgment immediately at and after death.
> I shall apply myself chiefly to the coming of Christ, at death, to his
> people. Because this doth chiefly concern us; the near approach of
> this will awaken, when apprehended near.[1]

On the other hand:

> By this coming of the Lord is (as hath been oft said) meant the
> coming of Christ to death or judgment; but especially and principally
> his coming to judgment, as may appear by the whole series of this chap-
> ter and the next, wherein the Lord answers to the second question, viz.,
> the signs and times of his coming, i.e., his second coming which is
> called his coming to judge the world.[2]

The idea of the general judgment in itself was complex, for it did by no

means only infuse horror, but also joy. Death as the particular judgment

was not only an end but also the beginning of an end. Its ultimate and

penultimate character found expression both in its historical use in the

funeral sermon as well as in the note of expectancy that prevailed in the

Ten Virgins. Death here was the "welcome in the way" for the saints,

"until the last trumpet shall blow" and "they shall meet the Lord in the

clouds coming in the air." In death Christ fetched the soul into the "bride

chamber." Even though it said in the same paragraph that then the soul will

be "there with him for ever and ever," such being referred to an intermedi-

ate state where Christ "will keep the dust of thy blessed body and not lose

one dust of it, and at the last day raise it." This last day is called the

"day of redemption" or "the day of judgment" when the husband will meet the

soul and "thou shalt go with thy beloved from the air up to heaven with a

shout, and live in his love and dearest embracing of thee."[3] The predomi-

nance of a death-consciousness in the sources which is usually taken as a

---

[1] Shepard, Works, II, p. 430.

[2] Ibid., p. 507.   [3] Ibid., p. 163.

self-evident "otherworldliness" (<u>Jenseitigkeit</u>) obscured that death itself

is hope rather than a terminal date. Shepard is emphatically opposed to an

ultimatizing of death. The desire to die before one's appointed time is to

put one's self above the Lordship of Christ and the service for him. Accord-

ing to Shepard, Lazarus was even brought back down from heaven for more

service.[1] If death be not severed from its connection with the daily life

of the spirit and the body, then it was also to be kept in relation to the

resurrection of the body at the day of judgment.

The interrelation between death and the second coming was but one

aspect of five other such comings. Shepard at one point deduced all six of

them logically from the second coming as the comprehensive scope.

> I confess the Lord speaks principally of his coming to judgment, yet
> it is true of any other coming of Christ to his people in this life;
> and because particular examples and instances are the roots of general
> truths (as circumcision a seal, so all sacraments are so; Christ is a
> savior of his people; it is meant of great salvation at last, yet it
> is true of all salvation beside), therefore I shall speak of the coming
> of Jesus Christ to his churches and servants in the general [<u>sic</u>]; and
> so involve the whole coming of Christ, for more use and comfort to us.[2]

In sixteenth century German the word <u>Zukunft</u> literally meant <u>Zu-Kommen</u>[3]

and it was in this sense that Shepard used the word <u>coming</u>. Coming here

referred primarily to someone or to something that was coming. A reality

that moved in on man rather than "someone who will be" (<u>Futurus</u>), or some-

thing that will move toward a goal. In Bacon's definition of the history of

prophecy we had met with a similar idea, but he phrased it in terms of a

continual presence rather than as an advent or arrival. While Bacon moved

---

[1] Shepard, <u>Works</u>, II, p. 163.

[2] <u>Ibid</u>., pp. 416-417.

[3] Joachim Staedtke, <u>Die Theologie des jungen Bullinger</u> (Zürich: Zwingli Verlag, 1962), p. 66.

from presence on to its complement of gradation, Shepard gave more material

content to this view of presence which he described with the biblical term

coming. Christ came in answer to prayers, in fulfillment of promises and

returned providentially after withdrawing. He was present in ordinances and

defended and preserved the oppressed saints as king, and he came in death.

As far as the latter was concerned, Shepard noted specifically "that some

would have all Christ's coming here, but there is some hereafter."[1]

As a means to highlight Shepard's insistence that these elements were

indeed as it were part of a crystalline structure, we can utilize the his-

tory of exegesis itself. Shepard was, as we have seen, concerned in par-

ticular about a comprehensive view of death and therefore the interpretation

---

[1]Shepard's enumeration of the "sixfold coming of Christ" contained in
mnemotechnic rather than systematic form essential elements for a comprehensive investigation of the view of history that prevailed in New England.
Since this list has come to our attention in the course of an explication of
the second coming as the scope of the parable of the Ten Virgins we must
point out that not only providence in general nor providences in particular
can be the sole focus of an investigation into the historiography of New
England, but death as well as ordinances and prayers ought to be included
for an adequate understanding of the historical self-understanding of New
England Puritanism. Thus, for example, the locus for the consideration of
the relation of time and eternity was the Puritan view of the Sabbath.
According to Shepard the Sabbath represented the weekly reminder and foretaste of the saint's return to the eternal rest. (Works, III, pp. 25-27.)
The Sabbath, therefore, was not primarily the rest from weekly labor, a view
which could easily lead to a moralistic-legalistic misunderstanding and in
reaction to it to a view of the Sabbath as a time of relaxation. The Sabbath
in Shepard's view was rather a time of active and hopeful recollection of the
eternal rest which seems to imply that eternity itself was conceived in terms
of a rest that was also activity. Prayer, furthermore, was looked upon as a
means to turn the wheels of providence. Edward Johnson expressed himself
very forcefully on this subject. New England was not simply a city on the
hill whose beacon shone afar and provided an attractive example. New England
was rather a disciplined praying camp on the mountain. Just as the prayer
of Moses was instrumental in bringing about the victory of Joshua over Amalek
in the valley, so the praying camp in New England was actively involved in
starting, furthering, and helping to complete old England's battle in the
valley. New England therefore had a "share with you in the works" of over-
throwing prelacy and it should have more than a voice of advice in terms of
how the results of this victory were to be shaped. (E. Johnson, Wonder-
Working Providence, pp. 155-160.)

of the parable of the ten virgins by Benjamin Colman was interesting for

its instructive contrast. In a series of "practical discourses" which

proved quite popular, B. Colman showed the same interest in the contempo-

rary background of the parable and the same insistence that its scope be

respected in interpretation.[1] In the definition of the scope, Colman

shifted the emphasis to the second coming of Christ in death.[2] Death for

him was more certain than the end of the world, the general judgment or the

historical events that lead up to it. He referred quite sympathetically to

those "good men" who tried to fix the periods of revolutions only in order

to see themselves confuted by the events themselves.[3] Colman therefore

asked the question: "Why should we not run to meet the smiling vision, as

those that are found alive at Christ's second coming will fly up to meet him

in the air?"[4] For Colman death primarily was the entrance to the marriage

feast itself and not preparation for the cosmic consummation of history

itself. An event like the calling of the Jews played no role in his sermons.

For Colman virgins or true professors were no longer confined to any one

---

[1] Benjamin Colman, Practical Discourses on the Parable of the Ten
Virgins (1713; Boston: Rogers and Fowle, 1947), p. 2. On parables themselves Colman said: "As to the parables of our Saviour in general, they
are Similitudes taken from known Customs and Actions of Men, and made use of
to inform us in spiritual doctrines. . . ." Colman even found that parables
could serve as a substitute for doctrines: "We find people will listen to
a story or an example in a Sermon, who are very careless while the doctrines
and laws of Christ are more simply pressed." On the scope of the parable
itself he made the observation that "it requires good thought and judgment
thoroughly to take the Sense of a Parable. Fanciful minds are very apt
abusively to overstrain them, unreasonably to twist and squeeze them. In
order to force some Divine Truth out of every minute circumstance in them.
This is to Press the Stalk with the Grapes; which would but soak up some of
the good wine, and spoil the rest."

[2] Ibid., pp. 1; 105; 135; 149-150; 157, 181.

[3] Ibid., p. 341.   [4] Ibid., p. 22.

particular church such as New England.[1] For him the true professors became
a catholic rather than an eschatological concept and while, therefore, those
professors in different churches, including the Roman Catholic, may not
share the same general goal in history, it could not be doubted that they
faced in their individual lives the same death. Death no longer was, as
Shepard put it, "a welcome in the way," but it was the way itself.

Even though all days from the ascension of Christ through his
second coming were called by Shepard the days of the son of man, and though
within it there were days where there was "some kind of coming of the Son
of man," as when he came to hear prayers, yet it was the "latter days" of
those last days which were properly called the "days of the coming of the
Son of man."[2] It was within these latter days that Shepard also spoke of a
"double coming" as the second instance of comprehension and differentiation
in addition to the already mentioned in examples in "sixfold coming."

Shepard's use of the Matthean apocalypse and 2 Thess. 2:1[3] as well
as his rejection of an earthly millennium in Revelations 20 pointed up continuity of themes and a discontinuity in their application with Calvin's
concentration on the same texts for his view of history and eschatology.[4]
In Calvin, Antichrist had to be discovered and destroyed. Destruction,
restitution of all things, and the second coming coincided. All of them
were preceded by the "universal call to the Gentiles" as a delay of the

---

[1] Colman, Practical Discourses, p. 246. Colman criticized Thomas
Shepard for making such an assumption in his exegesis of the parable.

[2] Shepard, Works, II, p. 24.

[3] Ibid., pp. 25, 26. See also p. 410.

[4] John Calvin, Commentaries on the Epistles of Paul the Apostle to
the Philippians, Colossians, and Thessalonians, trans. John Pringle
(Grand Rapids: Eerdmans, 1948), pp. 322ff.

second coming in order to give all nations a chance to accept or reject
the gospel. The second coming did not all happen in a single moment.
Therefore, the second coming already emitted rays of light into the anti-
Christian darkness. In Shepard, Antichrist also had to be discovered and
destroyed. Here, however, the destruction of Antichrist was identified
with the call of Jews and Gentiles as the first part of Christ's double
coming long before the second coming. Upon this destruction the churches
will be refined. This refinement was the last event before the second coming. Nevertheless, this refinement was followed by a delay which will
plunge the refined churches into a security out of which they were awakened
by the cry of the bridegroom before his final appearance. The notions of
the universal call, the gradual coming, and the delay were arranged in
Shepard in such a way as to reveal an interest in a periodization of the
future when he talked about the double coming. This very interest in turn
modifies his view of the rejection of an earthly millennium.

The very pattern of purity-delay-security-awakening cry and judgment
which characterized the period between the fall of Antichrist and the second
coming was being generalized by Shepard for the time prior to this fall of
Antichrist, for the virgin churches of New England also live in the "latter
days" or the "days of the coming of the Son of man." In this context,
Shepard's pattern served as a reminder for the virgin churches that their
removal from England had brought about a spatial separation from anti-
Christian pollutions and fornications,[1] but that this was as yet not the
predicted downfall of Antichrist. The two things could easily be confused

---

[1]Shepard, Works, II, p. 371.

and make purity into a security rather than into an opportunity. Just as

for Calvin the delay provided a space of history in which the gospel could

be spread, so Shepard warned not to turn the "day of forbearance" into "a

night of forgetfulness."[1] Both for Calvin and Shepard this delay is what

we today would call history and this history was for them a time of conver-

sion and of mission. We must be very careful here not to presuppose the

modern notion of the failure of the parousia,[2] for delay here has a positive

and not a negative meaning and function.

The call of the Jews and the Gentiles with the attendant downfall

of Antichrist was an anticipated epochal point. It was irreversible and

it marked the difference between the time of the virgin churches of New

England and the time of the universal expansion of the gospel afterwards.

At the same time, the pattern of purity-delay-security-cry-judgment applied

to both, since every coming of Christ was an awakening.

The calling of the Jews and the fullness of the Gentiles meant that

the truth will finally prevail and lead to a restitution of the churches

as a preliminary step to the restitution of all things in the second coming.

The virgin churches were a spiritual resurrection of the churches to which

would be added the Jews and Gentiles. What happened with virgin churches of

---

[1]Shepard, Works, II, p. 405.   ". . . For if the Lord should not delay
his coming, how many thousands would be swept away before any peace made
with God or before any work finished for God."

[2]For a recent account that tried to come to terms with the question
of delay and which in the pursuit therefore surveyed the different emphases
that are present in the eschatologies of the New Testament, see H. Conzelmann,
An Outline of the Theology of the New Testament (1968, E.T. New York: Harper,
1969), pp. 307ff. This does not mean that a comparison of the different views
of the delay could not prove helpful, but such a confrontation would lead
beyond the limits of this study.

New England in particular would then happen in the spiritual resurrection
of the Jews and Gentiles in general. In Shepard's thought there was a time
where the Endzustand corresponded to the Urzustand. In reply to a complaint
about the restrictiveness of New England church polity he gave an answer
that sounded almost like a description of the above mentioned downfall of
Antichrist and made the primitive church the model for a time when man
without a Christian education will be converted:

> I remember a godly divine, in answering an objection of late repent-
> ance from the example of the thief; having whipped it with many other
> rods, at least lasheth it with this, it is an extraordinary case; and
> hence not to be brought in for an ordinary example, hence he speaks
> thus: When, therefore, the time comes that Christ shall come and be
> crucified again, and thou one of the thieves to be crucified with him,
> and it fall out that thou be the best of the two, then shalt thou be
> saved by Christ, that, despising Christ now, puts off thy repentance
> till then; so I say here; there is somewhat imitable and ordinary in
> the apostles' example, in admitting three thousand in a day, but some-
> thing unusual, and far different from our condition now; and therefore
> this I would say when the time comes, that the spirit is poured out on
> all flesh; and that time is known to be the spring tide, and large
> measure of the spirit, when ministers are so honored as to convert many
> thousands at a sermon; and so God and reason call for quickness when
> elders of churches are as sharp-sighted as the apostles; when the con-
> version of men also shall be most emiment, and that in such places where
> it is death or half-hanging to profess the Lord Jesus, as that they
> shall be pricked at their hearts, gladly receive the word, lay down
> their necks on the block, cast down all their estates at the churches'
> feet out of love to God's ordinances; when men shall not have Christian
> education, the example and crowd of Christians from the teeth outwardly
> to press them to the door of the church, as those times had not, then,
> for my part, if three hundred thousand were converted, I should receive
> them as gladly and as manifestly as they receive Christ; but truly,
> there is such little takings now, that we have leisure enough to look
> upon our money. [1]

The New England churches had quite definitely not yet approached this spring
tide. Such a springtide seemed to indicate a move beyond the corpus
Christianum to include Jews and Gentiles. Shepard's view of the Jewish

---

[1] Shepard, Works, II, pp. 629-630.

role was less ambiguous than that of the Gentiles.[1] He said that after

antichrist is "consumed,"

> Not only the scattered visible Jews, but the whole body of the
> Israelites, must first be called, and have a glorious church upon the
> earth (Ezek. xxxvii). This glorious church scripture and reason will
> enforce, which when it is called shall not be expired as soon as it
> is born, but shall continue many a year.[2]

As a matter of fact, the place of the Jews in his theology is estab-

lished so much that he can use it as an argument in the Antinomian crisis:

"When the Jews shall be made the glory of all the earth, their glory shall

not consist then in immediate revelations, but in sanctification; there shall

be holiness and sanctification; there shall be holiness on pots and horse

bridles."[3] In Calvin's exegesis of 2 Thess. 2:1ff., the two key ideas had

---

[1]According to Shepard, Thomas Brightman had predicted that in 1650
the eastern Jews would repossess their land in a forty-year fight. Shepard
hoped that then the western Indians would soon "come in" and that the present
missionary beginnings in New England were preparatives for the day when east
and west would sing the song of the lamb. While the calling of the Jews
occurred several times in his writings unquestioned, Shepard did not award
such a definite prophetical status to the Indians. He was certain the
Indian mission was a work of God. He even hinted darkly the consequences
of missionary neglect: the old Saxons had rooted out the old Britons because
the latter had neglected to communicate the Christian religion when the
spirits of the Saxons were "at fit advantage"; "but I dare not discourse of
these matters." In any event, Shepard pointed out, it would be "for our com-
fort in the day of our accounts, that we have endeavored something this way."
(The Clear Sunshine of the Gospel Breaking forth upon the Indians in New
England, in Works, II, p. 482.) From this brief statement by Shepard it
seems that he was less sure of the part of the "American gentiles" (ibid.,
p. 486) in the universal reconstitution of the churches on earth than on
the problems created for New Englanders at the day of judgment if they neglected missions now. Still much later Cotton Mather (India Christiana,
Boston: Printed by B. Green, 1723, p. 46) said that the best way to inau-
gurate the mission to the heathen was through praying for the conversion of
the Jews as the appointed time for that mission. It seems, therefore, that
the expression "Jews and Gentiles" did not reflect an accidental phraseolog-
ical arrangement, but it implied a view of history which corresponded to the
same emphasis, that the Apostle Paul in his letter to the Romans put on
"the Jew first, but the Greek also" (1:17).

[2]The Sincere Convert, Works, I, p. 40.

[3]Works, II, p. 448.

been the universal call of the Gentiles as the time of history and opportunity as well as the restraining force of the gospel upon Satan during thi
time of the expansion of the reformation. This notion of opportunity we
found again in Shepard. Since he emphasized so strongly the transcendent
character of the eschatological scope, he could also speak positively of th
continued calling of the Jews in a context where his tradition without self
criticism had dwelt on the disobedience and rejection of Israel despite the
many providential judgments that had also been meted out to the church for
its acts of disobedience. Once the Jews were called, there shall be holiness on pots and horse bridles. While Shepard thus joined in the tradition
rejection of the earthly millennium, he also modified the view of the churc
as the present perfect estate and foresaw at the same time that there would
be a time of holiness upon the earth. For Shepard the focus was not a "new
earth," something which the Plymouth settlers had found out to be unworkabl
nor[1] was it a self-contained church, but a "new church" on earth. This
eschatological view received particular importance in the light of congrega
tionalist ecclesiology with its emphasis on the local parish rather than on
the church universal;[2] but we must also ask the question in light of Shepar
exegesis whether the preparation for the universal restitution of the churc
was not an anticipation and expectation of the church universal which in it
historical manifestation went far beyond the traditional mystical view of
universality which had excluded the Jews. If we use the term millennial,
then we would have to say that an understanding of the millennial element i
Shepard could lead only through an understanding of ecclesiology.

---

[1]William Bradford, Of Plymouth Plantation, pp. 120-121.

[2]L. J. Trinterud, The Forming of an American Tradition, a Re-
Examination of Colonial Presbyterianism (Philadelphia: Westminster Press,
1949), pp. 16-20.

An ecclesiastical vision of such grandeur also raised the question of how adequate an analysis of individual existence went along with it so that it would be possible, as it were, to get from here to there. To ask this question of Thomas Shepard is especially pertinent because of his intense interest in the analysis of soul-searching truths and because of his established reputation as a Pastor Evangelicus. For such an analysis his criticism of the antinomian view of Scripture was important. In his lecture series on the Parable of the Ten Virgins Shepard had applied the eschatological imagery of the bridegroom and the bride to a definition of Scriptural authority. For Shepard Scripture was like the correspondence which passed between the groom and the bride at a time of separation in which the bridegroom before his return revealed "by his letter his love."[1] This correspondence consisted of "letters, and syllabies, and words"[2] and contained in it not simply "a word," as the antinomians seemed to assume, but it included more specifically a "word of promise."[3]

For Shepard promise included the dialectic of faith and hope, for "faith entertains the promise as a faithful messenger, and sees that this message is true; hope runs out of doors, and leaves it with faith, and looks for the Lord himself."[4] In other words: Promise included the dialectic of assurance and glorification. Assurance was the beginning rather than the end of the quest. The way in which Shepard divided the parable pointed to this connection when preparation was conceived as the preparation of virgin believers and churches for the coming of the bride-groom. It would appear that the debate on preparationism has to be taken

---

[1]Shepard, Works, II, p. 518; see also pp. 599-600.

[2]Ibid., p. 144.   [3]Ibid., p. 605.   [4]Ibid.

this one step further in order to make it into more than a search for the
signs and criteria of a pre-temporal decree. Shepard told his congregation
that assurance by itself did not create a happy man. An assurance which
was analyzed only in terms of preparation and without regard to coming
assumed the character of a quest for possession and became legal as Anne
Hutchinson charged or turned moralistic, as we would say today, for
this analysis stopped short of the dialectic of sainthood. Historically
speaking, the search for signs of assurance in experience alone has no
doubt been a powerful option. But Shepard's exegesis indicates that for
him assurance is not just a _moment_ of transportation that settles down into
a stable character of cultivated self-hood, but it is also a _movement_. As
a matter of fact, the moment of assurance without the movement of hope was
not self-hood, but selfishness, for the promise did not only leave from
somewhere, it also led somewhere. For the sake of this second element
Shepard's insistence on the second coming is so crucial that therefore I am
inclined to speak of dialectic where Pettit speaks of dilemma.[1] Preparation
is the awakening from "sleep" and "dream" to a dialectic mode of existence.
The difficulty of this dialectic is that it is existential and not just
logical. For this very reason Shepard was skeptical about high enthusiasm
and deep depressions, about affluence as well as adversity because neither
could by itself prove anything. The form of the dialectic was pastoral and
casuistic, for in this way alone was it possible to indicate immediately for
every individual case of a diverse congregation what had to be done in order
to maintain or to achieve the dialectic. When we ask for the function of
the dialectic in historiography we certainly do not think of a thesis-
antithesis-synthesis triad of historical development. We might rather talk

---

[1] Norman Pettit, The Heart Prepared, Grace and Conversion in Puritan
Spiritual Life (New Haven: Yale University Press, 1966), p. 105.

about open and closed history. The dialectic was a means to ensure the

openness in any given situation in a saint's life. The saint may be "above

nature," but at no time is he above "improving his sainthood only" by

"nature." When the latter happened, he began to turn in and around himself

and lost history. It was at this point where the providences as judgments

or chastisements entered upon the scene in order to restore this openness.

Providences were thus no automatic ratifications for those who have

received the promise in assurance. Walther Zimmerli in his interpretation

of the promise put it thus: "Only Jahwe himself can by the work of ful-

fillment interpret his promise. This interpretation can be full of

surprises for the prophet himself."[1] Shepard put it this way:

> Nay, commonly, when the Lord brings any man to his hopes, having
> given him a promise and faith to believe it, the Lord, in the midway,
> seems to cross his promise. When the Lord promises life, glory, peace,
> honor, joy, fullness, heaven, they shall then and never so much before,
> feel darkness, shame, trouble, sorrow, hell. For the Lord tries them
> by this, and tribulation breeds experience, and experience hope.[2]

What happens upon the dissolution of the dialectic is described in this

way: "There is a lying still, no progress; so in carnal security the soul

stands at a stay, goes not backwards, grows not worse, but goes not forward;

such a one is compared to the door on the hinge."[3] This inertia was

described by him in more detail as the activity of "men that live in a

land and love the smoke of their own chimneys [and] never look to other

coasts and countries, or to a strange land."[4] Such complacency and self-

contentment could, in Shepard's view of the matter, also assume a highly

sophisticated character which he expressed by yet another image. The

[1]"Verheissung und Erfüllung," Ev. Theol., 12 (1952-53), p. 47.

[2]Works, II, p. 157.

[3]Ibid., p. 372.   [4]Ibid., p. 144.

absence of Christ likened men to "glowworms and stars that keep their shining and are very glorious because the sun is set."[1] The consequence was not so much a peaceful but a paradoxical existence in which the world appeared as "nothing more vain, yet nothing more glorious." Both of these alternatives were a loss of hope, because in neither was there to be found those groans and pains that reverberated throughout the Puritan literature and constituted those signs of experience which "breed" hope rather than doubt.

Summary

Shepard's lecture series on the Parable of the Ten Virgins was important for Edwards' own thinking. Their sermonic form pointed to a powerful sociological institution for ideological dissemination, and their main argument was largely focused on the psychology of religion. In light of these conditions, the successful analysis of the exegesis of this treatise in its hermeneutical and material consequences for a view of history was a first and crucial test for our interpretative thesis.

Shepard's selection of a text from the Matthean apocalypse, his scrutiny of the context of the pericope, and above all his insistence on the scope of the parable, led to a respect for the integrity of the story itself. Shepard thus restricted the ingenious allegorical-numerical interest in arbitrarily selected and irrelevant textual details; he avoided antiquarian research for its own sake, and he brought out the significance of prophetic exegesis. Shepard took the canons of prophetic exegesis for

---

[1] _Works_, II, p. 404.

granted, and while he admitted to be no exegetical expert, he nevertheless
evaluated carefully and critically the findings of such authorities as
Thomas Brightman or John Cotton.

Shepard's hermeneutical restraint in favor of the scope of the story
had several consequences. First, in his differentiation between the last
days and the latter days, Shepard opted for the priority of eschatology
over ecclesiology at a time when John Davenport still identified them.
While Shepard did not deny the Augustinian theory of the church as a perfect
society, he did reject an identification of this ideal of perfection with
the as yet unconsummated state of the virgin churches of New England. In
accordance with the Augustinian tradition, Shepard identified church and
millennium, but this ecclesiastical millennium was still to come and it was
to include the whole earth.   Second, the congregational theory of the
local church was thus put beyond charges of provincialism and elitist separation, for universality itself was no longer defined exclusively as a transcendent mystical universality or as a static unity of the **Corpus Christianum**,
but it was now conceived of beyond all constitutional issues as a restitution of all churches including those of Jews and Gentiles. Shepard was
therefore only consistent in his approach when his doctrine of preparation
did not address itself only to the dilemma of assurance, but when it also
focused on the dialectic of hope. Third, the comprehensive character of
the scope was furthermore illustrated by Shepard's eschatological interpretation of the Biblical concept of coming. Coming included for him the
periodization of history, and it also took place to the same degree in
providences, ordinances, prayer, the kingly office of Christ, death, and in
promises. The implications of this view appeared in a comparison with

Benjamin Colman's later exegesis of the same parable where his overemphasis on the ultimacy of death as the scope signalled a retreat from the
hope that was to be fulfilled in the course of history and its exigencies.
Instead, Colman concentrated on personal history and thus defined eschatology in a similarly restrictive way that we also find in the modern discussion on the delay of the Parousia with its notions of realized and futurist
eschatologies.

CHAPTER IV

SCRIPTURE AND HISTORY

In a polemic against historylessness, Edwards pointed to the necessity that Scripture be the basis of a "general view of the historical world,
or the series of history from age to age." As a means of emphasis Edwards
reiterated the same thought shortly afterwards in a slightly different form
when he spoke of the desirability of a "general view of the series of historical events, and of the state of mankind from age to age."[1] While John
Wesley cut these remarks of Edwards from his edition of the Religious
Affections[2] as a metaphysical backlash to the Great Awakening, Edwards
pointed out that it was Scripture itself which contained both a series and
a view of historical events. The approaches to history which underlay each
of these two aspects in Edwards' own time were different enough to warrant
a separate consideration of both in order to unfold our interpretative
thesis more fully.

For this purpose we shall orient the following discussion toward
observations which Thomas S. Kuhn has drawn from the historiography of
science and which he has incorporated into the concept of the paradigm.[3]

---

[1]Edwards, Religious Affections, pp. 303, 304.

[2]John Wesley, Works (Bristol: William Pine, 1773), Vol. XXXIII,
pp. 178f.

[3]Thomas S. Kuhn, The Structure of Scientific Revolutions, 2nd ed.,
International Encyclopaedia of Unified Science, 2 (Chicago: University of
Chicago Press, 1970), pp. 43f.

122

In its most general definition a paradigm included the threefold achievement of the constitution, continuance and reconstitution of a field, and
of a community of inquiry.[1] The constitution of a paradigm for the first
time will provide a generally accepted consensus that will allow for the
comprehensive inquiry into a particular subject. Prior to such an achievement there will be competing schools that study the same subject.[2] They
all will conduct inquiries of a scientific character which tend to explain
those facts best which are most akin to their respective beliefs. Out of
such an inchoate situation of much information and a diversity of investigations that school will emerge a winner which can establish a focus that
will hold out the promise aesthetically[3] and demonstratively to solve a
"few problems," and which will be able to attract practitioners from other
schools into a new community of inquiry. One of Kuhn's examples for the
constitution of a paradigm was   Isaac Newton's Opticks which for the
first time ever brought about a generally accepted definition of light.[4]
Such success will cause other schools to disappear and it will at least for
the ensuing time of "normal science" delimit the range of admissible
questions and reject others as metaphysical.[5]

The search for the reconstruction of a paradigm will commence as
soon as it is realized that the pursuit of the old paradigm leads to unexpected and unintended experimental discoveries as well as into theoretical
difficulties of a more fundamental nature than what the paradigm had led
to expect and had promised to solve. The normal reaction in such a

---

[1]Kuhn, The Structure of Scientific Revolutions, p. 10.

[2]Ibid., pp. 16f.   [3]Ibid., p. 158.

[4]Ibid., p. 23.   [5]Kuhn, pp. 19, 64.

situation will, however, at first be to adapt such fundamental difficulties
and subsume them under existing questions that can be solved within the
paradigm.[1]

According to Kuhn, the constitution and reconstitution of a paradigm
will always concentrate on particular subjects of inquiry and bring forth
particular communities of scientists. He therefore did not talk in an
essentialist manner about the one science that was constituted in the one
scientific revolution of the seventeenth century nor did he subscribe to a
notion of the progress of science in which constitution, continuance, and
reconstitution were elements of a universal and uniform dialectical development. He rather conceived of science as a process in which a few major and
many minor revolutions occurred and which all displayed similar "structures"
in the way in which paradigms were constituted as well as reconstituted.
Thus, for instance, Isaac Newton established optics as a particular inquiry
and he resolved the crisis into which the particular pursuit of physics
had moved. At the same time we might add, Newton continued to work out in
his historical researches the promise of still another paradigm.

When we take into consideration these observations for the question
of scripture and history, then we can say that the paradigm of a series of
historical events as well as the paradigm of a view of history arose out
of particular situations, and held out the promise of transferring particular problems into manageable puzzles and became the focus of particular
scholarly exegetical enterprises. Exegesis itself presented a process out
of which major and minor revolutions came and which next to the process of
the natural sciences was the oldest means of inquiry. The former paradigm

---

[1]Kuhn, The Structure of Scientific Revolutions, p. 78.

in and before Edwards' time was characterized primarily by an interest in chronology, while the latter paradigm arose out of a concern over coherence. Chronology constituted a broad movement of inquiry that ran into a major crisis. The discovery of coherence arose and was maintained as a minority voice in resolving a crisis. We shall therefore, in the following chapter, survey this chronological side of Scripture, then move on to the interest in coherence, explore its relation to exegesis, and conclude with an observation about the exegetical process as the matrix for the formation of different traditions of historiography that occurred during the rise of modern Christianity.

Chronology

Frank E. Manuel has observed that the "Biblical genealogies from Adam on down presented . . . a continuous reckoning in years unique amongst ancient historical records."[1] The impact of this peculiar feature was in evidence at the time of the Roman Empire in late antiquity as well as at the time of the revival of learning in early modernity. The process of detribalization and acculturation that took place within the οἰκουμένη of the Roman Empire is often discussed in terms of the efforts on the part of the educated classes to allegorize the literature of their diverse cultures into a common meaning. The golden age of the coincidence of the revival of learning and the revival of religion from the fifteenth century onward is often viewed as another chapter in the history of Christian παιδεία. Nevertheless, the consideration of the convergence of several

---

[1]Frank E. Manuel, Isaac Newton, Historian (Cambridge: Belknap Press of Harvard University Press, 1963), p. 38. See also J. W. Johnson, "Chronological Writing: Its Concepts and Development," History and Theory, 2 (1962-63), p. 127.

imaginative universes and the intellectual comprehension of the symbolic
interpretation of Hellas and Jerusalem must include the observation that
both transitional periods involved the basic issue of establishing a historiographical order for which these Biblical genealogies served as a
paradigm.

Both ancient Greek and Roman historiography showed a "lack of central purpose";[1] the Gentile nations as a whole had few certain elements
in their chronologies and Roman historians at the time of the Empire were
confronted in particular with the necessity of reconciling their national
records with the history of the then-known world. These factors go a long
way to explain the interest in Jewish history amongst the historians of
the Augustan period, for it provided the needed chronological paradigm and
answered in addition such questions as the continuance of man after the
Flood and the disappearance of the giants from the earth. The church
reinforced this tendency and made the series of events as they were
reported in the Old Testament the basis from which to synchronize and connect all history.[2] The success of chronology was therefore not only because
of its religious assumptions or the external success of Christianity, but
in that it also introduced the first successful and generally accepted
paradigm of universal history, which delineated these religious convictions
in terms of consistent and orderly historical documents.

Martin Luther is an instructive example for the acceptance of
Scripture as chronology in early modernity. He clearly showed a Humanist's
appreciation of antiquity when he acknowledged that the ancient historians

---

[1]Johnson, "Chronological Writing: Its Concepts and Development,"
p. 127.

[2]Ibid., pp. 128-130.

were respectable and industrious men, but that, nevertheless, their chronologies were not reliable. For one thing, they themselves complained that they had no certain knowledge of the reckoning of years and then their errors might be compounded through the additional mistakes that had accrued in copying them over the centuries, while Scripture, on the other hand, had a consistent and divinely ascertained order. For Luther himself the collection of such chronological tables was an aid to and a by-product of exegesis,[1] but the professionalism and specialization in this field increased more and more over the next two hundred years so that it came to be "recognized as an indispensable branch of knowledge, in short a science."[2] Affirmation of its popularity and confirmation of its wide diffusion came from many sources. Degory Wheare, the first reader of history at the University of Oxford, recommended in his influential Method and Order of History that the Bible was to lead the civil historian in everything including chronology.[3] In his New Offer to the Lovers of Religion and Learning, Cotton Mather projected as one of his sections in the ambitious Biblia Americana a biblical chronology and in his later proposals for the education of evangelical ministers he listed chronology as one of the areas of

---

[1]WA 53, pp. 22ff. See Also Klaus Scholder, Ursprünge und Probleme der Bibelkritik im siebzehnten Jahrhundert (München: Chr. Kaiser, 1966), pp. 82ff.

[2]Paul Hazard, The European Mind 1680-1715 (1935, ppb.; New York: Meridian Books, 1968), p. 41.

[3]Degory Wheare, The Method and Order of Reading Both Civil and Ecclesiastical Histories, E.T. (London, 1685), pp. 39, 41, 81, 316. The first edition of this introduction had been published in Latin and had run into three more editions before it was translated into English (H. A. Lloyd Jukes, "Degory Wheare's Contribution to the Study and Teaching of Ecclesiastical History in England in the Seventeenth Century," in Studies in Church History, ed., G. J. Cuming, 5, Leiden: E. J. Brill, 1969, pp. 193-203

the study of history.[1] John Locke in Some Thoughts Concerning Reading and
Study for gentlemen said that "to the reading of history, chronology and
geography are absolutely necessary," and suggested some literature for the
purpose.[2] The English Samuel Johnson in turn looked upon chronology as a
criterion by means of which to separate factual from romantic and fabulous
history.[3] Finally, the very interest in the history of prophecy clearly
needed and encouraged chronology in order to locate the dates of fulfillment.

Isaac Newton's work was a good example for this approach to history
when it reached its peak at the turn of the eighteenth century. He barely
wrote any historical narrative,[4] but compiled exhaustive chronological
tables which were built on three principles: Scripture as the paradigm,
astronomical calculations, and the whole accessible range of the literature
of Christian and pagan antiquity. In his overriding concern for the ascertaining of dates and time sequences, Newton collected his historical evidence indiscriminately from the pages of poets, historians, or theologians.
He took the genealogical tables from Greek mythology and conceived of them
in terms of actual historical successions of human generations. A critical
principle entered into the discussions at the point where such tabulations
were compared to the paradigm and either dismissed as fanciful or reduced
to their true historical proportions. Against the background of such

---

[1]Cotton Mather, A New Offer to the Lovers of Religion and Learning
(Boston: Bartholomew Green, 1710), p. 1; Manuductio ad Ministerium, p. 69.

[2]John Locke, "Some Thoughts Concerning Reading and Study," Works
(London, for W. Otridge, 1812), III, pp. 269-270.

[3]J. W. Johnson, "Chronological Writing," p. 124. See also here for
more examples of the reputation of chronology at the time.

[4]For the following summary see Manuel, Isaac Newton, Historian,
pp. 48ff., 68ff., 192-193.

128

"shifting verbal sands,"[1] astronomical dating set out with a great liability and Newton himself applied the method only in three cases.[2] While he was able to improve the method over his predecessors, the added criterion tended to enhance the antiquity of the paradigm when it led him to foreshorten Greek history by several hundred years.[3] The kind of history which emerged from such laborious research and which had disappointed the readers of Thomas Prince was very well epitomized by Paul Hazard:

> From the creation of the world to the coming of Christ there is an interval of 4000 years, or, to be quite precise, 4004. By the year 129 the population of the earth had considerably increased, and so had evil-doing. In the year 1656, came the flood; in 1757, men set to work to build the Tower of Babel. The vocation of Abraham dates from 2083. The written law was entrusted to Moses 430 years after the vocation of Abraham, 856 years after the deluge and the same year that the Hebrew people were delivered out of Egypt. . . . So delightful was it to fare along that road that minds innocent and quiet furnished their whole lives with memories of its mile-stones, recalling not only the year but the month, nay the exact day, on which occurred this or that memorable event recorded by holy writ. The faithful opened their books of devotion: on the 18th February in the year 2305 before the birth of our Lord, Noah sent forth a dove from the ark. On the 10th March, Jesus received tidings of the sickness of Lazarus; on the 21st March, Jesus cursed the fig-tree; on the 20th August, in the _Annus Mundi_, 930, died Adam, the first man.[4]

The achievement of such precision was one of the "intellectual passions of the age"[5] in which Isaac Newton lived. Such a quest in turn was in accord with the pervasive contemporary concern to defend and redefine order itself, whether it be the order in society, the laws of the universe, or the historical order of the world viewed through the perspective of Scripture. The single-minded attention to the clarification of this latter order aided in

---

[1] Manuel, _Isaac Newton, Historian_, p. 49.

[2] Ibid., p. 65.   [3] Ibid., pp. 92, 102.

[4] Hazard, _The European Mind_, pp. 40-41.

[5] Manuel, _op. cit._, p. 13.

:he eventual dissolution of the paradigm from which it had started, but in
:he process the paradigm had brought about some definite chronological
*oints of reference for Western man which are now largely assumed, but
.hich then could not be taken for granted. This even more basic search
*ust be kept in mind in order to see what was at the heart of a rather
:haracteristic claim that one of the contemporary chronologists made for
:heir dry and fact-studded outputs:

> For the Masse of Historians would prove but a confused Heape, and
> be like a Monster, if Chronology did not held to forme and frame them
> into fashion, by digesting them into a certainty of articulate Times.
> And Lastly, it is termed the Soule of History giving life to it, as
> the Soule doth to the body.[1]

As more historical material became known and as the same material continued
to be searched by different chronologists, we begin to perceive a gradual
trend in which the focus shifted from a synchronization of secular with
sacred history toward the use of various devices that were put forward in
order to harmonize sacred with secular history. The English chronologist
John Marsham, for example, found a simple way to reconcile the antiquity of
Egyptian history with the paradigm. He admitted the authenticity of the
list which contained the names of thirty royal Egyptian dynasties, but the
list itself according to him followed a consecutive order for some cases
and a collateral order for others. Since, therefore, some kings must have
reigned in different parts of the country at the same time, Egyptian history could not have reached back beyond the date set for Creation in the
paradigm. The Frenchman Père Pezron seemed to have an even simpler solution in the same matter. He discovered that the Septuagint version of the
Old Testament was 1,500 years in excess of the chronology that the Hebrew

---

[1]Manuel, Isaac Newton, Historian, pp. 37-38.

text provided. He suggested that the Septuagint chronology be used in orde to accommodate Egyptian history to the paradigm.[1] The simplicity of the proposal was compounded by its impiety, for such an adaptation would have abandoned the Hebrew text as the inspired standard for chronology. The pressures on the paradigm finally increased to the point where discrepancie in the dating of Creation went beyond the admissible margin of scholarly tolerance that could be explained in terms of the idiosyncrasies of individual authors.[2] Such ambiguity raised disbelief in Scripture as a paradigr of the series of historical events and it also provoked doubts with regard to its claim to antiquity. While the very beginning of the series began to be blurred, the documents that had caused this development did not inspire confidence enough to become the basis of another paradigm.

When we look at one example for a resolution of this historiograph-ical crisis we can see that doubt and skepticism about the antiquity of the paradigm alone did not resolve the issue positively. Voltaire had origi-nally planned to complete Bossuet's Discours sur L'Histoire Universelle (1681) which presupposed the old paradigm of Scripture chronology.[3] Insteac he set out with a chapter on China, and then moved on to India, Arabia, and the Islam before he dealt with Judaism and Christianity. Scripture was no longer the paradigm of world history, but at best a source for a history of the West. It has therefore been suggested that the claim to antiquity on

---

[1]The examples of John Marsham and Père Pezron are taken from Hazard, The European Mind, pp. 43ff.

[2]Manuel, Isaac Newton, Historian, p. 40; Hazard, op. cit., p. 47, quoted a contemporary who listed between the extreme dates of 6984 and 3749 years for the age of the world another seventy more intermediate dates.

[3]W. Kaegi, "Voltaire und der Zerfall des Christlichen Geschichtsbilde Historische Meditationen, I (Zürich: 1942), pp. 223ff., 232.

the part of the paradigm was discovered to be false first and foremost

through the increasing acquaintance in the first half of the eighteenth

century with the much more ancient civilization of the Chinese people.

When, therefore, the paradigm proved insufficient, then the whole and

universally accepted Christian view of history for which it had provided

the substructure also fell. The Swiss historian Kaegi who argued in this

way gave a very graphic and concise description of this view of history:

> The very ancient portrait of the Christian view of history repre-
> sents the course of man through this world as it were like an altar
> piece with three biblical scenes. The center part has as its theme
> the birth of Christ or his death; of the two side pieces the one on the
> left describes Adam's expulsion from paradise or another subject from
> the history of creation; the piece on the right tells about the second
> coming of Christ and the general judgment. These are the main epochs:
> history of creation, life of the redeemer and the end of the world.
> Historical and literary narrative depicts the course of man throughout
> the centuries in between these main scenes like an infinite predella.
> It begins with Jewish history according to the records of the Old
> Testament and occasionally it expands into the history of the great
> empires of Egypt and Mesopotamia. Shortly before the birth of Christ
> it interpolates a section on Roman history, and beginning with the
> life of the Savior it merges into Roman imperial history and culmi-
> nates in a broad portrayal of the time of the respective historical
> writer. The mood which sustains the whole alternates between two
> emphases: devout confidence when it has in view the salvation pre-
> dicted by the prophets, proclaimed by Christ and to be perfected by
> his second coming; somber melancholy when it has in view the corrup-
> tion of man, the degeneracy of public affairs and the arrival of the
> judgment.[1]

According to Kaegi, one extensive factual flaw in the piece on the

left side of the altar made the other pieces also obsolete as pieces of art.

Such an explanation made two assumptions which require comment. First,

Kuhn had pointed out that a paradigm shift always included a new view of

things and therefore proceeded from a process of "conversion"[2] as much as

---

[1] Kaegi, Historische Meditationen, I, pp. 225-226. The translation of
the quotation is my own.

[2] Kuhn, The Structure of Scientific Revolutions, pp. 151f.; see also
pp. 78, 146.

from a process of falsification. While the impact of Chinese civilization
may have been the single most successful continued demonstration of the
limitation of the old paradigm, Voltaire's achievement consisted in the
use of a different paradigm that could deal with the new situation positively. His view of the immutable moral law no longer needed these
chronological unities and units of time, because his was a story of manner
and morals[1] and not a drama with a beginning, middle, and end. Second, the
comparison is instructive for another reason. It was taken for granted
without any discussion that the right side of the altar, the future or the
end of the drama, had no role of its own to play. It was as though only a
new past and not a new future could burst in upon or penetrate slowly into
the restricted present and change it. Kaegi's graphic summary of Scripture
as a coherent view or drama of history, the chronological researches into
Scripture as a series of events and Voltaire's departure from both seem to
have in common that they merged the future with the present. They could in
this way provide a perspective on history without a vision of its goal.

Coherence

Edwards' concern for Scripture as a view of history and his active
search to locate its connections arose out of a community of scholarly
inquiry and exegesis which was specifically engaged in finding out the role
of Scripture and relating it to the mission and ministry of the church.
Jonathan Edwards was an heir to the Reformed branch of the scholastic theology of Protestant Orthodoxy in the sixteenth and seventeenth centuries.
The tradition in turn had assumed its scholastic character in the painstaking endeavor of its supporters to assure the transmission of the

---

[1]*Essai sur les Moeurs et L'esprit des Nations*, 1757.

Reformation by building a fence around it. They pursued their goal by

applying much thought to the clarification and conceptualization of all the

nuances and ramifications of this heritage.[1] Their systematic-rational

drive towards doctrinal elaboration extended also to a careful and minute

exposition of Scripture as the basis of all such efforts. In the course of

making Scripture an object as well as a source of doctrine, assumptions

about the inspiration of Scripture itself were introduced which in their

predominantly mechanical and indiscriminate orientation by-passed crucial

elements of Scripture despite many discriminating, correct, and clear

definitions.[2]

---

[1]Protestant Orthodoxy is not to be confused with modern fundamentalism. Orthodoxy was a constructive movement of thought which anticipated, provoked, accompanied, and partially absorbed the incipient Enlightenment. It conducted its business in reference to the past history of theological and philosophical thought. It provided a bridge in its terminology for modern philosophy (J. Freudenthal, "Spinoza und die Scholastik," in Philosophische Aufsätze, Edward Zeller zu seinem fünfzigjährigen Doctor-Jubiläum Gewidmet; Leipzig 1887, pp. 85-138). It was an aggressive as well as subtle controversialist movement whose engagement in the intellectual field left it exposed when it came to practical application. Modern fundamentalism on the other hand has none of this search for the ramification of meanings. It is a true heir to the Enlightenment quest to reduce things to a few fundamentals. At the same time, it uses these fundamentals often unwittingly in order to fight modernity. Despite many similarities in their respective views of inspiration, it could be said that Orthodoxy defined Scripture so well that it can be used as a most effective criterion by which to criticize the fundamentalist view of inerrancy. In a series of lectures on the history of theology (Perspectives on Nineteenth and Twentieth Century Protestant Theology, ed. Carl Braaten, New York: Harper, 1967), Paul Tillich called the age of Protestant Orthodoxy of the sixteenth and seventeenth centuries "the abutment against which the bridge of all later Protestant theology leans" (p. 11). What Tillich had to say on modern Protestant theology also applies to fundamentalism: "The vagueness of much theological thinking in modern Protestantism stems from this lack of a knowledge of Protestant orthodoxy" (p. 11). For a recent, though very general, survey which does not include Western Europe, see Lewis W. Beck, Early German Philosophy, Kant and His Predecessors (Cambridge: The Belknap Press, 1969), pp. 115-138.

[2]Heinrich Cremer, "Inspiration," Realenzyklodädie für Protestantische Theologie und Kirche, Ed., Albert Hauck, 3rd ed. (1896-1913; rpt., Graz: Akademische Druck- und Verlagsgesellschaft, 1969), IX, 183-203; Otto Weber, "Inspiration," in Religion in Geschichte und Gegenwart, Ed., Kurt Galling,

The view of inspiration that prevailed can be characterized as mechanical insofar as the personal role or commitment on the part of the authors or of the persons in Scripture were of no relevance. The Biblical authors in particular were looked at simply as the deliverers of goods or as the passive flutes on which the Holy Spirit performed. Just as the catechism at the time had to be learned by rote and not by understanding participation, so the prophets in Scripture were mainly the doctores who had been set in motion in order to promulgate doctrines that were to be learned and to be accepted. This same view of inspiration can be called indiscriminate insofar as the distinction between content and expression, the differentiation between individual authors and the tension of the human and the divine lost all significance, for in its strictest manifestation this view of inspiration required that every fact, form, and function of the written biblical document be divinely inspired to the same degree and extent. Coherence, structure, and integrity of the biblical account faded and whatever doctrinal system stood in need of easily accessible, safe, and infallible proofs (dicta probantia) could find them there. Scripture as a formative influence on the life and experience of the believer and as a frame of history had no room in such a static view of inspiration and therefore two reactions arose within the Orthodox tradition itself[1] in which experience and history became points of departure to complement, correct, and reconstitute doctrine.

3rd rev. edition, III (Tübingen: Mohr-Siebeck, 1959), 775-779; see also a detailed and extensive study for the Lutheran side of Protestant Orthodoxy in Robert Preus, The Inspiration of Scripture, A Study of the Theology of the Seventeenth Century Lutheran Dogmaticians (Edinburgh: Oliver and Boyd, 1955).

[1] Interest in the Orthodox doctrine of inspiration is usually restricted to the role it played in provoking the reactions which led to the rise of historical criticism (e.g., Hans Joachim Kraus, Geschichte der

The reassertion of the personal commitment and the application of
doctrine in the experience of conversion led to a historiography of the
saintly life which reinstated the existential-spiritual aspects of Scripture
as a guide to devotion beyond its use as a rule of doctrine. This achievement of Puritanism was taken for granted by Jonathan Edwards at the outset
of the draft of the History of the Work of Redemption.[1] The most impressive
synthesis of this whole tradition was set forth in Religious Affections and
found here also practical application in his refutation of contemporary
efforts to string together dicta probantia in the form of "scripture-chains"
and hold them forth as truth.[2] Insofar as Edwards brought together Scripture
as experience and Scripture as history, it can be said that his reconstitution of Scripture as the basis for the doctrinal formulation of the mission
and the ministry of the church was complete. We shall take up this question later on[3] and focus now on the reassertion of the Scripture paradigm
of coherence and history as a means to explicate our interpretive thesis.

For a consideration of coherence and history in Scripture we shall
first turn to an essay entitled Some Considerations Touching the Style of
the Holy Scriptures by Robert Boyle which had been published in 1663.[4] In

historisch-kritischen Erforschung des Alten Testamentes (Neukirchen: Verlag
des Evangelischen Erziehungsvereins, 1956, p. 34). Another line of development in which we are interested here and which aims at a constructive criticism from within orthodoxy is usually only mentioned in passing in this type
of historiography (ibid., pp. 33, 49ff.).

[1]Works, V, pp. 16-17.

[2]Edwards, Religious Affections, p. 294.

[3]See Chapter VI, pp. 311ff.

[4]The Theological Works, ed., Richard Boulton (London: W. Taylor,
1715), III, pp. 94-195. For the date of the original publication of this
essay see DNB II, p. 1031.

this treatise Boyle dealt with various arguments that had been brought forth
against Scripture. One of these criticisms contended that Scripture was
"Seldom coherent and Scarce anywhere discursive." Boyle traced this opinion
to the bad example of "pious Persons" who had employed the "Scriptures as a
repository of Sentences and Causes, as incoherent as Nero thought Seneca's
style, viz. arena sine calce." Boyle's literary allusion to Seneca's style
and its comparison with the Roman sports arena suggests that he considered
Scripture to be a marked field where an orderly game was going on. For him,
therefore, Paul's syllogisms were as "acute and as solid" as those of
Aristotle. He underlined this contention by reference to the saying of the
Psalmist according to whom man was created with eyes, ears, and knowledge
in order to see, hear, and reason. Of this human ability to behave teleo-
logically, God made also providential use in the Scriptures so that the
assumption must be that Scripture and the men who wrote it were coherent.
Boyle backed up his claims by the philological observation of a "Scripture-
logic," which neither pious persons nor their despisers had cared to find
out about. Thus, for example, he recognized the "figurative abrupt way of
arguing" in Scripture as something quite logical when it was explained in
reference to the customs in Eastern countries where parables left "much to
the discretion and collection of those they dealt with." If such coherence
did not come to light the fault was not an inherent defect of Scripture, but
ignorance that stemmed from the "unwillingness of divines to let the context and the scope of the argument regulate their choice of the significatio
of ambiguous words and phrases." We might sum up Boyle's charge of manipulation against the pious by saying that they used Scripture much as the
joker is used in the card game: it can serve many needs in the process of
completing rather than mapping out a strategy.

When Boyle admitted that there were many things in Scripture of
which his "reason cannot give a satisfactory account," then he did not
concede any incoherence in Scripture, for he used reason here not in the
sense of a logic of contradiction but rather that of a logic of
discovery. He pointed out that his own experience in the study of the
Bible had convinced him that initial impressions of incoherence will give
way to the discernment of "connections"; for

> the books in Scripture expound one another; Genesis and the
> Revelations being reciprocal comments, and like the Mariners Compass,
> though the Needle stand North; yet it discovers both east and west;
> and so do some Texts help to explain one another though much distinct
> in the Bible, and seem to be so in Sense.

While Boyle was concerned to show that individual parts of Scripture cohered
in themselves, here he looked beyond individual contexts as examples of
"heavenly extraction" toward the "contexture" of the whole which according
to him will be "admirable." As we have seen before, Edwards in his programmatic outline for the History of the Work of Redemption made this "admirable
contexture and harmony of the whole" goal and context in which all doctrines
would appear to greatest advantage.[1]

Boyle made his point about coherence even more cogently through the
comparisons he drew between art[2] and the investigation of nature on the one
hand and Scripture on the other. The latter analogy he repeated several
times and observed that the contexture of Scripture "will manifestly appeal

---

[1] See p. 2.

[2] Boyle did not elaborate on the analogy of art and Scripture. "The
Bible loses much by not being considered as a System; for though several
Books are like Cloath of which a Pattern is like, yet the Bible may be compared to a piece of Arras, of which though a shred may assure us of the
fineness of the Colours, and the richness of the Stuff, yet it's greatest
advantage appeared when displayed at its full Dimensions." (Ibid., p. 124.)

to be the work of the same wisdom that composed the books of nature, and the Fabrick of the World." In a situation that had been caused by the Protestant Orthodox view of an indiscriminate inspiration he pointed out that Scripture had as much order as nature, that the difficulties which were encountered in it would lead to a progressive understanding of the whole, and that in such an undertaking knowledge was also reserved for later ages. Boyle had taken an active and decisive part in the successful study of the "books of nature." He introduced this example as an encouragement for a thorough investigation of Scripture. The study of natural philosophy had done away with the criticisms of providence and Boyle anticipated that as the result of a similarly sustained exploration of Scripture the criticisms of revelation would be swept away also. In one of his _Miscellanies_ on Scripture, Jonathan Edwards followed a similar line of reasoning:

> If God gives mankind his word in a large book, consisting of a variety of parts, many books, histories, prophecies, prayers, songs, parables, proverbs, doctrines, promises, sermons, epistles and discourses of very many kinds, all connected together, all united in one grand drift and design; and one part having a various and manifold respect to others; so as to become one great work of God, and one great system; as is the system of the universe, with its vast variety of parts, connected into one grand work of God: It may well be expected that there should be mysterious things incomprehensible and exceedingly difficult for our understanding; analoguous to the mysteries that are found in all the other works of God, as the works of creations and providence; and particularly such as are analoguous to the mysteries that are observable in the system of the natural world, and the frame of man's own nature.[1]

For Edwards these forms, parts, and books within the one great book of Scripture were interdependent. Their relationships were characterized by unity, connections, difficulties, and mysteries. Unity, however, did not exclude mystery, but included it, for unity itself was not uniformity. Difficulties were not logical contradictions, but mysteries, and mysteries

---

[1]Edwards, _Works_, VIII, p. 210.

in turn were not rationalized difficulties or ahistorical mysticism. The

reason for Edwards' confident assertion is to be found in the three systems

which he appealed to as analogies: the system of the universe in general

and the system of nature and of human nature in particular.   In his treatise

on the Chief End for which God created the World, Edwards referred to the

same subject and mentioned that the whole system of the universe "in all

its actings, proceedings, revolutions, and entire series of events" moved

as though "actuated and governed" by "one common soul."[1]

The idea of a "common soul" if not the name was widespread and influ-

ential in English thought before Edwards' time and the first to have fully

articulated it was Ralph Cudworth in his Intellectual System of the

Universe.[2] What he there called a "plastic nature" was developed in part

as a reaction to and as a corrective of a Cartesian mechanism with the

premise that a "saddled horse has no more sense than its harness."[3]   In this

concept Cudworth combined the Platonist tradition of the real, substantial,

and invisible forms and the nascent investigative interest into animal and

plant life.   Edwards' own early empirical observations on the spiders[4] was

indicative of the spheres of nature into which such investigations did move.

In Cudworth's case the recognition of such a plastic nature in plants and

animals became the point of departure for larger generalizations.

---

[1]Edwards, Works, I, p. 455.

[2]The Cambridge Platonists, ed., Gerald R. Cragg, A Library of
Protestant Thought (New York: Oxford University Press, 1968), pp. 234-257.

[3]C. E. Raven, Natural Religion and Christian Theology (Cambridge:
Cambridge University Press, 1953), I, p. 109.

[4]Jonathan Edwards, Representative Selections, ed., Clarence H. Faust
and Thomas H. Johnson (rev. ed.; New York: Hill and Wang, 1969), pp. 3-10.

Cudworth described this plastic nature or common soul as something in its own right, as pairs of opposites and as one side of an opposition. Thus it was neither mechanical nor magic, but vital. Furthermore, it included order and force, spirit and matter, the invisible and the visible, seed and structure, ontology and teleology, identity and process, the angelic as well as the demonic. It was irresistible and it had flaws. It was penultimate, not ultimate; it was divine art, but not the deity; active but not directive; spermatic, but not perileptic. While Cudworth identified it with the vegetative and put its existence below the rational and the sensible, neither of the two latter could subsist without the former.

From this brief summary of the aspects of the idea of the common soul, it becomes understandable why those who were acquainted with it should strike out in so many different directions. Through Shaftesbury it became a constitutive paradigm of the field of aesthetics,[1] for John Ray it provided the backdrop of his investigations into the system of nature,[2] and for both Boyle and Newton it played a paradigmatic role in natural philosophy.[3] The persuasive force of this concept and its universal applicability make clear why Boyle should refer to natural philosophy as a model by means of which Scripture could cease to be a "repository of Sentences and Causes"

---

[1]Anthony, Earl of Shaftesbury, Characteristics of Men, Manners, Opinions, Times, ed., John Robertson, The Library of Liberal Arts (1711; ppb., Indianapolis: Bobbs-Merrill, 1964), ii, pp. 110-111. See also Ernst Cassirer, The Philosophy of the Enlightenment (E.T., Princeton: Princeton University Press, 1951), pp. 315f.

[2]John Ray, The Wisdom of God Manifested in the Works of Creation, Eleventh Corrected edition (London: W. Innys, 1743), pp. 46-47. See also Charles E. Raven, John Ray Naturalist, His Life and Works (Cambridge: Cambridge University Press, 1942), p. 428.

[3]John Hermann Randall Jr., The Career of Philosophy (New York: Columbia University, 1962), I, pp. 488, 489, 511.

and why Edwards should also employ it for the purpose of describing the
grand "drift and design" of Scripture. Edwards, like Boyle, presupposed
that natural philosophy had already provided a successful model for providence. In fact, Ralph Cudworth had applied the idea of plastic nature as
a means to assert and assure the solemnity of the present as the middle
part of the drama of history and providence,[1] but Edwards went one step
further, for the scope of his observations on the drift and the design was
redemption.

In another of his _Miscellanies_ on Scripture, Edwards gave one
example for the natural world and for Scripture in order to demonstrate
the particular character of the difficulties that arose in both areas. In
the former instance he pointed out that this "lower world"[2] has been created
for man's living in it and yet parts of the earth seemed to be of no use to
man because of the "innumerable stones and rocks that overspread so great a
part of the earth, which to anything known, were altogether useless and
oftentimes were rather an inconvenience than benefit." Edwards here
referred to more than an everyday problem of agriculture in rural
Northampton. In the ongoing geological debate on the significance of the
rocky debris on the surface of the earth,[3] he did not take the position
that these ruins were indicative of the effects of the flood and the sin of
man, but for him these stones were "insuperable difficulties" and "unintel-
ligible mysteries" of the kind that provided opportunity for study and

[1]_The Cambridge Platonists_, pp. 207ff., 213ff.

[2]_Works_, VIII, p. 211.

[3]Marjorie Hope Nicolson, _Mountain Gloom and Mountain Glory, The
Development of the Aesthetics of the Infinite_ (1959; ppb., New York: The
Norton Library, 1963), pp. 144ff.

improvement in the future, for history had shown that difficulties such as these had been solved either partially or totally in the past.

The interpretation of Scripture was faced with a similar issue. Its "stones and rocks," as it were, consisted of the fact that revelation was contained in "ancient languages, used among people whose custom and phraseology are but imperfectly understood." Once again, however, such difficulty left room for "vast improvement" of knowledge in the course of time. But even beyond that the increase of knowledge in this field will not only contribute to research, but will signify that the church progresses towards the end. The resolution of every difficulty or mystery opened up another part of the road toward the goal of history. In order to avoid misunderstandings at this point Edwards pointed out that Scripture already now showed sufficiently what was necessary toward "happiness."[1] In doing so he adopted the Orthodox definition of _sufficientia Scripturae ad salutem_,[2] but he applied it in a historical and not a rationalistic manner. Scripture was not primarily a paradigm for world chronology, but it was being projected as the paradigm for a history with a purpose.

What Boyle had called "Scripture-Logick" seemed to be compatible or even required more than one analogy in order to articulate all the possible aspects of coherence and history in Scripture. In another _Miscellany_ Edwards wrote of "the analogy there is to be observed in the workes of nature, wherein the inferior are images of the superior, and the analogy holds through many ranks of being, but becomes more and more languid."[3]

---

[1] Edwards, Works, VIII, p. 211.

[2] Heinrich Heppe, _Reformed Dogmatics, Set Out and Illustrated from the Sources_, ed., Ernst Bizer, rev. ed. (1934; E.T., London: Allen and Unwin, 1950), p. 28.

[3] _Images and Shadows of Divine Things_, ed., Perry Miller (New Haven: Yale University Press, 1948), pp. 84-85.

As we move down from man through animals and plants to inanimate objects,
the analogy decreases in clarity but it does not cease substantially.
This particular view of nature is taken from the notion of the chain of being
in which individual ranks and degrees are related to each other by means
of "mirrors"[1] through which the higher levels are reflected in the lower
ranks. At the end of the note Edwards mentioned that the "same can be
observed of the types of Scripture." The types of Scripture were thus a
gradated scale of representations of the spiritual. In the draft of the
History of the Work of Redemption, the types were very obscure at the beginning, but they increased in clarity continually through the time of David
and Isaiah.[2] In our exploration of coherence and history we can now add
the aspects of degree and gradation to those of a pervading unity with its
manifold connections, difficulties, and mysteries.

Such analogies were not only employed in order to point to similarities, but their imagistic potential could also be used to visualize
and point out differences and distinct identities, for Scripture was not
interchangeable with nature as a plastic force nor with nature as a chain
of being. In an extended meditation on the subject of the wheels within
the wheel in Ezekiel 1.15ff., Edwards wrote:

> Things in their series and course in providence do, as it were,
> return to the same point or place when they began, as in the turning
> of a wheel but not yet so, but that a farther end is obtained than
> was at first, or the same end is obtained in a much further degree;
> so that in the general there is a progress towards a certain and final
> issue of things, and every revolution brings nearer to that issue, as
> it is the motion of the wheel upon the earth, as in the motion of the

---

[1]Arthur O. Lovejoy, The Great Chain of Being, A Study of the History
of an Idea (1936; ppb., Cambridge: Harvard University Press, 1971), p. 63.

[2]Edwards, Works, V, pp. 32, 46, 51, 61-62, 77, 95, 96.

wheels of a chariot, and not like the motion of a wheel by its axis,
for if so, its motion would be in vain.[1]

Edwards did not deny or belittle this "motion by its own axis." He did not
simply postulate a circular motion for the cosmos and a linear progress for
the moral world. He jotted down a near exhaustive list which showed that
the observation of nature, experience, and Scripture itself was against such
an easy division: there were the steady seasonal changes in year, month, and
day; there was the "sphere of the fixed stars which was the greatest wheel
and includes all the others"; there was the flow of ebb and tide, the circulation of the blood, the circuit of the winds and the circular movement of
the water from the sea through the clouds, springs, and rivers back to the
sea. There was also man who came from dust and who will return to dust,
and the empires that rose and fell. Edwards quoted Ecclesiastes that
"there is no new thing under the sun,"[2] and concluded a meditation on this
particular verse with the sentence: "That which goes around in a link,
let it continue moving never so swiftly, and never so long, makes no
progress, comes to nothing new."[3]

Nevertheless, Edwards spoke of a system of wheels rather than of
individual arbitrary wheels. While the wheels within the wheel did thus
not represent the wheel of fortune, or a continual return of things where
the earth remained the only constant fixed point, Edwards did not conceive
of this system of interlocking changes in the world as a machine or clock
either. In reference also to Ezekiel's vision he understood the world to

[1]Edwards, Works, IX, p. 256.

[2]Ibid., pp. 254-256; 259.

[3]Ibid., p. 223.

be a "chariot"[1] in which God guided the motions and changes toward progress
and purpose. The larger and the smaller wheels of the chariot described the
shorter and longer periods of history based on Scripture as the paradigm.[2]
The sometimes incommensurate character of certain aspects of the image of
the chariot only underlined that we deal here with a comprehension of reality
on the level of the imagination with its attempt to unite opposites rather
than with a desire to simply add up individual uniformities. Thus, whenever
such a wheel had completed its circle, something had also been achieved, for
while human things "rise from the earth and return to the ground again . . .
spiritual things begin their revolution from God on high, and thither they
return again."[3] At the conclusion of his draft of the History of the Work
of Redemption, Edwards addressed himself to the same question of the eternal
return of revolutions and the progress which was made through it. For him
it was Scripture which made the difference between motion by its own axis
and the motions of the wheel of a chariot, for

> If we behold events in any other view, all will look like the
> tossing of the waves, things will look as though one confused revolu-
> tion came after another, merely by blind chance, without any regular
> or certain end. But if we consider the events of providence in the
> light in which they have been set before us, and in which the Scriptures
> set them before us, they appear an orderly series of events, all wisely
> directed in excellent harmony and consistence, tending all to one end.
> The wheels of providence are not turned round by blind chance, but are
> full of eyes round about (as Ezekiel represents them) and are guided by
> the Spirit of God. Where the Spirit goes, they go. All God's works of
> providence, through all ages, meet at last, as so many lines meeting in
> one center.[4]

---

[1] Edwards, Works, IX, pp. 259ff.; see also Edwards, The Chief End for
Which God Created the World, Works, I, p. 513. "The whole universe is a
machine, or chariot, which God hath made for his own use, as is represented
in Ezekiel's vision."

[2] Works, IX, p. 257.

[3] Ibid., p. 259.   [4] Ibid., V, p. 275.

This summary of history bore a superficial resemblance to the chronologists' warning of confusion. While the latter, however, achieved order through calculating it, Edwards here spoke of the orderly movement toward a center in which all parts converged and within the whole of which opinions like those of Ecclesiastes must be seen. It was not just this or that part of Scripture, but Scripture as a whole which displayed such a resourcefulness of the Spirit. Both Boyle and Edwards had insisted on the importance of Scripture as a whole for the view of history. It was therefore a highly questionable procedure on the part of Harvey G. Townsend in his edition of Edwards' _Miscellanies_ to leave out a "paragraph declaring that the Christian revelation informs man of God's plan."[1] Edwards in this particular instance had argued that for intelligent being something was being obtained as a result of all the historical revolutions and that God therefore had served notice of this purpose to men in a historical revelation. To omit the mention of revelation in an edition of Edwards' work is like presenting the summary of someone's research or working with the conclusions of a scientific experiment while maintaining at the same time that the way in which these results were reached was immaterial. While Townsend probably only meant to delete the more obscure parts of Edwards' thought and while he was representative in this procedure rather than unique, he did in this way render obscure that part of Edwards' argument which he did find fit to print. Townsend's elimination of Scripture removed the paradigm on which the argument for history was based and the method of explication which it followed.

---

[1]_The Philosophy of Jonathan Edwards from His Private Notebooks_, ed. Harvey G. Townsend (Eugene: University of Oregon Press, 1953), p. 136.

Exegesis

The analogies of plastic nature, the chain of being and the wheels within the wheel have displayed a mosaic of characteristics that represent Scripture as a paradigm of coherent history. When we now move from a survey of these analogies to the analysis of an example of Edwards' exegesis, we shall attempt to demonstrate how through it the coherence of Scripture and its history appeared. For this purpose we shall focus on Edwards' Miscellany on the "Types of the Messiah" which has come down to us incomplete, but which nevertheless contained a consistent argument.[1] This analysis will be followed by some general observations on the history of exegesis which are pertinent to Edwards' place in it. In conclusion, some comments on the subject of the different outcomes of the exegetical process itself will be offered.

It was Edwards' intention to prove that the types of the Messiah were not only intrinsic to the Old Testament, but that they could also be demonstrated from its pages through exegesis. For this reason he began his argument with a general exegetical observation on types in the Old Testament and then moved on from there to the question of the types of the Messiah. In the exegesis of types the relationship between the two major parts of the Bible had usually been viewed as one picture in which the Old Testament represented the rough draft and first delineation and in which all the lineaments, colors, and perfections had been drawn forth to characterize the New Testament. This difference between the outline and the full

---

[1] Works, IX, pp. 401-494. The "Types of the Messiah" is a reprint of Edwards' Miscellany 1069 (Mason I. Lowance, "'Images and Shadows of Divine Things' in the Thought of Jonathan Edwards," in Typology and Early American Literature, ed., Sacvan Bercovitch (Amherst: University of Massachusetts Press, 1972), p. 217.

picture was therefore commonly described in terms of the relation of the
shadow *skiá* or type to its image $\overset{?}{\epsilon}\iota\kappa\acute{\omega}\nu$ or antitype.[1] The Old Testament
was only a shadow with regard to the New Testament, while the image of the
New Testament itself was only the image of things to come. This theory
translated into exegesis in such a way that, whenever there was a reference to the Old Testament in the New Testament, then the former could and
should be elaborated more fully. In cases where such references were
implicit rather than explicit a comparison between the Apostolic teaching
and the Old Testament prophets[2] could legitimately draw out such a hidden
type. Edwards for his part, however, set forth to derive the types from
the Old Testament prophecies without so much as using the New Testament
directly. The total effect of this exegesis resembled very much the tradition of natural theology within Christianity which in its individual representatives always assumed some aspect of the revelation that it was about
to prove, and which has, despite this somewhat circular reasoning, enjoyed
continued respectability for its sophisticated arguments.

For Edwards prophecy was not only expressed in dreams and visions or
in the spoken words of the prophets, but also in outward historical events.
All three of these aspects of prophecy, however, had in common that the ful
fillment as the goal of the prophecy was indirectly represented "under the
name of other things."[3] In the "Types of the Messiah" Edwards was most
interested to relate the events of prophecy to the words of prophecy. He
observed that the prophets usually engaged in "symbolical representations"

---

[1] Samuel Mather, The Figures and Types of the Old Testament (Dublin, 1683), p. 213; Kraus, Geschichte, p. 21.

[2] Mather, The Figures and Types, p. 70.

[3] Works, IX, pp. 401-402.

in which their verbal message was dramatized by an action. Thus, for
example, Isaiah was commanded by God to go naked and barefoot in order to
"typify the Egyptians and Ethiopians going naked and barefoot in their
captivity."[1] Prophecy thus included as it were both pre-diction and pre-
action as distinguished from fulfillment. The fact that the Old Testament
in itself showed examples of such a correspondence made it possible to
generalize the pattern for the Old Testament as a whole. Edwards agreed
with contemporary Jewish rabbis that the "substance, main drift, and end of
all prophecies of the Old Testament was the Messiah and his kingdom of
salvation."[2] It was therefore only logical to assume that in the case of
Messianic prophecies the pre-actions corresponding to the pre-diction ought
to abound.

The prophetic books and the psalms in particular showed that the
future salvation was "expressly spoken of" as "represented" by historical
events.[3] In page after page Edwards ran down the evidence for the various
aspects in which "the redemption out of Egypt is very often in the Old
Testament spoken of as a resemblance of the redemption of the Messiah."[4]
He found that the correspondences between pre-dictions and pre-actions,
between word and event, were so close that their characterization as "representations" was not accurate enough because "one is spoken of under the
other, as though one were contained in the other, or as though one were the
other." Thus, for example, in Psalm 72 "the peace and glory of Solomon's
reign and the reign of the Messiah are spoken of under one."[5] Not only was

---

[1]Works, IX, pp. 407f.

[2]Ibid., p. 409.   [3]Ibid., p. 412.

[4]Ibid., pp. 412-419.   [5]Ibid., p. 420.

the word of prophecy represented by an event and not only was the word and event joined together but also the events themselves were sometimes mentioned as "signs and pledges of those great things of the Messiah."[1] Pre-actions or historical events were consequently not simply the pedagogical illustrations for some other purpose, but they were a history of promise. Gerhard von Rad has pointed out that Old Testament scholarship for a long time adhered to a pedagogical interpretation of the prophets, where pre-actions were not considered as events instrumental in helping to bring about the events that were predicted.[2] Edwards' observation about pre-actions, types, and events meant therefore quite literally the avoidance of allegory as a technique in which history was used as so many disposable examples at the discretion of a moral philosophy.

Edwards' exegesis did not only provide an arsenal of individual proofs for these correspondences, but one of his examples itself gave an opportunity to look at the Old Testament as a whole, something that the interpreter of Edwards will notice when he makes at least sample checks by consulting a Bible along with Edwards' exposition of it. He mentioned Psalm 78 which laid out the history of Israel through the time of David.[3] The introductory annotations to this Psalm in the Geneva Bible called it "the sum of all God's benefits to the intent the ignorant and grosse people might se in fewe wordes the effect of the whole histories of the Bible." In the Psalm itself the story of the mighty acts of God to Israel and the disobedience of the people were introduced as a mystery. This combination of a

---

[1] Works, IX, p. 412.

[2] Gerhard von Rad, Theologie Des Alten Testamentes (München: Chr. Kaiser, 1968), Vol. II, pp. 104ff.

[3] Works, IX, pp. 418-419.

"plain summary rehearsal or narration" which pointed to its own mystery or meaning was for Edwards a concluding proof that not only the predictions were represented by pre-actions, but that the pre-actions themselves called for their own interpretation. What seemed especially remarkable to Edwards from the standpoint of philological exegesis was what we would call today the mixed form of the Psalm. Modern commentators located both the didactic and the puzzling elements of this riddle in the wisdom literature. Edwards used a rendering of this word riddle in terms of "parable and dark-sayings." He said that the usual meaning of parable was that of "a set discourse of things appertaining to divine wisdom." In this case, however, the addition of "dark sayings" pointed the plain didactic parable in the direction of a typical parable. In his commentary on the Psalms H. J. Kraus stated that the historical context in which the author of the song spoke of the "mystery of history," was no longer ascertainable. Much, therefore, seems to depend on the context from which a commentator viewed it: Kraus called God's faithfulness and the people's apostacy the mystery;[1] A. Weiser said that in modern terms we would say that the Psalm dealt with the irrationality of history.[2] If someone were to approach the question from the point of view of Ecclesiastes he might take the riddle to mean that history itself is the mystery. Edwards, on the other hand, looked at this Psalm from a well-documented exegesis of the relation of pre-diction and pre-action and he discovered a history of promise and redemption in the Psalmist's description of the mystery of history.[3]

[1] Hans Joachim Kraus, Psalmen (Neukirchen: Neukirchener Verlag, 1960), I, pp. 539, 542, 548.

[2] Arthur Weiser, The Psalms, A Commentary (Philadelphia: Westminster Press, 1962), p. 538.

[3] Nevertheless, the very thoroughness of the exegesis to relate prediction and pre-action also revealed its limits and linked Edwards finally to the orthodox doctrine of Scriptural inspiration with the only difference

One of the main results of Edwards' exegesis in this particular
instance is to be seen in the view that the kingdom of the Messiah and of
salvation was the subject of eschatology as well as of history. The whole
cluster of ideas associated in the Bible with the Exodus from and the redemption out of Egypt were the subject of remembrance as well as of expectation
so that in more abstract terms we can offer this formulation that according
to "Scripture-logick" doctrine itself was a statement that consisted of
prophecy as well as of history. Scripture as a whole could therefore be
referred to in a chiasmic expression as a "prophetical history and a

---

that in his case coherence became the dogma that had to be found everywhere.
Unlike in the search for chronology the distinction was not simply between
order and confusion, but between the "significant" and the "impertinent" or
between the meaningful and the meaningless: "Some of the historical events
of the Old Testament, if they are not typical, must needs be impertinently
taken notice of in the history." (Works, IX, p. 420; see also pp. 434, 479.
In a very literal sense Edwards had shown how the pre-diction contained a pr
action. Now he turned the argument around and maintained that every event i
the historical books of the Old Testament had to be such a pre-action even i
no correspondence to a pre-diction could be found. In order to maintain thi
shift in his exegesis he made the only reference (Works, IX, p. 493) in "The
Types of the Messiah" to the Epistle to the Hebrews in the New Testament as
locus classicus in typological exegesis. According to Edwards' understandin
of Hebrews 9, 3-5, it was not necessary that all types were explained in
Scripture themselves, a position he had thus far argued in relating pre-
action and prediction. This meant he was free to look for correspondences
of his own and revert to allegory for the dogmatic purpose of making sure
that not one part of the Old Testament remained unedifying or meaningless.
The idea that the Old Testament could report anything that was at all "imper
tinent" to the work of redemption did not occur to Edwards. In his article
on Edwards' typology, Mason I. Lowance had argued that in his work Edwards
moved from a conservative historical typological approach in the draft for
the History of the Work of Redemption to a liberal allegorical spiritual
approach for which he found examples in Perry Miller's edition of the Images
and Shadows of Divine Things. Lowance used the "Types of the Messiah" as a
way to illustrate an intermediate stage between these two poles. Our own
analysis has shown, however, that the reversion to the allegorical method
was more dictated by a dogmatic position than by a movement from the conservative to the liberal. As long as the historical and prophetic aspects
of the doctrine of redemption can be proven in a literal sense, Edwards will
do it, but beyond that he will revert to allegory.

historical prophecy,"[1] and the programmatic outline for the History of the Work of Redemption Edwards summarily referred to Scripture as a whole in terms of "history and prophecy."[2] The close relationship which his exegesis of the "Types of the Messiah" here exhibited between doctrine, prophecy, and history was also one proof for the contention that Scripture in fact was "one grand drift and design" in which many things including doctrines, prophecies, and histories have manifold relationships to each other.

Edwards' exegesis of the "Types of the Messiah" proceeded as it were from prophecy as the end of history toward history as a process so that the coherence of history was constituted through its end. The peculiar nature of the sources which led to this point of view is best seen when we put it against the background of the several meanings that the word "histories" in the grand drift and design could assume. For Edwards histories included the Biblical stories which he himself would use for catechetical instruction[3] and the abuse of which as romances he criticized amongst his congregation in the draft for the History of the Work of Redemption.[4] In addition, philological attention to the Old Testament record as well as the search for legitimate precedents for historiography led to the recognition of the explicitly composite character of the Old Testament itself. Here were mentioned several different works of history such as the history of Creation, the book of generations from Adam, and the Book of the Wars of the Lord.[5] The same philological inquiry also turned up the evidence that

[1] John Cotton, A Brief Exposition, p. 3.

[2] See p. 2. [3] Ibid., V, p. 131.

[3] Works, I, p. 52. [4] Ibid., V, p. 131.

[5] Isaac Newton, Observations Upon the Prophecies of Daniel and the Aoocalypse (London: J. Darby and T. Browne, 1733), p. 45.

154

the Scriptures themselves were "but very brief abridgements of large histories" and acknowledged that much by referring to them.[1] Edwards therefore did not regard Scripture in terms of a perfect history in the Baconian
manner but as a

> very concise history in which only some particular facts and circum-
> stances that concern the special purpose of that relation are men-
> tioned -- and innumerable others are omitted that would be proper to
> be mentioned, if the main design were to give a full, clear, connected,
> continued history of such a people, or such affairs as the history
> mentions -- it is no wonder that many doubts and difficulties arise.[2]

"Such a people" for Edwards was no one else but Israel, and the
detailed attention that he gave to the record of the Old Testament in his
exegesis of the "Types of the Messiah" constituted as it were the paradigm
within the paradigm for Scripture as a coherent view of history. Not only
did he therefore disapprove of "some who are ready to look on the Old
Testament as being out of date, and as if we in the days of the gospel,
have but little to do with it," but it provided Edwards with a view of the
Old Testament that made it essential to his understanding of the content
and the form[3] of the History of the Work of Redemption.

---

[1]Sibley's Harvard Graduates, 5, p. 350.

[2]Works, VIII, pp. 211-212.

[3]Edwards observed that the very form and shape of the Old Testament
document was expressive of the theme of redemption: "The history of the
Old Testament is large and particular where the great affair of redemption
required it; even where there was most done towards this work most to typify
Christ, and to prepare the way for him. Thus it is very particular in the
history of Abraham and the other patriarchs; but very short in the account
we have of the time which the children of Israel spent in Egypt. It is
large in the account of the redemption out of Egypt, and the first settling
of the affairs of the Jewish church and nation in the time of Moses and
Joshua; but much shorter in the times of the Judges. So again, it is large
and particular in the times of Solomon, and then very short in the history
of the ensuing reigns. Thus, the accounts are large or short, just as there
is more or less of the affair of redemption to be seen in it" (Works, V,
p. 130).

There was an affinity in Edwards between his point of departure in the exegesis of the "Types of the Messiah" and the place in time that he accorded to the Old Testament prophets in general and to Isaiah in particular. In Edwards' attempt at the periodization of the history of Israel in terms of several wheels, Isaiah came on the scene when the Jewish church had reached the height of its wheel.[1] The prophets as it were could both pre-view the future and re-view the past. The implications of this approach become clearer when we hold it against Isaac Newton's conception of the prophets, for it seems that a different approach to this subject went along with a different approach to history. In his Observations upon the Prophecies of Daniel and the Apocalypse of St. John,[2] Isaac Newton first discussed the books and authors of the Old Testament in their chronological order and concluded this review with the statement that "amongst the old prophets Daniel is the most distinct in order of time, easiest to be understood and therefore in those things which relate to the last things he must be made the key of the rest."[3] Both Edwards and Newton maintained that prophetic language was figurative, but their understanding of the key to the figurative understanding was different. Newton wrote a whole chapter on prophetical language which consisted for him mainly of natural images, and were to be understood in terms of the analogy of the "world natural and an empire or kingdom politic."[4] For Edwards, on the other hand, the figurative language of the Messianic kingdom represented the actual history of

[1] Works, IX, pp. 257-258.

[2] J. Darby and T. Browne, 1733.

[3] Newton, Observations, p. 15.

[4] Ibid., pp. 16ff. See also Manuel, Isaac Newton, Historian, pp. 68-70.

Israel. In Newton's view of prophetic language such a connection of the
predictions with the Old Testament at large did not exist, for his linguistic key was the correspondence between the natural and the political.
For Edwards, in "Types of the Messiah" it was redemption in which prophecy
and history cohered, whereas in Newton's Observations the integrating factor between history and prophecy was a chronological one insofar as he was
primarily interested in the chronological order of the books and also
insofar as the prophet Daniel is chosen for he was the "most distinct in
order of time."

While the attention to the text by both men is painstaking, while
both use the available tools in order to carry out their investigations
and, finally, while Edwards belonged to the same conservative[1] branch of
chronology as Newton did, they both arrived at significantly different conclusions. In Newton there was no room for the imaginative in history and
his inclusion of prophecy in the overall enterprise of laying the foundations for the "connections" between sacred and secular history was matched
by Edwards' quest to find the "connections" of sacred history itself.
Newton in other words dealt with Historie, Edwards dealt with Geschichte.

---

[1] By conservative we mean that the Old Testament chronology as the
basis for world history was nowhere in doubt (Manuel, Isaac Newton,
Historian, pp. 39f.). Edwards defended it strongly (Works, V, pp. 126-127).
While a man like Arthur Bedford (1668-1745) attacked Isaac Newton's chronology vigorously (Manuel, p. 169f.), and while Newton disagreed with the
opinion of the noted orientalist Humphrey Prideaux (1648-1724) as to the
great antiquity of Assyrian history (Manuel, pp. 98-99), Edwards did use all
three of them for his notes on individual passages of Scripture. He was
familiar with Isaac Newton's Chronology of the Ancient Kingdoms Amended
(Thomas H. Johnson, "Jonathan Edwards' Background of Reading," Publications
of the Colonial Society of Massachusetts, 28 Dec. 1931, p. 208). Edwards
used Bedford's Scripture Chronology Demonstrated by Astronomical Consideration
(London: printed for James and John Knapton, 1730), extensively (Works, Ix,
pp. 55, 86, 96, 122, etc.). Reference was also made to Humphrey Prideaux,
The Old and the New Testament Connected in the History of the Jews, 9th ed.
(London: printed for R. Knaplock, 1725), see Works, IX, p. 236, etc.

The inclusion of such detailed analyses of Edwards' exegesis as a way
to explicate our interpretative thesis is an indispensable part of our argument throughout this study. The adoption of such an approach is a reflection
on the absence of a comprehensive historiography of exegesis[1] that could have

---

[1]Attention to the undoubtedly great exegetical achievement of
Reformers like Luther and Calvin, the focus on the theoretical definition
of the doctrine of verbal inspiration in Protestant Orthodoxy and the interest in the rise of historical criticism have had the combined effect to lead
to a historiography which encouraged the view that exegesis in the seventeenth century originated from great men, descended to the level of epigones,
and was followed by a group of liberators. A more comprehensive understanding of exegesis in this century must, however, also take into consideration
that amongst the Puritans of the seventeenth century an "unparalleled diffusion of the knowledge about the Bible" took place which "created a popular
religious intellectualism" that has never since been found (M. Weber,
Sociology of Religion, pb.; Boston: Beacon Press, 1964, p. 134). Such an
intellectualism may not always have reached the heights of Luther's or
Calvin's understanding of the Bible, but it was an expression of the penetration of the depths of a culture. If it is furthermore correct that both of
these Reformers were instrumental in disseminating the knowledge of the Bible
in an unprecedented degree, then a cultural diffusion like this should be a
necessary part of every history of exegesis that sets out from their achievement. It seems, however, that elitist assumptions, a lack of interdisciplinary cooperation and national lines of interest in historiography
have thus far prevented such an approach.

For a more adequate appraisal of exegesis in the seventeenth century
several other aspects must be added. Since the reading and interpreting of
Scripture was widespread we must take into account men like John Locke. He
also wrote commentaries on the Bible and was anxious to find Isaac Newton's
approval for his achievement in this field (Manuel, Isaac Newton, Historian,
pp. 11, 141-142). Poets like John Donne and John Milton were also expositors
of the Bible, an aspect of the history of exegesis which has been forgotten
by theologians, but kept alive by literary scholars (Brevard S. Childs,
Biblical Theology in Crisis, pp. 139-140). This long-standing interest by
scholars in the field of literature has recently received a new impetus by
a focus on the typological tradition within the exegetical process as a means
to trace the origins of literary symbolism and to define the character of
Puritan historiography (Bercovitch, "The Historiography of Johnson's Wonder-
working Providence," p. 140). -- Furthermore, the approach to the Orthodox
view of inspiration often creates the erroneous impression as if these orthodox divines had not engaged in exegesis at all (R. Preus, The Inspiration of
Scripture, pp. 193f.). In addition Protestant Orthodoxy itself was not a
monolithic movement. The contemporary complaints that the use of Aristotle
for the scholastic formulation of theology diverted the attention from exegesis were indeed justified (A. Tholuck, Das Akademische Leben des Siebzehnten
Jahrhunderts mit besonderer Beziehung auf die protestantisch-theologischen

helped to provide more points of reference in order to present the relation

of exegesis to history in a more systematic manner for Edwards and the back-

ground to which he belonged. The particular interest in the rise of

---

Fakultäten Deutschlands, Halle: Eduard Anton, 1853, p. 212), but then there
were also those theological groups who followed a Ramist methodology and continued to show a more biblical character (ibid., p. 206). Finally, if we
look at the five Folio volumes of the Synopsis Criticorum Aliorumque Sacrae
Scripturae Interpretum which Matthew Poole collected over ten years (DNB,
XVI, 99) we find an impressive testimony to the character and achievement of
exegesis in the seventeenth century (Ludwig Diestel, Geschichte des Alten
Testamentes in der Christlichen Kirche, Jena: Mauke's Verlag, 186, p. 349)
which in turn provided Jonathan Edwards with one of his exegetical tools
(Works, IX, p. 493). Another important -- and English-written -- source
which was compiled over many years is Cotton Mather's Biblia Americana (for
a description, see C. Mather, Magnalia, Vol. I, p. 33). This was to be not
only a digest of all exegesis but also a digest of recent science as it bore
upon exegesis. In A New Offer to the Lovers of Religion and Learning
(Boston: printed by B. Green, 1710), Mather quoted extensively Robert Boyle's
treatise as a means to recommend his huge project for subscription. The work
was to have twelve parts: "Philological Emendations," "Antiquities," which
included subjects like politics and music; "Laws of the Israelitish Nation"
and a "History of the City of Jerusalem" from Melchisedek down to the millennium; Types; Collections from the Talmud; Natural Philosophy; Biblical Chronology and harmony of the Gospel; "A sort of Twenty-ninth chapter of the
acts"; church history in the form of prophecy and fulfillment; Chiliad; "Some
Essays to Illustrate the Scriptures from Experimental Piety." Steps in the
direction of such a history of exegesis must proceed from an analysis and
comparison of commentaries themselves (Basil Hall, "Biblical Scholarship:
Editions and Commentaries," in Cambridge History of the Bible, The West from
the Reformation to the Present Day, ed. S. L. Greenslade, 3, Cambridge:
Cambridge University Press, 1963, p. 76). For such questions as atomism in
philosophy and for learning, the comparison of several exegetes has been used
with success (Danton B. Sailor, "Moses and Atomism," JHI, XXV (1964), 3-16;
M. Hattoway, "Paradoxes of Solomon: Learning in the English Renaissance,"
JHI, XXIX (1968), 499-630). A theoretical formulation of such an approach
in its importance for church history in particular has been provided by
Gerhard Ebeling ("Kirchengeschichte als Geschichte der Auslegung der
Heiligen Schrift," Sammlung Gemeinverständlicher Vorträge aus dem Gebiet der
Theologie-und Religionsgeschichte, 189, Tübingen: Mohr-Siebeck, 1947). One
way, therefore, to approach Edwards' exegesis in relation to its background
would be, for example, to pursue the theme of the "Wheels within the Wheel"
in Ezekiel 1, 15ff., in the work of several commentators.

historical criticism and its controversies with orthodoxy have assigned a

whole tradition of interpretation as well as the question of the overall

cultural diffusion of the Bible into a historiographical limbo. The result

of the first development was that "Spinoza, Hobbes, Colenso and Strauss are

treated in every standard history while one searches usually in vain for

even a mention of the English Puritan expositors, the French Jensenists, or

the influence of Matthew Henry and Adam Clarke."[1] These critical remarks

stem from the self-criticism of a Biblical scholar who is concerned that

the pursuit of the historical-critical method today shows signs of insuffi-

ciency in dealing with the aesthetic aspects of Scripture,[2] displays serious

difficulties in integrating the past and the present, and reveals a pervad-

ing sense of antiquarianism. For these reasons Childs thought it of "prime

importance to recover this tradition" which was by-passed by the rise of

historical criticism and which is too often and too easily dismissed as

"pre-critical" or metaphysical. While Childs offered only general observa-

tions about the character of this exegetical tradition these remarks never-

theless provide a valuable confirmation of the observations that we have

made on the subject of Scripture as a paradigm of history. He characterized

the exegesis of a man like Matthew Henry whose commentaries Edwards used[3]

---

[1]Brevard S. Childs, Biblical Theology in Crisis (Philadelphia: Westminster Press, 1970), p. 139. Adam Clarke (1762-1832) was a Methodist minister, biblical commentator, theological writer, and a scholar with an acknowledged reputation for wide learning. The eight volumes of his commentary on the Bible were published from 1810-26. (DNB, IV, 413-414.)

[2]Ibid., pp. 141ff.

[3]Works, IX, pp. 127, 129, 218. Matthew Henry (1662-1714) did not conform to the uniformity act of 1662. He had originally prepared for a career in law, then became a minister and served for most of his life as the pastor of Presbyterian church of Chester, England. His main work was the Exposition of the Old and New Testaments (RE, 685-686; Rgg[3] III, 226). From 1704 on, Henry published parts of his commentary. The first complete edition of six volumes came out in 1815.

as that of a man who had an appreciation of the canon as a whole, who could
move from a detailed study of syntax to the anatomy of the soul, and who
had the ability for a penetrating analysis of themes and motifs in the
whole of the Bible.[1]

While we know little of the history and hermeneutics of the exegetical tradition to which Edwards belonged, it is nevertheless possible to
illustrate the context and content of his achievement by relating it to a
particular case history from the field of the history of exegesis. In 1678
John Eliot had published a Gospel Harmony. In it he had collected for the
purposes of an extended sacramental meditation all those texts from the
various parts of the several gospels which dealt with the sufferings and
the death of Christ. His thorough search of the record led him to the
observation: "Why the Lord hath said so little of his eminent life and so
much of his sufferings and death is a point worth searching into."[2] For his
own part, however, Eliot decided that "Where the Scripture is silent why
should we speak."[3] Later interpreters no longer asked why there was no life
of Jesus, but they were convinced that such a life had been obscured by and
had to be rescued from the doctrinal corruptions as they appeared in the
theology of the apostle Paul and its perpetrations through the history of
the church. From the latter half of the eighteenth century onward, interpreters therefore turned to the synoptic gospel as the basis for Jesus
biographies.[4] In the ensuing controversy between life and history versus

[1]Works, IX, p. 146.

[2]John Eliot, The Harmony of the Gospels in the Holy History of the
Humiliation and Sufferings of Jesus Christ from His Incarnation to His Death
and Burial (Boston: John Foster, 1678), p. 18.

[3]Ibid., p. 12.

[4]Albert Schweitzer, Geschichte der Leben-Jesu-Forschung (1913; rpt.,
Tübingen: Mohr-Siebeck, 1951), p. 13ff.

doctrine the view of Jesus was no longer shaped exclusively by the various doctrinal assumptions of different churches, but it was increasingly replaced by the varying presuppositions which individual biographers brought with them and applied in order to recreate Jesus in their own image.[1]

At the turn of the twentieth century the history of religion did in fact discover the life of Jesus, but it so happened that its description of Jesus as a Jewish eschatological prophet did not square with the views that either the biographers or the doctrinalists had of him.[2] For the biographies he proved a great embarrassment because their quest which had set out from an Enlightenment protest against and criticism of doctrine came now up against a historical fact that turned its subject of attention into a character which answered all the specifications of an enthusiasm to which the Enlightenment tradition had an aversion as deep as to doctrine. Those who had upheld the importance of doctrine in the New Testament were, however, equally embarrassed. Their approach to the New Testament followed a tradition best epitomized by William Perkins and initiated by Martin Luther and John Calvin. Perkins had recommended that students begin their reading of Scripture with the letter to the Romans and the gospel of John, not only because they were the most difficult books, but they were also "the keys to the New Testament itself."[3] In the two great reformers this focus within

[1]Schweitzer, Geschichte der Leben-Jesu-Forschung, p. 4.

[2]Jürgen Moltmann, Theologie der Hoffnung, Untersuchungen zur Begründung und zu den Konsequenzen einer Christlichen Eschatologie, 6th improved ed. (Munich: Chr. Kaiser, 1965), pp. 31ff. Richard Hyde Hiers and David Larrimore Holland, ed.; Jesus' Proclamation of the Kingdom of God, by Johannes Weiss (1892, E.T., Philadelphia: Fortress Press, 1971), pp. 9, 15, 19, 25.

[3]William Perkins, "The Art of Prophesying," in The Works of William Perkins, ed., Ian Breward, Courtenay Library of Reformation Classics, 3. William Perkins (1552-1602), Fellow at Christ College, Cambridge, was a Calvinist and became the theological father of Puritanism in his theoretical, practical, and devotional writings (DNB, XV, 892-895).

162

the New Testament had coincided with a very reserved attitude over against
Revelations as the only prophetic book in the New Testament and both of
them had by-passed it in their extensive exegesis of the whole canon.

The discovery of the manifest eschatological character of the mission
of Jesus was therefore either repressed or reinterpreted in individualist
existential terms which were in keeping with both the biographical and the
doctrinal traditions. When almost sixty years later Jüurgen Moltmann began
to give systematic articulation to the implications of this discovery of
eschatology he could do it -- within his European and German context -- with
great emphasis on its novelty only, because his theology of hope did not
include the exhilarating and frustrating history of the unique quest for
this hope that had already taken shape and had been played out in the civilization of a Christian America. From its beginnings this enterprise had
bestowed a marked interest on the prophetic book of the New Testament and on
the prophetic literature of the canon as a whole. It is in the light of
this particular case history that the characteristic thrust of Edwards'
exegesis of the "Types of the Messiah" as an effort to include history and
doctrine as well as prophecy can be appreciated as well as assessed in its
relation to the pursuit of Scripture as a paradigm of coherent history.

(Appleford, Abingdon, Berkshire, England, 1970), p. 337. The sixteenth
century Zurich reformer Heinrich Bullinger referred to Paul's letter to
the Romans as "Methodus Totius Scripturae" (Joachim Staedtke, Die
Theologie des Jungen Bullinger, p. 58).

Summary

Thomas S. Kuhn's description of the function of paradigms served as
an aid to find a language in which to express the significance of Scripture
as the other part of the hermeneutical circle. Edwards himself differentiated in Scripture between a series of historical events and a view of
history. We conducted therefore a twofold investigation of Scripture as a
paradigm of chronology and of Scripture as a paradigm of coherence. Scripture as a paradigm of chronology had had a long and distinguished career in
the history of the mind of the West, but at the turn of the eighteenth century it became vulnerable to the ever increasing flow of historical information which produced internal strains in the paradigm, led to skepticism
against it, and facilitated its abandonment (e.g., Voltaire). The treatment of this particular aspect of the paradigm crisis by the Swiss historian
Kaegi was instructive, for in a typically European fashion he unconsciously
excluded future as a category of its own and thus prejudged a complete
understanding of Scripture as a paradigm of history. We found that Scripture
as a paradigm of coherence was a response to an internal crisis in early
modern Protestantism and led to a view of history which Edwards in his
descriptions approximated through such different and mutually exclusive
metaphors as plastic nature, the chain of being, and the wheels of fortune.
This view of history constituted a minority voice, but it held its own
against the rising tide of historical criticism.

Such an understanding of Scripture as a whole provided a contrast
to chronological antiquarianism and arbitrary doctrinal prooftexting. It
was also built on an intensive and extensive reading of Scripture itself.
We have already demonstrated the importance of exegesis for Edwards'

background in the investigation of Thomas Shepard. Since no substantial

research into the history of exegesis for this period is extant, it was

not   possible to give a detailed and continuous account of the exegetica.

process in its relation to history. Nevertheless, an inquiry into Edwards

understanding of typology and a brief review of the exegetical emphases in

New Testament interpretation outlined in a general way how and in what con-

text Edwards set out to articulate and to defend a view of history which

included America and was indigenous to it.

CHAPTER V

SCRIPTURE AND REVIVAL:

JONATHAN EDWARDS' DEFENSE OF HISTORY

Virtue and History: Prejudice, Pride, Prudence

Jonathan Edwards in his writings on the Northampton revival and

the Great Awakening was concerned over the bad press[1] which both of them

drew. In order to counteract such misrepresentations with an adequate

coverage of events, Edwards wrote not only A Faithful Narrative, A

History, but also Distinguishing Marks, and Some Thoughts Concerning the

Revival, both of which were interpretations of a historic event. Toward

the end of Some Thoughts Concerning the Revival he also proposed a collec-

tion of accounts to be compiled and published at fortnightly or monthly

intervals in Boston.[2] This design was carried through in part by Thomas

Prince, Jr., with the full cooperation of his father. Between March 1743

---

[1]Press is here to be understood in a literal sense, for newspapers
were one of the media through which revivals became known. Thus, for
example, Charles Chauncy's Seasonable Thoughts on the State of Religion in
New England (Boston: Rogers and Fowle for Samuel Eliot, 1743) relied for a
good deal of its information on the Boston Weekly Newspaper (p. 58), The
Boston Evening Post (p. 68, 147, etc.), and the Boston Post Boy (p. 96),
106). In addition to public means there were also letters on a private or
semiprivate level which supplied the news. To determine how far this newspaper coverage helped shape the image of the revival and contributed to its
historiography is not part of this study (cp. Jonathan Edwards, The Great
Awakening, ed. by C. C. Goen [New Haven: Yale University Press, 1972], p. 38).
All subsequent references to Goen's critical edition of Edwards' writings
on the revival will be referred to as "The Great Awakening, ed., C. C. Goen."

[2]The Great Awakening, ed., C. C. Goen, p. 529; see also pp. 224, 538.

and 1744 they published two annual volumes of the periodical <u>Christian</u>
<u>History</u>.[1] Both men were conveniently situated in Boston where Thomas
Prince, Sr., was a man of widely established reputation prior to the Great
Awakening not only in the field of meticulous chronological scholarship
and antiquarian research, but according to Charles Chauncy he also
"possessed all the intellectual powers in a degree far beyond what is common." While Chauncy ranked only "Dr. Cotton Mather" higher, he was particularly grieved that a man of such excellent attainments should succumb
to such a "strange disposition"[2] as that of collecting and publishing under
his name the fantastic stories of the ongoing revival.

The rationale for such accounts derived from the experience that
the propagation of the news of the revivals also aided considerably in the
promotion and propagation of the revivals themselves.[3] Publication of histories for the sake of promotion was no novel device. Like seventeenth
century accounts that were written to promote settlement, such a projected account on the revival walked the thin line that separated promotion
from propaganda. In the present case promotion was not for emigration to
a new land, but it undertook promotional activities to spread new events
across and beyond the new land. The attempt to attract attention and to
appeal for participation could easily become stereotyped into promotionalism

---

[1] <u>Christian History</u> was "the first specifically religious magazine in
the western hemisphere" (<u>The Great Awakening</u>, ed., C. C. Goen), p. 18. The
assessment of its historical character in relation to the portrayal of religion in later magazines proved impossible, since the Harvard Archives could
not locate in its holdings the unpublished thesis by R. C. White on "Writing
pertaining to Religion in Eighteenth Century Magazines" which was mentioned
in Nelson R. Burr, ed., <u>A Critical Bibliography of Religion in America</u>
(Princeton: Princeton University Press, 1961), p. 22.

[2] <u>Sibley's Harvard Graduates</u>, 5, p. 357.

[3] <u>The Great Awakening</u>, ed., C. C. Goen, p. 120.

In light of the fact that Jonathan Edwards and Thomas Prince[1] helped shape
a tradition of reporting on and promoting of revivals, one of the questions
that must be asked is whether and in how far Jonathan Edwards in his own
several attempts to come to grips with the challenge of the revivals did
or did not provide more than an account for the sake and in terms of
promotion.

It was fortunate that Jonathan Edwards interspersed in his work
remarks which provide the reader with clues as to the change and development
of his own thinking. In a letter written from Stockbridge[2] to the Reverend
Thomas Gillespie[3] in Scotland, Jonathan Edwards looked back on the
historiography of the revivals and commented:

> And there is this inconvenience attends the publishing of narratives
> of a work of God among a people: such is the corruption that is in the
> hearts of men, and even of good men, that there is great danger of mak-
> ing it an occasion of spiritual pride. There is great reason to think
> that Northampton people have provoked God greatly by trusting in their
> privileges and attainments, and the consequences may well be a warning
> to all God's people far and near, that hear of them.[4]

Here was a clear awareness of the dangers involved in the historiography of the revivals. Edwards did not deal here with such questions as
method or hermeneutics. We shall see that matters of that kind did not

---

[1] Glenn T. Miller, "The Rise of Evangelical Calvinism, A Study in
Jonathan Edwards and the Puritan Tradition," unpublished Th.D. dissertation,
Union Theological Seminary, New York, 1971, p. 386. An elaboration of this
tradition does not fall strictly within the area of an investigation of
Edwards' view of history.

[2] July 1, 1751.

[3] Gillespie (1708-74) studied at the University of Edinburgh and at
Philip Doddridge's Northampton Academy. Pastor at Carnock, Scotland, from
1741 to 1752, when he was deposed for refusing to help settle a minister
resisted by the people, Gillespie founded the Relief Church of Scotland in
1761. Cf. The Great Awakening, ed., C. C. Goen, p. 561, n. 1.

[4] Ibid., p. 563.

escape his attention. At this point he cut deeper and went beyond such
issues as those of bias or point of view in history to that of "spiritual
pride." Not just pride in general, but the pride of those who through
their conversion had obtained forgiveness of sin. In a passage that sounds
very much like Henry James' The Turn of the Screw, he described this
spiritual pride thus:

> It is a sin that has, as it were, many lives; if you kill it, it
> will live still; if you mortify and suppress it in one shape, it
> rises in another; if you think it is all gone, yet it is there still.
> There are a great many kinds of it, that lie in different forms and
> shapes, one under another, and encompass the heart like the coats of
> an onion; if you pull off one there is another underneath.[1]

Such a statement in historiography was the kind of observation to
end all observations, for it took the question of historiography to a level
of inquiry compared to which other issues such as those relating to style
and method seem to be merely derivative. And yet one wonders whether Edward
in his graphic and offensive way has not given an adequate description in
the several layers of the onion of the promise and plight of the historian.

With such a sweeping appraisal before us we can only ask the preliminary question as to how early and where Edwards became aware of the
danger of pride for historiography. If we look at Edwards' autobiographical
statements throughout the writings on the revivals the quotation from the
letter to Gillespie was not a retraction in the classic sense in which
Augustine practiced it. Toward the end of his life Augustine surveyed what
he had written and detailed where, how, and why his mind had changed; Edward
on the other hand, marked his changes as he went along. The reason why the
statement in the letter sounded so general was precisely because he had

---

[1]Great Awakening, ed., Goen, p. 417.

been considering the problem on the basis of many particular insights. Thus, at the end of the Distinguishing Marks he wrote: "I once did not imagine that the heart of man has been so unsearchable as I find it is. I am less charitable, and less uncharitable than once I was."[1] This almost paradoxical statement indicated that for Jonathan Edwards the issues have become more complex while he himself has become more discriminating. He had been both too credulous and too critical. Both attitudes have led into errors and disappointments but neither can be given up, for between them they have fully discovered the unsearchableness of the heart which demanded both trust and discrimination. The learning process now began. At first Edwards saw that something was going on; now he has learned that when something is going on, some things also go wrong. He did not capitulate, but he moved on and wrote in the preface to Some Thoughts Concerning the Revival: "I think I have been made in some measure sensible and much more of late than formerly of my need of more wisdom than I have. I make it my rule to lay hold of light and embrace it, though held forth by a child or any enemy."[2]

If we compare the earlier Faithful Narrative and the later Some Thoughts Concerning the Revival, we can see that the former included the case history of a child, whereas the latter contained only the case history of an older, unidentified person.[3] This circumscription of the range of sources he intended to embrace was not merely hyperbole. He would listen both to those who could not speak for themselves and those who could hold their own in an argument. The children belong to that group in Edwards which, like the illiterate people, the common sort, the Indians, and the Negroes, fall

---

[1] Great Awakening, ed., Goen, p. 285.

[2] Ibid., p. 292.　　　　　　　　　　[3] Ibid., pp. 331ff.

outside the view of most of his contemporaries. His association of these
groups was not at all unusual because indentured servants and apprentices
at the time included all children, Negroes, and Indians. From the way
Edwards introduced this subject one would expect the quotation to end "by
a child or an older person." Instead we read "by a child or any enemy."
It was observable that from Distinguishing Marks onward, Edwards increasingly articulated the Great Awakening as a youth movement, and tried to
find out why the contingent of older and converted people was so small and
why the majority of the older people was so hostile. Where in A Faithful
Narrative we found "Young and Old" as one of the distinctive features of
the revival at Northampton, we now find "a child or any enemy" in an attempt
to at least learn from those who opposed the revival. This particular
stance of openness for more wisdom stood in contrast to those of his
opponents of whom Edwards said: "Indeed, I know not what persons may deny
now, to defend themselves in a case they have had their spirits long
engaged in, but I know those things don't use to be denied, or doubted of."[1]
Edwards here seemed to have found his "antitype" which he charged with
self-love and self-indulgence. To top the argument, he used the familiar
device of claiming that the opinions of those people were in effect novel
notions and departures from a well-established tradition.[2]

These autobiographical remarks tied in with a posture that was
intimately related to a reflection on the nature of reporting which the
revival required. The peculiar challenges in reporting on the revival were
to be found in the partially metalinguistic character and impact of its

---

[1]The Great Awakening, ed., C. C. Goen, p. 302.

[2]Ibid., pp. 301-302.

events. For some cases, at least, Edwards maintained that the work of God found its participants literally speechless. There was a biblical saying that "the words that the mouth utters come from an overflowing heart."[1] Here Edwards referred to the opposite: the heart was full to the point of speechlessness, for "there may be language sufficient in such a case in their behavior only."[2] This metalinguistic character was an independent variable, for it could be seen both in those with weak and in those with strong reasoning powers. Nor were the events wholly commensurable in terms of an affectionate style of preaching or reporting. In other words, in the language that was in behavior or actions there was transparent a charismatic quality which was self-authenticating and which was not so much verbally communicative as it was contagious upon personal encounter. Such charismatic "examples"[3] did not simply provide instruction or demand imitation. As living examples they exerted influence and initiated as well as propagated a movement.

The reader at this point may be somewhat surprised at the emphatic apology of Edwards on behalf of the rationality of example. Both before and during the Enlightenment "example" served as the link between history and moral instruction. The reading of appropriate classical or other histories was to inculcate moral precepts and to discipline one for action.

---

[1] Matthew 12:34.

[2] The Great Awakening, ed., C. C. Goen, p. 239. Here Edwards obscured his own point in his presentation because of a leap in his thought. The context plainly showed that his point was that not even an affectionate style could effectively communicate the events of the work. At the same time he said that it was impossible for a dull and unaffected narration to represent and communicate the events. The latter was what we would expect him to say, normally, the former is more radical.

[3] Ibid., p. 238.

More often than not the life of the ancients, of kings, of bishops, of the
Fathers, including the fathers of New England, as they were for example
enshrined in Cotton Mathers' Magnalia, had to serve this purpose. For
Edwards, on the other hand, example was not a literary model for the character and vocational training in civility, but it was a charismatic example
that could snowball into a common movement that was not dependent on just
one charismatic leader. Unlike what we know of the preceding Stoddardean
Harvests, Edwards' own experience at Northampton in 1735 showed how quickly
such "examples" aided in the growth of a movement. Living through events
like these seemed to have provided the means to understand the expansion
of primitive Christianity and the Reformation. In early Christianity,
according to Edwards, "one person was moved by another, so one city or
town was influenced by the example of another."[1]

An account of the revivals therefore which held examples to be unrea-
sonable will not perceive the dynamics of the situation and will probably
see nothing but confusion in it. By the same token a view which was to
allow for example, but at the same time did not account for or did exclude
the charismatic character of it, would be too restrictive and would thus
be unable to evaluate the dynamics either. Finally, an account that used
an affective kind of preaching and reporting could take charismatic
examples seriously, and provided a movement history as distinct from a
"dull narration of one that is unexperienced and insensible himself."[2]
Even in this case, however, the reporting and the example were not
identical.

---

[1] The Great Awakening, ed., C. C. Goen, p. 239.

[2] Ibid., p. 339. See also p. 386.

Of the three preceding types, the first and the third immediately emerge from the text. The second type suggests itself when we look at the peculiar insistence by Edwards on the rationality of example and view it in the light of a widespread tradition of historiography which cannot have been unknown to him. In fact, this tradition was so common that one could feel tempted to assume that Edwards for polemical purposes belabored the obvious!

When we now try to characterize the first and the third type, our considerations, which set out from autobiographical remarks of Edwards, come full circle. The danger of the third type was the pride which he pointed to in his letter to Gillespie and which he touched upon in his treatment of examples. If the problem here was the overshooting of the mark, the first type came short of the mark by prejudging the case. Besides prejudice and pride, however, there also occurred the counsel of prudence which did not do justice to the situation either. To wait and see what the issue will be: "That will be like the fool's waiting at the riverside to have the water all run by."[1] You can't cry it down, you must not cry it up, you can't sit it out, you must live in it and with it. To leave behind prejudice, pride, and prudence were the first steps toward the historiography of the revival, because only then Edwards' own understanding of the revival as a historic event of passage could come into view. Prejudice, pride, and prudence were so many attempts to ignore, exaggerate, or evade history as a crisis and dynamic.

The metaphor of the river expressed the dynamic and critical dimensions of this rite of passage. Furthermore, it also clarifies for us the

---

[1] The Great Awakening, ed., C. C. Goen, p. 273. For positive views on prudence, see pp. 323, 384, 448.

movement in his autobiography. He always was in the middle of the river, not safe on the shore.

The Great Awakening both as a line of demarcation and as a crisis in American history has been recognized increasingly. Historians have attempted to identify and evaluate the religious, intellectual, social, political, and economic factors that went into this crucial event. Jonathan Edwards, the first historian of this crisis, has not yet received the attention due him. In a way, he suffered a fate similar to the one that Alan B. Howard observed in the case of William Bradford who as a ready source has been exploited for all sorts of purposes, but whose own historiography was neglected or ignored partly because it did not fit the uses that it was being put to.[1]

In part, the difficulty of considering Jonathan Edwards as a historian could be minimized if we could find some point of departure for the very concept of "historian" held by his contemporaries. In 1649 the English scientist and theologian John Wilkins[2] preached and published a sermon under the title, Discourse on the Beauty of Providence in all the Rugged Passages of it. Date of publication and content put the sermon in close proximity to the crisis of the English Civil War. The sermon was reprinted several times. There was a seventh edition in 1704 in London.

---

[1] Howard, "Art and History," p. 238.

[2] John Wilkins (1614-1672), Bishop of Chester. Wilkins studied at Oxford, owed his early academic preferment to his political and personal ties to the parliamentary party. Even then the Royalists appreciated his moderation. He survived almost unharmed the restoration, to become one of the key figures in founding the Royal Society of which he was the first secretary. Later on he became Bishop of Chester. (DNB XXI, 264-267.)

The edition I have used was issued at Boston in 1720 and claimed to be the
fifth edition of the sermon. John Wilkins wrote:

> Tis commonly observed, that though smooth and peaceable times are
> best for the liver, [sic], the Man that lives in them. Yet times full
> of change and vicissitudes are best for the writer, the <u>historian</u> that
> writes of them; so though quiet seasons may best suit our desires and
> outward conditions, yet these disturbed confused times, may be best
> improved by observation and do most set forth the wisdom of providence.[1]

The 'historian' was not a man for all seasons, but only for crises and
extraordinary periods. In such times he set forth providential continuity.
The historian did not narrate a story, relate a life or describe a country.
The mention of the commotions in church and state in Wilkins' sermon provided a very real background, but they are incidental to the pattern of
thought in the sermon, for Wilkins the preacher was also the historian.
The historian helped to search the "dispensations" where "there have been
many new, unusual emergencies, such as our forefathers have not known."[2]
The preacher-philosopher-historian thus aided in the common "duty with
<u>Diligenca</u> to observe the passages, and with patience to attend to the
issue."[3]

Edwards, also the participant in a contemporary crisis, faced a
similar challenge of diligent attention to events and their meaning. It
is from these two angles that we can approach him as a historian in his
writings on the revival. Nor do we phrase the question in a way alien to
his own understanding, for he began the application section of <u>Distinguishing
Marks</u> which had originally been preached as a sermon at Yale College in
1741:

---

[1]John Wilkins, <u>A Discourse Concerning the Beauty of Providence in
All Rugged Passages of It, Very Seasonable to Quiet the Heart in these
Times of Public Confusion</u>, 5th edition (Boston, 1720), p. 4.

[2]Ibid., p. 43. [3]Ibid., p. 42.

176

> There are but two things that need to be known in order to such a
> work being judged of, viz facts and rules. The rules of the Word of
> God we have had laid before us;[1] and as to facts, there are but two
> ways that we can come at them, so as to be in a capacity to compare
> them with the rules, either by our own observation, or by information
> from others that have had opportunity to observe.[2]

Unlike John Wilkins whose historical work was also done in a sermon, Edwards

gave explicit methodological instruction as to the way in which one was to

proceed in the present crisis. What Edwards gives us in his case is not

simply a "historical meditation" on a crisis in which we can read between

the lines how the author was coping with the facts of the situation, but

rather a glimpse as it were of the "historian at work." We shall therefore

now pursue his use and description of the two criteria of facts and rules

which he has given us.

Facts, Observations, and Experience

In the opening section of Part I in Some Thoughts Concerning the

Revival, Jonathan Edwards called for the events of the revival to be judged

a posteriori: "We are to observe the effect wrought."[3] Such an idea of

observation was present in the revival writings of Edwards from the letters

that lead to A Faithful Narrative through Some Thoughts Concerning the

Revival in which the statement is to be found. Observation belonged to a

whole cluster of terms such as "observation and experience,"[4] and "fact

and experience."[5] These terms complement each other. If we pursue a

terminological analysis of the terms it is helpful to see that the

---

[1]This probably referred to the marks that he had found earlier in
opening his text.

[2]The Great Awakening, ed., C. C. Goen, pp. 260-261.

[3]Ibid., p. 293.   [4]Ibid., p. 452.   [5]Ibid., p. 472.

combinations just mentioned gravitate toward the word experience. On the other hand, this focus complicates rather than simplifies issues, for experience in his writings has a number of nuances which should not be reduced to a single principle even if it be broad.

First of all, observation of the effect took "time and experience." Such time was necessary in order to provide the ministers with an opportunity to give "birth" to "rules" for people's conduct, since rules as they had previously been worked out in the writings of divines no longer applied.[1] For most ministers, 1740 ushered in a new situation and time was needed to sort it out. Variety mediated meaning and such meaning took time to emerge and to be assimilated.

Furthermore, the word appears to be used in both the singular and plural. This grammatical differentiation corresponded -- even though not necessarily and at all times -- to a semantic differentiation: experience helped assess experiences: "And experience plainly shows that Christians may have high experiences in some respects, and yet their circumstances may be unhappy in this regard, that their experience and discoveries are not more general."[2] Experience as a term, therefore, referred both to individual religious experiences as well as to the deliberate observation and evaluation of these experiences.

Finally, there is also the assumption that a growth in experiences will establish experience: that is, an increase in awareness was simultaneously an increase in discriminating self-awareness. Experiences grew into experience:

---

[1] The Great Awakening, ed., C. C. Goen, p. 318.

[2] Ibid., p. 464.

> I know by experience that there is a great aptness in men, that
> think they have had some experience of the power of religion, to
> think themselves sufficient to discern or determine the state of
> others' souls by a little conversation with them; and experience has
> taught me that this is an error.[1]

The point was made in an indirect manner because the semantic differences
in the word "experience" came almost without any grammatical differentiation. Edwards implied that the rudimentary stage of a saint's experience
made him look down upon serious conversation and time as of little value.

Edwards was a thinker who could insist on a carefully defined use
of words; as a matter of fact, he was convinced that it was because of the
lack of such precision that much harm and confusion was brought into the
world and in turn hurt man's well-being.   When he entered into an argument as he did in Freedom of the Will, he proceeded from a distrust of the
ambiguity in words and defined carefully.[2] In the case of the different
shades of meaning of experience, however, he abided by a largely allusive
use of "experience" and refrained from giving it the kind of denotative
preciseness and restriction of meaning that had become the stylistic ideal
of Augustan England.[3]

---

[1]The Great Awakening, ed., C. C. Goen, p. 318.

[2]Jonathan Edwards, Freedom of the Will, ed., P. Ramsay (New Haven:
Yale University Press, 1957), pp. 144, 149, 150, 163.

[3]The differentiation between experiences and experience that we can
find here was far more characteristic in the case of providences and providence, promises and promise. In each case the plural has an existential
or "experiential" dimension and the singular provides a transindividual
frame. John Wilkins never talked of providence in the plural; Thomas
Shepard did so most of the time.

An illustration that may help to clarify the connotative use to which
experience was put can be drawn from a distinction that the German language
makes. What was rendered by Edwards as experience would have to be translated either as Erlebnis or Erfahrung. Edwards' own use of experience did
not resolve its inherent incongruities by a dissociation of sentiment and
science. In a review of the history of modern philosophy the German

Such experience carried authority, for the pattern into which
Edwards cast it related positively to the traditional cases-of-conscience.
Thus it was the ministers who were to have "time and experience" in order
to find out rules.[1] For his observations on the revival he confidently
said that what he had observed "won't be at all wondered at by those who
have had much to do with souls under spiritual difficulties." Since there
was such a professional element involved, an interpretation of Edwards the
historian cannot take lightly or ignore Edwards the minister and
professional counselor.

It was against this background that Edwards reported for his own
person of "all the observation that can be made by all that is heard from
them and seen in them, for many months together,"[2] and spoke of his cases
as "many of them being persons that I have long known and have been intimately acquainted with in soul concerns, before and since."[3] In a more
programmatic statement he said that such professional experience presupposed
a "most critical observation, under all manner of opportunities of observing."
Experience consequently arose out of the application of the rule of comparison to the experiences. Experience resulted from the skill of observation.[4]

---

historian Wilhelm Dilthey pointed out that the exclusive attention to experience as Erfahrung in British empiricism tended to arrest the growth of historical thinking. In his own attempts to equip the humanities in general
and historical study in particular with a foundation he therefore applied
to experience both terms. While the latter could only explain the parts,
the former would help to understand the incongruities of the parts in terms
of their manifold relationships toward a whole. Dilthey himself found confirmatory evidence for his exploration of the psychological basis of history
in the work of William James. (Wilhelm Dilthey, Gesammelte Schriften, 8, Ed.,
B. Groethuysen, Leipzig, B. G. Teubner, 1931, pp. 22, 23.)

[1] The Great Awakening, ed., C. C. Goen, p. 318.

[2] Ibid., p. 262.   [3] Ibid., p. 263.   [4] Ibid., p. 297.

le of comparison was not identical with the rules of Scripture that
entioned in the quotation on method from which we set out. The rule
was comparison and comparison required time. "All manner of opportunities'
took into consideration temporal as well as spatial extension. Edwards
spoke of the "difference that there was in different places, and in the
same places at different times according to the diverse examples and conduc
that they have."[1]

Because of the professional background, the references to experience in Edwards often assumed a confident and self-evident air and character, even though there was the important reservation that observations
could be made only insofar as things were accessible to the "observation
of a bystander."[2] Thus Edwards could say: "Let others that have much
occasion to deal with souls in spiritual concerns, judge whether experience doesn't confirm it."[3] Jonathan Edwards even went so far as to offer
a challenge along these lines. Since we know things by information or
observation, on authority or experience, he said:

> It is to be wondered at, that those that have doubted of the work
> that has been attended with such uncommon external appearances, should
> be easy in their doubts, without taking thorough pains to inform them-
> selves by going where such things have been to be seen, and narrowly
> observing them, and diligently inquiring into them; not contenting
> themselves only with observing two or three instances, nor resting
> till they are fully informed by their own observation. I don't doubt
> but that if this course had been taken, it would have convinced all
> whose minds are not shut up against conviction, in a great degree
> indeed. How greatly have they erred, who only from the uncertain
> reports of others, have ventured to speak slightly of these things.[4]

In the Faithful Narrative Jonathan Edwards cited a precedent for this
approach when two ministers came to Northampton on a fact-finding tour and

---

[1] The Great Awakening, ed., C. C. Goen, pp. 472-473.

[2] Ibid., p. 263.   [3] Ibid., p. 236.   [4] Ibid., p. 275.

thereby had their misconceptions about the revival of 1735 dispelled.[1]

In Distinguishing Marks where Edwards voiced his challenge, he also added

this edge by means of a play on words: "It [observation] would have con-

vinced all whose minds are not shut up against conviction, in a great degree

indeed." Since conviction was one of the cornerstones of New England

preparationism,[2] everyone who was orthodox in New England could be con-

vinced merely by taking a field trip. Any such observations irresistibly

led to Edwards' conclusion. One of those who professed allegiance to

preparationism as staunchly as did Edwards was Charles Chauncy. Whether

it was this statement by Edwards that set Chauncy on a fact-finding tour,

I cannot tell, but Chauncy reported of himself:

> I have been a circle of more than three hundred miles, and had, by
> this means, an opportunity of going thro' a great number of towns in
> this, and the neighboring Government of Connecticut, and of having per-
> sonal conversation with most of the ministers, and many other gentlemen,
> in the country, and of settling a correspondence with several of them,
> with a particular view to know, as nearly as might be, the truth of
> things, upon better evidence than that of mere hearsay.[3]

This statement by Chauncy had the marks of complying with the challenge

voiced by Edwards. Nevertheless, we might wonder why Chauncy only talked

to ministers and gentlemen and why he did not mention any direct contact

with what was going on. In this way Chauncy sounded as though he went

---

[1]The Great Awakening, ed., C. C. Goen, pp. 108-109.

[2]New England Preparationism was that peculiar modification of traditional ordo salutis that emerged from the conflict between scholastic definitions and spiritualizing tendencies in the late 1630s. Although based on
the Ramist elaboration of salvation by Perkins, Ames, and other English
thinkers, its elevation to the status of an article of faith was the result
of American conditions. See Norman Pettit, The Heart Prepared, chs. 2 and 3;
E. S. Morgan, Visible Saints, esp. chs. 3 and 4; Glenn T. Miller, "The Rise
of Evangelical Calvinism," Part I.

[3]E. S. Gaustad, The Great Awakening in New England (1957; ppb.,
Chicago: Quadrangle Books, 1968), p. 93. I have checked Gaustad's source
for this quotation, but was unable to verify his reference.

around the country less in an effort to observe, than to organize by "settling a correspondence" and in an attempt to establish the credibility of the selected prospective correspondences by personal conversations. What followed in the first and largest part of Chauncy's Seasonable Thoughts was a compilation of and extracts from letters by ministers and gentlemen across the country. They provided the factual basis for his judgments. References to his participant observations as a basis are minimal and negligible.

Edwards himself became bewildered also because experience and observation did not yield the expected results in every case. His writings on the revival provide a unique opportunity to see how he at least in part went over the same ground again and in the course of it added to or changed the argument.

Edwards opposed "immediate revelations" in the Distinguishing Marks because he had observed that they led to a depreciation of the value of the Bible and finally to its elimination. He was, however, confident that this particular error would vanish in the course of time, for these immediate revelations or prophecies were proven vain by the events. Thus, if the work wrought was judged by the effects it produced, such prophecies would be abandoned. In Some Thoughts Concerning the Revival, on the other hand, his "late experience" or observation showed him that, despite the repeated failures of these prophecies, no experience of self-awareness had grown up even amongst "religious persons." This observation that experience did not automatically teach a lesson, but that old mistakes were repeated over and over again was truly "astonishing" for Edwards. Instances of this "disposition" not to learn from experience were so frequent that they would -- as

Edwards said -- furnish him with enough material for a "history."[1] The

chronique scandaleuse which Edwards did not write was contained in Chauncy's

Seasonable Thoughts, where he reported one case that concretized very well

what Edwards only vaguely called the depreciation of the Bible. According

to Chauncy, the Reverend Timothy Allen was deposed by his consociation

because "He had publicly said, that the Word of God, as contained in the

Old and New Testament, is but as an Old Almanack."[2] For Edwards, on the

other hand, one of the crucial events of the earlier Northampton revival

had been a new delight in the Bible "especially the book of Psalms, the

prophecy of Isaiah, and the New Testament."[3] We have already pointed out

in the last chapter how important both the Psalms and the prophets were

for his view of history.

When we look for the reason why Edwards talked of experience with

such assurance and why at the same time he was surprised by its obvious

---

[1] The Great Awakening, ed., C. C. Goen, pp. 289 and 433; another
example where Edwards has also become more cautious can be found in comparing his statements on zeal in Distinguishing Marks, p. 287, and Some
Thoughts Concerning the Revival, p. 450, respectively.

[2] Chauncy, Seasonable Thoughts, p. 215. Timothy Allen (1715-1806)
had been a student at Yale College where he came under the influence of a
fellow student, David Ferris, who was well on his way to becoming a Quaker.
(Daniel B. Shea, Jr., Spiritual Autobiography in Early America, Princeton:
Princeton University Press, 1968, pp. 23-24.) In 1738 he was ordained to
the Congregational Church in the village of West Haven. He became a supporter of the Great Awakening. The incident reported by Chauncy occurred
in 1742. Franklin B. Dexter (Biographical Sketches of the Graduates of Yale
College, Oct. 1701-May, 1945, New York: Holt and Company, 1885, p. 552)
quoted the charge against Allen and added a parenthesis in order to show its
thrust: Accordingly Allen had maintained "that the reading of the Scripture
[without the concurring influence and operation of God] will no more convert
a sinner than reading an old almanac." After his dismissal by the New Haven
Association, Allen was put in charge of "the Shepherd's Tent" by a group of
New Lights in London in order to train ministers and exhorters. A bill passed
later in that year by the Connecticut legislature forced the academy across
the border into Rhode Island where it soon ceased to exist. After a "full
and satisfactory confession," Allen was reinstated in 1748, but he continued
to move from one place to the other until he died, ninety and a half years
old, leaving behind 150 dollars and 125 volumes of books.

[3] The Great Awakening, ed., C. C. Goen, p. 184.

184

failure to work with other people, we arrive at the Northampton revival as
one yardstick by which he measured the revival in the early 1740s. He
compared the two revivals. Unlike most present ministers, he already had
"experience, and time to see the tendency, consequences and issue of
things." Thus he said: "The happy influence of experience is very manifest
at this day, in the people among whom God has settled my abode. The work of
God that has been carried on there this year, has been much purer than that
which was wrought there six years before."[1]

All those who in the 1740s began to criticize and misrepresent the
events could be directed for correction to the history of the revival as an
argument in its favor. Edwards did not have to admit simply that there
were negative aspects in the revival, for he could prove by comparing
Northampton in 1735 and in 1741 that what he claimed to be temporary and
irregular features were indeed temporary and irregular features. In a way,
this argument was the reappearance on a different level of the principle
that events be observed under "all manner of opportunities." A comparison
of the revivals of 1735 and 1741 in Northampton showed that the laughter
which Chauncy found so reprehensible[2] and which was prominent in the
Northampton of 1735 had disappeared in the Northampton of 1741. The
"experience" that Edwards derived from this comparison of Northampton in
two chronologically separate revivals helped him refute objections that had
been made both in 1735 and that were being made now. The reason why Edwards
was so surprised that religious persons would not learn from experience may
be explained in a similar way: one man was reported to have been temporarily
deluded by prophecy in the 1735 revival. He was set straight easily.[3]

_____

[1] The Great Awakening, ed., C. C. Goen, p. 269.

[2] Chauncy, Seasonable Thoughts, p. 126.

[3] The Great Awakening, p. 207.

A Faithful Narrative contained basic elements of Edwards' view of
history which were at the heart of his historiography. This recognition
is important because the concern with the millennium was explicit only
insofar as he established the point that the interpretation of the prophecy
belonged to the ministerial office.[1] The Faithful Narrative was the only
descriptive account of Edwards about a revival, and if it is compared to
his final thoughts in Religious Affections, it looked plain and not very
philosophical. It seemed less freighted with meanings and problems than
the latter.[2]

It comes as a surprise that A Faithful Narrative anticipated many
of the attempts in modern historiography to interpret the Great Awakening.
Edwards listed quite a few factors that played a role in the Northampton
revival and also compared them to each other in order to assess their
ultimate significance. He did indeed observe under "all manner of opportunities." Edwards was aware of the frontier situation of Northampton which
made it less accessible to novel and different outside influences.[3]
Northampton as a town was settled very compactly so that communication,
including the communication of religion, was very swift and easy.[4] This in
turn led Edwards to consider seriously whether the revival in such an isolated spot with such a peculiar settlement pattern was not a cheat.[5] Again
he used the comparative method by setting the events in Northampton against
those around it and came to the conclusion that, since in 1735 revivals

---

[1] The Great Awakening, ed., C. C. Goen, p. 207.

[2] See William Cooper's preface to the Distinguishing Marks, ibid.,
p. 224.

[3] The Great Awakening, p. 113.

[4] Ibid., pp. 114, 145.   [5] Ibid., p. 262.

sprang up independently at the same time in different places, it could
neither be only a local custom, as in the days of Solomon Stoddard, nor a
local delusion which could be attributed solely to the pattern of settlement. Just as there were external factors that favored the revival, but
did not completely explain it, so there were external factors that diverted
attention and energy from it and helped towards its decline: arrival of
the governor and the General Court, and the conclusion of a treaty with
the Indians.[1] Then there was also the building of a new meeting house
which we might perhaps understand literally as the "institutionalization"[2]
of the revival.

A contemporary comment on the Faithful Narrative by Isaac Watts in
his preface to the London edition was probably one of the first and influential interpretations of any revival and thus in a crucial position to aid
in shaping the image of the revival as a phenomenon in modern history. He
commented on the absence of "any sudden and distressing calamity or public
terror."[3]

There was indeed no mention of any natural catastrophes, epidemical
diseases, or Indian wars in A Faithful Narrative. The special chapters on
memorable accidents in William Hubbard's General History, the book in Cotton
Mather's Magnalia[4] that was devoted to the same subject, and also the
Jeremiads showed that such events belonged to the tradition of "providences"

---

[1] The Great Awakening, ed., C. C. Goen, p. 208.

[2] Thomas F. O'Dea, The Sociology of Religion (Englewood Cliffs, N. J.:
Prentice-Hall, Inc., 1966), p. 104.

[3] Ibid., p. 133.

[4] Vol. II, pp. 339-486.

which were to lead men to repentance and reformation. The absence of such
"cosmic" providences in <u>A Faithful Narrative</u> did not mean that Edwards
moved outside this tradition, for in the historiography of providences the
death of a sinner or of a dear friend was as much of a standard topos as
the arrival of an earthquake. Since Edwards gave such a detailed description of all the external factors we could not even assume that his use of
the topos indicated a spiritualizing and a withdrawal from natural causes.
An interpretation like that of Watts could easily lead into that direction
once the conventions of the historiography of providences became less
familiar. On the contrary, Edwards did not have to look out for all kinds
of providences as signs of what the divine counsel might be, because he
could report that in fact the death of a young woman[1] had become the initi-
ating cause of the reformation of the community. Providences here were no
longer solely the admonition to reform, but its arrival in history. In
addition, the fact that a great revival should spring from such a rela-
tively small event was for a Puritan like Edwards even more reason to take
this revival as a true work of God. The God who knew all the hair on man's
head was the same who could bring great things out of small ones. This
theme of God and his respect for the small things was woven into the very
fabric of Puritan spirituality.[2] Both Isaac Watts and modern scholarship

---

[1] <u>The Great Awakening</u>, ed., C. C. Goen, pp. 116, 149.

[2] Increase Mather in a sermon on the <u>Doctrine of Divine Providence</u>
(Boston: By R. Pierce for T. Brunning, 1684) said in one of his applications
that "little improbable things do occasion great matters" (p. 29). Moreover,
"God maketh little matters like the small wheel of a clock which sets all the
rest a going or like the hinges of a great gate upon which all turns. 'Great
Revolutions' in the world have been occasioned by mere contingencies. . . ."
(p. 30). In a sermon on the same subject which is now bound together with
the <u>Doctrine of Divine Providence</u>, Samuel Mather pointed more particularly

have come to the same conclusion as far as the absence of any such cosmic causes for the Northampton Revival was concerned. E. S. Gaustad on the basis of all the available sources[1] or -- to use Edwards' own phrase -- after a "critical observation under all manner of opportunities" cannot but agree with the observation of Watts that was ultimately based on the attested reliability of Edwards' account itself.

The notion of comprehensiveness which encompassed these individual factors was more important in the Faithful Narrative than an anticipation of different modern interpretations. Isaac Watts' reference to historiography fell short of expressing the spirit of comprehensiveness that pervaded A Faithful Narrative. The revival in Northampton included all classes, all ranks, all races, all sexes, all ages, and all of the area round about: it was widespread within the town and it extended beyond it, too. To call Edwards arrogant for believing that God had his glory dwell at Northampton forgets that Edwards simply did not make an unsubstantiated claim. As we have shown, he provided the circumstantial evidence that made his point convincing to many. If only for a time, heaven had indeed come down close to earth and gave a foretaste of things to come. Even the Indians and Negroes were included.

---

to the scriptural side of this theme. He referred to the parable of the mustard seed when he wanted to illustrate the small historical beginnings of the gospel. The theme of smallness itself was not an exclusive Puritan property for Francis Bacon gave for his preference of lives over chronicles the reason of "the workmanship of God, that he hangs the greatest weights on the smallest wires" (VIII, 425). A clearer understanding of similarities and differences here would depend on a greater interest in Puritan studies to trace thoroughly such themes as God and the smallness of things.

[1]Gaustad, The Great Awakening, pp. 20ff.

The archetypal experience of the comprehensiveness of community was matched by the "variety" of responses to this event by the several participants. The community represented "multitudes of all kinds of capacities, natural tempers, educations, customs and manners of life."[1] Edwards did justice to this variety in the style of A Faithful Narrative by giving as complete a description of the variety of these responses as possible. He took every kind in society seriously. The list was long and exhaustive and the descriptive style went somewhat like this: "To some happened this, and to some happened that; many were convinced then and many received grace here, but commonly such and such was more frequent than such and such. Thus some had scripture come to their minds, others had none of this sort at all."

As far as the order of the responses goes, Edwards arranged them in a preparationist order.[2] Within this order, however, there was considerable variety. All the different steps were assumed to be necessary, but they did not have to be taken in an identical order. Unlike Chauncy,[3] who in his criticism of Edwards at the time of the Great Awakening insisted on "uniformity," Edwards himself already in A Faithful Narrative dealt with order in terms of "universality," and "proportion" a position that made it possible for him to say in the Distinguishing Marks during the Great Awakening that "we need not be sorry for the breaking the order of the

---

[1] I have taken this quotation from Some Thoughts Concerning the Revival (The Great Awakening, ed., C. C. Goen, p. 317) because it formulated more concisely what we found in A Faithful Narrative (ibid., pp. 185, 189).

[2] See fn. 2, p. 170.

[3] Chauncy, Seasonable Thoughts, p. 107.

[4] The Great Awakening, ed., C. C. Goen, p. 157.

means, by obtaining the end to which that order is directed: he that is going on a journey to fetch a treasure, need not be sorry that he is stopped by meeting the treasure in the midst of his journey."[1]

The nature of these various responses remind one of a classroom situation: all students have had the same assignment to prepare. The question of the teacher in class addressed to all students will draw quite different responses, if the students know that they are not to learn by rote and can really let go rather than guess about what the teacher wants to hear. The very familiarity with the assignment and an over-eagerness to respond can be responsible for a proportional lack in the distinctness and correctness of the answers, for each one in his or her answer addresses himself or herself to that part of the assignment that struck home. In this way the situation becomes dramatic rather than dogmatic.

This example is not far from the reality of the New England situation where L. A. Cremin has shown how a common background is mediated through the many agencies of the community. If we picture this common background in terms of catechism or dogmatic textbook, we can see that the variety of responses described by Edwards represented a pluralism defined by the circumference of the exposition. In this sense, the different people in the Northampton revival represent each one of them one fraction of the total catechism in their initial responses.

When Edwards talked about the way that conviction arose, he mentioned that some were struck by the sin of unbelief, some by a sense of general sinfulness, some by a recollection of past sins, some by a sense of particular sins.[2] The question therefore also arose as to how this variety

---

[1]The Great Awakening, ed., C. C. Goen, p. 267.

[2]Ibid., p. 169.

of initial responses could be prevented from developing into a variety of
fixed attitudinal convictions. Thus, someone who starts off with a conviction of particular sin may never get to the meaning of general sinfulness of the human condition. The history of theology and the incipient
Arminian controversy which already reverberated through the Faithful
Narrative[1] make this point abundantly clear.

The situation which A Faithful Narrative described can be put this
way: In the revival the whole catechism came alive and became dynamic,
but how could this dynamism be kept alive? A Faithful Narrative described
a whole, but was it also a whole? The description of the primordial character of the event in Northampton was one thing, the articulation and
defense of it was still another. How then did Edwards deal with variety
and universality? Where was, as it were, the body to the movement that we
see emerge in his history of the Northampton revival of 1735?

It is with his use of the word variety that we get to the heart of
the discussion of history. He characterized variety with terms like
"endless," "manifoldedness," "unsearchableness."[2] Such a view was by no
means startlingly novel, for the variety displayed in history had always
been taken to be mystifying and defying comprehension for that reason.
What was different in Edwards when held over against this tradition was
that he affirmed such "unsearchableness" to be something different from
confusion, something positive. "Unsearchableness" here is a judgment in
favor of further pursuit of the matter rather than a dismissal of it.

---

[1] The Great Awakening, ed., C. C. Goen, pp. 116, 148.

[2] Ibid., p. 185.

The range of this variety seemed to be more defined by intensive
penetration rather than by extensive knowledge. Voltaire's knowledge of
the variety of cultures, European or non-European, superseded anything
that Edwards ever could know. Edwards was indeed a provincial and he knew
it. He was, however, desirous to know more; he kept a large catalogue of
books on the subject of history.[1] There are many books he had listed to
which we would have liked to know his reaction, but he probably never saw
them. If he could not use -- what we now think to be the "best of his
time" -- we might ask and inquire as diligently whether he made the best
out of the situation in which he lived. A handicap can also be a chance:
Edwards did not integrate in his thought far-away cultures and countries;
he discovered instead the complexity of his own community. As Walden Pond
became for H. D. Thoreau the mirror of the universe, so the Northampton
revival became for Edwards the mirror of history. The revival of 1735
opened up territory beyond the accustomed traditional perspective and
Edwards was forced into comparison. To put it more succinctly: the rise
of the revival from a local to a regional -- and eventually to a provincial
and national -- phenomenon seemed to have brought him as many insights and
questions in looking at the world as if he had dealt with other than
European cultures as it happened in the European Enlightenment.

At this point a brief recapitulation of our argument may help. We
began with an explication of the three vices of prejudice, pride, and prudence which all deny, disrupt, or detach themselves from the movement of
history. We then attempted to gain a perspective on his confidence in and

---

[1]James Stillman Caskey, "Jonathan Edwards' Catalogue," B.D. thesis,
Chicago Theological Seminary, 1961, especially Appendix A. Stephen Stein,
loc. cit.

use of the notion of observation. Edwards defended it as a means for ministers to shape rules of conduct in a new situation. We also saw that the characteristics of participation and detachment could not as easily be transferred to other people and consequently he was surprised but not shocked to find out that the experience of repeated failures in prophecy did not teach a lesson nor establish a rule of conduct even with religious men. History in this case was not _magistra vitae._[1] The source of Edwards' confidence was found in A Faithful Narrative which in later treatises served as a criterion. In an attempt to elucidate his historiography from this narrative we found that he described different points of entry into the preparationist scheme. Now we come back once more to the ambiguity of experience, for Edwards attempted to deal with the different manifestations of the revival. He did so in the passage on custom from which the programmatic statement on "critical observation" had been quoted previously.

From what Edwards told us, there was apparently an attempt by some to minimize the importance of external manifestations of the revival by reducing them to "custom and fashion." The implication of such a reduction seemed to be: such outward manifestations were _merely_ accidental, they were no more than "custom and fashion." Therefore, they could be dismissed and condemned. Custom and fashion were so incidental to what was going on that they could not even be admitted as positive circumstantial evidence. What Edwards here took custom and fashion to mean was the conduct of ministers who shaped the different styles of the different churches. He observed that a change of minister may also involve a change of style, so

---

[1]Cotton Mather, Magnalia, Vol. I, p. 28, quoted Cicero to the effect that "historia est testis temporum, Nuntia vetustatis, Lux veritatis, vita Memoriae, Magistra Vitae."

that the same churches at different times and different churches in different parts of the country would show considerable variation in styles. This defense of different styles on the part of Edwards also reflected back on the Stoddardean Harvests, for one could easily argue that this was simply a local custom and fashion that came and went and thus be done with it.

The variety of styles which Edwards observed ranged along the spectrum of the churches. From A Faithful Narrative[1] onward, Edwards insisted that there has to be a proportion in experience between fear and joy. Here he said that in actual fact such a balance was reached only approximately. This approximative nature of proportion in turn made for the variety of styles.

Edwards ended on a note of ambivalence about styles: even though empirically ("fact and experience") and metaphysically ("reason and things") custom and fashion are to be accepted, neither of these methods can come to grips with them fully and prove "any proper design or contrivance of those in whom there is this alteration."[2] The churches themselves changed their styles unaccountably, for they did not even notice that they did. Only Edwards as an observer could see it. What Edwards described here came close to what we today would call conditioning. The crucial factor in conditioning is that it is like a rucksack on our back which everyone but ourselves can see. While Edwards thus took variety of styles seriously, he was also baffled by them, but even at the high point of the Great Awakening with its admitted threats to orthodoxy, Edwards abided by

---

[1] The Great Awakening, ed., C. C. Goen, pp. 151ff.

[2] Ibid., p. 472.

195

the variety that we have found in <u>A Faithful Narrative</u> where there arose

out of the revival no serious threat to orthodoxy.

Edwards' concern with observation was not accidental or peripheral.

When he was still a boy he had conducted an investigation of a spider in

the field of nature. Two versions of the description of this inquiry are

extant, of which one was the draft of a letter that had been sent to an

unnamed correspondent of his father in England.[1] These two reports between

themselves showed that young Edwards had a gift for observation and had

received training as well as encouragement in it. Edwards' curiosity at

that time had been aroused by the "pleasing as well as surprising" event

when a large spider that obviously had no wings sailed right past his eyes.

He set out to find an explanation and after he had performed a series of

four experiments he arrived at a point of view where his observation was

successful. At first he had simply provoked a spider to leave the bush

on which he had found it on one of his trips into the nearby woods. When

he could not find out anything this way he then had the idea of whisking

a stick around the bush in order to make sure that there were no already

existing invisible webs that the spider could use. Since this improvement

in his apparatus yielded no results either, he put the spider on the stick

in order to be able to observe it more "narrowly." While he could now see

how a web proceeded from the tail of the spider, he wanted to eliminate

any error on his part and made sure of that by clearing the air around the

stick. Then he repeated the experiment so often until all "conjecture"

---

[1]S. E. Dwight, <u>The Life of Jonathan Edwards</u> (New York, 1830), pp.
23ff. The version which gives Edwards' argument in full is reprinted in
<u>Representative Selections</u>, eds., C. H. Faust and T. H. Johnson, pp. 3-10.

was removed. His findings were twofold: as soon as the web touched a
tree the resistance that occurred would signal to the spider that it could
now begin its march through the air. If, however, the web found no tree,
the increasing length of the web would reach the point where its levity
would outweigh the gravity of the spider so that the updrift of the wind
could turn the marching spider into a flying spider. The ascent itself
would reach an equilibrium, according to Edwards, as soon as the air became
lighter than the web.

The account of the investigation did not proceed with the description of an inquiry into the causes of the descent of the spider. Edwards
pointed to several plausible, though unproven hypotheses for a descent
such as violent means, rain, or the spider's own action of reducing the
length of the web. After he had thus far literally strained his eyesight
in order to gain some insight, he did not pursue any of these possible
hypotheses. Instead his interest in causes yielded to his concern over
ends. The individual links in the causal explanation were for him so many
parts of the story of the spider which in the fall of each year would
ascend for the purposes of a journey that provided it the highest pleasure
and which led it to the sea where it perished. In this way Edwards' essay
combined experimental observation, explanation, the time for observation,
and theodicy. Interpreters usually ignore these aspects of time and
teleology and focus on the precocity that young Edwards displayed in the
causal explanation, not without strongly emphasizing the point that this
early promise of a successful career as a naturalist came to a premature
end through Edwards' aberration into theology.[1] We do find, however,

---

[1] Interpreters have usually relied on the version that was printed
in Dwight, The Life of Jonathan Edwards, pp. 23-28. In 1890 E. C. Smyth
("The Flying Spider - Observations by Jonathan Edwards when a boy,"

already here that strong comprehensive teleological interest which was
similar to the combination of meticulous observation and an awareness of
its limits in those later writings on both the Northampton revival and the
Great Awakening which we have just reviewed.

Observation, Observance, and the Rules of Scripture

When we now go on to "observe" A Faithful Narrative on the one hand
and Distinguishing Marks on the other, "under all manner of opportunities,"
then we shall also see a different argument for variety. In one of the
first points that Edwards made in Distinguishing Marks he wrote: "The
spirit of God is sovereign in his operations; and we know that he uses
great variety; and we can't tell how great a variety he may use within the
compass of the rules he himself has fixed."[1] "We know" can refer to three
things. First, it could refer to the knowledge that we have of the "reason
of things." Second, it could refer to the "observation and experience" of
variety in the Northampton of 1735 and in the Great Awakening in 1741.
Finally, there are the "prophecies of Scripture"[2] or "Scripture prophecy"[3]

Andover Review, Vol. XIII (Jan. 1890), p. 16) published the longer version
which showed no signs of being a draft for the letter to England. We can
therefore with a great degree of probability conclude that Dwight's text
was later than that published by Smyth. In the former version theological
reflections were cut to a minimum. A comparison of both documents casts
great doubt on the simple distinction between Edwards as the naturalist
that he promised to be and Edwards as the theologian that he unfortunately
became. In his letter Edwards was to address himself to a specific purpose
and had to observe the "decorum" of a particular style. Consequently, he
chose from his investigation mostly the factual information that had been
requested. If we disregard literary criteria such as style we would actually
have to conclude not that Edwards' theological interest increased, but that
it had decreased, for in the later and shorter piece considerably less than
one-eighth of the text was taken up by the reflection on the "Chief End of
this Faculty of Flying" that had been given to the spiders (Dwight, The Life
of Jonathan Edwards, p. 16).

[1]Ibid., p. 229.   [2]Ibid., p. 228.   [3]Ibid., p. 230.

which give "reason" to think that new things are still ahead. We have
shown that for Edwards "variety" was indeed accessible to empirical observation and metaphysical reasoning. As to the rules of variety, however,
the context of the quoted passage introduced the subject of what Edwards
later on called the "sure word of prophecy."[1] In addition, "within the
compass of the rules," Edwards could also refer to the "latitude the spirit
of God uses in the methods of his operations."[2]

For the average colonist, latitude was part of the mechanics of
trade. By knowing the latitude of a city or a ship, one could compute
its location on a north-south axis, and with the addition of longitude,
compute its precise location. In church politics, the idea of latitude,
also, rested on a spatial relation. By standing in the center of the
spectrum, the latitudean could safely relate himself to men at either
extreme. Edwards explained the connotation of latitude, which was primarily linear (Raum) to the more historical idea of space-time (Zeitraum)
in which the point is defined by simultaneous reference to all real points.
It was, consequently, not only a means for location or the basis of an
ecclesiastical politic, but a totality that united past, present, and
future into one framework of reference. It was not monotemporal -- not
locked in three dimensions -- but multitemporal or, in more theological
language, prophetic and eschatological.

---

[1]Dwight, The Life of Jonathan Edwards, p. 282. The passage was
taken from the second epistle of Peter, 2:19. This place was a Locus
Classicus for prophetic exegesis (Thomas Sherlock, The Use and Intent of
Prophecy, in the Several Ages of the World, London: printed for John
Whiston, at Mr. Boyle's head in Fleetstreet, 1749, pp. 21, 23).

[2]The Great Awakening, ed., C. C. Goen, p. 242.

Such orientation toward the world not only permitted the variety of the Awakening without the danger of confusion. This prophetic dimension thus made it possible for present observation as well as former observation to be related in such a way that the present was confirmed and corrected, that the past could be criticized, and that the past and present could be displayed with full continuity. In pursuit of Edwards' understanding of the "Rules of Scripture," we shall now proceed to delineate these various uses of the past in his historiography.

For Edwards, historical change was "the beginning of something extraordinary 'and it involved' a great deal of noise, and tumult, confusion and uproar, and darkness mixed with light."[1] Edwards' affirmation of variety was therefore a recognition of strife as a part of change in which it played more than the role of the necessary evil but was not the creative instigator or spring of development. The passage from the coldness of winter to the serenity and calm of spring, according to Edwards, always led through "very dirty and tempestuous weather." To Edwards, his opponents in the Great Awakening must have looked like men who asserted harmony without struggle and strife in the well-intentioned but ahistoric attempt to walk in the rain without getting either wet or dirty. Edwards found confirmation for his view in his survey of church history which showed him that the epistles of Paul were not just doctrinal exercises but were pieces written in periods of strife and disorder. He also saw that Reformation of the sixteenth century was not a smooth restoration of the Golden Age of apostolic antiquity. Likewise, early New England had not arrived on the scene full-grown without strife and disorder.[2] The indistinct beginnings

---

[1] The Great Awakening, ed., C. C. Goen, p. 318.

[2] Ibid., p. 246.

that were such a distinctive mark of the description of conversion in
A Faithful Narrative as well as the strife that characterized the Great
Awakening were discovered to have been a mark in history at large.

What Edwards had discovered as a mark of historical change was
advocated, however, by some of his colleagues as a "maxim"[1] so "that the
more division and strife, the better sign; which naturally leads persons
to seek and provoke it." The more opposition these men could create and
the more persecution this engendered, the more to their liking. In
English ecclesiastical historiography persecution and the hope for its
end had played a dominant role. Edwards, however, attacked here the per-
version of this tradition and criticized the evaporation of the strife of
persecution into a coarse persecution mentality that had been programmed
for continual conflict and that would feed and live out "whatsoever is
found to be of present and immediate benefit . . . without looking to future
consequences."[2] For the correction of such a consciousness Edwards again
referred to the authority of the early church and of the example of Luther.
According to Edwards, in ecclesiastical antiquity abolition of the cere-
monial law was not accomplished quickly, but the transition to the new
covenant happened gradually. In the General History of the Reformation of
the Church by Johann P. Sleidanus,[3] Edwards found proof for his contention

_____

[1]The Great Awakening, ed., C. C. Goen, p. 447.

[2]Ibid., p. 444.

[3]Ibid., p. 450. Johann P. Sleidanus (1505-1556), politician and
historian, was born in the region of the upper Rhine. He studied law at
Liège, Cologne, Louvain, and received his doctorate from Orleans. He
served in various capacities as aide and diplomatic emissary to various
French officials who were anxious for an alliance between France and the
Protestant league of Schmalkald in Germany against the Hapsburg dominated
Empire. The secret diplomacy in some of his assignments exposed him to

that such presentist behavior must be corrected if it was not to harm the

revival as it had harmed the Reformation. In his affirmation of strife

and in his attack on a crusade mentality and confrontation behavior

Edwards felt akin to Martin Luther who was fought by the traditionalists

and yet fought in part as a traditionalist.

In addition to the confirmative and the corrective use of the past,

Edwards also kept a critical distance toward it. In this attitude he fol-

lowed a line of thinking which was akin to the position of Benjamin

Whichcote (1609-1683) who is considered by scholars[1] to be the father of

the group of thinkers known as the Cambridge Platonists who in turn were

---

unjustified suspicion. At Bucer's urgent request the league employed him
as historian, a position which was, however, financially as well as politically insecure and at one time he received a pension from the King of
England. His reputation as a historian rested on two works. Shortly before
his death he published De Quattuor Summis Imperis which was translated into
many languages including English and which served as a textbook in schools
until the eighteenth century. His magnum opus, however, to which Edwards
referred, was a translation of the De Statu Religionis et Reipublicae Carolo
V Caesare Commentarii Libri XXVI. It was first published at Strassburg in
1555 and with the addition of the posthumous twenty-sixth volume it carried
the story of the German Reformation down to the year 1556. The work was
based on archival materials from Hesse, Strassburg, the Palatinate, and the
Electorate of Saxony. It "remained through the nineteenth century when
archives were made officially available the basic work on the History of the
German Reformation" (Religion in Geschichte und Gegenwart, 3rd ed., VI, p. 110).
Sleidan's historiographical model were the Commentaries of Caesar. His focus
on contemporary history which seems to have been of such advantage for
Edwards was also what led to several attempts by Catholics and Protestants
alike to pressure the city of Strassburg into stopping publication. Even
though Sleidanus had already told less than he knew, Melanchthon's reaction
to this history of the Reformation was typical. He said that he could not
recommend the book for it put indecent actions into a decorous style and
told many things that would better have been buried in eternal silence. Above
all, however, he hoped that the young people would not read a history that
was a history of error and confusion and showed all too clearly the folly
and wretchedness of those of the older generation who shaped it.
(Realencyclopädie für Protestantische Theologie und Kirche, XVIII, 446.)

[1]The Cambridge Platonists, ed., G. R. Cragg, p. 35.

influential in articulating the emergent latitudinarianism in the church
of England in the latter half of the seventeenth century. In an exchange
of letters with his former teacher, Whichcote had objected that in "former
times some, whose names and memories I otherwise honor and value their
writings, have been sharp and censorious."[1] Edwards in his critique of the
three extremes of severity, enthusiasm, and superstition[2] to which Satan
could drive the zeal of Christian professors added to such general allusions
specific names. He called attention to the severity of the factional disputes of the early church in Corinth. He went on to comment that in the
"days of Constantine the Great, the zeal of Christians against heathenism
ran out into a degree of persecution." Edwards also struck much closer home
when he disapproved that in "some of the most eminent Reformers, as in the
great Calvin in particular," the zeal for the cause led them into persecution of those who differed "in some points of divinity."[3] Edwards furthermore offered his observations on "ecclesiastical story" in which "some eminent servants of Jesus Christ"[4] were mistaken in the belief that they had
the same kind of immediate revelations which had been formerly accorded to
the prophets and apostles. Such a dangerous enthusiasm proper Edwards found
in the case of Martin Luther and warned that the young New England divines
must "vastly exceed Luther, the head of the Reformation, who was guilty of
a great many excesses, in that great affair in which God made him the chief
instrument."[5] Thus Luther was fought by the traditionalists, he was fought
as a traditionalist, but he also had to be criticized as an enthusiast.

---

[1] The Cambridge Platonists, p. 243.

[2] The Great Awakening, ed., C. C. Goen, p. 319.

[3] Ibid., p. 243.   [4] Ibid., p. 442.   [5] Ibid., p. 410.

When Edwards dealt more specifically with the question of the novelty
of bodily effects in the revival, his criticism of the tradition expanded
from general comments into a detailed argument of historical proof which
did not simply submit insights to others for further consideration.[1] Edwards'
research on this topic included ten examples, one of which reached as far
back as the seventeenth century. We shall approach Edwards' handling of
his sources through the eyes of his opponent Charles Chauncy, and proceed
from there to an evaluation of the novelty and continuity argument. Since
C. C. Goen in his edition of Edwards' writings on the Great Awakening has
critically collated both Chauncy and Edwards with their sources, we shall
begin with a summary of Chauncy's opinions on Edwards' historical research.

Chauncy assaulted Edwards' arguments one by one.[2] Thus he pointed
out that the absence of any mention of terror in a source could not be made
up by embellishing it with the authority of William Perkins whose name did
not appear in the source either. In two more cases Chauncy maintained that
the proclivity to bodily effects resulted either from character deficiencies
in the case of a man who had incurred a mental condition prior to conversion, or they could be explained in the case of the Reformer Guillaume Farel
by the latter's well-known quarrelsome temper. Chauncy in a somewhat con-
descending manner did, however, concede in the latter case that Edwards
could not possibly have checked out his source because he did not have access
to "some of the best and largest libraries in New England." As a provincial
Edwards was not -- as Peter Gay would put it much later -- familiar with the
"best of his time." Even in a case where Chauncy could not find such adverse

---

[1] The Great Awakening, ed., C. C. Goen, pp. 442, 468.

[2] Ibid., pp. 307-313.

personality problems, he was convinced that second causes would go far in explaining such divine influences on the body. In two more cases, however, where even for him the textual evidence was strong he ruled that abstinence was not a bodily effect and that the report of the minister of Dedham which stemmed from a time before the revivals was simply inadmissible because it tended to discredit religion. Finally, three more of the examples given by Edwards, including a testimony of his own father, were not commented upon at all.

If we concede Edwards' failure to attend to questions of a correct transmission and a critical evaluation of his sources, and if we furthermore accept the charge that he did not do justice in his selection of examples to the aspect of secondary causation, we are still faced with the fact that Chauncy missed his opportunity to polemicize in three instances and that in two other cases he did not understand the first and misunderstood the second. Edwards had quoted at length from a life of a popular Puritan saint in the early seventeenth century which dwelt extensively on the joys attendant upon the conversion of this particular saint. We have already pointed out that from A Faithful Narrative onward Edwards had been concerned to show that the initial appearance of joy as laughter had developed into a positive and essential element of sainthood. For this reason he wanted to include a historical example for this distinctive feature. With regard to these joyous aspects of religion, Chauncy also most clearly misunderstood Edwards. For Chauncy the bodily effects were associated only with things like swooning or instability, and therefore abstinence which presupposed a high degree of concentration and discipline did not at all belong for him in such a discussion, whereas already in A Faithful

Narrative Edwards had observed some cases where it was the new "spiritual delights" that caused the appetites of saints to fail.[1]

Such misunderstanding arose from the way in which Edwards and Chauncy looked at these historical examples. Thomas S. Kuhn has suggested that the difference between Aristotelian and Galilean mechanics can be explained by the fact that representatives of both schools literally looked at heavy bodies in different ways. Where the Aristotelian, for example, saw something that was fastened to a chain and swung back and forth until it came to a rest, Galileo saw a pendulum which could repeat the same motion almost ad infinitum.[2] In a similar way it must be recognized that Chauncy could look at these historical examples only in terms of a circumstantial and causal sameness of past and present. Edwards, on the other hand, viewed the relation of past and present in terms of a substantial similarity and circumstantial differences which made him interested not only in doctrinal demarcation, but also in doctrinal development.

Traditional preparationist teaching had held that favorable external signs or circumstances were not sufficient in order to indicate or to infer a state of grace in all cases. For that reason Edwards rejected the charge that the momentary and partial likeness between the Quakers and the Great Awakening could be made the basis for a doctrinal identification of both in order to discredit the latter.[3] In his introduction to the presentation of his historical research Edwards was, however, more immediately interested in the continuity with the past of such new circumstances as "new scenes"

---

[1] The Great Awakening, ed., C. C. Goen, p. 183.

[2] Thomas S. Kuhn, The Structure of Scientific Revolutions, p. 118.

[3] The Great Awakening, p. 313.

206

and "new things" and in the defense and definition of such novelty as a
positive rather than as a deficient mode of history. In this way Edwards
shifted his focus from a search for like, ancient historical precedents,
to the finding out of historical antecedents that led up to and prepared a
new situation. When he therefore maintained that new things "are not so
new as has been generally imagined,"[1] he meant to direct the attention of
his opponents to a historical distinction. There had been cases, such as
his historical examples, which "have been found and well approved of in
the church of God from time to time," but the "appointed time" or fullness
of time for these cases may not yet have come. The difference between
these two kinds of time he described in terms of an increase in frequency,
swiftness, and degree from the former to the latter so that the antecedents
and their corresponding event were not distinct goods, but the same good
in different degrees. The meaningfulness of this notion of the antecedents of novelty depended both on its teleological and typological definition. The creation of the world "was carried on through six days and
appeared all complete, settled in a state of rest on the seventh." The
progress from one day or stage to the next was each time a step that
brought about something new. Nevertheless, new events did have their forerunners, for the various types of Christ scattered throughout the Old
Testament were so many antecedents of the being and the new event of Christ.
Since every new or extraordinary event in turn was a type of the Christ
event, each such event could have its own antecedents which would be similar and more or less distinct, but which would not have to be circumstan-
tially identical or uniformly distinct. The being as well as the novelty

[1]The Great Awakening, p. 307.

of an event was, consequently, a direct corollary of the application of christology to history. Even if Edwards would have taken greater care in the selection of his examples, his teleological emphasis would have remained at odds with Chauncy's predominant interest in causal uniformity.

Edwards, in order to show that an ancient and pure practice had fallen into abeyance and decayed, did not leave the argument from precedent untried. In his draft for the History of the Work of Redemption, he followed a martyrological tradition of historiography which maintained that throughout the Middle Ages there was "an uninterrupted succession of many witnesses through the whole time, in Germany, France, Britain and other countries; private persons and ministers, some magistrates and persons of great distinction."[1] In the same way he maintained that "great outcries under awakenings were more frequently heard of in former times in the country than they have been of late, as some aged persons now living can testify."[2] While it had been the polemic intent of this argument from precedent to show the traditionalists that the circumference of their view of tradition was smaller than they claimed, Edwards himself even went beyond this view of combatting the ancient by the even more ancient, since both were antecedents of the new which included the confirmatory, corrective, critical, and continuous uses of the past.

The Faithful Narrative was, as we have seen, chiefly taken up with the description of comprehensiveness. This delineation of the situation in Northampton seemed to roll present and future into one under a millennial experience. In his treatise on the Distinguishing Marks and Some

---

[1] Edwards, Works, V, p. 211.

[2] The Great Awakening, ed., C. C. Goen, p. 310.

Thoughts Concerning the Revival, the explication of the relation of the

Great Awakening to past and future took place and the debate over history

was on in earnest. This shift was not arbitrary. In the five years that

had intervened between the revival at Northampton in 1735 and the outbreak

of the Great Awakening in 1740, and in the period that had elapsed between

the publication of the final version of A Faithful Narrative in 1737 and

and the Distinguishing Marks in 1741, Edwards had begun to deal with the

questions of history in 1739 in a series of sermons that were then published

posthumously under the title of the History of the Work of Redemption. We

have already seen how its findings entered the argument on continuity. Its

results were present when Edwards pointed to the role of strife by reference

to the "Spirit of God that first moved upon the face of the waters, which

was an occasion for the great uproar and tumult."[1] Furthermore, Edwards

reminded his present-minded colleagues of the task of the minister "as a

wise builder or architect, who has a long reach and comprehensive view; and

for whom it is necessary, that when he begins a building, he should have at

once a view of the whole frame, and all the future parts of the structure,

even to the pinnacle that all may fitly be framed together."[2] It was under

this image of the building that Edwards introduced and held together the

series of sermons that he had preached on the work of redemption.[3] In his

criticism of tradition and former observation he applied the story of

Israel's revival in the wilderness and the Babylonian captivity. That

revival had been mainly an affair of the young and the later captivity

---

[1]The Great Awakening, ed., C. C. Goen, p. 318.

[2]Ibid., p. 445.   [3]Ibid., pp. 17, 18.

lasted just long enough for those of them to "waste away . . . that were
adult persons when they were carried away."[1]

The significance of the draft of the History of the Work of
Redemption becomes thus more transparent and accessible through its application in a particular and polemic situation in which its paradigmatic
character was being tested for its capacity of differentiation as well as
integration. The draft itself is a document that is difficult to tackle,
and an explanation of it as the "cosmic rationalisation of the revival" was
to assign too easy a reason for the work of revision that went on in it.
What went on in the draft for the History of the Work of Redemption is a
process well known to the professional historian and can itself be clarified through a story. In one of his classes on American colonial history,
Richard B. Morris mentioned that in the thirties the labor movement became
so very much a part of the American mainstream that the novelty of this
event sent him and others back to American history in order to find out
what they could on this phenomenon and its development. In his case, the
outcome was the monograph on Government and Labor in Early America. The
situation was similar with Edwards. The Northampton revival sent him back
to history in order to find out how this event was related to the past of
universal history in Scripture. The experience of the Northampton revival
led to a revitalization of history which in turn made the draft for the
History of the Work of Redemption into a cosmic explication and the
treatises on the Great Awakening into a cosmic application of the historicity of the revival, through a re-reading of Scripture. The dimensions
of such a revitalization cannot be exhausted by an interpretation which

---

[1]The Great Awakening, ed., C. C. Goen, p. 505; Works, V, p. 63.

focuses only on cosmic rationalizations which by definition suggest the

subconscious or conscious projections of needs and interests for the

purpose of a new ideological ritual as a means to reduce anxiety.[1]

Our analysis of Edwards' use of the past as one aspect of his con-

cern over history has exemplified his awareness of the dangerous conse-

quences of the omission of one perspective at the expense of such use for

another. As a result, Edwards' admission of all the perspectives was pro-

vided by the Scriptural referent of the work of redemption. Edwards

therefore opened his argument in Some Thoughts Concerning the Revival by

taking aim at both the friends and the foes of the Great Awakening for

their "foundation error . . . of not taking the Holy Scriptures as a whole

seriously."[2] Throughout the treatise he showed that if they had paid close

attention to it, then the traditions of the past could not have deteriorate

into traditionalism. Likewise, the example of the fathers would not have

turned into a filipietistic adulation of patriarchs. The interpretation

of providence could have remained more than the success story where the

preacher counted his blessings by the conflicts he had engineered for his

self-aggrandizement. Faith in prophecy would still deal with the future

instead of proliferating into illuministic fantasies. Nor was contemporary

observation which we had described in the first part of this chapter exempt

from such deterioration. In Edwards' connotative use of language "obser-

vation" meant both empirical observation and habitual observance where the

positive inquiry into the new could become a habitual empiricism. This

---

[1]The term "revitalization" I owe to Anthony F.C. Wallace, Religion:
An Anthrological View (New York: Random House, 1966), pp. 31ff.

[2]The Great Awakening, ed., C. C. Goen, p. 296.

latter attitude Edwards characterized elsewhere in a critique of Matthew

Tindal on Christianity as Old as the Creation as the kind of worldview in

which everything depended on the "existence of that idea, or those few

ideas which are at this moment present in our minds, or are the immediate

objects of our present consciousness."[1] What Edwards had put forward in a

general way at the beginning of Some Thoughts Concerning the Revival, he

summarized specifically and systematically at the beginning of the end of

the same treatise.

> There is a good use to be made of the events of providence, of
> our own observation and experience, and human histories, and the
> opinion of the fathers and other eminent men; but finally all must
> be brought to one rule. The Word of God, and that must be regarded
> our only rule.[2]

Edwards' summary here read almost like a review of some of the major genres

of historical writing which we had surveyed earlier in this study as part

of the general climate against which he himself must be seen. There was,

however, this one basic difference between Bacon's polyhistoric classifi-

cation and Edwards' concluding summary of the categories of historical

thinking: the former had been arranged according to an abstract essential-

ist scheme,[3] whereas the latter related its categories concretely to the

essential structure of Scripture as the paradigm of coherent history. More-

over, in Edwards' case Scripture did not only include the several temporal

and categorial interrelations of history, but it also did away with spatial

discrimination in history and became the intercontinental connecting link

---

[1]Edwards, Works, VIII, 198.

[2]Ibid., p. 452.

[3]See Chapter I, p. 33f.

and medium of meaning: "Nor does God send beyond the seas, nor into past ages, to obtain a rule that shall determine and satisfy us. But we have a rule near at hand, a sacred book that God himself has put into our hands, with clear and infallible marks. . . ."[1] Few if any people in New England at the time would have professed their allegiance to Holy Writ in terms less definite than Edwards did here, but Edwards in addition spelled out the consequences of such a conventional stance and confronted all parties that emerged in the controversy over the revival with Scripture as the Geschichtsbibel.[2] He demonstrated throughout the Distinguishing Marks and Some Thoughts Concerning the Revival that every merely particular conceptualization of history would -- under the unpredictable pressures of strife and crisis -- become just one of several similar, but variant, shade of the same historylessness unless Scripture provided the rule to turn them into the various aspects of one history of Redemption. In that case Script functioned both as the categorial center for different kinds of histories in Edwards and its paradigm preceded their rules in the way in which Thomas Kuhn has described the priority of the paradigm over the rules.[3] When Scripture did not function in this manner, it was well on the way to being used as a rubber-stamp approval in a merely religiously saturated culture that felt the perpetual need to be biblistic without remaining Scriptural.

---

[1]The Great Awakening, ed., C. C. Goen, pp. 330-331.

[2]The term "Geschichtbibel" comes from the title of the Chronicle of World History of the sixteenth century mystic and dissenter Sebastian Franck (1499-1542). See Steven E. Ozment, Mysticism and Dissent, Religious Ideology and Social Protest in the Sixteenth Century (New Haven: Yale University Press, 1971), p. 148.

[3]Kuhn, The Structure of Scientific Revolutions, pp. 43f.

When Edwards therefore translated his concern over the Scriptural
mediation of history from a polemic argument into a positive statement of
its narrative structure, the term "Scripture-history" assumed a full and
complex meaning. The reading of this history did not serve a curious or
traditional interest only as did those human histories mentioned before.
Nor did this history attract only the skilled participant observer or the
prudent bystander. But acquaintance with this history could lead to several
conversions of attitude that moved man from the role of reader through that
of participant observer to that of the participating actor in the drama in
which the whole and the parts, the love and concern for the small things,
as well as their suggestive omission, and in which, also, sophistication
as well as childlike plainness was blended into the perfect way:

> There is a strange and unaccountable kind of enchantment, if I may
> so speak, in scripture history, which although it is destitute of all
> rhetorical ornaments, makes it vastly more pleasant, agreeable, easy,
> and natural, than any other history whatever. It shines bright with
> the amiable simplicity of truth. There is something in the relation,
> that, at the same time, very much pleases and engages the reader, and
> evidences the truth of the fact. It is impossible to tell fully what
> I mean, to any that have not taken notice of it before. One reason
> doubtless is this: the scripture sets forth things just as they hap-
> pened, with the minute circumstances of time, place, situation, gesture,
> habit, etc., in such a natural method, that we seem to be actually
> present; and we insensibly fancy, not that we are readers, but spec-
> tators, yea, actors in the business. These little circumstances won-
> derfully help to brighten the ideas of the more principal parts of the
> history. And, although the scripture goes beyond other histories, in
> mentioning such circumstances; yet no circumstances are mentioned, but
> those that wonderfully brighten the whole. So the story is told very
> fully, and without in the least crowding things together, before one
> has fully taken up what was last related; and yet told in much less
> room, than any one else could tell it. Notwithstanding the minute
> circumstances mentioned, which other histories leave out, it leads
> along our ideas so naturally and easily, that they seem to go neither
> too fast nor too slow. One seems to know as exactly how it is from
> the relation, as if we saw it. The mind is so led on, that sometimes
> we seem to have a full, large, and particular history of a long time:
> so that if we should shut the book immediately, without taking particu-
> lar notice, we should not suppose the story had been told in half so

little room; and yet a long train of ideas is communicated. The story is so narrated, that our mind, although some facts are not mentioned, yet naturally traces the whole transaction. And although it be thus skilfully contrived, yet things are told in such a simple, plain manner, that the least child can understand them. This is a perfection in the sacred writers, which no other authors can equal.[1]

Such claims for "Scripture-history" were considerable. In the last chapter we introduced the imagistic and exegetical dimensions of this view of history and in the following chapter we shall attend more closely to his positive-systematic statement. The argument from history was, however, not only reserved for special polemical or philosophic occasions. Edwards' concern over history was not simply an agitation over historiography that came and went with crucial moments, events, and years of New England's passage, but it also entered his theoretical and practical decision-making process. In order to perceive the background of his claim and consequences that followed from it, we shall broaden the base of our study by drawing out some implications of the above interpretation of A Faithful Narrative and compare them to an argument in Religious Affections.

One of the results of the revival of 1735 was the transformation of the strife-ridden and factious frontier town of Northampton into a community of common concern. Neither the external force of the secular arm nor the application of means of ecclesiastical sanctions brought this about, and while promotional activities in the form of small societies provided a nucleus, the event itself was more than the sum total of the constitutive elements. It converted the ecclesiastical and civil spheres as well as the persuasion of the societies into one praying community. Edwards' view was like Edward Johnson's understanding of New England as a disciplined praying camp in the way an imaginative hyperbole was matched with ascertainable fact

---

[1]Edwards, Works, VIII, 179-180.

In the Northampton of 1735, vision and fact merged and in turn set
forth a historical model. No longer could it be said that the hopes of
New England nor the often fanciful expectations of Europe about America
were still only a matter of unfulfilled imagination, imaginative anticipation or imaginary substitution. Here the perennial dream of and aspirations toward community itself as communion rather than as coercion had
become a datable event in church history. In this event artistic veri-
similitude as the means to account for and to conceal the literal "nowhere"
of literary utopia could be shed for the beauty of history itself. This
event also pierced through the abstractions of the social covenant and
social contract that had served as viable theoretical constructs in the
endeavors to rationalize an increased participation in or a prolonged conservation of once established societal relationships. In this event, however, both literary and social theory are confronted with community as it
became incarnate in space and time for a brief period in the revival at
Northampton. Unlike the later nineteenth century communitarian experiments,
no emigration from space or time, be it that of Europe or the settled part
of America, preceded this exhibition of community. The promise lay not
wherever more space was left. On the contrary, the occurrence of this
archetypal community experience came about within an established town and
within a mainline, not a sectarian ecclesiastical body; in fact, it came
to pass in a church that had piloted admission standards which had made it,
since the time of Solomon Stoddard's ministry, more churchly than other New
England churches. To be sure, Northampton was too small to be the focal
point for the fulfillment of the expectation of thousands which Thomas
Shepard had looked forward to as the sign of the springtide of the churches

216

and of which Jonathan Edwards may have read in Shepard's <u>Parable of the
Ten Virgins</u>.[1] Yet, still this event marked in an unprecedented way the
reconstitution of most citizens into one local congregation and thus provided a model for community itself as concrete manifestation as well as
social and spiritual comprehension. It was the internalization of these
interrelated historical, social, and spiritual processes in this occurrence
and event of community which Edwards also insisted upon in <u>Religious
Affections</u>[2] as the necessary and perfect correlate to the "internal evidences
of assurance on the part of the saint, which dwelt extensively on the joys
attendant upon the conversion of this particular saint. These processes
in turn Edwards defended by reference to the "general view of the historical world" as contained in Scripture and pointed to the consequences that
would ensue for socialization, historical hermeneutics, and civilization if
the event of community or Scripture was being disregarded.

Edwards at this particular point in <u>Religious Affections</u> criticized
a situation where learned history became the sole arbiter and authority of
salvation and where consequently erudition in historical matters rather than
the event of community in history became the yardstick. He pointed out that
the attitude inherent in such a mentality would lead to results which were
socially discriminating because they were intellectually exclusive and
would therefore endanger the durability of the socialization of values.
This particular learning was very much in agreement with the nature and
temper of its authors rather than with the objective and existing needs of
every member of the community. The benefit for the authors themselves was

[1]See Chapter III, p. 112.

[2]Edwards, <u>Religious Affections</u>, ed., John E. Smith, pp. 303f.

considerable and those in the community who were less articulate would give "much credit" to such efforts, but a credibility gap still remained, for the concern for the community in this type of historical erudition was self-love. In Edwards' view, self-love was the extension of self-interest and its projection on to the community at large which then became only an echo. Such historical reasoning was preoccupied with the absence of vice, but it could not do much towards the presence of positive well-being as the otherness of the inferior other did not come into view. The resultant admiration of and participation in prestige, but not participation in authority, was but "negative moral goodness."[1]

This credibility gap could indeed be activated at such times when those who are "illiterate and unacquainted with history" faced severe tests with regard to their own convictions and commitments. Under such circumstances they would simply no longer accept things out of social convenience, but challenge the intellectual credentials on which this convenience had been built. For a group of people who had been referred to as "illiterates" these challenges as Edwards listed them sounded very sophisticated. We must therefore see Edwards here in his role as a minister to others. For he acted as spokesman for those who could not speak for themselves, in exposing the shaky foundations of this erudition:

> After all that learned men have said to them, there will remain
> innumerable doubts on their minds: they will be ready, when pinched
> with some great trial of their faith, to say, how do I know this, or
> that? How do I know when these histories were written? Learned men
> tell me these histories were so and so attested in the day of them;
> but how do I know that there were such attestations then? They tell

---

[1] Edwards, The Nature of True Virtue, Works, II, p. 63.

me there is equal reason to believe these facts, as any whatsoever
that are related as such a distance; but how do I know that other
facts which are related of those ages, ever were?[1]

Such solidarity was not unlike what we can find later on in Marxism where

intellectuals began to speak out for the working classes whom they had come

to see as the focus of social discrimination and who like the "illiterates"

here could not care less to defend a culture of learning or a society in

which they had no stake. Under persistent questioning, therefore, the

authority of erudition turned out to be no more than an antiquarianism that

operated on an insufficient hermeneutical base.

For purposes of defense the learned historian -- as Edwards saw him

-- retreated from one part of antiquity to another. In the process this

learned historian levelled the distinction between church history and his-

tory in general. Even though he exposed his own hermeneutics in such a

compromising way, the main thrust of Edwards' criticism here was that such

a mere shifting of the ground avoided a reconsideration of the issue insofar

as for the "illiterates" it did not make a difference which past was being

talked about as long as the "attestation" procedure remained the same, for

one past was as distinct for them as the other. The argument from erudi-

tion thus involved an infinite regress in which at one point the supply of

authoritative antiquities will be used up and in which skepticism will arise

because the distance of past and present was being bridged without regard

to the dynamic or spiritual processes that obtained between them. This

dilemma and another solution to it we shall review in an analysis of

Shaftesbury's view of Scripture in our last chapter.

If this kind of erudition could not stand up to the test of inte-

grating the Christian community socially or historically, then it could not

---

[1]Edwards, _Religious Affections_, ed., J. E. Smith, p. 303.

be expected that it would be more effective in removing cultural discrimination in the propagation of Christianity outside of the Christian community
where the "illiterates" were red rather than white, and pagan rather than
nominal members of the corpus christianum. Edwards pointed out that for
the Houssatunnucks, acceptance of Christianity on such premises would be
"immensely cumbersome" and "infinitely difficult"[1] and would thus certainly
not lead to the kind of "joy in Christ"[2] which for him was one of the two
operations of true religion.

This impediment to Indian missions he identified more precisely as
the "acquaintance with the histories of politer nations."[3] A look at the
draft for the History of the Work of Redemption and at his correspondence
make it clear that one of these histories at least was that of England.
England for him was the "principal kingdom of the Reformation" and was
looked upon by the church history of the times as a replica of ancient
purity as well as the climax of civilization. For Edwards to maintain that
such a climax of Christian civilization could not be the unqualified model
of imitation was indeed radical, but both the general view of the historical
world as well as observations on the mission scene itself tended to bear out
such a relativization of English history as the road to civility.

Further along in the same section in Religious Affections Edwards
left no doubt that the rise of infidelity[4] in England at that present time
would have made the history of that church a "cumbersome" model of instruction and imitation indeed. "Cumbersome" could mean in addition that historical erudition will here also bring convictions of the truth of

---

[1] Edwards, Religious Affections, p. 304.

[2] Ibid., p. 94.   [3] Ibid., p. 304.   [4] Ibid., p. 305.

Christianity only to some choice few individuals, and will set them up as authorities and will deny to all others full assurance and conviction with the contention that in this life only in "very extraordinary circumstances will there be a "full and absolute assurance of hope."[1] Those who follow such a double standard step outside the "doctrine of Protestants" which over against the "papists"[2] had always maintained that complete assurance is possible. In Edwards' time, Charles Chauncy was a proponent of this view of the impossibility of full assurance.[3] Unlike Edwards, he displayed a positive attitude toward indigenous Indian culture, but again from Chauncy's own view of assurance, this is but consistent: if only a few can have assurance and in the meantime learned men and historians like himself assume authoritative guidance, then indigenous culture can also be tolerated.

For Edwards, however, conviction and assurance were accessible to all, and while England was the principal kingdom of the Reformation, it was nevertheless not the principle of the Reformation, for neither English nor Indian nor any other kind of particular Christian community and its civilization could be the ultimate yardstick with which to measure the conviction of the truth of Christianity. Religious Affections was published in 1746, five years before he himself moved to Stockbridge to take over as a missionary to the Indians. The straits in which he found the mission

---

[1] Edwards, Religious Affections, p. 167.

[2] For this central assertion and the danger of a relapse, see Moltmann, Praedestination und Perseveranz, Neukirchen, 1961, Chapter I, and Perry Miller, From Colony to Province, 1953, p. 224, where he analyzes the unsettling effects of a continual renewal of the covenant that takes away assurance and leads to scepticism.

[3] Conrad Wright, The Beginnings of Unitarianism in America, 1955, p. 45.

station at that time was enough to vindicate his criticism in terms of the

clearly observable facts. His predecessor, John Sargent, had held to the

idea that Indians ought to emulate the example of godly English families.[1]

He petitioned for and received from the state an allowance of land at

Stockbridge on which to settle four carefully screened English families.

Edwards in turn spent a good deal of his time and influence in politicking

in order to offset the schemes devised by these God-fearing Englishmen for

the purpose of victimizing and cheating the Indians out of what they had.

While we had seen in our analysis of Edwards' uses of the past that he,

like Martin Luther, found himself pitted against and between two opposing

theological camps, we must now also add here that Edwards' community experi-

ence of the revival at Northampton and his defense of it in terms of the

general view of the historical world included a self-critical attitude of

his own theological tradition as a civilizing force in its tendency to con-

fuse the priorities of gospel and civilization. The importance of this

latter point may easily be overlooked because of Edwards' style. His com-

ments were not specifically advertised but tucked away in a diversion to his

main argument and the persons to whom he addressed this criticism remained

unidentified.

[1]R. Pierce Beaver, Church, State, and the American Indians, Two and a Half Centuries of Partnership in Missions Between Protestant Churches and Government (St. Louis: Concordia Publishing House, 1966), p. 37.

222

Summary

Edwards' writings on the revival in Northampton and on the Great
Awakening as well as a section from Religions Affections were the main
textual basis for an inquiry into the crucial elements and consequences of
Edwards' defense of history. His argument touched on moral questions,
involved empirical concerns and focused both of them on Scripture as the
paradigm of the historical processes which entailed definite understandings
about the interdependence of mind and society.

In the course of his own deepening insight as it evolved during the
Great Awakening, Edwards concluded that the necessity as well as the dangers
of reporting on the revival could not be solved simply by adherence to a
party, class, or group. Thus, for example, his evidence comprised the
experiences of women and the young as much as those of older people. Edwards
had set out to write on the revival in order to counteract the prejudice of
its opponents and to reach the prudence of the cautious. He now added to
this criticism of others the criticism of himself who as a committed historian had realized that pride like an onion has many layers. With this
ability for self-criticism, he avoided the danger of emergent enlightenment
historiography which took its own moral principles to be so self-evident
as to subordinate history to the function of a mute replica of them.

Edwards was confident that a minister who had been trained in the
tradition of the cases of conscience could through a protracted and comparative observation develop the rules of conduct required for the new situation occasioned by the Great Awakening. For his own part, at least,
Edwards had given a striking example of this comparative approach in A
Faithful Narrative which must therefore be considered his masterpiece as a

historian. In it he did not only pay attention to the variety of external factors that had led to the rise, progress, and decline of the Northampton Revival. Nor did he simply attend to the variety of unsearchable spiritual manifestations of this revival, but in both cases his intense analysis of the space of a small province had cosmopolitan scope and led to a novel and positive attitude to variety which provided at least for Edwards standards of comparison and gave him the edge over others in ascertaining responses to and establishing rules of conduct for the events of the Great Awakening.

Scholars have singled out for praise this gift of observation already in the young Edwards and have viewed his essay on the spider primarily as the sign of a precocious talent in the natural sciences. It is frequently overlooked, however, that experiment and explanation, empirical curiosity and metaphysical interest were inseparable in this early essay as well as in his later writings on the revival. In addition his forthright observations on the revival made him realize that neither observation nor metaphysics as they were understood then could account positively for the frequently changing styles of ministries in different locations. Edwards, therefore, dealt with the historiographical issues that arose out of his empirical findings by comparing the facts of observation with the rules of Scripture-prophecy.

This focus on Scripture had several historiographical and ideological consequences. First, Edwards' view of latitudinarianism was not only spatial but also temporal. Second, Edwards presented a sophisticated and coherent theory of the uses of the past in which the Reformers, for example, confirmed and criticized the present, but in which the present also criticized the Reformers so that past and present could be seen as a continuity as well as a discontinuity. It is therefore not possible to maintain that the draft for the History of the Work of Redemption was a cosmic ex-post rationalization of the revival. Third, of Bacon's classifications Scripture appeared in Edwards as the most comprehensive of all historiographical modes. According to Edwards, the absence in the Great Awakening of the Scriptural paradigm perverted providence, prophecies, tradition, lives, and observation into ahistorical even if religious and biblicistic substitutes. The conversion of providence into a success story which Edwards criticized here became a common staple of an American ideology later. Fourth, the paradigm of "Scripture-history" set the positive example for the problems of unresponsive prejudice, uncommitted prudence, and over-zealous pride that he had encountered in the reporting on the revival. The literary quality of this Scripture-history moved man from the role of reader through that of participant observer to that of participating actor in a drama. Fifth, Scripture helped to articulate and to sustain the historical view of community which had emerged in the Northampton Revival. Scripture also guarded community against the dangers of a socially divisive and ahistoric intellectualism and spelled out the consequences of community for the relation between Christian Englishmen and Christian Indians as coequal partners in the work of redemption.

CHAPTER VI

SCRIPTURE AND METAPHYSICS:

THE EMERGENCE OF A HISTORICAL SYSTEM

Principles and Forms of Systematic Theology

Jonathan Edwards himself did not leave a complete systematic theology of his own, even though a treatise like The Chief End for Which God
Created the World can be considered the prolegomena of such a projected
future system. In order to find, therefore, at least a working definition
of systematic theology, we turn to Edwards' pupil Joseph Bellamy who published his systematic account under the name of True Religion Delineated
to which Edwards contributed a preface. This preface was a strong plea
that both over against the New England of former times and over against more
acted countries these obscure parts were now ready to make an original contribution to the understanding of Christianity, for "we cannot suppose that
the Church of God is already possessed of all that light, in things of this
nature that God ever intends to give it."[1] Bellamy's account therefore
filled a gap and in the course of his endorsement of Bellamy's systematic
work Edwards summarized the principles on which this account was built. Not
only did Bellamy include the "careful consideration of important facts
(which he has had great opportunity to observe) and a very clear experience

---

[1]Joseph Bellamy, True Religion Delineated; or, Experimental Religion
(Boston: S. Kneeland, 1750), in Great Awakening, ed., C. C. Goen, p. 510.

in his own soul; but the most diligent search of the holy scriptures, and
strict examination of the nature of things."[1] A systematic articulation of
theology thus included the religious experience of the author as well as
the exegesis of scripture, metaphysics, and observed facts. Even though we
cannot necessarily conclude that these principles were Edwards' own, nor tha
he would have executed them in the same manner if he shared them, we can at
least assume that Edwards in a preface of this kind would not have gone on
record, had he had a major disagreement with the inclusion of any of the
principles listed. Edwards' summary of these principles included facts and
metaphysics. These facts were the events of the Great Awakening that had
brought about a unique and particular situation which had to be accounted
for. We have dealt with the crucial importance of Scripture for the historiographical argument that had been precipitated by these facts and events
We shall now turn to the inquiry as to how far the measure of positive metaphysical articulation and evaluation of this historical situation was also
maintained by means of scriptural exegesis.

Such a positive inclusion of historical facts into the construction
of a system transformed the belief of history as ceaseless change into a
view of history as the locus where new things can happen, and do happen. At
this point we must be especially careful in our attempt to set limits to ou
discussion. The idea of newness as something positive had been voiced befor
Edwards defended his belief that there was to be more light, that an ultimat
end could be a subordinate end at the same time, and that reformation was no
simply the recovery of something corrupted, but also the addition of something new. Thus we find that John Robinson, theological mentor and spiritua

---

[1]Bellamy, True Religion Delineated, p. 571.

director of the future Plymouth settlers, maintained that the "Lord had more truth and light yet to break forth out of His Holy Word."[1] We also find that in the field of systematic theology, Cotton Mather set down his intention to try something that had never been attempted before except for a few "feeble essays": he wants to "go thro' a Body of Divinity" and relate every article that he deals with to Christ.[2] A positive awareness of the new itself as well as plans to articulate it occurred at different times, in different contexts, and related to different subjects for which the style of a treatise or sermon may have been sufficient. Some of these plans, like Cotton Mather's project, never moved beyond the planning stage. Therefore, when we deal with the positive appreciation of history as the consequence of a new event in a new land, it is important to state that in this chapter we shall confine our inquiry to the field of doctrinal theology. Within the field of theology this discipline in particular usually carried out the most sustained efforts to conceptualize a tradition and its changes. Edwards was not only aware of the new and planned to articulate it, but he made enough progress in this endeavor for us to see the direction in which his systematic thought was headed.

Edwards' enumeration of history as one of the four constructive principles directs our inquiry primarily toward the material and not to the formal aspects of his systematic thought in divinity. Neverthess, an

---

[1]Robert Ashton, ed., The Works of John Robinson, Pastor of the Pilgrim Fathers, 3 Vols (Boston: Doctrinal Tract and Book Society, 1851), Vol. I, p. xliv. It should be mentioned that this famous utterance of Robinson from his farewell sermon to the ship population of the Mayflower was taken from a report of it rather than from his own copy.

[2]Cotton Mather, Diary, 2 Vols. (Frederick Ungar Publishing Co. of N. Y., 1911), I, 519 (July 27, 1705).

arbitrary separation of form and content could easily falsify the overall
picture and therefore a brief look at the role of some formal elements in
systematic theology in the light of the history of this discipline is
appropriate.

The example of a systematic exposition closest home to Edwards was
Samuel Willard's Compleat Body of Divinity.[1] Willard at the outset of his
commentary stated that at all times and at all places in the history of the
church, doctrines had been reduced into such bodies. In this way the ministers received a help for preaching and the laymen had a guide to Scripture.
Moreover, such aids were a means to break in the young as well as to promote
deeper understanding on the part of the advanced professors. Willard indicated that in this work he aimed at the advanced students of the Christian
faith. The task itself was one that had been undertaken over many years in
his weekly lectures which drew "many of the most knowing and judicious persons both from town and college,"[2] and which led posthumously to the largest
book printed and published in New England up to that time.[3] In his introductory remarks, Willard observed that "there have been various methods
observed in the compiling of these systems, but that which hath of late most
generally obtained with us is that of this Catechism." The catechism which
he referred to was the Westminster Assembly's Shorter Catechism. Willard's

---

[1]Samuel Willard, A Compleat Body of Divinity in Two Hundred and Fifty
Expository Lectures on the Assembly's Shorter Catechism (Boston, printed by
B. Green and S. Kneeland for B. Eliot and D. Henchman, 1726).

[2]Ibid., p. i.

[3]Ibid., p. iv. C. Mather, Magnalia, mentioned two bodies of divinity
by New England ministers which were never published. Their authors were
Richard Denton (I, 399), and Samuel Stone (I, 438). Samuel Willard, A
Compleat Body of Divinity, p. iv.

body of divinity was therefore the exposition and interpretation of a system
Unlike William Ames earlier and Jonathan Edwards later, Willard did not
contribute a system of his own.

Willard's adherence to the Westminster Assembly's Shorter Catechism
was a deliberate choice on the part of a man who was known for his learning
and who had a reputation for being a "recommender of divinity systems."[1]
Of all the options of which he was aware he chose that one which was current
in the churches of New England at the time in order to facilitate the catechetical and paedagogical effort which he had in mind. A different model
and method was suggested by Willard's contemporary, the Dutch Arminian Jean
LeClerc.[2] In his Epistolae Theologiae LeClerc advocated the use of the
"historical method" in which doctrines were to appear in the order in which
they occurred in Scripture from creation onward. In addition, the "form"
of the doctrines was to be explained for every age of the church.[3] We had
already seen in our introductory chapter that Jonathan Edwards who lived
later than Willard or LeClerc went on record in his letter to the trustees
at Princeton that his projected History of the Work of Redemption was to
follow the "historical order," by which he meant that all parts of divinity
were to follow each other in "that order which is most scriptural and most
natural."[4]

---

[1] Willard, A Compleat Body of Divinity, p. 2.

[2] Jean LeClerc (1657-1736) studied at the Calvinistic Academy in
Geneva. He became Professor of Hebrew and Philosophy at the Remonstrant
Seminary in Holland. He was known for his exegetical work (compare Edwards,
Works, IX, 36, 94), which relied on reason rather than on dogma as the crit-
ical standard of exegesis. For this reason he was used by the Deists as an
authority even though he was not a freethinker himself. (Rgg[3] I, 1839.)

[3] Alexander Schweizer, Die Glaubenslehre der Evangelisch-Reformierten
Kirche, I (Zürich: Orell, Füssli und Comp., 1844), p. 115.

[4] See p. 2.

This formal principle of the historica series of Scripture as a tool in the formulation of theology is usually traced back to a statement in the preface to the 1559 edition of Philip Melanchthon's Loci Communes in which he wrote:

> Nunc De Ordine partium aliquid praefandum est. Ipsi libri Prophetici et Apostolici Optimo ordine scripti sunt et articulos fideli aptissimo ordine trahunt, est enim historica series in libris Propheticis et Apostolicis, ordiuntur a prima rerum creatione et conditione Ecclesiae, et deinceps omnium temporum series a conditione rerum usque ad Cyri Monarchiam continentur in his libris Propheticis. In hac serie multae narrantur Instaurationes Ecclesiae, et insperguntur narrationibus doctrina legis et promissio Evangelii, deinde Apostoli testes sunt de Chris exhibito, nato, crucifixo, resuscitato. Haec sunt historica. Et in concionibus Christi, continentur articuli fidei, explicatio legis et Evangelii. Accedunt et Pauli disputationes, qui ut artifex instituit disputationem in Epistola ad Romanos de discrimine legis et Evangelii de Peccato, de Gratia seu Reconciliatione, qua restituimur ad vitam aeternam.[1]

Melanchthon spoke of history in the Old Testament as a narration in which the doctrine of the law and the promise of the gospel were scattered throughout. He also mentioned history in the New Testament as a witness to the Christ event. Both aspects together were summarized as "haec sunt historica" or as "historica series." Furthermore, the "conciones" or speeches of Christ were looked upon as the "explicatio" of doctrine, but the Apostle Paul in the epistle to the Romans became the "artifex" of a "disputatio" which provided the "discrimen" or discrimination of doctrine into its several Loci Communes. Ernst Troeltsch has suggested that Melanchthon himself introduced the idea of the historica series as a means to establish an objective counter point to his own earlier and more narrow focus on the benefits of Christ's salvation.[2] Such an interest of reaching back as far as creation would have

---

[1] Corpus Reformatorum, XXI, 605-606.

[2] Quoted in O. Ritschl, "System und Systematische Methode in der Geschichte des Wissenschaftlichen Sprachgebrauchs und der Philosophischen Methodologie," in Programm zur Feier des Gedächtnisses des Stifters der

been in keeping with a conviction that established authority by invoking
antiquity for the task in hand which in this case was the task of doctrinal
discrimination.

The positivistic adherence to the historica series became a part of
the textbook tradition of Orthodox Protestant theology and led to an arrangement of the individual doctrines in the order from creation to judgment.[1]
In a discussion of the historiography of chronology we had already seen that
its interest was above all in the series of dates and events, but that it
had no concern over their connection. The idea of the "temporum series"
which was mentioned in Melanchthon's preface belonged to this historiography
of chronology to which was added an interspersion of doctrines.

As soon as the trend became strong enough to connect the individual
doctrines of this serial arrangement at least two possibilities of doing
so became conceivable and were conceptualized. Thus, for example, the very
sequence of the historica series with its beginning and end could be turned
into the consequence of a principle or principles from which all followed,
and by means of which a summary of separate doctrines could be forged into
a consistent system. The method which was employed for the purpose had a
certain affinity to the historica series itself, because it was a "com-
positio, quando ordimur a principiis et per media procedimus usque ad finem."[2]

Universität, König Friedrich Wilhelms III...am 6. August 1906 Heraugegeben
vom Rektor und Senat der Rheinischen Friedrich-Wilhelms-Universitat (Bonn:
Carl Georgi, 1906), p. 20.

[1] Paul Althaus, Die Prinzipien der Deutsch Reformierten Dogmatik im
Zeitalter der Aristotelischen Scholastik (Leipzig: A. Deichert, 1914),
pp. 45f.

[2] Ritschl, System und Systematische Methode, p. 20.

The Latin term "principia" as it was used by the authors of Protestant
Orthodoxy could refer to beginnings as well as to principles. As soon as
any particular concerns such as either the knowledge of God, the decrees
or the covenant became a sufficiently dominant interest they would supply
the principle and cause from which the other doctrines were deduced. On
the other hand, a question could be addressed to the historica series not
with regard to the first principles, but in consideration of the final end
to which these doctrines related and toward which the actions of men led.
In this case it was the end which introduced the subject matter of the individual doctrines as means and principles of preparation: "A fine ad media
quae ducunt ad finem progrediendum."[1] These respective interests in the
nature of doctrine or in its end resulted in either a theoretical or practical approach to theology as a discipline. In the history of theology
these two methods were referred to as synthetic and analytic respectively.
According to Paul Althaus, the clearest formulation of these two formal
principles of systematic thought were worked out under the influence of a
renewed interest in Aristotelian logic by the Reformed theologian B.
Keckermann.[2] While the objective trend in the synthetic method tended to
encourage speculation and assign the analytic method solely to Scriptural
exegesis and the catechetical literature, the analytic method on the other
hand and its widespread reception in Lutheran systematic thought at the time
focused on the salvation of man.

---

[1]Althaus, Die Prinzipien, 54.

[2]Bartholomäus Keckermann (1571-1609), Professor of Theology and
Hebrew at the Reformed Academy of Danzig, East Prussia, opponent of Peter
Ramus. (RGG[3], III, 1234.)

While the serial character of the historiography of chronology became
a substructure of various systematic methods, there were also attempts to
take the history of doctrine seriously. The premium which chronology had
placed on facts and events such as the monarchy of Cyrus could slight the
intellectual content of history or what Bacon had called the history of
learning. The Reformed theologian Heinrich Alting,[1] for example, charged
that the history of the church in the Old and New Testaments "non tantum est
rerum Gestarum, sed etiam Dogmatum narratio." Alting engaged in an effort
for which he for the first time used the term Theologia Historica and which
he distinguished from the Theologia Dogmatica with the purpose in mind that
"historia religionis et omnium dogmatum colligenda certisque capitibus juxta
locos doctrinae dispescenda."[2] As a means of defending his program of a
history of doctrine Alting referred to Psalm 78 which he called a historical compend of doctrine.[3] We have already seen that Edwards used the same
Psalm as a basis from which to generalize his own findings on the relation
between doctrine, history, and prophecy. Alting did not integrate doctrine
and history in the way Edwards did, but he planned to add to each chapter
of dogmatic theology a monograph on the history of the respective doctrine.

This brief sketch of the role of the historica series in its relation
to systematic theology and to the history of doctrine indicated that there

---

[1]Heinrich Alting (1583-1644), Professor of Theology at Heidelberg
and Groningen. He was author of a Church History of the Palatinate and
was one of its representatives at the Synod of Dort.(Rgg[3] I, 294.)

[2]Quoted in Ritschl, Dogmengeschichte des Protestantismus, I (Leipzig:
Hinrich, 1908), p. 31.

[3]Gustav Adolf Benrath, Reformierte Kirchengeschichtsschreibung an der
Universität Heidelberg im Sechszehnten und Siebzehnten Jahrhundert,
Veröffentlichungen des Vereins für Pfälzische Kirchengeschichte, 9 (Speyer,
1963), p. 65.

were antecedents as well as parallels to Edwards' programmatic proposal for

a divinity in "an entire new method being thrown into the form of a history."

We have also seen that this formal principle itself could be understood in

divergent ways. For our study it is therefore not as important to know if

and to what extent Edwards was aware of these and other instances of the

principle of the historical order. The subsequent inquiry will rather

explore how novel an application of this formal principle Edwards intended

to put forth. In pursuit of this goal, we shall as it were go one step

behind the draft as well as the outline of the History of the Work of

Redemption in order to locate the material principles of Edwards' emergent

system. For this purpose we shall concentrate largely, though not exclu-

sively, on the interpretation of arguments from his treatise, Chief End for

which God Created the World. This approach is methodologically consistent

with the findings of the last chapter where the historiographical and prac-

tical consequences of Scripture as a coherent view of history had been made

explicit in a similar indirect way.

The treatise itself was most orderly in design, most abstract in its

level of thought, and somewhat incomplete in its execution. Each of these

aspects is both advantageous and disadvantageous for an adequate

understanding.

Edwards divided the treatise into two chapters and an introduction.

Within the chapters he provided subsections. The subsections in turn were

often numerically ordered or transitions in the argument were made clear

otherwise. The introduction was devoted to an extensive and intensive

clarification of the term end (pp. 443-450). The first chapter consisted

of a statement of the thesis (p. 452) which was summarized with the brief

phrase that God did not forget himself in his creation (p. 456). This statement was followed by a detailed argument from reason in support of the thesis that included two subsections (pp. 457-466). The subsequent section answered objections to the argument (pp. 467-481) and aided in the clarification of the argument. The second chapter dealt almost exclusively with the argument from revelation or Scripture (pp. 481-575). This part culminated in an exegesis of the terms glory and name (pp. 515-524) and concluded in a section that summarized lines of reasoning from both chapters (pp. 526-533).

The great advantage of this clear design is that it becomes possible to define quite clearly to which section an interpreter refers. By the same token, this clarity made it easier to select according to considerations which ignore or neglect the unity of the treatise. P. Miller, for example, was of the opinion that "the second half of Concerning the End for Which God Created the World is a study of what may be learned from Scripture. Fixing upon texts which the Arminians were constantly citing, Edwards argued them in a literalistic -- and to us unrewarding -- vein, elaborating still one more polemic against his foes."[1] It is nothing less than ironic that in one of Edwards' most clearly organized treatises it should be so easy simply to read out one chapter despite the fact that it provided a series of propositions that form a key to this "literalistic vein." Perry Miller was a master of the literary interpretation of the New England sources of the seventeenth and early eighteenth centuries, but he could not or did not see that significant parts of this literature arose out of a sophisticated study and interpretation of Scripture.[2]

---

[1] P. Miller, Jonathan Edwards, p. 297.

[2] Miller's verdict on Edwards' use of Scripture and its obsolescence was not an isolated instance. In fact, in The New England Mind, the Seventeenth Century, he was even more outspoken on this subject. Because of

Miller's influence on Puritan studies and because we have advanced a different view it seemed appropriate to collate some of Miller's statements
on the subject, for in the course of using Scripture as the negative foil
Miller also summarized some of the main principles of his own interpretation of New England Puritanism. Miller wrote:

> The colonial leaders believed that they had Scripture on their side,
> yet careful analysis [sic] of their arguments show again and again that
> the polity was established upon the Bible only at several removes, only
> after the Bible had been pressed by logic to yield up deductions which
> are not always obvious in the texts, or else it was established openly
> upon the laws of reason and nature upon the political ideas of contract
> and government by consent [p. 461].

The Puritans were not intentionally hypocritical, "but while they
were sincere, precisely because their sincerity was uninhibited by any
'higher criticism' or by any sense of the relativity of logic, they proceeded all the more freely to interpret the Bible with methods supplied by
the intellectual heritage" [p. 461]. Miller named three such ingredients
of the intellectual heritage in particular: "Piety," the tremendous thrust
of the Reformation, "The Living force of theology" [sic]. The other two
elements were the "deep and worldless sense of the tribe," and "newer political and economic forces." Therefore, Puritan thinking about church polity
as a "system" testifies not so much to a profound reading of the New
Testament as to a profound response to "several forces molding the thinking
of all men in the seventeenth century" [p. 440]. Miller concluded that
"were we to take them at their word, and assume that the only determinants
in their thinking had been the Bible and logic, we should be justified in
dismissing the whole enterprise as an eccentric, fantastic, and absurd per-
version of Holy Writ" [p. 440]. This statement was topped only by one
other final comment which did not only read between the lines but inverted
the evidence from between those lines: "The so-called Bible commonwealths
of New England were Biblical only insofar as an intellectual heritage, which
was not Calvinist [sic], nor even Christian in origin, determined the meaning of the Bible" p. 439 .

The determinative tradition which Miller had in mind was the influence
of the Renaissance -- George M. Marsden ("Perry Miller's Rehabilitation of
the Puritans," Church History, 39, 1970, pp. 91-105) has shown how Miller's
rehabilitation proceeded at the expense of minimizing Scripture, systematic
doctrine, Christology, and the influence of Calvin. Marsden particularly
emphasized the blatant evidential inaccuracies of Miller's references to
Calvin and his consequent claim for doctrines like the covenant of grace
in the development of thought which cannot be maintained in such a one-sided
manner [pp. 97, 103]. Marsden's defense of "biblicism" in Puritanism was a
minor aspect of his critique of Miller. A neglect of Calvin can be proved
more easily, but it also seems that church historians by a critique of
Miller's critique would like to make their case for the Puritans as Christians
rather than renaissance intellectuals. Over against such a tradition of
ignorant as well as fair criticism of the role of Scripture in New England

The language of the treatise is abstract or, as Edwards preferred to say, it was "indistinct." Hopkins in his preface to the posthumously published edition referred to this when he said that "the manner in which these subjects are treated is something above the level of common readers."[1] In this treatise Edwards played the role of the theologian's theologian which made his purpose quite different from the catechetical intentions of Samuel Willard. Since much of the vocabulary used is archaic to us, the indistinct nature of the language keeps the treatise also somewhat above our level and makes it easy to hold on to whatever seems most comprehensible to us. Beyond this initial stage of difficulties, however, the abstract character of the treatise also means that it opens up to the persistent student a wide range of "second meanings." Abstraction therefore is not equivalent to empty forms or dead and dry conceptions, but to density in the way in which an abstract mathematical formula yields expected and unexpected deductions. This may be a risky comparison, but laborious attempts to move beyond the hermeneutical barrier that separates Edwards from us have indeed shown glimpses of a mind capable of concentration and vision.

Samuel Hopkins also mentioned that in the _Miscellanies_ there were ideas related to the subject discussed in the treatise.[2] That the treatise was not complete is apparent even from internal evidence. Thus Edwards made several attempts[3] at explaining the meaning of "communication through

---

Puritanism must be understood the surprise on the part of Alan B. Howard when he discovered that "here, as in so much of _Plymouth Plantation_, the use of Scriptural and historical models does not simply divert Bradford's gaze from the world of nature to that of idea." ("Art and History," p. 265.)

[1] Edwards, _Works_, I, p. 441.

[2] _Ibid._, pp. 441-442.

[3] _Ibid._, pp. 466, 531f.

eternity" without a clear resolution of the question involved. This incompleteness coexisted with structural order in the treatise, and it is not to be confused with the abstractness of the language.

In the Chief End for Which God Created the World Edwards set about a doctrinal interpretation of the view of the end. We shall deal with this subject and its bearing on Edwards' view of history by focusing on seven related aspects of the same question. The delineation of the state of the question will deal with his view of doctrine and its history. His affirmation of doctrines of revelation will lead to an exploration of the type of argument that he thinks has successfully been used in order to settle doctrinal issues. The definition of the question will lead both into the ecclesiastic context and the logical questions of the end and present an unsatisfactory attempt that tried to deal with the issue of the end. The Scriptural foundation of the question will first establish Edwards' exegetical credentials, present his exegesis of glory, and view it in the light of Protestant Orthodoxy and modern exegesis. A discussion of the question of the conceptualization of the end will be prepared by a paraphrase of all the issues involved. The conceptualization of the end will be prepared by a paraphrase of all the issues involved. The conceptualization of the question and its operation as the integrating principle will then lead to a presentation of the consequences for the range of Edwards' view of history and the consequences for systematic theology.

The Place of Doctrine

The Enlightenment helped shape our view of dogma as something negative and detrimental to morality. "Dogmatic" is either considered to be hostile or naive. In the first case it "refers to a belief or opinion that is handed down by authority as true and indisputable and usually connotes arbitrariness, arrogance, etc."[1] In the latter case it can be said that "the dogmas of the quiet past are inadequate to the stormy present."[2] Since the Enlightenment achieved a consensus that there were certain fundamental truths that are self-evident, the artificial formulation of doctrines or precepts for morality became dispensable.

Edwards joined the critique of arbitrariness that had come to be associated with doctrine. He objected to doctrines which were made into a means of coercion rather than of conviction. His criticism therefore concerned not a rejection of all doctrine or of the notion of doctrine in itself, but it referred to the manipulation of doctrine for political purposes and its elimination as a means of interpretation. Whenever that happened, doctrine became a tool of governance rather than a means toward grace and glory. The end of doctrine was redemption, not repression. For this reason doctrine was an expression of saving religion and it was the relation to this center that gave it its authority. S. Willard made the same point when he pointed out that a body of divinity was "necessary for ministers of the Gospel for their profitable preaching, and helped to reduce all their doctrines to the proper foundational article they relate to."[3] Willard seemed to presuppose that every minister has some favorite articles of his own which will, however, falsify his preaching if they are not related to the center. Jonathan Edwards charged the "papists" for their "fiery zeal" with which they "insist

---

[1] Webster New World Dictionary, College Edition (New York: World Publishing Company, 1964), p. 429.

[2] Abraham Lincoln, as quoted in American Heritage Dictionary of the English Language (New York: American Heritage Publishing Company, 1969), p. 388.

[3] Willard, A Compleat Body, p. 1.

on the profession of a great number of doctrines, and several of the doctrines of pure revelation as the Trinity, etc." for the sake of the "domin-
ion of their hierarchy over man's faith."[1] He rejected a triad of tradition
tyranny, and trinity, as we might put it, for the doctrine of the trinity
which he mentioned was often turned into a loyalty test or oath simply for
the maintenance of the particular tradition handed down from former generations. This criticism was followed by a kind of self-criticism, for Edwards
concluded his observation: "Some Protestants have a zeal for doctrines from
like views, doctrines indeed for which they have no great value in themselves considered."[2] Edwards has thus committed himself to the explication
of doctrine in relation to the center of "saving religion." In order to
avoid all misunderstandings at this point, it must be insisted that this
emphasis on a center for doctrinal interpretation was not the end, but the
beginning of dogmatic theology. Edwards did not share an attitude of contemporary and later Pietists that such an evangelical center made doctrinal
interpretation a metaphysical luxury. The evangelical religion as a center
was not something that could be taken for granted, not even as a pious
possession. The center of this religion was dynamic and to assume possession of such a center of value could become indistinguishable from a rationa
self-evident principle. The aversion to or refusal of a closer elaboration
of the content and circumference of such a center of value was inconsistent
with the affirmation of the power that this center radiated.

We can take the rejection of doctrine as a political expedient one
step further and say that such an abuse was inconsistent with the fact

---

[1] Edwards, _Works_, VIII, p. 256.

[2] _Ibid._

that doctrines do have a history when they are related to and understood
in terms of evangelical religion. This notion is quite important for an
understanding of the intent of The Chief End for Which God Created the
World.

In his writings on the revival, Edwards noted that, on the one hand,
unlike the apostles who were infallible, he must find out the right way
through history, experience, and error. On the other hand, however, he
also recognized that the apostles themselves still did not know fundamental
things even about the revelation they themselves had received.[1] In Edwards'
treatise on the trinity we find the idea that the churches in the course of
their history were told "more about the incarnation and the Satisfaction
of Christ and other Gospel doctrines."[2] He did not elaborate where, when,
and how this happened, in the particular case of the "Gospel doctrines"
mentioned. However, since these were examples that he introduced in order
to justify his own interpretation of the trinity, we might say that Edwards
was of the opinion that his time was the occasion for such advancement and
that he himself was the interpreter.[3] In a more general way he represented
the times at which the center of evangelical religion is seen in different
doctrines in terms of a man who walks toward an object in nature:

> He that looks on a plant, or the parts of the bodies of animals, or
> any other works of nature, at a great distance where he has but an
> obscure sight of it, may see something in it wonderful and beyond his

---

[1] The Great Awakening, p. 320,449.

[2] An Unpublished Essay of Edwards on the Trinity, G. P. Fisher, ed.
(New York: Scribner's, 1903), p. 129.

[3] Ibid., p. 128: "I humbly apprehend that the things that have been
observed increase the number of visible mysteries in the Godhead in no other
manner than as by them we perceive that God has told us much more about it
than was before generally observed."

comprehension, but he that is near to it and views them narrowly indeed understands more about them, has a clearer and distinct sight of them, and yet the number of things that are wonderful and mysterious in them that appear to him are much more than before, and, if he views them with a microscope, the number of the wonders that he sees will be much increased still. But yet the microscope gives him more of a true knowledge concerning them.[1]

Three different postures of the observer were mentioned and the obscure sight that was obtained far away from the object was taken to be characteristic of the times of the Old Testament.

When we now return to The Chief End for Which God Created the World World we see Edwards mention two more doctrines:

Nor is it to be supposed that mankind--who, while destitute of revelation, by the utmost improvements of their own reason, and advances in science and philosophy, could come to no clear and established determination who the author of the world was--would ever have obtained any tolerable settled judgment of the end which the author of it proposed to himself in so vast, complicated, and wonderful a work of his hands.[2]

If Edwards did not specifically refer to author and end as "gospel doctrines" he clearly considered them to be doctrines of revelation. In this statement he made it clear that he was about to solve a problem: What revelation had done for a doctrine of the author of the universe he will now show on the basis of revelation to be accomplished for the doctrine of the end. What has been done and accomplished before in the case of one doctrine is to be done now for the other. As he put it before: the churches were to be told more about the end this time and Edwards will do it. Even his use of the microscope bears on our treatise here, for Edwards' microscopically minute exegesis of Scripture in this treatise increased both the mysteries and the knowledge of the end.

---

[1] An Unpublished Essay of Edwards on the Trinity, p. 129.

[2] Edwards, Works, I, 451

We have thus seen that Edwards believed that all doctrines must be related to evangelical religion as their center. What we see now in the case of The Chief End for Which God Created the World is that Edwards set out to develop another fundamental doctrine, but with a slight difference: this doctrine was not to be valued as any other in its relation to the center of value, but it was the center itself to which all others were to be related. Now at this time in history and in New England was the time when to set forth the "foundational article" of evangelical religion: "Revelation not only gives us the foundation and first principles of all learning, but it gives us the end, the only end, that would be sufficient to move a man to the pursuit."[1]

The self-confidence with which Edwards put the state of the question is borne out in an academic and scholarly way by a review of the actual treatment of the doctrine of the last judgment in the textbook tradition of Protestant Orthodoxy. In his survey of the field in which he drew on examples from both Lutheran and Reformed theologians, James P. Martin came to the conclusion that "if we may speak of an orthodox understanding of history, it must be in general restricted to an interest in the history of the salvation of the individual."[2] He pointed out that both the synthetic and analytic methods with their respective causal and theological emphases led to inadequate elaborations of a doctrine of the end as an integrated part of a system. In the former case he observed that the end was simply looked upon as a result. In the case of the other approach

---

[1] Edwards, Works, VIII, p. 143.

[2] James P. Martin, The Last Judgment in Protestant Theology from Orthodoxy to Ritschl (Grand Rapids, Mich.: Eerdmans, 1963), pp. 25-26.

244

he found only evidence for a switching of places so that the doctrine of
the end would be moved up from the end of the system and be placed in the
vicinity of such other doctrines as predestination or providence.[1] The out
come of such arrangements was not a greater integration with other doctrine
and in those instances where the idea of the end did become the determinative principle of the system, the understanding of the end itself was
restricted to the goal of individual salvation. Therefore, the way in whic
the nature of the end as well as its scope had been treated within the text
book tradition left ample room for improvement and required considerable
rethinking in order to do justice to an understanding of history. Edwards'
decision to enter upon a systematical exploration of the doctrine of the
end was a major departure in the teaching about eschatology which included
the this-worldly interest of the postmillennial view, but did not stop ther

In concluding this section it is important to understand better what
Edwards meant by his assertion that revelation had successfully settled the
issue of the doctrine of the author of the universe. Such an illustration
of the import of his statement and an exposition of the argument that went
along with it will be facilitated by an excursus beyond the context of The
Chief End for Which God Created the World. To do so requires the presentation of an exegetical argument that will anticipate but not pre-empt our
separate consideration of the Scriptural interpretation of the end later
on; for this presentation will also establish a background against which it

---

[1]Martin, The Last Judgment in Protestant Theology, p. 7. The exampl
which Martin gave was that of the Lutheran theologian Georg Calixt (1589-
1656) who taught at the University of Helmstedt in Germany. He supported
the rapprochement between Protestants in theology. Because of these irenic
leanings he became the subject of great controversies in which he was
accused of syncretism.

can be seen not only that the doctrines of author and end were settled the same way, but also that in Edwards' thinking these two doctrines themselves could not rigidly be kept apart. We have quoted earlier the passage from The Chief End for Which God Created the World, in which Edwards stated that one of the achievements of revelation had been the "great attainments in the habitual exercise of reason." Revelation, as it were, had created its own civilization. Edwards did not deny that there were "advances in science and philosophy" apart from revelation, but he insisted that the two be not confused. He pointed out, for example, that the abolition of idolatry was the fulfillment of a prophecy to Israel as well as the outcome of a historical education of Israel that had come to fruition with the appearance of Jesus Christ.[1] From then on the abolition of idolatry could be taken for granted. In the draft for the History of the Work of Redemption he pointed out that the Deists[2] and Moslems as well as the Jews now owed their continued belief in the one and only God[3] to the contact with Christianity as the representative of revelation.

Edwards therefore rejected as false the Deist assertion that natural reason was sufficient to arrive at the notion of the one and only God. The Indians of America,[4] for example, had lived far away from civilization for thousands of years, but they had not arrived at a position comparable to that of the Deists. On the contrary, the Indians drew their beliefs from a sense of "tradition and history," and did not follow an "imaginary light"[5]

---

[1] Works, VIII, p. 145.

[2] Ibid., pp. 124, 145, 188, 191.

[3] Works, V, pp. 200-201

[4] Works, VIII, p. 142.

[5] Ibid., p. 188.

of nature. Edwards' criticism of the discrepancy between the claims of
Deist theory and the facts as he knew them in this particular case amounted
to an inversion of the contemporary argument that revelation was a republi-
cation of nature: "If Christianity came too late into the world, what is
called natural religion came full as late; and there are no footsteps of
natural religion in any sense of the words to be found at this day, but
where Christianity hath been planted."[1] While the certainty with which the
Deist argument was put forward stemmed from revelation, its conceptualization in terms of natural religion, natural philosophy, or natural morality
was based on a circular reasoning that proved what it already assumed, but
could not admit because it studiously ignored the tradition of the particular Christian civilization in which and from which it lived. According to
Edwards, Deism talked about the human condition without reference to its
historical conditioning and therefore ended up to be more provincial and
less original than it conceived of itself.

Edwards formulated his position in even more sweeping and general
terms. According to him, observations in the field of social morality show
that "no legislator ever founded his scheme of government on any supposed
dictates of nature, but always on some pretended or real revelation."[2] The
crucial question therefore was one between genuine and false revelation and
not one between reason and revelation. As far as the whole issue of the
dictates of nature was concerned, he also stated in one of his Miscellanies
that "there has never been any trial how it would be with mankind in this
respect without having anything from revelation."[3] Edwards backed up this

---

[1]Works, VIII, p. 195.

[2]Ibid., p. 188.

[3]Ibid., p. 142.

thesis with two related arguments which culminated in a third still more
basic view that in turn provided the presupposition for his thinking of
natural religion in historical terms and which also showed that an argument
like that of the doctrine of the author achieved its full force only because
for Edwards the beginning implied the end.

In a pointed way, Edwards stated that at the time of the Old Testament
it had been the example of the "practices and principles" of Israel as the
"light of nations"[1] and not the consequences of a thinking along the lines
of the light of nature which had supported "the neighboring nations in remembrance of traditions which they had from their forefathers and so kept them
from degeneration so much as otherwise they would have done." Thus, for
example, wise men from these neighboring nations would travel and transplant
from Israel what they thought fit. The character and authority of those
ancestral traditions was nevertheless not something worthless or inferior,
for it pointed back to the "ancient founders of nations."[2] Edwards stated
that the "Chinese, descended probably from the subjects of Noah, that holy
man, have held more by tradition from him than other nations, and so have
been a more civilized people."[3] The degree of a nation's civilization therefore either depended on the tenacity of adherence to a corporate memory that
went back to a crucial juncture in the History of the Work of Redemption or
the corporate memory as the root of such civilizations needed the proximity
to the supportive influence of a particular stage of the work of redemption
as it became manifest successively in Israel and Christianity. In both cases
nations "had a great deal more of truth in matters of religion and morality,
than ever human reason would have discovered without help."[4]

---

[1]Works, VIII, p. 142.

[2]Ibid., p. 244.   [3]Ibid., p. 142.   [4]Ibid., p. 224.

248

In the draft for the History of the Work of Redemption, Edwards mentioned sacrifice as that tradition of which it could be said that "no nation
however barbarous, was without it."[1] In this case it did not matter how far
away a nation was located from Israel, because the institution or sacrifice
had preceded the levitical laws and the very existence of Israel itself.
Through Noah, the father of nations, who had received this divine institution from his ancestors, the custom of sacrifice had passed on to all
"founders of nations." Since sacrifice was a type of Christ's sacrifice and
since the purpose of this institutional type was to establish the necessity
for an atonement of sin, "all nations of the world had their minds possessed with this notion, that an atonement for sin was necessary." Such
consent of "all the heathen nations" as well as such a diffusion of sacrifice as a genuine revelatory tradition throughout all religions contributed
to make this institution for Edwards the prototype of every argument on the
relation of revelation and natural religion, for "it need not seem strange
that what natural religion they had amongst them, came the same way."[2]
In this way typology itself appeared in a universal protological role which,
for example, allowed Edwards to go over the field of Roman history for types

The significance of the role which Edwards assigned to sacrifice
will become more evident, if we see it in the light of conclusions that
Claus Westermann arrived at in an exegesis of Genesis 1-11. According to
Westermann, past research on the creation stories in Genesis had dwelt primarily on questions of their literary dependence on or uniqueness over
against the creation myths of the ancient civilizations of Egypt and
Mesopotamia. An increased and more general knowledge of the history of

---

[1] Works, V, p. 27.

[2] Ibid., p. 142.

religions has shown that parallels to these stories were far more widespread, that equivalents also occurred in preliterate societies, that the
total number of possible motifs was limited, and that in all of Genesis
1-11 a great concentration of these motifs had come together that made
these chapters the "traditions of all peoples which are bound as such to
no special people or culture."[1] Westermann therefore referred to this part
of Genesis as "primal history" and described the universal view contained
in it as the background against which the "special history of God with his
elect people" is possible, and because of which the special history itself
"can flow into a final event which again widens into the universal end
history of mankind and the world."[2]

In a similar manner history for Edwards in the draft for the History
of the Work of Redemption began after the fall and the expulsion from para-
dise. From here he proceeded to the interpretation of stories which showed
that, despite the guilt and limitation incurred by the fall, man lived on
and precipitated through his actions the dissolution of the universal dimension with which the History of the Work of Redemption had begun. The incident that marked this watershed in history was the unsuccessful attempt to
raise the tower of Babel. At the same time, however, that the work of
redemption focused more narrowly on the salvation history of Israel, the
universal dimension remained throughout as the hope of the end. Edwards
described two stages of separation in the history of Israel. The first
state commenced with Abraham's founding of the family church. But Abraham

---

[1]Claus Westermann, "Creation and History in the Old Testament,"
The Gospel and Human Destiny (Minneapolis: Augusburg Publishing House, 1971),
p. 16.

[2]Ibid., p. 17.

received a promise of numerous posterity which Edwards understood in terms
of the prophecy of Isaiah as a prediction of the "future victory which the
church shall obtain over the nations of the world."[1] The second state of
separation led to the even more restricted establishment of a national
church by Moses. The very exclusiveness of this church and the subsequent
rejection of the nations came about in Edwards' view of the matter as a
preparation for an end that would include Jews as well as Gentiles. This
paradoxical interconnection[2] of the universal and the particular in the
draft for the History of the Work of Redemption can be best defined in
Edwards' own words which came to him originally through the Platonist
tradition: "Here is both an emanation, and remanation."[3]

An understanding of Genesis 1-11 which exploited the various nuances
of this text had not been the rule in the history of theology which was
mostly committed to an exposition of chapters 1-3 in general and to an
interpretation of the fall itself in terms of a one-sided view of guilt
which discouraged the development of its relation to history and focused on
how much or how little man had lost of his original natural ability to know
of God. Westermann set forth the different nuances in Genesis 3-11 by using
the tools of modern source criticism and tradition history:

> P merely makes the point that mankind was very corrupt.... While J
> says the same thing in a series of stories which tell of the offenses,
> each the violation of imposed limits, for which God punishes man. In
> each case the punishment is a limitation of human existence, but man is
> allowed to go on living.[4]

---

[1] Works, V, p. 45.   [2] Ibid., pp. 55-56.   [3] Works, I, p. 529.

[4] Claus Westermann, Beginning and End in the Bible, Ed. John Reumann,
Facet Books, Biblical Series, 31 (1969; Philadelphia: Fortress Press, 1972),
p. 13. P and J are the symbols used to designate the different sources and
traditions on which Genesis was based. P referred to the so-called priestly
source. J derived its name from the fact that this source consistently used
"Jahwe" as the name for God whereas still another source usually is referred
to as "E" because in it the name for God was "Elohim."

The repeated assertion of guilt on the one hand and its transformation into a theme of history in the form of stories represented two nuances
present throughout these chapters. The importance of Edwards' view of
sacrifice was that it was part of a historical understanding of these chapters and that it could therefore constitute a type that endured beyond the
dispersion and apostacy of the nations. Sacrifice as a type was therefore
a token that mediated the universal beginning with the universal end and
showed that even the most barbarous religions were not beyond the pale of
the History of the Work of Redemption. On the "Ruins of Revelation" on
which heathendom was built there remained the reminder of the reconstitution of mankind. The atonement to which the type of the sacrifice pointed
was the anticipated at-onement of all nations in one church. If, as Edwards
maintained, sacrifice was the prototype of doctrines of natural religion
such as the being of God and providence, then the definition of these doctrines in terms of typological knowledge could not be isolated from a history, the peculiar characteristic of which it was to point continually to
its own end.

The View of the End

In a consideration of the doctrine of the end, it is easy to draw a
false line of distinction between theory and practice. The authors of the
textbook tradition were not only the academic teachers of students whom they
sought to train to become learned ministers, but the teachers themselves
were ordained clergy who in their thinking and working responded to the
experience of the community of the church. In Puritan studies we have
learned much about the polity and philosophy of the New England Puritans,
but we know little and may never get to know enough about the significance

that the church qua church had for them and which, for example, made men
like Shepard and Edwards conceive of the millennium in terms of an ecclesiastic state. J. P. Martin's selection of the textbook tradition as his only
source of interpretation was therefore representative of a modern Protestant
attitude which identified the minister of the church with an intellectual
who addressed himself to society on his own behalf. Generalizations in the
study of history are necessary and undoubtedly the intellectualist tendencies and their concomitant dangers in Protestant Orthodoxy were real, but
if generalizations are taken too far they cease to be helpful and begin to
become tendentious. In a society where everyone still had his place and in
a culture that delighted in classifications or logic, even the textbook
could claim and did command no more than one compartment of interest even
if a substantial one. This left room for other enterprises which in turn
could influence the questions to be raised and the forms to be adopted in
the systematic exposition or explication of theology itself. Samuel Willard
used the Westminster Assembly's Shorter Catechism because it had become
meaningful for and accepted in his own church; Edwards used the same catechism in order to instruct his own children,[1] and his treatise on The Chief
End for Which God Created the World did not only allude to but was mainly
concerned with the first question asked by this same catechism.

The catechisms in the seventeenth and early eighteenth centuries,
whether in New England or outside of it, constituted a diverse body of
literature which cannot easily be subjected to generalizations, for they
were all written out of particular situations. In this "endless variety"[2]

---

[1]S. Hopkins, "Memoirs," Works, I, p. 46.

[2]David D. Hall, The Faithful Shepard, A History of the New England
Ministry in the Seventeenth Century (Chapel Hill: University of North
Carolina Press, 1972), pp. 168-169.

we nevertheless find two examples which pointed systematic theology in a direction where the main concern would not be so much the attempt to integrate the doctrine of the end with the other doctrines and where the alternative of an inquiry into principles or a focus on the end arose in a different form. Since the time of Calvin's Geneva Catechism of 1542 which had found international dissemination the question as to the chief end had become the lead question for much catechism instruction. Out of the way in which this chief question was handled subsequently the problem had to arise sooner or later whether or how the doctrine of the end itself could be understood in a definite way. In order to illustrate this point, our first example is taken from Thomas Shepard's The Sum of the Christian Religion in Way of Question and Answer. The first two questions and their answers in this catechism ran as follows:

Question. What is the best and last end of man?

Answer. To Live to God (Rom. VL 10, 11. Gal. III. 9. 2 Cor V, 3, 15).

Question. How is man to live unto God?

Answer. Two ways, first, by faith in God (Ps. XXXVII. 3). Secondly, by observance of God (Eccl. XII, 13).[1]

The answer to the lead question and the emphasis on faith and sanctification put into catechism form the issue which had agitated the generation of New Englanders to whom Shepard belonged and which in its preparationist resolution became a part of New England orthodoxy. On the other hand, the Westminster Assembly's Shorter Catechism began:

---

[1]Shepard, Works, I, p. 337. This catechism went through five editions between 1648 and 1747. See Wilberforce Eames, Early New England Catechisms, A Bibliographical Account of Some Catechisms Published Before the Year 1800 (Worcester, Mass.: Charles Hamilton, 311 Main Street, 1898), pp. 32-34.

Question. What is the Chief end of man?

Answer.   Man's chief end is to glorify God and enjoy him forever.[1]

Here the emphasis was not so much on grace, but on glory as the end and

consequently the situation of the church required that the "affair of

Christian theology" take up and work out this problem of the end.

There was general agreement that the importance of the question of

the end went beyond the convenience of its affirmation in the context of

catechism instruction. Shepard, for example, tried to **recall** for his

parishioners their own experiences when he addressed them:

> Nay, you know that whatever we make our last end, it will swallow
> up all our desires after any other thing. This is the center, and
> rest, and journey's end of our tired, weary spirits. And the truth
> is, when we make it our last end, we cannot but desire it.[2]

Samuel Willard in turn pointed to the metaphysical necessity of the notion

of the end because man "must have a last end, else he can never be happy;

for if it were an infinite subordination in his ends, he could never be

happy; he could never come to his Resting Place, but must be an Everlasting

Seeker, wandering in his endless quest."[3] If there was no last end there

will be the more dead ends and continual motion without any aim or goal:

"Such an end there must be, or man can never be blessed; because he could

never come to his Resting Place, but must be left in a labyrinth and carried

in an endless Pursuit of Happiness."[4] Ralph Cudworth, on the other hand,

was engaged in the refutation of what he considered to be an atheistic

---

[1]S. Willard, A Compleat Body, p. 1.

[2]Shepard, Works, II, 161.

[3]Willard, op. cit.

[4]Ibid., p. 1.

caricature of the idea of the end by Thomas Hobbes whom he describes as
saying:

> When men going on further and further, and making a continual
> progress, without seeing any end before them, being at length quite
> weary and tired out with their endless journey, they sit down, and
> call the thing by this hard and unintelligible name, infinite.[1]

Beyond the agreement on the importance of the question, there was, however,
also a need for a clarification of the term end itself.

Samuel Willard distinguished between end and ends. According to
him, the "chief end" which makes possible a pursuit of happiness takes for
granted that "a man may have _diverse_ ends which he proposeth to himself in
his actions." He engaged in such ends "lawfully and regularly" and Willard
suggests that such ends are not simply only means. Such ends include man's
different roles in both church and state and in his involvement in the
"divers arts and sciences." He characterizes these ends as

> _Intermediate Ends_, some [of which] may be subordinate, others may
> be co-ordinate, but the _Last_ will admit of no Compeer: and as the
> _Chief_ is but _One_, so it is not a thing compounded but single: it
> cannot be made of the Meeting of Divers in One; for that which is com-
> pounded, is indeed manifold; and except there were an equality between
> those things so concurring, they cannot be of a like Weight: and
> therefore the One must needs stand in Subordination to the other.[2]

Willard's description of the end and the ends stood out both for its solemnity and practicality. To these aspects Jonathan Edwards added a note of
subtlety in a short but complex definition of the end. This definition
appeared outside of the introductory chapter of the treatise and showed more
clearly while more casually the aspects that Edwards absorbed into the notion
of the end in the description of the man Christ at the commencement of his
sufferings:

---

[1] The Cambridge Platonists, p. 223.

[2] Willard, A Compleat Body, p. 4.

> Now, it is the <u>end</u> that supports the agent in any difficult work
> that he undertakes, and above all others, his <u>ultimate</u> and supreme end;
> for this is above all others valuable in his eyes; and so, sufficient
> to countervail the difficulty of the means. That end which ultimately
> terminates his desires, is the center of rest and support; and so must
> be the fountain and sum of all the delight and comfort he has in his
> prospects with regard to his work.[1]

Some of the various shades of meaning of the term end here are: it is the
goal of striving, the view of prospects, the point of spatial and chronological termination, the fulfillment and result ("sum"), the center of
rest. It is intention, execution, termination, and result.

Such a view of the end made it all the more demanding to furnish a
definition or formula that would avoid "confusion" as Edwards himself said.
The affirmations Willard made notwithstanding, he talked about more than
he actually dealt with: which of the intermediate ends were coordinate and
which were subordinate? What was the difference between a subordinate and
a coordinate end? What did he mean by his observation that if there was an
"equality between those things so concurring" they would be of "like weight"
and lead to a positive "meeting of divers in One"? Did he polemicize,
reject, or rhetorically concede another possibility besides the one presented to him? In the somewhat aphoristic way in which Edwards set out on
his exploration of terms, this particular echo in Willard came into focus:
"Though the chief end be always an ultimate end, yet every ultimate end is
not always a chief end."[2] That is to say, the sentence was not reversible,
but in order for it to make any sense, Edwards must press toward a clearer
definition of the "ultimate." Otherwise it remained doubtful if "ultimate"
could retain its meaning over against "chief" in such a way as to be not

[1]Edwards, <u>Works</u>, I, pp. 494-495.

[2]<u>Ibid.</u>, p. 443.

only semantically but also functionally more than "subordinate." Edwards
defined an ultimate end as "that which the agent seeks, in what he does,
for its own sake." An ultimate end was thus something which was valued
on its own account and not for any further end besides it. It was the difference between loving a person because of the person itself and not because
of the person's reputation that could be channelled in such a way as to promote one's own good. Consequently, the opening statement by Edwards aimed
at proving that there was the chief end that was valuable on its own account
and that there were also ends which were valuable on their own account.
The chief end and the ends could thus no longer be understood to function
in a relationship of the subordination of the many under the one, for the
chief end and the ends all came to be within the same sphere of ultimacy
in which the ends were inferior, but not subordinate. The ends had
identities, but they were not identical with the chief end. Edwards spoke
also of higher and lower, more and less within such ultimacy. There were,
as he put it, "two sorts of ultimate ends" which were differentiated in
terms of degree rather than of kind, because they were within the same
sphere of ultimacy. In order to bring out this differentiation more clearly
beyond what was said in the initial somewhat aphoristic thesis, Edwards
called these two sorts of ultimate ends an original, absolute, independent
ultimate end and a consequent, hypothetical ultimate end respectively. The
way the word hypothetical is used here in disjunction with absolute suggested that Edwards here used the language of Orthodox scholastics in talking about the decree and rephrased the language in such a way that the
expression "chief" is replaced by the more suggestive nomenclature of the

"original ultimate end" which he said will be what he means when in the
treatise he speaks of end in the "highest sense." Both ultimate ends were
related; they were the same in different respects. Within this ultimacy
the consequent presupposed an occasion, the absolute did not.

Edwards had thus provided a definition by means of which Willard's
"coordinate" ends became more than simply a rhetorical flourish. The question of the one and many was resolved by giving something to each, but
Edwards went even further. In proposition 5, which contained the differentiation of the two ultimate ends, Edwards radicalized the issue by putting
the question of the one and the many on the level of the absolute itself.
If thus far it was possible at least to assume that he spoke of one original ultimate end and several consequent ultimate ends, he had now gone one
step further and had sharpened the issue under consideration as a basis for
subsequent argument. He wrote:

> If there be but one thing that is originally, and independent of any
> future supposed cases agreeable to God, to be obtained by the creation
> of the world, then there can be but one last end of God's work, in this
> highest sense, but if there are various things, properly diverse from
> one another, that are absolutely and independently agreeable to the
> Divine Being, which are actually obtained by the creation of the world,
> then there were several ultimate ends of the creation in that highest
> sense.[1]

Edwards thus epitomized the metaphysical problem of the relationship of the
one and the many which will engage his skills in the treatise itself, but
which also prompts the question whether he can come up with a model of
thought that will give substance to and deliver on the promises made in
these subtle logical distinctions. In order to set the stage for a clearer
understanding of Edwards' own argument, we shall proceed e contrario and

---

[1] Edwards, Works, I, p. 450.

inquire what, if any, model Samuel Willard used and in how far the question
of the many received positive consideration from him.

In what follows we shall entertain only such arguments as relate
to Willard's doctrine of God. In his systematic exposition, Willard took
his departure from the statement in the Pentateuch that Moses only saw the
back parts of God. Only this part of God could be the subject of theology.
The part apart from the back parts remained unknown and incomprehensible.
This distinction was very important. It functioned like the theme in a
fugue by Bach. It was announced at the beginning, and while the music
developed it reoccurred in all kinds of different shapes throughout. Some
were more easily identifiable than others. The Ramist structure of
Willard's Body of Divinity was like a frame in which these variations were
carried out. To change metaphors, it could perhaps be said that the
methodical arrangement of his catechism was like the instrument on which
Willard could vary the theme. The exposition provides him with the keyboard
on which to play.

The object of faith was God. When Willard talked about God, he distinguished between what God is and what God does, between God's all-
sufficiency and his all-efficiency. The former was "his divine fulness, by
virtue whereof he hath enough in himself to answer all his own ends."[1] This
sufficiency or fulness in turn was described as essence and subsistence,
which corresponded to the other pairs of being and mode of being, oneness
and variety, essence and existence. The former dealt with the deity, the
latter dealt with the trinity:

---

[1]Willard, A Compleat Body, p. 46.

> Man, as he is a <u>reasonable</u> creature, stands in need of a Deity to
> make him happy; and as he is a <u>sinner</u> he wants a <u>Trinity</u> to save him:
> and we have both these fully displayed to us in Scripture. The
> essence is first in order to be considered of; and that because the
> Godhead is the ultimate object of our Faith; it must ascend thither,
> and rest there. The Absolute Being of God is the subject of all his
> relations and we believe in all the Divine Persons, because they are
> God. Joh 14, 1.[1]

When Willard took up the question of the one and many, he did so

under the heading of essence as well as dealing with it in terms of the

subsistences or persons of God. In the first case, his main concern was

with the attributes of God. Of these attributes he stated that they "may

more properly be said to be ascribed to him than to be really in him."[2]

The attributes were real in our minds and likewise they were distinct from

each other conceptually. In being itself, however, any gradation or contra

diction would argue changeability and therefore any differences of attri-

butes such as they existed conceptually were to be excluded, for essence

and being were "devoid of composition." Willard compared the attributes

to words that make up a name, but it seemed as though the words were in our

minds and the name was in God and if there was a way by means of which the

two met it happened when all words were forgotten in order to get to the

name! Was such a view of essence and the one not actually a way to say

that it was not only independent but also something other than its attri-

butes? His thinking on the one emerged more clearly when he set out to

define the difference between the three persons of the Godhead. Tradi-

tionally, the notion of "relations" in connection with the trinity were

used as a way to describe that there was an order in the Godhead:

---

[1] Willard, <u>A Compleat Body</u>, p. 49.

[2] <u>Ibid</u>., p. 50.

A relation is less than an Essence, and yet it is more than a
thing merely rational: it is True, though it be not essential:
things differ <u>really</u>, when there are Two Essences, <u>Rationally</u> when
the Difference is only in our Conception: <u>Modally</u> or <u>Relatively</u>,
when the Being itself differs from the several respects that it
bears.[1]

While we have seen that in the case of the attributes differences
occurred only conceptually but not really, we find now that Willard outlined a gradation of reality in order to keep all gradation out of the
Godhead and of being. Thus, between essence and concept there was a third
which was more than a concept and less than an essence. Willard in fact
suggested a modalist doctrine of the trinity. The reason why he did so
was as interesting as the conclusions that followed from it. We have quoted
that he thought that the three persons were part of the scripture testimony
while at the same time he was committed to a concept of being that did not
allow for any variety except for sheer modes of being: "Thus a <u>man</u> differs
modally from himself considered as a man, and as a master, and as a servant."
The essence of man was hid behind the masks of man, master, and servant.
He offered this as a <u>vestigium trinitatis</u> and continued to show that in the
case of God the Father there was no such thing as fatherhood, but this
designation father held only in relation to the Son.[2] In brief, the slight
increase in "essentiality" that he was forced into by Scripture did not take
away anything from his view that the one was single and uncompounded.

Willard consequently had to defend the trinity as an "article merely
of faith" which is "above the comprehension of human understanding" and when
the question arose, "How can these things be?" he had to rely that "Faith
must silence the Uprisings of Carnal Reason."[3] The irony of this statement

[1]Willard, <u>A Compleat Body</u>, p. 98.

[2]Ibid.   [3]Ibid., p. 97.

was that the same reason all along argues from a concept of essence which
did not allow any diversity in being. The trinity became something supernatural which was not only above reason but was presented as being against
reason, at least against a reason that was morally of dubious standing.

Since the three persons were something that could only be believed
and not known, the work of redemption was a mode or mask; or, to put it in
more technical terms: the work of the trinity in redemption was economical
only and not ontological. We do not have to enquire into the works of
creation and providence, for they belong to the deity, not the trinity.
Redemption may and did happen "in the Concrete, and not in the Abstract."[1]
For in the abstract Willard followed a view of the deity that was unrelated
to redemption. If we now try to summarize the argument, we can say this:
In the order of essence there was a deity which was one and to whom belonged
the work of creation and providence. In the order of subsistences there
was a trinity to whom belonged the work of redemption. In the case of the
first no history was desirable or necessary because the deity was one and
difference and change were unreal. In the latter case some existence of
change was admitted, otherwise conversion as the beginning of redemption
could not be explained. If conversion was a new birth, then differences had
to exist. But still in this particular case, history was not possible since
we only believe and do not know.

Only insofar as Scripture was included into the argument did he admit
the consideration of a positive minimum of history. Willard, as it were,
set the end so high and made the divine being so independent that the essential and real things remained hidden and secret. This did not happen becaus

---

[1]Willard, A Compleat Body, p. 98.

an affirmation of the historical process and its variety had wiped out the possibility of knowing unity metaphysically, but because history was not essential to this unity. In the final analysis, the two ends of grace and glory did not meet in Willard's exposition. In it a general view of the historical world remained a mask or mode. In his thinking, history was a kind of twilight that was flanked on the one side by an essence and that became most concrete on the other side in the individual life stories of saints. There was one God who was something other than his attributes and there was a triune God who was something different from what he did.

End and Exegesis

In the case of Thomas Shepard we had seen that a passage in Scripture had to be understood in terms of its scope. Edwards, in addition, was concerned with a general formulation of a view of the end itself. These exegetical and metaphysical concerns merged in Edwards' analysis of glory. In the Edwards corpus this interpretation of glory was not the outcome of an isolated or random exegetical effort, but it occurred against a broad spectrum of detailed observations of great variety as his Notes on the Bible show. It was this meticulous care that went into the inquiry of the literal sense in any given biblical context which led into mysteries and it was the persistent and gradual elaboration of themes and the clarification of terms which helped to build up that background of expertise and self-criticism that made it possible for him to exploit the one theme that permeated them all once he had worked it out. Typology was only one part of these efforts and in order to introduce the subject of glory and its significance for the understanding of history we shall therefore start out with a loosely connected series of five illustrations from the variegated exegetical process in which Edwards was involved.

264

The reading of Scripture did not simply confirm, but it also changed
Edwards' opinions. A good example for such a development occurred in his
explanation of the expression "in the ages to come" in two separate entries
of his Notes on the Bible, both of which referred to Chapter 2:7 of the
letter to the Ephesians in the New Testament.[1] The whole verse read:
"That in ages to come he (God) might show the exceeding riches of his
grace, in his kindness towards us through Christ Jesus." At first Edwards
arrived at the conclusion that the expression aimed at the "present and all
future ages" and at what was "brought to light for the last ages of the
world which were now begun." Then, however, "upon second thought," Edwards
found out that the phrase referred to eternity. In support of this change
of mind he quoted the Greek original: τοῖς αἰῶσι τοῖς ἐπερχομένοις.
He pointed out that in the New Testament αἰών by itself was mostly equivalent to "world," while ἐπερχόμενος or μέλλων always referred to the
"world to come." In his second note Edwards developed that insight more
fully. First he reassured himself of the history of interpretation on
this verse through an extract from the works of Thomas Goodwin. He then
went on to present his own reasons. The main difficulty with the text
proved not to be the assertion of eternity, but the plural form in which
it was described and which presented a question that had already occurred
to him in his first entry. How was it possible, so ran the objection now,
that there "are ages, in the plural, taken for the times after the day of
judgment to eternity, where there is no flux of time"? We can see now how
the reading of the phrase "ages to come" in terms of events relating to
this world was facilitated and determined by a philosophical presupposition

---

[1]Edwards, Works, IX, pp. 367-370.

which overrode part of the philological evidence. For this philosophical
attitude it was not possible to relate the "riches of grace" in this verse,
to anything but this world with its "flux of time." Edwards' own adherence
to the full meaning of his observations on the linguistic and semantic context required of him to oppose a position which defined the relation of
time and eternity in terms of a negative contrast between change and change-
lessness. Edwards described eternity positively with the biblical term
"age of ages" and the traditional Latin "secula seculorum."

Psalm 45[1] was a song which described the marriage of a king and his
spouse. In it Edwards found points of contact to the description of the
Shulamite in the Song of Songs. He ran down these similarities in considerable detail as a means to prove that the Song of Songs was canonical
and that its theme was the "union and mutual love of Christ and his church."
This indirect defense of canonicity included at the same time the correction
of a traditional neglect in the interpretation of the Song of Songs. According to Edwards the reference to the "conjugal embraces of the bridegroom"
and the spouse was not "liable to a bad construction," for a comparison with
the corresponding verses of the Psalm showed that "what is most naturally
understood as the most direct meaning" was not an "allegory or mystical meaning," but the view "that the spouse had not only glorious clothing, but was
yet more glorious in the parts of her body within her clothing, that were
hid by her clothing." Psalm 45 and the Song of Songs were "Songs of Love."
"In both the lovers spoken of are compared to a man and a woman, and their
love which arises between the sexes of mankind." Edwards did not give up
the spiritual interpretation of the two Songs of Love, but he changed the

---

[1]Edwards, Works, IX, pp. 203-206.

266

meaning of spiritual by including it in the this-worldly aspect of love
or the churches' existence. For Edwards the Psalm was a type and not an
allegory of the union of Christ and the church. Typology included rather
than excluded the story and thus helped to make the literal meaning of
the Song of Songs into more than simply a bad construction.

In a long piece with the somewhat misleading title "the Pentateuch
written by Moses,"[1] Edwards set out to show at length that the Old Testament
was no patchwork, but that in it events were minutely recorded over long
periods of time and that they cohered meaningfully. The same dedication
to observation that had characterized his essay on the spider and his
reporting on the revival was here applied to his interpretation of Scripture
itself which he approached descriptively through the "bare inspection of the
writings, as it stands."[2] In the course of this pursuit he analyzed the
"words of the covenant" in Deuteronomy 29 and identified five different
components in it:

1. "A history of the transaction."

2. "Moses' rehearsal of past transactions and wonderful dealings of
God with them, with reproofs for their insensibility and unaffectedness, as
introducing what he had further to say.

3. "He then proceeds to charge them to serve the true God and to
avoid idolatry."

4. "And then to enforce this charge with awful threatenings and
predictions of judgments that shall come upon them when they transgress,
with the circumstances of these judgments, and promises of forgiveness and
repentance."

---

[1] Edwards, Works, IX, pp. 1-37.

[2] Ibid., p. 15.

5. "And the whole concludes with various arguments, pressing
instances, solemn appeals, obtestations, exhortations to enforce their
duty."[1]

Edwards' method of procedure in this instance resembled that of
modern form criticism for he started out with an analysis of the smallest
unit and then branched out to the larger context: "If such a miscellany
is called words of the covenant, we need not wonder, if the whole book,
that is called the Book of the Law, should be a similar miscellany." In
addition, out of the close reading of the text there arose an interpretative thesis in which history appeared as "introductory, concomitant and
confirmatory"[2] to the "Words of the Covenant." Therefore, it was impossible
to argue as the Orthodox, the Deists, and the extreme Revivalists had done
that moral precepts could be isolated from history. For as long as Scripture
was admitted as a model and medium of reality its exegesis showed that history and law were inseparably intertwined. In the Latin textbook language
of Protestant Orthodoxy, Edwards' formula had been identified even more
succinctly in terms of the providence which was the praecursus, concursus
et succursus virtutis Dei.[3] This "virtue of God," however, was according
to orthodox doctrine the work of the Holy Spirit ad extra.

When Edwards commented on Psalm 49:3,4 he observed that "perhaps a
future state is here more plainly spoken of than anywhere else in the Old
Testament."[4] For Edwards the context of a passage did not necessarily

---

[1] Edwards, Works, IX, p. 11.   [2] Ibid., p. 8.

[3] Quoted in Karl Barth, Church Dogmatics, III, 3, p. 96.

[4] Edwards, Works, IX, pp. 206-207. Gerhard von Rad also has argued
that life after death is the subject of the Psalm, but he took Psalm 73 to
be a clearer example of this doctrine. (Theology of the Old Testament, I,
pp. 406f.)

refer to the immediate context of a chapter, or to the immediate context
of a single book, but here it comprised the whole of the Old Testament.
Edwards in this case gave us the results of rather than the reasoning
behind his exegesis and his emphasis on the uniqueness of this Psalm identified his observation not simply as a process of exploration of terms but as
a constructive element for the project of the History of the Work of
Redemption which was to introduce doctrines in the "order of their existence,
or their being brought forth to view in the course of divine dispensations."

In none of these examples was Edwards only the disinterested investi-
gator nor do they show that he followed one simple line of argument. His
"opening" of the text for his lecture series on the History of the Work of
Redemption provided an example that indicated his concern with a terminological exegesis[1] that was methodologically similar to his handling of glory.
Isa. 41, 86 reads: "But my righteousness shall be forever, and my salvation
from generation to generation." Edwards showed that at different places
in Scripture "for ever" could mean "as long as the world shall stand, or to
the end of the generations of men." It could also refer "to all eternity,"
to the life span of an individual and to the duration of the Jewish church.
Since in the present case "from generation to generation" referred to the
history of mankind, the first part of the parallelismus membrorum must be
understood in terms of its second part. This clarification of the meaning
"for ever" had an immediate bearing on the selection of the subject matter
of the draft of the History of the Work of Redemption, for this history did
not include the subject of eternity that was to be a part of the later projected outline on the same subject which he communicated to the trustees as

---

[1] Edwards, Works, V, p. 13.

Princeton. While in this particular instance exegesis led to precision
it could also lead to the resolution of a metaphysical problem.

The importance of this observation is evident when Edwards presented
the results of his exegesis of "glory" in The Chief End for Which God
Created the World, for here did he not only find different meanings in
glory, but he found -- and "this is manifest to everyone acquainted with
the scripture"[1] -- that all these meanings cohered. One could probably
put it this way: He took the word "glory" like he took "for ever" and
established all its reference points and saw in it a structure. Edwards
did not divide his exegesis by signifying that such and such places refer
to God and others refer to man. He was interested in glory itself, as it
covered both.

Edwards set out to ask for the meaning of the root of the word
7|בֹד itself in its manifestation as verb, adjective, and noun. Accord-
ing to him, all of them shared in the root meaning of "weighty."[2] Especially for the noun he saw the meanings "gravity, nerviness, greatness,
abundance" as a consequence of the root meaning "weighty." We can best
explain what he meant if we refer to our own everyday language where we say
positively that someone carries weight with someone else or negatively that
someone throws his weight around. Man is this weight, but at the same time
-- to use a colloquial phrase -- he is also loaded with it. He is and he is
rich. It would seem that in the two phrases from everyday usage such a
differentiation shows because what is resented in the second case is the
abuse of the richness of weight, whereas the first seems to focus on the

---

[1] Works, I, p. 523

[2] Ibid., pp. 516ff.

270

inherent quality of it. Somehow weight is both very abstract and very concrete. Weight is, as it were, both an ontological and a dynamic principle,
or even better, weight was inherent and influential, for otherwise we would
speak of dead weight. Weight is both the charismatic character and its
power. This summary is a fair and full description of Edwards' basic definition of כבוד. Edwards also showed that as far as glory was concerned
the two testaments of the Bible were basically of one mind since the New
Testament δόξα according to Edwards took most of its meaning via Septuagint
from the Old Testament. Therefore in his own summary statement Edwards
said:

> The Hebrew word (כבוד) which is commonly translated glory, is
> used in such a manner as might be expected from this signification of
> the words from where it comes. Sometimes it is used to signify what
> is internal, inherent, or in the possession of the person: and some-
> times for emanation, exhibition, or communication of this internal
> glory: and sometimes for the knowledge, or sense of these, in those
> to whom the exhibition or communication is made; or an expression of
> this knowledge, sense, or effect.[1]

What Edwards apparently suggested when he said that glory sometimes meant
this and sometimes meant that was what Gerhard Kittel wrote about in a
recent terminological exegesis of the term. According to Gerhard Kittel
the analyses of all these separate individual meanings could only be an
aid, for in the New Testament

> the meanings 'divine honour,' 'divine splendour,' 'divine power,'
> and 'visible divine radiance' are fluid, and can only be distinguished
> artificially. In content, however, there is always expressed the
> divine mode of being, though with varying emphasis on the element of
> visibility.[2]

Beyond such basic observations there was also congruence between Edwards'
particular exegetical conclusions and some recent interpretations. In one

---

[1] Works, I, p. 516.

[2] Theological Dictionary of the New Testament, Ed. G. Kittel, II
(Grand Rapids, Mich., 1964), pp. 247-248.

instance Edwards listed about forty places of Scripture in his margin in
order to support his exegetical conclusions for what he called "internal
glory." Three of these references were Isaiah 10:8; 35:2; 60:3.[1] All of
these places spoke of the דבכ of the forest and served Edwards as a
textual base for his conclusion about glory as beauty. In an interpretation of these three places which were taken to be representative of still
others, Gerhard von Rad pointed out that glory consisted "not in description of its aesthetic or material value, nor as a botanical term, but in
definition of its nature."[2] Von Rad saw the aesthetic, concrete, and
natural connotations and aspects of glory, but in this particular case he
focused on its essential side and seemed to make glory something essential
while beauty itself was not. Edwards, on the other hand, included beauty
as something essential to glory. Furthermore, for Edwards glory can be
something that is possessed rather than inherent: "Anyone may be called
heavy, that possesses an abundance." The example which Edwards chose in
order to make his point was Genesis 30:1 which von Rad also uses as a means
to point out that glory refers to all the movable belongings of Jacob as
his possession and fullness.

The importance of Scripture for Edwards' thinking on glory was confirmed by Thomas Schafer's observation that the evidence throughout the
Miscellanies right up to the time of The Chief End for Which God Created
the World showed that it was the study of the Bible which led Edwards into

---

[1]Edwards, Works, I, p. 517. There is a printing error in the list.
It must read 35:2 and not 35:21.

[2]Theological Dictionary of the New Testament, p. 238.

272

an increasing awareness of a complexity of meaning in the term which went beyond the simple views of glory as human benevolence which had played such an important role in shaping the climate of moral discourse in the eighteenth century.[1] Edwards' mature position on this subject was similar to that of a pietist orthodoxy as it was represented by Petrus van Mastricht in his Theoretico-Practica Theologia.

Van Mastricht's system stood out amongst other presentations of theology like those by William Ames and Johannes Wolleb not only because of its bulk, but much more so because within the textbook tradition of the Reformed branch of Protestant Orthodoxy it represented a transition from the straightforward theological compend and system to an elaborate theological encyclopaedia. Van Mastricht, for example, added to the second edition of his work amongst other things a complete church history and a separate moral theology. In his Manuductio Ad Ministerium Cotton Mather recommended this work with these words: "I hope, you will next unto the Sacred Scripture make a Mastricht the storehouse to which you may resort continually, for in it the minister will find everything." If we consider furthermore the isolated situation in which many New England ministers including Edwards found themselves, then the investment into this encyclopaedia went a long way to meet basic professional and scholarly needs, for here, as Mather said, ministers "in one or two quarto volumes will enjoy a well furnished library," for "I know not the sun has ever shone upon an humane composure that is equal to it."[2]

---

[1] Thomas A. Schafer, "The Concept of Being in the Thought of Jonathan Edwards," unpublished dissertation, Duke University, 1951, pp. 68ff.

[2] Manuductio Ad Ministerium, p. 85.

In the treatment of each doctrine Van Mastricht followed a set
pattern which started out from the appropriate locus classicus in
Scripture. For this verse or passage he then provided a minute and con-
densed analysis. He proceeded from there to the explication of doctrine,
to the controversies surrounding the doctrine and to the practical conclusions to be drawn from the doctrine. In his discussion of "De Majestate
Et Gloria Dei,"[1] van Mastricht set out from Isaiah 42:8 which read: I am
the Lord, the Lord is my name; I will not give my glory to another God, nor
my praise to any idol." In order to do justice to the intent of the verse
von Mastricht's analysis dealt separately with the being of God ("I am the
Lord"), with the name of God ("the Lord is my name") and with the glory and
praise of God ("I will not give my glory to another God, nor my praise to
any idol"). After the analytic description of the content of the verse
the doctrinal explication of the verse focused on glory and was accompanied with Scriptural proof. In van Mastricht's overall understanding of
glory as "infinitae eminentiae fulgor, agnoscendus &c manifestandus" four
elements concurred: In the glory of God the "eminentia" as foundation consisted of "essentia" and "attributi"; moreover, glory was "perfectionis
eminentiae istius fulgor"; glory was also "agnitio istius eminentiae, qua
facies dei dicitur," and this acknowledgment of eminence in turn led to
"celebratio seu manifestatio, quae magis proprie glorificatio; quam gloria
appellatur." The first three meanings were also taken more closely
together by van Mastricht, for "eminentia, fulgor agnitio, gloriam internam
constituunt, deoque coaeternum." Van Mastricht's explication of glory went
beyond what he had said about it in the analysis of the verse, for his

[1]Theoretico-Practica Theologia, pp. 225-230.

description of glory included the being as well as the attributes of God
in addition to the praises that were being returned to God. Unlike
Willard's negative definition of God as a single, uncompounded essence,
van Mastricht's view of glory was positive as his definition of the internal
glory in terms of the coeternal "eminentia," "agnitio," and "celebratio"
showed. Karl Barth has pointed out[1] that of all Reformed dogmaticians
van Mastricht was the only one who based his textbook exposition of glory
thus squarely upon the results of an exegesis of the variegated use of
glory in Scripture. The ideological affinity between the exegesis of
Edwards and that by van Mastricht most probably indicated a relationship
of influence, for Edwards was familiar with van Mastricht's work. In
Edwards' Notes on the Bible one verifiable source reference to the second
edition of the Theoretico-Practica Theologia occurred in which Edwards
mentioned that van Mastricht had compared the ascension of Christ to the
"many ways the Roman triumphs were like Christ's ascension."[2] From one
of Edwards' extant letters we know that he loaned "a Mastricht" to Joseph
Bellamy in exchange for other books.[3]

Van Mastricht's analysis of "the Lord is my name" was at variance
with his Scripturally informed explication of glory. A review of this
incongruity will help us to understand a characteristic aspect of Edwards'
exegesis in The Chief End for Which God Created the World, which would
otherwise easily escape attention.

---

[1]Kirchliche Dogmatik, I, 2, p. 791.

[2]Edwards, Works, IX, p. 207.

[3]Thomas H. Johnson, "Jonathan Edwards' Background of Reading," p. 200

When we compare in the passage from Isaiah, "The Lord is my name"
and "I will not give my glory," we notice that "is" and "give" put these
two sentences into two different classes of statements and made them point
in different directions. Such logical and grammatical peculiarity was not
lost on men like Mastricht and Edwards who had undergone a thorough training in grammar and logic within their respective liberal arts curricula.
In addition, such philological observations were not dissociated from
philosophical conclusions where the "is-statement" pointed toward ontology
and the "give-statement" referred toward relation and revelation. Both
statements, however, occurred in the same inspired sentence of Scripture
and therefore both the ontological significance of "name" and the revela-
tional use of "glory" had to be taken equally serious. As soon as attention was paid to the fact that both statements were not simply propositions, but that they occurred as parts in the same sentence or context,
then the meticulous attention that was given to grammatical and philological
detail could come to fruition. The crucial point of Mastricht's exegesis
for this verse was that in one case he treated of a part of the sentence in
isolation and in the other case he treated of it in relation. In order to
show the relation of glory to the rest of the sentence, van Mastricht
enlarged the context of the sentence by the context of the term glory and
did thus show that glory included being and name, but he did not do the
same thing for the term name in order to indicate at least whether and how
it was related to glory.

The Reformed tradition had as a distinctive characteristic of its
textbooks in divinity a chapter on the "names of God."[1] This specialty

---

[1] O. Weber (Grundlagen der Dogmatik, I, p. 458) quoted as an
example J. Wolleb's statement: "Essentia dei cum ex Nominibus eius tum ex
Proprietatibus Intelligitur."

was one of the testimonies to the continued significance of the exegesis of Scripture within the Reformed branch of Protestant Orthodoxy. The names of God as they appeared in the Old Testament were taken and analyzed as a means to arrive at an understanding of the essence of God. Unlike in the case where the adjectival designations of God were formulated into a doctrine of attributes this "nominal" approach seemed to provide a philological short-cut by means of which the distortions could be eliminated or reduced which were said to arise from using terms which were not as central to Scripture for an interpretation of Scripture. On the whole, however, this approach led to a "theologizing philology"[1] where beyond and behind those names a common denominator was sought which rather than doing justice to the diversity of these concrete names arrived at a being unrelated to history.

In addition to this special doctrinal feature in the Reformed tradition, the early Enlightenment also had a great interest in the idea of the "name of God."[2] Edwards in his exegesis of God's name in The Chief End for Which God Created the World was anxious to establish a link to his elaboration of glory. Edwards for this purpose collected a whole series of examples of the expression "for his name sake" which referred to God and which corresponded functionally as well as semantically to the various meanings of glory. He came to the conclusion that "God's name and his glory, at least very often signify the same things in Scripture."[3] As long as the idea of the name of God was not brought into line with the interpretati

---

[1] Weber, Grundlagen der Dogmatik, I, p. 467.

[2] Rgg[3] IV, pp. 1298-1299.

[3] Edwards, Works, I, pp. 502; 504-505.

of glory the name could always behave like a boomerang which would in the
name of some abstraction reopen the dichotomy of being and act and lead
thereby to an insufficient view of history.

The variety of connotations which these terms glory and name represented and comprehended raises the issue whether an attention to so many
literal meanings of the term glory in particular was not based on a faulty
exegesis in which the elaboration of complexity covered up unexplored or
unexplained contradictions. Edwards himself was not of this opinion and
in a series of Miscellanies he criticized Matthew Tindal for a resolution
of complexity into contradiction.[1] In its various forms, modern critical
understanding of Scripture has made this principle of contradiction its
axiom of knowledge and its maxim of conduct. At this point in time, however,
Biblical criticism itself has acquired a history and while the principle
remains valid, its application is no longer as axiomatic as when the method
of literary criticism and source separation dominated the field and led to
scientifically meticulous distinctions of the various origins of the different Scriptural sources. The advent of the history of traditions approach
introduced an attitude that was aimed not simply at the facts, but also at
their interpretation, meaning, and coherence. The serious consideration of
facts as well as of their interpretation, of their syntax as well as of
their style, opened up two possible emphases within one inquiry. On the one
hand, it was possible to take the different nuances of a text and distribute
its various meanings over the several successive layers of tradition that
make up the final form of the document called Scripture. In this way, for
example, the less palatable aspects of the variety of glory could be said

---

[1] Works, VIII, pp. 197ff; 210.

to belong to those levels that have passed away and do no longer concern either the past or the future. The total impact of this emphasis, therefore, resembled that of a historical dictionary in which obscure and defunct meanings are usually listed along with those that are still current in contemporary usage. On the other hand, this approach could also lead to a conclusion that, despite different successive layers and contradictions, a continuum existed. It is the interest in such a common concern as it was exhibited in the Scriptural sources which provides a point of contact between Edwards and recent exegetical scholarship even though the ultimate understanding of the character of this concern might differ.[1] In the particular case of glory that meant, for example, that the history of traditions approach showed at least in a negative way that glory could not be only explained by a distribution or separation over several strata of source formation, Gerhard von Rad observed:

---

[1] What we have briefly outlined here for the subject matter of exegesis is already a widely accepted premise for the study of other areas of Edwards' thought. Thus, for example, the fact that both Whitehead and Edwards had metaphysical concerns and that both shared a Platonist background for their philosophizing has been justification enough to embark on full-scale interpretations of comparative achievements of the two thinkers. Consequently, our occasional use of illustrations of Edwards' exegesis from that of recent scholars is likewise not prompted by an attempt to discredit or by a desire to modernize. As long as there is no objection to embark in the philosophy of religion on a systematic comparison of William James and Jonathan Edwards because of their illuminating insights into the question of religious experience, so long does it stand to reason that an occasional illustration of Edwards through the work of recent exegetes for the purpose of mutual explanation is also admissible. Apart from such involved methodological considerations it is the conviction of this author that for pragmatic reasons alone a modern interpreter of Edwards' exegesis is dependent on a measure of help from the specialized knowledge of modern exegetes in order to find his way into Edwards' knowledge of the Bible in an intelligent way.

> To give a history of the term is not really possible; indeed it is
> certain that the signification of כבוד has met with changes, but still
> the differentiations arising from these cannot be explained in terms
> of a chronological sequence and in addition it must be observed that
> it is those places in the [Old Testament] literature that are late
> which are distinguished by poetic archaisms or priestly religious
> traditionalisms.[1]

The uses to which such an acknowledgment of a common concern in the sources
could lead pointed in different directions. כבוד or corresponding paradigms
like mana and charisma have furnished scholars with the nuclei for the construction of theories of religion and their use as interpretative theses
aided in the empirical investigation of the psychological, sociological, and
institutional consequence and the significance of the impact of the numinous.
Edwards' own theory of religion as it was expressed in his interpretation of
glory and as it was mediated by Scripture and elaborated in the exegesis of
it included further the consequence of the numinous for a view of history
which comprised being and change.

This particular meaning of glory as history was more succinctly
formulated in the phrase "from glory to glory" which was used in the New
Testament and which Gerhard Kittel summarized as follows: "The bridge
between the present and eschatology is contained in Ἀπὸ δοξης εἰς δοξαν.
The now to be sure is ἐν δοξη but at the same time the εἰς carries the view
towards a perfection yet to come."[2] Edwards did not use the formula "from
glory to glory." Instead he employed in The Chief End for Which God Created
the World other scriptural phrases such as that God or glory was the beginning, the middle and the end, and that everything was created of Him, in
Him, and to Him. Scripture in general and glory and name in particular

---

[1]Theological Dictionary of the New Testament, p. 242.

[2]Ibid., p. 251.

therefore constituted the model of that level of ultimacy which gave content to his explanation of terms, in which the one end and the many ends could be sustained in such a way that the originality of both was safeguarded and which provided the foundation for Edwards' conceptualization of his view of history in terms of the idea of communication.

End and Trend

The prominent role which Scripture has played in this study thus far could easily create the impression as though Edwards was the representative of a kind of Biblical Theology which, according to a popular academic opinion, has as its only interest exegesis and which either ignores or is ignorant of concerns for and questions of conceptualization. In our review of Edwards' treatment of the phrase "ages to come" we have seen that in his case such a separation would be artificial because for him exegetical and philosophical orientations interpenetrate.[1] The very structure of the treatise on The Chief End for Which God Created the World furnished evidence for this relationship. Edwards' arguments from reason in chapter one and his proof from revelation or Scripture in the subsequent chapter both culminated in the affirmation of the indistinct and obscure character of our knowledge because of the "sublimity" of the subject matter which it considered. The transition from the first argument to the second did therefore not lead to a negation, but to a positive affirmation of the obscurity and mystery of the sublime.[2] The particular character of this harmonious relationship between reason and revelation had its basis in Edwards'

---

[1]See p. 264f.

[2]Edwards, Works, I, pp. 480-481, 526.

conviction that doctrine and exegesis were the two sides of the same truth.
It has been pointed out, however, that in any given situation these two
sides may be like the aggregate states of ice and water. In such a situation it became necessary to "melt the rigid form of this truth--be it doctrine or be it scripture--in order to make it liquid, so that we can drink
and incorporate it."[1] Neither doctrine nor exegesis, neither Biblical
Theology nor Philosophical Theology, neither biblicism nor speculation was
immune from such rigidity and each would, could, and did try to pose as an
authority which impeded the saint's vision of the goal of the pilgrimage.
The next step of our inquiry into the foundations of Edwards' view of history will therefore be to describe the range and the impact which Edwards'
exegetical explication of the end as glory had on the articulation of the
body of doctrines that had been handed down to him through tradition.

For the purposes of such an inquiry we shall paraphrase a section
in The Chief End for Which God Created the World, where Edwards dealt with
the one and the many and where he set out specifically "to consider what
thing or things are actually the effect or consequence of the creation of

---

[1]Hans Joachim Iwand, Nachgelassene Schriften, Ed. Helmut Gollwiteer,
I (München: Kaiser, 1962), p. 57. Current designations such as Biblical
Theology or Philosophical Theology are equally unsatisfactory to describe
this relationship. Biblical theologians usually suspect the philosophical
theologians of by-passing Scripture as a normative element of thought and
the representatives of Philosophical Theology commonly complain of a bias
against philosophy and a poverty in the field of systematic reflection in
the case of their counterparts. For a Biblical theologian of this kind,
Edwards is too speculative, and for the Philosophical theologian, Edwards'
exegesis is not philosophically attractive. Both, however, are united in
the suspicion that Edwards was a biblicist because he did not use the critical tools deemed necessary for an interpreter or because he did not fully
exert his creative powers as a thinker. For both there is too much doctrine
in him, even though one side sees it in his speculation and the other in
his adherence to Scripture.

the world, that are simply and originally valuable in themselves." Or,
to put Edwards' expression into a slightly different order: what thing or
things that are simply and originally valuable in themselves are _actually_
the effect or _consequence_ of the creation of the world. The things which
Edwards here had in mind were the several doctrines that had customarily
been used in order to define the concept of revelation. The degree of
interpretation and the lucidity of the conceptualization that Edwards was
able to achieve between these things or doctrines will be a measure by
which to evaluate in how far his emergent systematic thought went toward
a convincing solution of the problem that he had taken up in this treatise,
how far his thinking went beyond Protestant Orthodoxy by making doctrines
so mutually transparent to each other that he could through the medium of
these doctrines as a newly wielded tool correct a rigid philosophy of
happiness in his own time through his view of history.

The following paraphrase will not aim at criticism, but at the
reconstruction of Edwards' vision in such a way as to follow the main drift
of the several propositions of this section. Not the partial selection of
characteristic traits, but the delineation of the trend and spirit contained in these propositions is the aim of this paraphrase. Such an approach
is in accord with the theory of discourse as it was set forward by Edwards
in the treatise. The language of The Chief End for Which God Created the
World combined descriptive and discursive elements in such a way that mystery _and_ logic were equally respected. This meant that no "short definition" of the subject was possible, but that an exact description of essential relations within the subject matter could be given by using "a variety
of expressions, by a particular consideration" of them.[1]

---

[1]Edwards, Works, I, p. 526.

Before we enter upon the paraphrase itself it may be helpful to
anticipate its trend and make it more comprehensible by means of an
extended analogy from twentieth-century materials in the field of the
arts. A musician, for instance, can have in his mind an idea for a piece
of music. He can cherish this idea and go on and on with it all in himself
and by himself. He can leave it right there and be quite happy with it.
Merely to think it up can produce enormous pleasure and satisfaction. No
one can suspect from any outward signs what is going on in his mind. On
the other hand, we might also assume that the musician exercises this idea
outside of his own mind, by writing it down or by trying it out on an
instrument. He may want to go no further than this and only those who
accidentally hear him practice or who find a score later on will know about
this idea. But then our musician will probably go one step further. Not
only does he have an idea and exercise it, but he actually expresses and
performs it to other people. He likes others to know and like it. Again,
the musician may be interested most of all in his performance, the show he
puts on, and the excitement which he creates in his audience. The impression of his expression will not last. On the other hand, such a performance
may become part of the life of the audience, add to their lives, and elicit
a continued response. Each of the actions by the artist musician is good,
but, if each one of the actions is taken by itself, then such independence
is not good enough, for none of the individual aspects taken by themselves
and none of them that are taken in partial or random combinations will give
the whole story.

In order to see the connection between this analogy and the text of
the subsequent paraphrase we shall set out from the idea of God's "all-
sufficiency." Samuel Willard, for example, followed the established

tradition of the textbooks in distinguishing between the sufficiency and the efficiency of God.[1] This distinction between the sufficiency and the efficiency of God reoccurred here in The Chief End for Which God Created the World as that between self-sufficiency and the "sufficiency to certain acts and effects."[2] Self-sufficiency for Edwards was a kind of divine self-reliance which did not invest any value in the relation between itself and others. When Edwards talked about sufficiency we can best understand the thrust of his statements when we remember a related case in human behavior where only if a person is a person in its own right can it enter into a relationship. Such independence and transcendence included rather than precluded relationship. Edwards did not object to the metaphysical side of the question of sufficiency, but his thrust was: if self-sufficiency was to be the dominant question, then thinking about the world would remain always in the area of the first principles and the search for sufficient reasons why the world should and must exist would not come to an estimate of what value or significance that sufficiency could give to the world. The roles here were the reverse from what they usually are in a proof for the existence of God, for in the case of sufficiency it was a question of the existence of the world. In neither case, however, did the sufficient reason for the existence of God or the world inform about the value of the relation that was established. A. Lovejoy pointed out how Leibniz simply by means of addition turned his world into the best possible world after he had found sufficient reason for it to exist.[3] To ask, therefore, the

---

[1] Willard, A Compleat Body, p. 46.

[2] Edwards, Works, I, pp. 487f.

[3] A. O. Lovejoy, The Great Chain of Being (Cambridge: Harvard University Press, 1936), pp. 180f.

metaphysical question was necessary and good, but to ask only this question of sufficient reason was not that necessary and not good enough.

When Edwards now dealt with the question of the "sufficiency to certain acts and effects" he proceeded both carefully and syllogistically:

> But then, if the attributes which consist in a <u>sufficiency</u> for correspondent effects, are in themselves excellent, the <u>exercises</u> of them must likewise be excellent. If it be an excellent thing, that there should be a sufficiency for a certain kind of action or operation, the excellency of such a sufficiency must consist in its <u>relation</u> to this kind of operation or effect, but that could not be, unless the <u>operation itself</u> were excellent.[1]

In this definition Edwards was not concerned with the attributes themselves nor with the results they produced, but with the operation itself that took place in the execution of attributes. It was not the attributes themselves nor their results but their operation which was "excellent." Since there were several operations they were all excellent or originally valuable in themselves. Edwards provided a whole list of these operations himself, but he also quoted a sermon by Gilbert Tennent[2] which mentioned design, action, and doing good as the end of the operations of wisdom, power, and goodness respectively. Each of these operations, therefore, was to be originally valuable in itself. Thus it looked as though the end of creation was indeed several ultimate ends instead of one thing. Since Edwards had invested so much in the question of the one and the many by insisting that there was more than one thing which was originally valuable in itself, we might take a short look at the history of the relationship of such divine attributes as wisdom, power, goodness, and justice. Usually the affirmation that all of them were divine operations was followed by the more or less overt

---

[1] Lovejoy, <u>The Great Chain of Being</u>, p. 258.

[2] Ibid.

selection of one of them as the chief end by means of which the others were interpreted and made into subordinate rather than into ultimate ends. A very good example of this can be seen in John Ray's Wisdom of God in Creation. Here judgment became justness and power was understood as plasticity or as a life force. All fit the design and nothing upset it.[1]

It is understandable that Ray, after a generation of political upheaval, religious strife, and doctrinal acrimony, reacted against a period in which power and the claims of justice had all but submerged notions of wisdom and goodness as subjects of thought and a principle of conduct. Such a pattern of action and reaction to the operations of the divine attributes was common and makes it possible to see the discrepancy between the theory of operations and its actual application. Groups as diverse as the metaphysically inclined, the Deists, the Orthodox, and the Evangelicals can be distinguished as parties by virtue of the particular operation that dominated their thinking and that was used to deliberately draw lines of demarcation to other groups. What in fact happened under the affirmation of all operations was that wisdom turned into rationalism, justice into vindictiveness, power into arbitrariness, love into moralism, and beauty into aestheticism. The disenchantment with this actual proliferation of

---

[1]Even if we allow that Ray represented the position of an understandable reaction against the misuse of power and discontinuity for events of providence, it is nevertheless noteworthy that his investigations of nature also disregarded signs of power in this area which did not easily fit the idea of design. Ray was aware of contemporary discussions which tried to square geological findings with the Scriptural account of the flood. The physical character of the earth could not be conceived of as a continuous growth out of one seed as it was true in the case of plants. Insofar as Ray formulated a philosophy, such aspects of discontinuity did not enter into it.

the operations into separate attitudes was best expressed and summed up

by the English poet Shelley:

> The good want power, but to weep barren
> tears the powerful goodness want; worse
> need for them the wise want love; and
> those who love want
> wisdom
> and all best things are thus confused to ill.[1]

Edwards reacted against such extreme insistence on an individual operation

in the case of wisdom. In one of his Miscellanies that dealt with the ques-

tion of the end, he stated that to see the "highest end in the world" in the

usefulness of the individual parts to each other was like a man who was

fascinated by the wheels and workings of the clock and who never looked at

the hands in order to find out the time.[2] "Sufficiency to certain acts and

effects" had thus become too independent and needed to be related to

sufficiency.

Whereas the danger in the case of self-sufficiency lay in the trend

toward a negative assertion of one simple essence, the one-sidedness in the

sufficiency toward operations occurred in the selection and generalization

of single-minded affirmations about God. In the first case the world was

not taken seriously. In the latter instance the world was taken too seri-

ously. The former position was afraid of change in the world, the latter

---

[1] M. H. Abrams, Natural Supernaturalism, Tradition and Revolution in Romantic Literature (New York: Norton, 1971), p. 306.

[2] Townsend, p. 127: "For most certainly, if the highest end of the world be to have its parts useful to each other, the world is good for nothing at all. To illustrate it by example: if the highest end of every part of the clock is only mutually to assist the other parts in their motions, that clock is good for nothing. The clock in general is useless. However, every part is useful to turn around the other parts. . . . But as in a clock, one wheel moves another and that another till at last we come to the hand and there we end. The use of that immediately respects the eye of man."

position halted operations by selecting one operation. Both of these
views were independent of man which was good and necessary, for essence
and world are more than a function of human consciousness. Nevertheless,
this independence was not that necessary and that good because it did not
take man himself seriously.

The phrase "exercises and expression" occurred twice in the course
of the propositions. In both cases the italicized printing of either
"exercises" or "expression" indicated a shift of emphasis from one element
to the other in order to make clear that the phrase could have two different orientations. At its first occurrence the emphasis was to introduce
the operations of the attributes in the world, and the second time the
phrase referred to man's knowledge of those operations. To exercise the
operations was good and necessary but it was not that good and necessary
unless someone knew about them. Such a syntactical means of providing for
nuances had a semantic parallel, for individual terms in the treatise
occurred in such a way that the same word could signify different things
in different contexts throughout the chapter in which he was engaged in the
argument from reason. One such word was expression itself and in this
respect it was like experience which we analyzed in the last chapter, and
it was not unlike what we found in the exegesis of glory. Edwards, for
example, pointed out that God did not find, but make objects of his benevolence "by flowing forth, and expressing himself in them, and making them
to partake of Him, and rejoicing in himself expressed in them, and communicated to them."[1] In this context the idea of self-expression in the sense
of "create" emerged as a meaning of the term expression. In the context

---

[1] Edwards, Works, I, p. 480.

of the propositions expression occurred in the sense of "appear," "be
known" and become public to human beings.[1] In another reference we read
of that which has become known as the "external expression, exhibition and
manifestation of the luminary."[2] Expression could thus refer both to the
revelation of God to man as well as to the creation of man through God.

As Edwards proceeded expression itself had to be considered more
fully beyond an external manifestation of knowledge. It was good to know
of operations, but that was not good and necessary enough unless such knowledge carried along with it acknowledgment, esteem, and love. Neither knowledge nor love could be subsumed under each other without the destruction of
the moral world as something valuable in itself, for both knowledge and love
were original ends that constituted this world. While this equal affirmation raises once more the question of the one and the many, a neglect of
love did cause serious problems also, for without it the moral world tended
to be turned into a mere appendix to speculation or into corollary of an
investigation of nature according to whether individuals were inclined to
take up metaphysical or non-metaphysical models of thought. Edwards' inclusion of love as a proposition of its own was therefore a challenge to current views of ontology, or plastic nature and of psychology which all kept
love and joy subordinate and at arm's length. In order for love to be not
only a good but also a necessary thing and end, it had to be considered not
in terms of expressions of appreciations, but as expressions of participation.[3]

---

[1] Edwards, Works, I, p. 428.

[2] Ibid., pp. 526f.

[3] The difference between appreciation and participation is in evidence
in our standard invitation after a lecture: "I think we all want to express
our appreciation to Mr./Ms. So-and-So for his/her lecture."

The paraphrase of the propositions thus far provided an opportunity
to characterize those dialectical pairs of independence and relation which
Edwards considered necessary for an adequate understanding of history. The
neglect or elimination of even one of these doctrines would turn a world-
view either by default or by ignorance in the direction of the non-
historical. It was nevertheless not enough for him only to state, as it
were, negatively the minimum requirements which a team must display in order
to play a game. Edwards has introduced the members of the team. But with
so many original talents on the team the expectation increases to see whethe
they can and do make a play on the field.

Since independence and relation had to be equally guarded for the
sake of reality, Edwards introduced yet another proposition which was "a
thing amiable and valuable in itself," and which led to a positive comprehending formula for the other original ends. Edwards here talked about "an
infinite fulness of all possible good in God -- a fulness of every perfection, of all excellency and beauty, and of infinite happiness -- and this
fulness is capable of communication, or emanation _ad extra_."[1] This statement presupposed a distinction of the Godhead as it was traditionally
applied in theology in order to differentiate between the internal and the
external works of the trinity. Some of those original ends and things that
have been mentioned in the paraphrase were identifiable in this statement
as part of the internal Godhead or being itself. This was true of "infinite
as something valuable in itself, for it referred to essence, and of "fullness" which included all the attributes of God in general, and which later o
in the text was specified in terms of "knowledge and understanding,"

---

[1]Edwards, _Works_, I, p. 459.

"excellence and beauty," "joy and happiness." Finally, this infinite
fullness was capable of "communication" ad extra.

The key to the import of the statement and what distinguished it
from all the previous original propositions is the place and meaning of the
word "communication." A focus on the idea of "communication" in the following will require two things: it will be shown how in the concluding
section of The Chief End for Which God Created the World, Edwards formulated his argument in terms of communication. In the next section we shall
then develop more closely Edwards' view of communication against the background of other writings by him and with the question in mind what this
argument yields for our own thesis. Edwards summarized his argument by
means of the term communication in the following two sentences in the last
section of his treatise:

> God exercising his perfection to produce a proper effect, is not
> distinct from the emanation or communication of his fulness; for this
> is the effect, viz., his fulness communicated, and the producing of
> this effect is the communication of his fulness; and there is nothing
> in this effectual exerting of God's perfection, but the emanation of
> God's eternal glory.[1]

> When God was about to create the world, he had respect to the emana-
> tion of his glory, which is actually the consequence of the creation,
> both with regard to himself and the creature. He had regard to it as
> an emanation from himself, a communication of himself, and as the thing
> communicated, in its nature returned to himself as its final term. And
> he had regard to it also as the emanation was to the creature, and as
> the thing communicated was in the creature as its subject.[2]

Communication here preceded as well as succeeded each of the previously mentioned doctrines or things such as, for example, sufficiency, exercise,
effect, and expression. Each of these terms had nuances of its own and
could also occur along with synonyms which enlarged the complexity of

---

[1] Edwards, Works, I, pp. 527, 528.

[2] Ibid., p. 530.

meaning cumulatively, but communication was the most comprehensive term for the most-comprehensive doctrine and thing. We have seen before: Edwards had set out to deal with the doctrine of the end; he had sharpened the issue by an equal admission of the one as well as the many to his considera-tion; he had outlined a view of the end as a complex interaction of ideas of goal, center, support, and termination; he had given content to the end through an exegesis of glory as inherent and influential weight which expressed itself in a communication of knowledge and love. For all these various logical, devotional, and exegetical concerns the concept of com-munication provided doctrinal explication, conceptualization, and integra-tion. The philological evidence for the pervasive use of communication throughout the treatise was therefore not accidental to its three-fold argument of terminological exploration, reasonable explication, and Scriptural proof. On the contrary, communication was essential to the treatise as the underlying theme for it was the foundation of the sys-tematic formulation of Edwards' paradigm of the view of history.

These far-reaching conclusions from our paraphrase are confirmed by the way in which Edwards' own argument developed beyond that section which contained the series of propositions. In this treatise Edwards had put a premium not on short definitions, but on considerations of a kind that helped him to deal with the same subject "in its different respects and relations." Since the propositions had presented more of an enumeration of several original ends or things, Edwards now went on to consider more fully the aspect of "how a value to these things is implied in his (God's) value of that infinite good that is in himself.:[1] For this purpose Edwards set

---

[1] Edwards, _Works_, I, p. 461.

about to reconsider the same propositions. He argued the affirmative
that expression as well as sufficiency to certain acts and effects par-
ticipated in the one end of God. Both arguments were brief and compared to
the former propositional arrangement he contracted the propositions about
knowledge and love into one small paragraph. Only when he came to the
subject of the communication of fullness did he launch forth on a full-
scale elaboration and give as a consequence of it an explication of his
positive comprehending formula of communication.[1]

At the end of the section that contained the series of propositions
Edwards concluded his argument with the definition of "a disposition in
God" which was the cause as well as the end of the creation of the world.
Here Edwards spoke of emanation, not communication. This definition in
terms of emanation provides a convenient means of relating Edwards' own
argument to the pervasive ontological tradition of the occident as it has
been traced and described by A. O. Lovejoy. Since this story is primarily
concerned with Edwards' thought we shall not interpret Edwards' knowledge
of this tradition, but proceed to summarize what he added to it by means
of his conceptualization of communication.

Communication

In pursuit of his argument that communication also had to be considered in different relations, Edwards mentioned that communication was
implied in the Godhead itself. He spoke of that "good disposition in his
nature to communicate of his own fulness in general"[2] or he referred to

---

[1] Edwards, _Works_, I, pp. 461–462.

[2] Ibid., p. 462.

the "communicative disposition in general, or a disposition in the fulness of the divinity to flow out and diffuse itself."[1] This disposition which Edwards also called a desire belonged to the nature of the Godhead itself and therefore had the same claim to generality that belonged to God as the Summum Ens. Conversely the Godhead itself was conceived of as having its own end because it included a disposition or desire. Edwards referred to this disposition as an "original ground" in both of the possible meanings of this expression. First, its ontological status made disposition or desire the ground of being which was originally valuable in itself. Since, however, desire was something that by definition aimed at an end, the meaning of the ontological status of desire was that the end preceded the beginning. Second, while this disposition or desire therefore "cannot have any particular present or future, created existence for its object," it was also at the same time "the very source of the futurition of its existence." The "original ground" was thus to be understood to be the turning point between the ground of being as the original foundation and between the origin of history as a source. This way of putting it agreed with his exegesis of glory as an influence of inherent excellence as well as of internal riches. To put it in slightly different terms, we can use the traditional phrase that the disposition in the Godhead was the source as well as the river which originated from the source.

In his definition of the "original ground" Edwards made assumptions in the brief argument and implied consequences which were not fully dealt with at that point. Thus, for example, his contention that the "original ground" or disposition preceded present as well as future superseded both

---

[1] Edwards, Works, I, p. 460.

[2] Ibid., p. 462.

sides of an argument which he had conducted in his <u>Miscellanies</u> with
Matthew Tindal.[1] Edwards had charged that Tindal took the present as the
only measure of judgment while Edwards had contended that Scripture had
been given to all people in all ages including the time of the future.
Here in turn he indicated that the future as well as the present was dependent on this divine disposition which was "equally present"[2] to both so that
neither the immanence of the present nor the transcendence of the future
should be confused with the transcendence and goal of this disposition.

A further identification and explanation of the idea of disposition
is found when we return to Edwards' exegetical argument for the doctrine of
the trinity which had been published posthumously from his <u>Miscellanies</u>:

> The word spirit in Sacred Scriptures when used concerning minds,
> when it is not part of the spiritual substance or mind itself, is put
> for the disposition, inclination or temper of the mind; Numb. 14, 24.
> Caleb was of another spirit. . . . When we read of the spirit of a
> spirit or mind it is to be thus understood, Eph. 4, 27. Be renewed in
> the spirit of your mind. So I suppose also we read of the spirit of
> God who we are told is a spirit. It is to be understood of the dispo-
> sition or temper or affection of the divine mind. If we read or hear
> of the meek spirit or the kind spirit or pious and holy spirit of a
> man we understand it of his temper. So I suppose we read of the Good
> Spirit and Holy Spirit of God, it is likewise to be understood of God's
> temper.[3]

When Edwards spoke of a disposition in the Godhead he did not mean an uncompounded essence, but a person. His exegesis in this particular case set out
from human psychology and moved on to the statement that love in the Godhead
was infinite and perfect and could not therefore be distinguished into habit
and act.

---

[1] Edwards, <u>Works</u>, VIII, p. 210.
[2] <u>Ibid.</u>, I, p. 469.
[3] <u>An Unpublished Essay</u>, pp. 95-96.

This disposition or person within the Godhead was the Holy Spirit.[1]
For Edwards the Holy Spirit was the "sum of all good things. Good things
and the Holy Spirit were synonymous expressions in sacred scripture." The
Holy Spirit was the sum of the Godhead or its "bond of perfectness" by means
of which the father and the Son were in communion and through which they
were being communicated, for the Holy Spirit is "the common excellency
and joy and happiness in which [God and man] all are united; 'tis the bond
of perfectness by which [men] are one in the Father and the Son as the
Father is in the son."[2] Even more pointedly Edwards said that "the blessing
from the holy ghost is [God] himself, the communion of himself."[3] Thus, on
the one hand the Holy Spirit was equal with and essential to both Father
and Son and constituted their communion. On the other hand, the Holy Spirit
was more specifically the love with which the Father and Son loved each
other and therefore the Holy Spirit _flowed_ forth from Father and Son and
was the communication of their communion and became as such the foundation
of the community of believers. This breathing or flowing forth was mentioned by Edwards specifically as the unique feature of the Holy Spirit in
Scripture which employed "similitudes and metaphors" such as "water, fire,
breath, wind, oil, wine, a spring, a river"[4] in order to identify this
distinct mode of the Godhead. The Holy Spirit as the disposition within
the Godhead was the communion as well as the communication.

In the case of this particular definition of the doctrine of the
end in terms of the Holy Spirit, Edwards explicitly drew the line between
his understanding of it and that understanding which had preceded him.

---

[1] _An Unpublished Essay_, p. 121.

[2] _Ibid._, p. 109.   [3] _Ibid._, pp. 109-110.   [4] _Ibid._, p. 106.

This interpretation, Edwards explained, never went beyond peremptory

declarations on the subject that God was the "alpha and omega in this

affair of redemption," for it did not formulate a doctrine of the Holy

Spirit that went beyond the conceptualization of binity and a half instead

of a trinity.

> If we suppose no more than used to be supposed about the Holy
> Ghost [then] the concern of the holy ghost in the work of redemption
> is not equal with the father's and the son's, nor is there an equal
> part of the glory of this work belonging to him: merely to apply to
> us or immediately give or hand to us the blessing purchased, after it
> was purchased, as subservient to the other two persons, is but a
> little thing. . . .[1]

Such an immediate subordinate application was no general sustained communi-

cation and turned the Holy Spirit into a machinery without a clearly-defined

context of its own.

This brief review of the origin of "communicative disposition in

general" makes clear why Edwards had chosen communication as a means to

integrate the propositional arrangement of doctrines and when we now return

to our section in The Chief End for Which God Created the World, we are

also able to see the thrust with which Edwards employed the positive formula

of communication in pursuit of the question of the completion of the Godhead.

"God looks on the communication of himself, and the emanation of his own

glory to belong to the fulness and completeness of himself; as though he

were not in his most glorious state without it."[2] The meaning of this con-

tention was not to indicate that God can find completion only by means of

communication, but that the completeness of God insured the fact of any

communication at all. In his treatment of Edwards' ontology, Thomas Schafer

---

[1] An Unpublished Essay, pp. 123-124.

[2] Edwards, Works, I, p. 463.

criticized that in this statement and others like it Edwards betrayed a strong necessitarian bent which we might characterize not just as desire, but as a compulsive or inevitable desire to communicate. It is true that the emphasis in the treatise was on the works ad extra, because in The Chief End for Which God Created the World, Edwards was concerned with the Holy Spirit as the turning point of the ground of being and the origin of history. Nevertheless, necessity here cannot refer to a blind drive of some kind. If we want to use the term necessitarian at all, we must be more precise and say that in order for the history of the work of redemption to be concrete, real history itself must be represented in the Godhead. Edwards said that unless the will of God had equal status with his understanding the suspicion would remain "that God had pleasure in things that are brought to pass in time, only figuratively and metaphorically" and that "he exercises will about these things and makes them his end only metaphorically."[1] God in other words may have the "foresight" that something will happen, but he will not get involved. We have already observed that Edwards on the other hand emphasized the ontological aspect of communication by rejecting the present and the future as self-contained ends. Edwards' so-called necessitarianism was actually a defense of the Holy Spirit.

We have seen that communication served to integrate doctrines in a twofold way, for communication according to Edwards was simultaneously a systematic-ontological and a dynamic-historical principle. We shall now review in particular the several dimensions of reality which Edwards comprehended within this conceptualization as the necessary prerequisites for

---

[1] Edwards, Works, I, pp. 470-471.

arriving at a full-blown view of history. These dimensions, according to
Edwards, were "the nature and circumstances of the communications of God's
fulness."[1] Furthermore, "that communication of himself which he intended
through all eternity"[2] and the "increasing communication of himself through
all eternity."[3] The first dimension contained his consideration of the
course of historical events; the second described his positive view of
eternity; and the third dealt with his attitude to infinity or the goal of
progress.

According to Edwards, the "nature and circumstances" of the "communications" were implied in the overall diffusion of the Godhead ad extra.
Knowledge in the creature here was "participation" in the "image of God's
own knowledge of himself." In holiness "the creature partakes of God's
own moral excellency," and the "creature's happiness" was a "participation
of what is in God." At the same time, Edwards pointed out that knowledge
and holiness each for itself also issue forth and are praise. Therefore,
Edwards summarized in the following formula the essential nature of all
communications and the way in which they nevertheless were the circumstances
of each other:

> God is all in all, with respect to each part of that communication
> of divine fulness which is made to the creature. What is communicated
> is divine, or something of God; and each communication is of that
> nature, that the creature to which it is made, is therefore conformed
> to God, and united to him: and that in proportion as the communication
> is greater or less. And the communication itself is no other, in the
> very nature of it, than wherein the very honor, exaltation and praise
> of God exists.[4]

---

[1] Works, I, p. 464.

[2] Ibid., p. 465.   [3] Ibid., p. 466.   [4] Ibid., p. 465.

Expressions like "God is all in all" point in the direction of the language that had been used in the course of church history for the explication of the doctrine of the trinity.[1] Two other concepts that were developed in this connection are particularly adequate in order to make explicit the thrust of Edwards' formulation. The concept of "relations" was used in order to indicate that there was a definite order between the modes of being in the Godhead. "Coinherence" on the other hand referred to the insight that the several modes of being in the Godhead moved within each other and contained each other. Coinherence, consequently, provided a safeguard without which the order of relations could easily be misconstrued as a hierarchy of ontological subordinations. When Edwards spoke of knowledge, holiness, and happiness as communications, he understood these communications to be such a coinherence where each of the three aspects were not only circumstances of each other, but also moved within each other and contained each other.

Edwards shared with his own time and tradition the assumption that gave priority to understanding and knowledge in the "order of nature. His insistence on communications as a process of coinherence relativized this position while it did not at the same time absolutize the affections. The communications were a trinitarian image and consequently the dynamism of the trinity was applied to history also. In The Chief End for Which God Created the World, it is impossible to speak of knowledge without also speaking about the affections. For without love and the diffusion of the Holy

---

[1]Cyril C. Richardson, The Doctrine of the Trinity, A Clarification of What It Attempts to Express (Nashville, 1958, p. 246), quoted the similar statement by Augustine: "So both are in each, and all in each, and each in all, and all in all, and all are one."

Spirit there would be no knowledge. Edwards' use of the trinity in this instance was not characterized by a desire to engage in a technically complete and expository defense of this doctrine for the sake of upholding and rehearsing the Orthodox position. On the contrary, Edwards applied this doctrine as an explanatory hypothesis in a concrete controversy and showed the significant consequences which this speculative construct entailed for a view of psychology. The aggressive use which Edwards made of the salient features of this doctrine was not dependent on the only and late occurrence of the triadic formula in the New Testament.[1] His confidence, however, arose out of a respect for the whole of Scripture, where it was not possible to separate within glory between the inherent and the internal or between knowledge and affection. Scripture as the paradigm pointed the way toward the elimination of dualism. Unlike later American critics of dualism in philosophy (R. W. Emerson, William James, John Dewey), Edwards did not develop his position as an alternative to religious dualisms, but maintained it by employing a religious paradigm. According to Edwards, man was created in God's image and, therefore, this view of psychology was a prerequisite to understand the kind of progress in the course of historical events. There have been theories which located knowledge, holiness, and joy each in a separate epoch of history, and then went on to construe a succession like that of religion, metaphysics, and science. There have been also opinions which assert and affirm the present as a time of celebration. Both ideologies, however, create only the illusion of historical movement, for what they discover and accept and what they ignore and explain away at critical points is some essential part of the image. In the former case,

---

[1]John 5:6-8.

the construction of a philosophy of history will provide the backdrop for
extensive generalizations around a theory of progressive secularization.
Reactions to this theory and the social and cultural conditions it sanctions make it appear in the latter case that the trend has reversed itself
in favor of a process of resacralization. Edwards' understanding of the
image excludes such theories of secularization and resacralization, be they
complementary or contradictory, for in either case they re-introduce a
dualism into reality that destroys the dynamism of the image.

The substantial participation of the Godhead in the image made
typology a more profound and less external description of the dependence
of man on God than the contractual-legal relationship expressed by means of
the covenant. In the way in which the covenant had come to be used it
signified a two-sided contract between two originally separate partners in
a state of nature. The image of the trinitarian God, on the other hand,
described community as a dynamic entity because it was the image of the
living God and because it had been experienced in the Northampton Revival
of 1735. By the same token emanation, like covenant, did not penetrate
deeply enough the historical world to which this revelation was addressed.
At one point in The Chief End for Which God Created the World Edwards,
therefore, differentiated between emanation as "effusion" and communication
as "diffusion."[1]

The meaning of the statement about "that communication of himself
which he [God] intended through all eternity" is self-contradictory as long
as eternity and time are conceived of in terms of absolute opposites. We
have already demonstrated that Edwards in one of his exegeses moved in a

---

[1]Edwards, Works, I, p. 473.

different direction and we shall now describe this dimension of eternity
more narrowly.

In his posthumously published essay on the trinity, Edwards objected
to a "maxim amongst divines that everything that is in God is God which
must be understood of real attributes and not mere modalities." He
rejected this position, for he could not find "any rational meaning" in it.[1]
Edwards' criticism at this point was all the more instructive, for it
showed explicitly that his contention in The Chief End for Which God
Created the World that there were several things originally valuable in
themselves did not lead him to the point of simply affirming the plurality
of attributes. The reason for Edwards' rejection of the maxim is apparent
in the consequences to which it would lead in the case of his two examples.
First, an identification of God with his providence and his government of
the world would reduce faith to a penultimate concern with providence to
the exclusion of everything else; and second, God's identification with
his own omnipresence would turn faith into no more than the experience of
a pervasive presence. Edwards here argued against a contemporary position
which accepted all these attributes as real insofar as they occurred in
Scripture, and which combined this point of view with an explicit refusal
to go beyond Scripture out of fear to impose false systematizations. The
distinction between incommunicable attributes like eternity, omnipresence,
immutability, and communicable attributes such as wisdom and power were
looked upon as such mistaken classifications. We have indeed seen in our
own analysis how Willard degraded one group of attributes into mere modalities. Edwards did not criticize the removal of the traditional distinction,

---

[1] An Unpublished Essay of Edwards, p. 112.

but he was not satisfied either with a seemingly unpretentious listing
of biblically endorsed attributes. For Edwards Scripture itself as the
paradigm of ultimacy contained quite literally the mandate for a dis-
criminate articulation of attributes which involved more than a hostile
reaction to their metaphysical abuses and which led to a positive revalua-
tion of their metaphysical significance. In Scripture, Edwards found that
the only attributes which were identified with God in an essential way
were understanding and love. Here were therefore two attributes which were
traditionally thought to be communicable but which were now thought by him
to be also incommunicable, or which in other words were considered to be
historical as well as eternal. As soon as Edwards began to think along
these lines, the traditional dualism and dichotomy between real incommunicable and conceptual attributes disappeared, while a levelling of all
differentiations was avoided.

If it be meant that real attributes of God, viz., his understanding
and love are God, then what we have said may in some measure explain
how it is so, for deity subsists in them distinctly; so they are distinct divine persons. We find no other attributes of which it is said
that they are God in sacred scripture or that God is they, but Λόγος
and Ἀγάπη , the reason and the love of God. John 1:1; I John 4:8, 16.[1]

In The Chief End for Which God Created the World, Edwards gave to
the traditionally incommunicable attributes like eternity and infinity a
positive meaning and function by looking upon them no longer as "a distinct
kind of Good." The infinity of the Godhead did not mean any more that God
was boundless and therefore totally other than understanding and love.
Infinity rather expressed that the Godhead possessed this good in the highest degree. The eternity of the Godhead in addition made clear that God no

[1]An Unpublished Essay of Edwards, p. 113.

longer was something timeless which eclipsed all understanding and love,
but rather eternity emphasized that God possessed the same good in its
duration. Finally, the immutability of the Godhead did not refer to something unchangeable beyond understanding and love, but immutability expressed
the same good with a negation of change in it.[1] The Godhead therefore had
duration, but a duration without change. "Eternal" therefore meant for
Edwards that there was a communication of highest degree which had variety
without the variableness[2] that adhered to the communications in the course
of human history.

   This definition of eternity as duration presupposed a notion of
extension. In his controversy with Descartes, Henry More had maintained
that extension was not only an attribute of matter, but also an attribute
of the spirit and of God. This meant that God was not just a power to
act, but that he was actually present, since his presence pervaded all
places at all times. Usually this idea of absolute space and time is
traced for English philosophy in relation to the scientific revolution of
the seventeenth century.[3] This idea of extension, however, had also affini-
ties with Edwards' exegesis of glory. For Edwards, glory was the highest
end and had therefore the most universal history, since "the more original
an end is the more extensive and universal it is." This notion of the
eternal and glory as extension made it possible to speak of the Godhead as
that which was at once beginning, middle, and end, as well as that from
which, to which, and in which everything was.

---

[1]Works, I, p. 527.   [2]Ibid., p. 469.

[3]John Tull Baker, "An Historical and Critical Examination of English
Space and Time Theories from Henry More to Bishop Berkeley," unpublished
dissertation, Columbia University, 1930, pp. 6ff.

While communication thus penetrated the course of historical events
and while it extended to all these events and endured, communication also
became more and more. Edwards expressed this latter dimension in the phrase
of the "increasing communication of himself through eternity." This progress
to the "infinite height" or to the highest degree meant for the creature to
advance toward oneness with the Godhead.

As far as the definition of the goal of the increase is concerned,
there was an ambiguity in The Chief End for Which God Created the World
which is no less than ironic when we consider all the thought that has gone
into the definition of the end. On the one hand, Edwards said with regard
to the "elect creatures" that "they were respected as brought home to him,
united with him, centering most perfectly, and as it were swallowed up in
him: so that his respect to them finally coincides, and becomes one and the
same, with respect to himself."[1] This view of the eventual "identity" of
God and the elect where the elect are swallowed up in God was offset by
long passages to the effect that "there never will be any particular time
when it can be said already to have come to such a height."[2] If we look at
both opinions from the point of view of communication, then the idea of a
final coincidence and identity looked more like an annihilation than a fulfillment and the idea that there will never be a time when a union comes
about looked as though communication has no end and could this per defini-
tionem be no full communication but only an unending process of transmission

If we look more closely, however, at the quotation about the final
coincidence we observe that the saints' respect to God was connected with

---

[1]Works, I, p. 466.

[2]Ibid., p. 531.

God's respect to himself. God's respect to himself was his son. When Edwards therefore described what he meant by the final coincidence and union he quoted John 17:21-23: "That they all may be one, as thou Father art in me, and I in Thee, that they may also be one in us; I in them and thou in me, that they may be made perfect one."[1] The goal of the increasing communication was thus the participation in the union of the father and the son. This union was a "conformity" and not a conformism where everything was annihilated into a nameless identity. The form of God was the Son. Just as these two were one, but not identical, so will the saints be co-opted into the Godhead through the church. The union which is mentioned here was thus the Holy Spirit who was the communion of the father and the son without being identical with them. How three persons can be the same while they are still different, that, according to Edwards, was the mystery of the trinity. The communion of the saints was where identity and community were no longer contradictory but each was open to the other as a perfect history.[2]

Summary and Conclusions

Through the Great Awakening the historical location of the theologian had entered for Edwards into the systematic elaboration of the Christian faith as something new and positive. Even though his own system remained

---

[1] Works, I, p. 466.

[2] Evidence for this possible resolution of the ambiguity exists in the Edwards corpus. In one of his numerous Miscellanies on the subject of heaven he wrote: "It seems by this to have been God's design to admit man as it were to the utmost fellowship with the Deity. There was, as it were, an eternal society in the Godhead in the trinity of persons; and it seems to be God's design to admit the church into the divine family." (Works, X, 70.)

formally incomplete, <u>The Chief End for Which God Created the World</u> showed
a clear design that supported the investigation of metaphysics as well as
of history as material principles of dogmatic theology in such a way as to
show that Scripture defined either one and related both. Research into
the background for Edwards' program of a divinity in the new form of a
history showed some instructive if inconclusive formal antecedents. We
found that a near contemporary of Edwards, the Dutch Arminian Jean LeClerc
had also endorsed this principle of the historical order. We had seen
that originally the idea of the <u>historica series</u> had been introduced by
Melanchthon, and had become a substructure to unfold theology either as a
theoretical or as a practical science which could pose a problem for the
systematician. The brevity of the treatise and the precision of its
argument required to go beyond it at points for purposes of illustration,
demonstration, and explanation.

We began our interpretation in this chapter with a description of
Edwards' positive, though critical attitude toward doctrine as a means to
determine the increase of knowledge and mystery for each age. His own
choice of the end as the one doctrine of central significance turned out
to be adequate and timely, for it had been neglected by the textbook tradition of Protestant Orthodoxy. Edwards proposed a scriptural method of
doctrinal explication of which he claimed that it had been successful befor
in settling the question as to the author of the universe. A reconstructio
of this latter argument showed a critique of the discrepancy between the
claim for a Deist view of nature and its actual conditioning by a historic
civilization. Moreover, in his theory of sacrifice Edwards advanced toward
a historicizing of natural religion and showed that in the draft of the
<u>History of the Work of Redemption</u> beginning and end cannot be rigidly
separated.

In order to sharpen the issue of the end we stepped outside of the limited situation of academia, touched upon the general concern about the end, and considered the catechism instruction of the church as a potential context that could force a resolution of conflicting views of the end. In a complex analysis Edwards unpacked the term end and made the decisive step to admit to this consideration not only the one, but also the many as "original ultimate" ends. Edwards' previous polemic against the exclusion of variety and his defense of the past as well as of the present and future were thus transformed into the point of departure for a constructive argument. A comparison with Samuel Willard then showed a contrast: as long as his argument dealt with the "deity" the many was inadmissible. As soon as he introduced the "trinity" and insofar as he used Scripture his attitude toward the many became more positive. He rejected the many as an ontological category, but he did not totally dismiss it as an economical notion.

Edwards' Scriptural method of doctrinal explication and the use of Scripture as a partial correction of the traditionally negative attitude toward the pluralism of the many led us to another and broader investigation[1] of Edwards' expertise in the area of exegesis. Examples from his shorter and longer exegetical arguments revealed that their diverse themes of eternity, life after death, the Song of Songs, and the question of moral precepts were either attempts to define a view of history or to locate individual doctrines within its progress. The consistent attention to the variegated literal detail of Scripture led Edwards, unlike Petrus van Mastricht, to the theme of glory in which end and ends, the one and the many as well as beginning, middle, and end cohere. This outcome of Edwards'

---

[1] See pp. 263ff.

exegesis can hold its own against modern exegesis. And if we compare his interpretation of כבוד to the role it plays in modern theories of religion, then Edwards' contribution was distinctive for its view of history.

Edwards was not only an exegete, but also a thinker who set out to conceptualize his findings about this central doctrine of the end in such a way as to correct, reinterpret, and integrate the body of traditional doctrines: the exegesis of glory led to his understanding of the Holy Spirit as a communication which included the ground of being as well as the origin of history. Communication, consequently, became an ontological-systematic as well as a dynamic-historical principle that served to integrate the ontological, cosmological, and anthropological propositions which we described in our trend analysis of Edwards' concept of revelation and which as a rational explication of Edwards' exegesis of glory can be looked upon as the prototype of his divinity in a new method.

A review of the dimensions of communication which are contained in The Chief End for Which God Created the World concluded this chapter. The application of the principle of communication led to an elimination of dualisms as a prerequisite of safeguarding the view of history. A certain reluctance to follow this principle consistently accounted for a "final ambiguity" at the conclusion of Edwards' own argument from communication and recalled Willard's distinction between a deity and a trinity.

On the positive side the removal of dualisms affected our understanding of Edwards' psychology, provided a basis for his typology, complemented the traditional theory of emanation, reminded of the nominalistic deficiencies of modern secularization and resacralization theories, and finally this removal helped redefine in positive terms the traditionally negative

incommunicable attributes of eternity as duration and extension and of
infinity as degree and as goal of progress.

We have indicated at the outset of this chapter that this treatise
of Edwards' was rich in "second meanings." In conclusion of this chapter
and its summary, we shall therefore emphasize three of these meanings as
they concern the Reformed tradition, the religious tradition of the West,
and the historiography of intellectual history in the West.

1. Edwards' exegesis integrated speculation and salvation in such
a way as to solve a particular problem in the textbook tradition of
Reformed Orthodoxy. This solution also suggested a material principle in
systematic theology which represented a distinctive type that cannot be
subsumed under any of the other varieties that already existed in the
history of theology.

In his basic work on the German Reformed tradition, Paul Althaus
observed that already in Calvin's theology a lively tension between speculation and salvation existed.[1] The extrapolation of this reciprocal
interaction transformed the subsequent history of the Reformed tradition
into a pattern of action and reaction defined by Theodore Beza's position
on the one hand and by that of William Ames on the other. Previously we
had viewed Ames' plea for application and for the life of the saint only
against his critique of scholastic speculation. Ames, however, did not do
away with this speculative aspect and we must therefore now also view this
scholastic background from its positive side which posed an unsolved problem
for systematic theology and was not exhausted only by a polemic. Paul
Althaus described the state of the question in the following terms:

[1]Paul Althaus, Die Prinzipien der Deutsch Reformierten Dogmatik im
Zeitalter der Aristotelischen Scholastik (Leipzig: A. Deichtersche Verlags-
Buchhandlung Werner Scholl, 1914), p. 67.

Der Calvinismus in seiner genuinen Gestalt griff von jeher über die Seligkeitsfrage hinaus. Gottes _gloria_ wird der Seligkeit neben-und vorgeordnet, und zwar nicht nur als bewusstes subjektives Ziel menschlichen Handelns, sondern als objektiver Zweck alles Weltgeschehens und der Menschheitsgeschichte. Daher liegt in der Reformierten Doktrin leicht ein "objektiver" Zug, der nicht als intellektualistisch, sondern als bezeichnender Ausdruck calvinistischer Frömmigkeit zu werten ist. Der Calvinist betet Gottes Herrlichkeit an, auch wo es nicht die Herrlichkeit der Gnade ist. Die religiöse Funktion greift über den Heilsglauben hinaus. Die Seligkeitsfrage ist nur _eine_ Frage in der objektiven Beschreibung des Weltwaltens Gottes, an der für den Calviniste religiöses Interesse hängt. Soteriologie und Theologie fallen nicht zusammen.[1]

Glory consequently was an ultimate objective as well as an objective purpose. In it final causes and finality, the practical-teleological as well as the theoretical-speculative could be merged. In his admittedly limited review of the Reformed tradition, Althaus expressed his amazement that this potential of glory was "not elaborated in such a way as to put glory at the head of the system." Edwards scripturally informed view of glory moved precisely in this direction. His treatment of the dimensions of communication included the salvational and the speculative interest and for that reason it is incorrect to speak of his program of a History of the Work of Redemption in terms of Heilsgeschichte as its scope reached beyond "Heil" or salvation.[2]

This objective or speculative interest in the Reformed tradition was not a deplorable aberration. In his detailed monographic treatment on the significance of Beginning and End in the Bible, Claus Westermann recently came to the conclusion that in Scripture the earth was "not merely the stage for the history of salvation," for "the message of the beginning and the end means that God is not confined to salvation history but extends to universal

---

[1]Althaus, _Die Principien_, pp. 62-63.

[2]RGG[3], III, 187-189.

history as well. According to Westermann's exegesis God intends to bring
this creation to a goal only he knows.   The same message also means that
the entire created universe beyond the planet Earth has a purpose and
therefore has "a history with a beginning and an end." Finally, he pointed
out that Scripture itself gave to beginning and end, to Genesis 1-11 and
to Revelations a transcendence which is foreign to our concepts and our
ways of thinking.[1] Westermann therefore referred to beginning and end as
"primal time" or origin and "end time" or goal respectively. He defined
their relation by means of the "function which is common to both and which
is possible because they share a common nature." This nature makes both
the "delimitation of time."[2] Westermann stopped short of explaining why
and in what way "the common nature" could be such a positive delimitation
of time. We had seen that in Edwards communication as ground of being and
origin of history performed this service. Based as it was on glory in its
inherent and internal aspect, in its "exercise and expression" communication described the ontological, cosmological, and anthropological character
of history. Edwards' conceptualization of the view of glory as the end of
creation which were prolegomena to a Christian theology included thus the
history of salvation, the history of the world, and the history of God.
Neither ontology nor anthropology, nor Heilsgeschichte by itself was
the material principle of his emerging system. Thus the history of the
work of redemption represented a divinity of a new kind.

2. In the context of the religious tradition of the West, Edwards'
view of the Holy Spirit marked a major point of departure. A question that

---

[1]Claus Westermann, Beginning and End in the Bible, p. 38; see also
p. 3.

[2]Ibid., p. 32.

had been posed for Christianity by Greek thought was the "basic metaphysical problem of the relation of God to motion, creativity, expression, and
non-being." It is a problem that within the tradition of the West "cannot
be avoided,"[1] and Arthur O. Lovejoy's history of the Great Chain of Being
is a good illustration for the perennial character of this issue.

Cyril Richardson observed that in the New Testament the Spirit was
creative, ecstatic, and connected with the end of history. Here the
Spirit's outpouring was a distinctive mark of God's kingdom at the end of
days."[2] The Spirit thus is a term of wide meaning. It covers all of God's
dynamic action and is closely related to, and even synonymous with, many
other expressions. However, the New Testament distinguished the Spirit
from Christ, and it is important to understand the ways in which the difference is conceived. The doctrinal development in the early church later
on restricted the Holy Spirit to the role of the "subjective appropriation"
of Christ as the "objective revelation."[3] In this way the distinction
between Christ and the Holy Spirit was obscured and an object-subject split
was introduced. This deficiency was seen before Edwards' time by men with
whose work he was familiar. Ralph Cudworth pointed out that "the genuine
Platonists and Pythagoreans" acknowledge the Spirit to be the "principle and
original of the whole world" while the "Nicene Fathers themselves" did not
even determine "that the Holy Ghost was an hypostasis, much less that he
was God."[4] In more general terms Samuel Mather in the introduction to his

---

[1] Cyril C. Richardson, "The Ontological Trinity, Father and Son,"
Religion in Life, XXIX (1959-1960), p. 9.

[2] Richardson, The Doctrine of the Trinity, pp. 45-46.

[3] Ibid., p. 47.

[4] Ralph Cudworth, The True Intellectual System of the Universe (1678;
Andover: Gould and Newman, 1837), p. 779.

treatment of the trinity stated that the divinity of the Holy Ghost had
never been stated as sufficiently as that of Christ.[1]

The reasons for this neglect were complex, but one factor was that
enthusiastic and prophetic movements in the ancient church helped to provoke
a backlash that made it easier for a domesticated and official view of the
Holy Spirit to win the day and that deprived prophetic exegesis of potent
and recognized institutional foci. It has been pointed out that the
proclamation of religious liberty in the United States marked a historic
occasion, for ever since the Christian religion became established under
Emperor Constantine in the Fourth Century A.D.[2] it had been taken for a
self-evident principle that a commonwealth could not endorse this liberty
and still exist. Likewise, it had been taken for granted that no community,
sacred or secular, could survive should all the scriptural manifestations
of the Holy Spirit be allowed. The Great Awakening in the American
Colonies proved this attitude to be a premature prejudgment, if not a
prejudice. This Great Revival can therefore not be ignored in the history
of the West in general and in its religious tradition in particular, for
it provided Edwards with the experiential impetus to remove an acknowledged
deficiency in the tradition by using its metaphysical sophistication and
by giving back to prophetic exegesis of Scripture a broad institutional
focus after it had undergone a revival in the seventeenth century and had
focused on the movement of the Spirit toward the end of history.

---

[1] Samuel Mather, A discourse concerning the Godhead of the Holy
Ghost, the Third Person in the eternal Trinity (London: Eman Matthews,
1719), p. xii.

[2] Handy, A Christian America, pp. 4ff.

3. Finally, the recognition of the importance of Scripture in Edwards' argument suggests a revision in the intellectual history of the West. A good example for the necessity of such a revision can be found in A. O. Lovejoy's classic work on The Great Chain of Being. Lovejoy used Edwards as the representative of a long tradition, for he "did not differ from most of the great theologians in having many Gods under one name." In Edwards, Lovejoy saw two Gods: one God who was "externally serene and impassibly absolute." As proof he quoted Edwards' statement to that effect from The Chief End for Which God Created the World. The other God, according to Lovejoy, was the "sadistic Deity" in Edwards' sermon "Sinners in the Hands of an Angry God,"[1] and the question was: How can a God eternally happy be interested at all to bring about change in man under the threat of hell?

Lovejoy traced this "polytheistic" way of thinking back to the strong influence even after centuries of a seminal cluster of ideas which were first announced by Plato and which later became endemic in the tradition of the West. This cultural a priori gave rise to the most characteristic strains and conflicts of the idea of a divine self-completion which yet was not complete enough:

> The concept of self-sufficient perfection, by a bold logical inversion, was -- without losing any of its original implications -- converted into the concept of a self-transcending fecundity. A timeless and incorporeal one became the logical ground as well as the dynamic source of the existence of a temporal and material and extremely variegated universe. The proposition that -- as it was phrased in the Middle Ages -- omne bonum est diffusivum sui here made its appearance as an axiom in metaphysics.[2]

---

[1] Lovejoy, The Great Chain of Being, p. 44.

[2] Ibid., pp. 49-50.

Phrases like "bold logical inversion" or the similar expression "happy inconsistence" are not enough to describe let alone conceptualize the relation between sufficient fecundity and diversity. Lovejoy thus stayed away just one step from getting involved where the issues were joined. He substituted boldness for an answer, and called the subject fascinating instead of formulating a thesis to account for this inversion.

We had seen that exegesis led Willard to a partial resolution of the question of the one and the many. Edwards even found a sophisticated solution to the different parts of this cultural a priori. Even though Scripture played a vital part in the intellectual tradition of the West, it did not come into view in Lovejoy's monograph and it is not generally recognized as one of the great fundamental themes of our tradition. Historians of idea thus far have exegeted the sources of the philosophical tradition and have ignored the history of the exegesis of the Scriptures in the West.

318

CHAPTER VII

SCRIPTURE AND NATURE: THE EXAMPLE OF SHAFTESBURY

In order to see that Edwards' view of history to a large extent
depended on Scripture, it is useful to show what possible consequences a
neglect, misunderstanding, or elimination of Scripture from someone's
intellectual pursuits had at the beginning of the eighteenth century.
Lord Shaftesbury in his time was a kind of representative man who like a
sponge absorbed different and diverse currents of thought. The language
and style of his Characteristics of Men, Manners, Opinions, Times[1] was quite
distinct from the earlier cumbersome and complicated modes of writing with
which divines and metaphysicians would treat of questions such as nature and
virtue. Insights buried in such tomes as Ralph Cudworth's True Intellectual
System of the Universe[2] attained in this way a more widespread dissemination.
It is not unfair to liken Shaftesbury's role for the eighteenth century to
the man in show business who feeds the lines to a comedian. The comedian
will take off on these lines and it is he who will be remembered.
Shaftesbury's career as a thinker followed this very pattern. Many great
minds in philosophy and literature throughout the eighteenth century

---

[1]Anthony, Earl of Shaftesbury, Characteristics of Men, Manners,
Opinions, Times, ed., John M. Robertson, The Library of Liberal Arts (1711;
ppb., Indianapolis: Bobbs-Merrill, 1964). This work will subsequently be
quoted as "Shaftesbury, Characteristics."

[2]Ralph Cudworth, The True Intellectual System of the Universe, 1678
(Andover: Gould and Newman, 1837). Cited below as "Cudworth, Intellectual
System."

recognized the importance of Shaftesbury for themselves. By the end of
the eighteenth century, Shaftesbury's value as a straight man had outlived
its usefulness and he lapsed into obscurity.

Edwards certainly knew Shaftesbury and used him.[1] On the other hand,
he did not bestow the lavish praise on him that came from men like Herder.[2]
Edwards as a student of Scripture had a universal view of history. In contrast, Shaftesbury -- who dissolved Scripture -- had only a view of tradition which was as indispensable for legitimating the existing social order
as it was religiously and aesthetically unsatisfactory beyond the maintenance of a civil religion. While Shaftesbury made comments on secular historiography in passing,[3] the question of historical knowledge itself was
joined over what we have previously called universal history and which
included Old Testament, New Testament, and church history. Joseph H. Preston
pointed out that the recent interest in the historiography of the sixteenth
and seventeenth centuries ignored church history and he set out to show a
sustained preoccupation with the question of impartiality for the later
seventeenth century church historiography in England.[4] An answer to this
question also played a significant role in shaping Shaftesbury's concept of
tradition.

Shaftesbury referred to "historical revelation"[5] as a subsequent act
of faith with which he was not concerned. He was concerned only with the

---

[1]Works, VIII, p. 184.

[2]Stanley Green, Intr., Characteristics by Shaftesbury, pp. xiv-xv.

[3]Shaftesbury, Characteristics, I, 52, II, 132, 146.

[4]Joseph H. Preston, "English Ecclesiastical Historians and the
Problems of Bias, 1559-1742," JHI, 32 (1971), pp. 208ff.

[5]Shaftesbury, op. cit., II, p. 92.

320

first act of natural revelation and was determined "to keep these provinces distinct and settle their just boundaries."[1] This division touched upon questions such as general _versus_ special revelation, natural _versus_ supernatural religion, and could also become an issue between natural and historical religion or simply between nature and history. To the extent that "historical revelation" receded, the view of history itself grew dim to the point where one would have to ask whether or not a failure of nerve was reflected in the retreat to the "solemn groves."[2] Proclamations of separation and their actual execution are usually two different kinds of things in the realm of the mind. Such a just settlement of boundaries as it was advocated by Shaftesbury leaves the historian with the task of finding out where Shaftesbury as his own lawyer found it just to settle the boundaries. Boundaries are usually drawn and redrawn in accordance with a strong desire to safeguard interests and get from the other side those things which seem most desirable. Thus, while there are distinct landmarks that make for unmovable boundaries, there are also those areas where the justness of the settlement is more flexible and a good deal of traffic and carry-over goes on. Shaftesbury, for instance, settled the boundary in such a way as to include the territory of enthusiasm which had previously belonged to historical revelation, and he transplanted miracle in different soil so that it reappeared under the form of wonder. History itself was excluded from this settlement. The following argument will describe this disappearance of history into a no-man's-land in which neither side, be it tradition, revelation, or nature, was interested in the subject.

[1] Shaftesbury, _Characteristics_, II, p. 323.

[2] Ibid., p. 126.

Church History

According to Francis Bacon, "registers are collections of public acts, as decrees of council, judicial proceedings, declarations and letters of estate, orations, and the like without a perfect continuance of contexture of the thread of narration."[1] Bacon called this "imperfect history" and drew a line between it and "perfect history" which included interpretation. A whole succession of church historians in England in the latter part of the seventeenth century made a distinction like this their basic concern in an apparent attempt to strive for objectivity in their own several historical narratives, and Preston found three approaches which in their respective ways tried to cope with a question that had become more pressing in the aftermath of the English civil war.

> Initially some historians made a distinction between partisanship and partiality, i.e., the assertion that one could be fairminded and abide by the rules of evidence (facts) even if one was a 'party.' Others proclaimed that they would eschew 'reflections' without considering the role of bias in deciding the relevance of facts. Another tactic was an increased emphasis on documentation and primary sources.[2]

All three approaches show a considerable increase in the sophistication with which evidence was handled. On the basis of the sources[3] which Preston

---

[1] Works, VI, p. 189. See also p.

[2] Preston, "English Ecclesiastical Historians," p. 218.

[3] Important to Preston's argument on bias was also the Catholic historian Hugh Tootel (1672-1743). He had studied philosophy at Douay. He had received minor orders in 1690, and from 1726-1743 he had led the Roman Catholic congregation at Harvington, Worcestershire. Under the pen name of C. Dod he published The Church History of England from the Year 1500, to the Year 1688, Chiefly Relating to Catholics (Brussels: 1737-42). Tootel attempted to formulate the sources of bias with which the historian must deal in his search for objectivity: "Ignorance, education, religion and passion, and party disputes, are in a kind of confederacy to seduce mankind" (Preston, op. cit., p. 215). Preston did not pursue the question of how much of this insight on the part of the historian of the Roman Catholic minority came actually to be incorporated in his historical craftsmanship. We shall therefore not include him in the following discussion.

322

· provided it is possible to delineate more sharply than he did the complexity

of the issues involved.

Both Heylin[1] and Burnet[2] implied a distinction between partisanship

and partiality, but their respective reliance on secondary and primary evi-

dence changed what they meant by "partiality." This difference can be put

into a catch phrase similar to that of partisan and partial: For Heylin

partiality meant that he still told the story, while Burnet claimed to tell

a story. For Heylin, whose formative years antedated the Civil War, evidenc

was still the testimony of "unquestioned authors" or "good authors." Conse-

quently, evidence itself retained an authoritative canon of judgment which

allowed for improvement but not for self-questioning. The burden of proof

always remained on the "adverse party." What Heylin seemed to contend for

was increased self-confidence in handling one's own tradition from its best

sources. The improvement of authoritative secondary evidence raised self-

esteem and improved the climate of discussion at the same time. It was no

longer necessary to resort to polemical and partisan tricks for fear of the

superiority of the arguments of the "adversary party." Such a view of

Heylin's case was not without foundation in the development of the interest

in church history at the time. Heylin was the spokesman for the Anglican

party which came to develop a specific, long-standing, and confident

patristic interest.[3]

---

[1]Peter Heylin (1600-1662), churchman, historian, and author of
Examen Historicum which represented a full-scale critique of Thomas Fuller's
The Church History of Britain. He had been associated with Laudian policy
and during the Civil War with Royalist forces.

[2]Gilbert Burnet (1643-1715), Bishop of London and author of the
History of the Reformation and the History of My Own Time.

[3]B.H.G. Wormald, Clarendon, Politics, History and Religion 1640-1660
(Cambridge: Cambridge University Press, 1951), pp. 246-247, 253.

Whereas Heylin claimed <u>the</u> point of view, Burnet presented <u>a</u> point

of view. It is probably inadequate to say that Burnet presented his per-

sonal point of view, for that sounds too modern. Burnet asked the reader

to assess "the truth of this history," he did not claim the truth as a

whole. He presupposed and accepted parties and therefore aspired to impar-

tiality.[1] Both John Strype[2] and he himself included primary documents so

that the reader could judge for himself whether the author had lived up to

the aspirations of impartiality. In point of fact, Strype left that judg-

ment so entirely to the reader that he, unlike Burnet, never got around to

the construction of an interpretative narrative. In the case of Burnet,

attention to these primary facts led him to revise the accepted hostile

view of Cardinal Pole, the apostolic legate of the Roman See at the time

of Queen Mary.[3]

Shaftesbury's criticism went further and drove deeper. He eliminated

such a Baconian appeal of and to primary evidence by pointing out that the

"registers" themselves did arise in a partisan way as the deliberations of

modern synods had shown:

---

[1]"I know the duty of a historian leads him to write as one that is
of neither party, and I have endeavored to follow it as carefully as I
could, neither concealing the faults of the one party, nor denying the just
praises that were due to any of the other side, and have delivered things
as I found them, many of them neither better nor worse than indeed were"
(Preston, "English Ecclesiastical Historians," p. 272).

[2]John Strype (1643-1737), ecclesiastical historian, biographer,
antiquarian.

[3]Preston, op. cit., p. 217, suggested that these church historians
were more conscious than the contemporary secular historians of the question of bias and objectivity. I cannot find support for this opinion in
the reference (Fussner, Historical Revolution, p. xvii) which Preston used
as his proof. Since Lord Clarendon was a contemporary of Burnet and
belonged to what can be called the origin of "partisan" historiography, a
comparison between the two might throw light upon Preston's suggestion.

We should easily be subject to heterodoxy and error when we had no
better warrant left us for the authority of our sacred symbols than
the integrity, candour and disinterestedness of their compilers and
registers. How great that candour and disinterestedness may have been,
we have no other histories to inform us than those of their own licens-
ing or composing. But busy persons, who officiously search into these
records are ready even from hence to draw proofs very disadvantageous
to the frame and character of this succession of men. And persons
moderately read in these histories are apt to judge no otherwise of
the temper of ancient councils than by that of later synods and modern
conventions.[1]

This negative view of the past initiated the search for criteria by means

of which it could nevertheless be shown that the history of Christianity

was not "pure invention or artificial compilement of an interested party

in behalf of the richest corporation and most profitable monopoly which

could have been erected in the world."[2]

Burnet's resignation to a party posture accepted a reality which for

men like William Chillingworth and also Shaftesbury was not that easy to

adapt to intellectually. For the former the disintegration of the

consensus quinquesaecularis[3] evoked comments on the confusion in the early

church: "Some Fathers against others, the same Fathers against themselves,

a consent of Fathers of one age against a consent of Fathers of another

age."[4] Shaftesbury has one of his characters say that there was no consen-

sus on the part of the Fathers with regard to the canonicity of Scripture,[5]

---

[1]Shaftesbury, Characteristics, I, 231-232.

[2]Ibid., II, p. 302.

[3]The phrase meant that the first five centuries A.D. provided the
authoritative and normative consent of church history for all subsequent
ages of the church. Peter Meinhold, Geschichte der Kirchlichen Historiographie (Freiburg: Verlag Alber, 1927), I, pp. 351-358.

[4]Chillingworth (1602-1644), The Religion of Protestants, quoted in
Wormald, Clarendon, Politics, History and Religion, p. 252.

[5]Shaftesbury, op. cit., II, p. 356.

and John Hales came to the conclusion that "those things which we reverence
for antiquity, what were they at their first birth? Were they false? Time
cannot make them true . . . the circumstance of time . . . is merely impertinent."[1] That was as much as to say: Who needs antiquity as authority in
the first place? It was merely a "circumstance of time." As the consensus
broke up and time lost its pertinence, time became "impertinent." Consensus theories in historiography seem to have a tendency to turn barren as
providers of meaning as soon as the increasing stream of historical research
points to their contradictions. One begins to wonder whether such consensus
is not unconsciously defined as uniformity rather than as an overall agreement. Once the tire had a puncture, it shrivelled into an unusable formless
mass. Such a consensus was like a wooden figure that a wind could blow over
and not like a body over which the wind will blow because it can adjust.
These few examples show that Shaftesbury's own comments on church history
related to a complex discussion: "Narrative or historical truth must needs
be highly estimable; especially when we consider how mankind who are become
so deeply interested in the subject, have suffered by the want of clearness
in it. 'Tis itself a part of moral truth."[2]

To the intellectual lack of clearness that we have explored thus far,
Shaftesbury also added that of human suffering. He seemed to say that up to
the present the popular arguments from history have only influenced the
course of history to the extent of plunging mankind into suffering. For
the purposes of such a clarification of the nature of "historical truth"

---

[1]John Hales (1584-1656), Of Enquiry and Private Judgment in Religion,
quoted in Wormald, Clarendon, Politics, History and Religion, p. 254.

[2]Shaftesbury, Characteristics, I, p. 97.

326

Shaftesbury did not become a practicing historian himself. He simply indicated the way in which this popular subject must be dealt with in order to
avoid suffering. He suggested a moral and critical approach. The critical
tools such as literature, languages, and also "chronology, natural philosophy, geography and other sciences"[1] were to guide the inquiry which would
locate the harmful bias and establish the disinterestedness and the "character" of an author in church history. Whatever testimony, witness or authority an author was allowed depended upon the outcome of such an inquiry.
Such a definition of the sources in terms of character witnesses excluded
for Shaftesbury any positive consideration of martyrs. Otherwise, "one migh
be a little scandalized, perhaps, at the history of many of our primitive
confessors and martyrs. . . ."[2] Jonathan Edwards, on the other hand,
observed on the basis of "fact and experience" that the "histories of the
many thousands that died martyrs for Christ since the beginning of the
Reformation" witnessed effectively, even though imperfectly to the truth in
persecution and torture.[3] Many of them were illiterate women and children
who did not have the benefit of hindsight. Shaftesbury's advocacy of disinterestedness therefore did not turn on the concern for the removal of the
abuses of suffering, but it eliminated suffering itself as something meaningful from the historical process and history writing. The apostle Paul
in his praise of love had criticized and corrected an attitude as nihilis-
tic which incurred physical death for Christ without love. While for Paul
martyrdom without love was nothing, for Shaftesbury this admonition meant

[1]Shaftesbury, Characteristics, I, p. 97.

[2]Ibid., p. 19.

[3]Religious Affections, p. 305.

that love made martyrdom superfluous, because "the spirit of love and
humanity is above that of martyrs."[1]

Scripture

When we move from church history to Scripture as the other major
element in the scheme of universal history we find that instead of its
becoming a "sufficient guide and rule"[2] for the settling of ecclesiastical
disputes, the authority of Scripture itself was in question to the point
where Shaftesbury has a character in one of his invented speeches ask:
"What is Scripture?"

There was a variety of manuscript readings and a variety of interpretations and in each case variety points to a deficiency. The different
and divergent manuscript readings of the scriptural text pointed to the
fact that the completion of the canon itself was a matter of partisan
controversy in the early church. Where the boundaries between the time of
Scripture and the church were removed in this way, Scripture could not serve
as criterion or appeal for the settling of problems. The history of interpretation likewise did not offer any authoritative support, since the
variety that this history displayed was itself "part of the disease." Even
amongst the early Fathers themselves there was no agreement of whether one
and the same verse or passage was to be taken literally or figuratively.
If already they who lived so close to the time of Jesus could not distinctly
discover the meaning of these passages, then it was even more impossible to
do so for the present-day generation of interpreters. A historical sense

---

[1] Shaftesbury, Characteristics, I, p. 19. I Cor. 13:3.

[2] Ibid., pp. 356ff.

such as Thomas Shepard insisted upon and which was for him a platform of

appeal had gone. From all this Shaftesbury concluded that there were

indeed

> Divers places in these sacred volumes containing in them mysteries
> and questions of great concernment, yet such is the fabric and the
> constitution of the whole, that there is no certain mark to determine
> whether the sense of these passages should be taken as literal or
> figurative.[1]

While Shaftesbury conceded that there were questions of great concernment

or appeal in Scripture, he also asserted that the "whole" to which all

partisan facts could meaningfully relate was no more, for no constitution

nor fabric was recognizable. As the whole departed, meaning emerged, for

"the matter is so profound and the manner so intricate." This complexity

made faith for him an exercise of charity, not an adventure in hope. The

problem that Shaftesbury had with the "whole" led him like other contempo-

raries to fasten upon those "mysteries and questions of great concernment"

which regardless of the total structure still had the power to make an indi-

vidual concerned. There was a reduction from a total concernment to a par-

tial concernment. Shaftesbury there reflected a change from a concern with

the whole to a concern with fundamentals. Thinking about the architectural

design gave way to an inquiry into the necessary foundations. Both without

and within the church the trend was away from the vision of the whole toward

a view and contentment with basics.[2]

---

[1]Shaftesbury, Characteristics, II, pp. 356-357.

[2]Ibid., p. 302. "'Tis the substance only of the narrative, and
the principal facts confirming the authority of the revelation, which our
divines think themselves concerned to prove, according to the evidence of
which the matter itself is capable."

For Protestant Orthodoxy, the authority of Scripture consisted of its perspicuity, sufficiency, and efficacy.[1] Perspicuity was understood to mean that Scripture in its concern for salvation was comprehensive if not always distinct to everyone. Sufficiency meant that no tradition as a complementary and improving principle was needed in order to make Scripture either perfect or more perfect, for the tradition of the church itself had no necessary existence without it. For Shaftesbury the authority of Scripture was unclear as well as insufficient, and when we review the grounds on which its style and miracles as testimonies for its present-day authority were excluded, then we can see even more clearly the extent to which also the efficacious aspect of Scripture had disappeared. Since Scripture was in doubt it could no longer serve as the main criterion for tradition, and Shaftesbury found other different means of support for tradition. He also used another mode of understanding and language, since the "enchantment" which flowed from the literary, not the learned, qualities of Scripture which Edwards had described as "Scripture-history" were not available.

Style

For Shaftesbury the style of Scripture was not "self-convincing." His attitude toward that subject was characterized by a simultaneous adherence to two different if not contradictory views on inspiration. On the one hand, he depended upon a poetical view of inspiration. On the other hand, he also asserted the then current notion of the doctrine of verbal inspiration. Each of these views implied a different conception of the

---

[1] Heppe, Reformed Dogmatics, pp. 20-37; O. Weber, Grundlagen der Dogmatik (Neukirchen: Erziehungsverein, 1959), I, pp. 269, 302, 310, 313.

whole and the appearance of the poetical view of inspiration indicated that
the resignation to complexity was but an unstable position that must be
resolved.

For Shaftesbury it was inconceivable that the divine should create
something that was "indifferent" to "art itself, for whenever something that
was without art demanded veneration and spontaneously received it, this was
a sure sign for the presence of a case of disorderly enthusiasm." The only
exception that he made occurred "where the supreme powers have given their
sanction to any religious record or pious writ."[1] Consequently, Shaftesbury
claimed both that there "can be no scripture but what must of necessity be
subject to the reader's narrow scrutiny and strict judgment" and that "it
becomes immoral and prophane in any one to deny or dispute the sacred authority of the least line or syllable contained in it."[2] While Shaftesbury was
consistent in his insistence on his deference to the traditional position,
he at the same time did not spare his criticism of this position by means
of his aesthetic standard. According to this judgment, Scripture was
"multifarious" when it should be "single," "voluminous" and not "short," "of
the most different interpretations" and not "uniform." For these reasons
Scripture could not be "self-convincing" in terms of the criteria of singleness, shortness, and uniformity. It had neither character, self, identity,
nor whole. There was no justness or proportion in it. He concurred with
the opinion of those "judicious divines" of the established churches "who
maintain the infallibility of the Biblical record," but who:

----

[1]Shaftesbury, Characteristics, II, p. 298.

[2]Ibid.

> Neither do . . . in the original itself represent it to us as a
> very masterpiece of writing, or as absolutely perfect in the purity
> and justness either of style or composition. They allow the holy
> authors to have written to their best faculties and the strength of
> their natural genius: A shepherd like a shepherd; and a prince like
> a prince. A man of reading, and advanced in letters, like a pro-
> ficient in the kind; and a man of meaner of capacity and reading, like
> one of the ordinary sort, in his own common idiom and imperfect manner
> of narration.[1]

This authoritative opinion put Shaftesbury both at a polemical advantage

and into an embarrassing situation. Over against the "mere enthusiasts

and fanatics" he could point out that the Bible was also a learned document.

By the same token, however, Shaftesbury also saw that Scriptural variety

included examples that from the literary point of view bordered on those

characteristics which he had denounced as deficiencies in enthusiastic

pieces of work.

Shaftesbury's learned defense and literary criticism of the Scriptures

derived from his inability to see the Scriptures as one book. His literary

theory operated from an identification of book and genre, but as we have

seen before, the Scriptures simply did not consist of one "single" genre.

The fact that there was more than one genre in it cancelled out a view of

"uniformity" in which the one was identical with one form (uniformitas).

Shaftesbury on the other hand could allow variety only as long as it was of

no concern to the genre and he would ignore the ignorant as long as they

did not conform to the genre. Shaftesbury was therefore not a historical

critic, but he followed primarily a line of aesthetic criticism in the con-

text of which Scripture could not be "self-convincing" because it did not

fit a certain theory of form. This in turn led to a selective reading of

the Scriptures which reminds one of contemporary efforts in which Shakespeare

---

[1]Shaftesbury, _Characteristics_, II, p. 302.

criticism and editing tamed the plays of the dramatist by reducing their
multifarious dimensions. In a similar way Shaftesbury did have an appreciation for the fact that "entire volumes" of Scripture were "plainly
poetry and full of humorous images and jocular wit."[1] He mentioned in
particular the books of Job, of Proverbs, and of Canticles. Insofar as
Scripture contained wit and wisdom he could agree with it, but not insofar
as it contained history. Unlike Shaftesbury's later admirer Herder who
combined a view of Scripture poetry with a general view of the historical
world, Shaftesbury's own attitude to Scripture excluded such a general
view and made his appreciation of the poetic qualities in Scripture
isolated and unassimilated instances of secondary importance.

The authoritative statement by the "judicious divines" made him confident that his views would gain additional support through a consultation
of the Scriptures in the "originals" and he expressed his unequivocal con-
tempt for those who only had the "sufficiency of the reiterate translated
text" as their basis. For Shaftesbury it was unfortunate that the vulgar
and the common were not only part of the cast, but also dramatis personae
as well as authors of Scripture. It was chiefly their presence which
interfered with the singleness, brevity, and uniformity of style.
Shaftesbury was quite sympathetic to those Greek philosophers who solved
the problem of the vulgar and the miraculous by means of an allegorization
of their own early literature. Allegorization can be described as a means
of control: the literal meaning of a passage was not its intended meaning.
The vulgar actually hid something very refined. The interpreter raised the
seemingly vulgar and built it up or "edified" it to the level of meaning

---

[1]Shaftesbury, Characteristics, II, p. 228.

shared by the interpreter's community. In this way the vulgar qua vulgar
lost its identity and historicity. The classic case of such a loss of
identity in Western history was, of course, the Christian interpretation
of the Old Testament both in its sophisticated and simplistic ways. On
the other hand the pervasive process of allegorization still testified
to a need to relate to Scripture as a frame of reference. This vitality
of Scripture no longer existed for Shaftesbury so that he did not need
allegorization as a means of achieving a dehistoricization. For him the
vulgar simply dropped below the horizon of his conscious perception of
reality.

The significance of Shaftesbury's aesthetic stance appears best in
a contrast with the positive analysis and critical defense of the relation
between variety and style by Robert Boyle who at the time of Shaftesbury's
birth had a well-established reputation as a scientist.[1] Boyle also was
not happy at the idea that "illiterates" wanted to dispute about the materials of the Bible, but his own extensive study of the originals convinced
him that the lowly were nevertheless an integral part of Scripture. Boyle
admitted that he had no gift for languages, but out of veneration for the
Book he learned the original languages that were deemed necessary to study
both the Book and its background.

Boyle distinguished "betwixt what the Scripture says and what is
said in Scripture."[2] The various words and actions that were reported in it
had to be distinguished from their design and drift, for, according to Boyle,

---

[1] Robert Boyle lived from 1627-1691. Shaftesbury lived from 1671-1713.

[2] Robert Boyle, Theological Works, Ed., R. Boulton (London:
W. Taylor, 1715), III, p. 99ff.

Scripture resembled the Royal realm which included many things that were
not Royal business and could not therefore be blamed on the King. Boyle's
point was that in this Scriptural realm "prophets, kings and priests" as
well as "soldiers, shepherds and women and others who might speak without
wit or eloquence" were part of the Royal business. This latter part of the
human situation and condition as the goal of divine activity was for Boyle
not a disturbing but a distinctive feature of the Biblical records and he
observed that the inspired penmen or "secretaries" "personate" both groups.
Boyle therefore saw to it financially and administratively that Bibles were
spread abroad.[1]

Boyle turned the charge of the alleged Scriptural deficiency "in
eloquence and wit" around and made it into a critique of men like
Shaftesbury who would explain away the implications of Scriptural style by
means of substituting a different theory of inspiration that was restrictive
as well as repressive:

> . . . though in Romances the speakers are made to express them-
> selves as well as the Historians, yet such were Embassadors, Orators,
> Generals, or eminent Men, whose Parts were extraordinary, as well as
> their Employments; or the Historian takes the liberty to make Speeches
> for them, and relates not what such Persons said, but what they ought
> to say upon such occasions. Whereas one of the sacred Writers confesses,
> that he followed not cunningly devised fables but faithfully recorded
> both their sayings and actions, observing the laws of truth more than
> the conditions of the speaker.[2]

The attempt to save the reputation of Scripture and its author by means of
placing the former in the vicinity of orations and a literate style was
dangerous, for the price for such a defense was the confusion of high social

---

[1] DNB II, pp. 1027-1028; R. P. Beaver, Church, State and the
American Indian, p. 37.

[2] Boyle, Theological Works, III, 101.

status with reality, of the "conditions of the speaker" with the "laws of
truth." Such a defense turned the deity into one group's conception of
the divine. A history that did not transcend the conditions of the speaker,
that dealt with the conventions of his group instead, and then took them
to be true, was a "romance." The result was so many roles and characters,
but no individuals.

Invention of speeches had been a typical trait of classical Greek
historiography, but Boyle did not explicitly reflect on this tradition here.
His criticism was directed at the social exclusiveness and the social illusion which such a perception of reality could create. In his critique he
appealed to one "sacred writer" who declared "that he followed not cun-
ningly devised fables." This was a reference to I Timothy 4:7, "But refuse
prophane and old wives fables, and exercise thy self rather unto godliness"
(AV). Usually this locus classicus[1] in Puritan Scriptural proofs is taken
only as a negative attitude toward the aesthetic, an approach that was made
easy by the pervasive moralism of Puritanism which strikes us first and
foremost. As soon as we look at this locus positively as the pointer to
reality which the moralism does represent, but not exhaust, then Scripture
emerges as a comprehensive model for the social construction of reality.
According to Scripture, as Boyle saw it, a faithful and non-faithful recording of the whole of reality included King and soldier, prophet and shepherd,
priest and women, the extraordinary and the others. In his History of the
Royal Society, Thomas Sprat listed as one of the main concerns of this
society the desire to leave behind fables and old wives' tales.[2] Boyle

---

[1]Herbert Schöffler, Neue Wege zur Englischen Literatur des
Achtzehnten Jahrhunderts, 2nd ed. (Göttingen: Vandenhoeck, 1958), p. 12.

[2]Cf. Basil Willey, The Seventeenth Century Background (1934; ppb.,
London: Penguin Books, 1962), p. 194.

himself was probably the most perceptive and critical of the members when it came to exposing such tales in the field of natural history.[1] At the same time he was a man who did not only uncover natural, but also social reality when he used Scripture as his basis to deal with a fanciful and elitist aesthetics.

The implications of Boyle's critique are very important when we compare it with Shaftsbury's attitude and project both views forward into the development of the mind in the West. Shaftesbury's view of art as harmony, justness, and proportion was predicated on the exclusion of Boyle's soldiers shepherds, women, and others. Reality was reduced to genre. The role that this lower social segment played in Shaftesbury's mind and thought was significant; it occurred as a potential enthusiastic threat, as an object of ridicule, or as idealized rustics in nature. They were either a threatening fact or a noble fiction, they were rebellious, and romantic.[2] They became the focal points of fascination and frustration. In the overall picture of generic harmony they floated as an incongruous dream at night and as the wishful projection during the day. Shaftesbury, the representative man and popular influence only highlighted a paradox at the heart of the emerging Enlightenment: its conviction of having removed or of being in the process of removing particularism and parochialism in favor of the general, universal, and the humanitarian as marks of progress from darkness to light was built upon an aesthetic abstraction from social reality. The species man and humankind or mankind did not include the people. It is one of the basic rules of hermeneutics that the way that question is put has more than an incidental bearing on the way in which the issue can be resolved.

_____

[1]Randall, Career of Philosophy, I, 509.

[2]Shaftesbury, Characteristics, II, 125.

If, as Peter Gay showed so clearly, the Enlightenment arose out of the
battle between clerics and philosophes and if the cleric is of the type
for whom the people are a quantité negligeable, then it comes as no surprise when Gay observed that the "question of the lower orders is the
great unexamined political question of the Enlightenment." According to
Gay, the private correspondence of the philosophes abounded with references
to the common people, but this abundance was the kind of variety of which
we saw that it could not fit into a consistent conception. Gay himself
attempted to improve on the unfinished business that the philosophes left
behind. Was it just an unfinished or more properly an unmanageable business
for them? Gay himself observed: "There is snobbery in these casual remarks
and a certain failure of the imagination. There is also something else: a
sense of despair at the general wretchedness, illiteracy, and brutishness
of the poor, which appeared by and large incurable."[1] If we compare this
attitude with that of Boyle and Shaftesbury, it is possible to recognize
that in their respective views of man Shaftesbury and the philosophes made
an omission where Boyle saw a commission. One of the pivotal discoveries
in the formative years of Karl Marx's own philosophy was the social and
productive processes beyond and underneath an abstract view of man and mankind as a species. In the case of Boyle it was the adherence to Scripture
as an inspired document which made him include the lowly. Inspiration for
him comprehended the extraordinary as well as the ordinary and puts both
relative to an anticipated goal. Inspiration includes all ages and more
than just one group, the social as well as the historical processes.

[1]Peter Gay, The Enlightenment: An Interpretation, The Science of
Freedom, II (New York: Knopf, 1969), p. 517.

Miracles

For Shaftesbury miracles raised the question of continuity and discontinuity between past and present. Miracles belonged to the past. They
have ceased to occur upon the completion of the canon of Scripture. Since
miracles as a means of divine self-disclosure had stopped, they could
therefore not serve as means of or medium for the conviction or confirmation that the God of the past was the same as the God of the present. In
order to bridge this gap between the past and the present, Shaftesbury
divided the question: the credibility of the past did not depend upon the
mediating force of miracles, but upon the credibility of the documents in
which the miracles of the past were reported. As long as an orderly conducted research into the historical record could establish the documentary
facticity of miracles, so long the continuity of past and present was
secured.

The solution of one problem, however, threw him into another. We
have pointed out earlier that for him the simple Baconian distinction
between fact and interpretation no longer existed. Since the record itself
was biased, neither the Fathers nor Scripture provided a disinterested
criterion towards their credibility as a historical record. For this reason he introduced the "collateral testimony" of classical antiquity. Accor-
ing to him, the New Testament referred to this disinterested criterion with
which the credibility of the record could be established. The New Testament
"not only alluded to the annals and histories of the ancient world but even
to the philosophical works, the regular poems, the very plays and comedies
of the learned polite ancients."[1] Like a theme with variations, the

---

[1]Shaftesbury, Characteristics, II, p. 303.

necessity of this argument was being played through in Shaftesbury's

Miscellany V:[1] "The language of the wisest and most learned of nations

is acknowledged to contain the principal and essential part of our holy

revelation."[2] As long as the ancient authors were in demand we need not

worry about the "support of the sacred volumes."[3] The interests of a pious

clergy" were therefore bound up with that of "ancient letters and polite

learning."[4] Shaftesbury became emphatic in his warning that "when they

(clergy) abandon this, they resign their cause. When they strike at it,

they strike even at the root and foundation of our holy faith, and weaken

that pillar on which the whole fabric of our religion depends."[5] "This con-

servation of these other ancient and disinterested authors they [Roman

Catholics] judge essential to the credibility of those principle facts,

on which the whole religious history and tradition depends."[6] The distinc-

tive feature of these exhortations was not the plea for a "learned ministry,"

but it was the urgency of the plea and the crucial role assigned in it to a

particular kind of learning. Since the "fabric and constitution of the

whole" of Scripture yielded no mark of certainty, it was now classical

antiquity "on which the whole fabric of our religion depends." Shaftesbury

---

[1]"Miscellany" here did not refer to that collection of thoughts which
Edwards accumulated for the purposes of clarifying problems and assembling
material toward a later system. Shaftesbury spoke on the contrary of "the
celebrated wits of the miscellarian race" which included "the essay writers,
casual discoursers, reflection coiners, meditation founders, and others of
the irregular kind of writers (Characteristics, II, p. 215). These writers
were content with insights that represented "cuttings and shreds of learning" improved "with various fragments and points of wit" (ibid., p. 159).
Shaftesbury himself used the miscellany as a means to complement and to
comment on facts of his own treatises.

[2]Ibid., p. 307. [3]Ibid.

[4]Ibid., p. 302. [5]Ibid. [6]Ibid., p. 305.

carried on with his exhortations by saying: "It must be owned that, as
those ancient writings are impaired and lost, not only the light and clearness of Holy Writ, but even the evidence itself of the main facts must in
proportion be diminished and brought into question."[1] Both factual basis
and interpretative coherence depended on the "collateral testimony" from
antiquity. Shaftesbury's statement can be summarized by translating it
into the concluding remark of a book review: "In brief, it must be said
that the contribution of the author consists almost exclusively in the
great skill with which he selected his sources. They account fully for
fact and argument." To put it still differently: Shaftesbury the
literateur resembled those who think it a satisfactory explanation of the
dramatic art in Shakespeare's histories when they have pointed out that in
some of them whole passages are simply lifted from Plutarch's Lives.

After so much thought had been given to the credentials and the
criteria of their evaluation Shaftesbury nevertheless did not come to a
firm decision. The result of such historical research and construction
did not close the credibility gap, but led only to the two attitudes of
"historical faith" and "implicit faith." As far as the former is concerned
he wrote:

> The best Christian in the world who being destitute of means or cer-
> tainty depends only on history and tradition for his belief in those
> particulars, is at best a sceptic Christian. He has no more than a
> nicely critical historical faith, subject to various speculations and
> a thousand different criticisms of language and literature.[2]

---

[1] Shaftesbury, Characteristics, II, p. 303.

[2] Ibid., p. 201. P. Miller quoted a contemporary definition of
historical faith: "A beleeving, not of the stories of the Bible only to
be true, but a beleeving of the whole word of God, the articles of the
faith; but beleeved onely in a historical manner generally, not applyed
particularly to himselfe" (The New England Mind, The Seventeenth Century;
1939, Rpt. Cambridge: Harvard University Press, 1954).

Besides those who had the special education and the office there were
those like Shaftesbury himself who were laymen. Whatever the experts with
their "historical faith" will say a layman will accept on their authority
and thus attain an "implicit faith." This he called "a kind of passive
scepticism":[1]

> His faith is not in ancient facts or persons, nor in the ancient
> writ, or primitive recorders (for of these he is unable to take cogni-
> zance). But his confidence and trust must be in those modern men, or
> societies of men, to whom the public or he himself ascribes the judg-
> ment of these records, and commits the determination of sacred writ
> and genuine story.[2]

We had seen before that Shaftesbury was concerned to bring clearness to
the harmfully confused field of "historical truth," but the clarification
of the issues which he effected here led into skepticism rather than
certainty and yielded a faith that did not bring assurance.

Even in the use of the word skepticism[3] Shaftesbury remained unde-
cided and vacillated between two meanings both of which he retained.
Skepticism for him meant both the maintenance of tradition as the status
quo or the present and the retreat from it into an eternal presence:
Skepticism arose out of the protest against "dogmatic" presumption and is

---

[1]Shaftesbury, Characteristics, II, p. 202.

[2]Ibid., pp. 201-202.

[3]Skepticism as a word and attitude was quite common at the time,
but often did not carry the kind of negative implications that we associate
with it. We can distinguish its use in theology and in natural science.
(1) It was an old scholastic doctrine that the believer in this life except
for a special revelation cannot obtain assurance, but lives in the practice
of charity (J. Moltmann, Prädestination und Perseveranz, p. 5); (2) Robert
Boyle in his Sceptical Chymist (1661) was of the opinion that "the absolute
elements of bodies may never be revealed to us. But if through experimental analysis we can discover certain constituent parts of bodies, such
relative elements are all that is needful and fruitful for our knowledge"
(cf. Randall, The Career of Philosophy, I, p. 509).

the affirmation of humility in the face of the great complexity of tradition; skepticism was also the doubt that in tradition qua tradition with
its "holy mysteries" there was no intelligibility to be found.

For an affirmative and a negative expression, for his skeptical
blend of humility and allegiance to tradition as civil religion[1] on the
one hand and doubt and retreat from tradition as individually unsatisfactory
on the other hand, Shaftesbury appropriately enough chose his illustration
from the field of heraldry which in the sixteenth and seventeenth centuries
had been one of the greatest contributors to the increasing flow of historical knowledge.[2] The clergy as distinct from the philosophers should have
the same privileges and prerogatives as those with which the College of
Heralds was invested:

> 'Tis agreed on all hands that particular persons may design or
> paint, in their private capacity, after what manner they think fit;
> but they must blazon only as the public directs. Their lion or bear
> must be figured as the science appoints, and their supporters and
> crest must be such as their wise and gallant ancestors have procured
> for them. No matter whether the shapes of these animals hold just
> proportion with nature, no matter though (sic!) different or con-
> trary forms are joined in one. That which is denied to painters or
> poets is permitted to heralds. Naturalists may, in their separate
> and distinct capacity, inquire as they think fit into the real exist-
> ence and natural truth of things; but they must by no means dispute
> the authorized forms, mermaids and griffins were the wonder of our
> forefathers, and, as such delivered down to us by authentic traditions
> and delineations. . . .[3]

The figures on these crests were lifeless. They were not images or symbols
which pointed to something, inspired the imagination or even provided
answers. They were "emblazoned" records of the past issued for present

---

[1]On civil religion, see Shaftesbury, Characteristics, II, p. 204.

[2]Fussner, Historical Revolution, pp. 42ff.

[3]Shaftesbury, op. cit., I, pp. 232-233.

currency. As such they represented a marked contrast to an appeal to the mythological past of the immemorial rights of Englishmen. Indeed, such a possibility was intentionally excluded, for the privileges and powers which these heralds once proclaimed and enforced in civil wars have now given way to civilization. History was an affair of the past, civilization had now arrived. This past was not a living or organic past as it is known through Romanticism. As long as the heraldic "science" for example was able to establish that the mermaid on a contemporary crest was handed down without fraud, so long the legitimacy of the crest was secure. The point was not what was on the crest, but that it had gotten there and had stayed there correctly. The two basic criteria of heraldic science were, therefore: the critical validation of the original source of the crest and the critical verification of the process of transmission of the crest. Whenever these two criteria were met, a crest was entitled to authority.

The dissociation of legitimacy and meaning in the process of transmission led to the support of the status quo. It replaced meaning by a "legal fiction," for as soon as one looked at the content and meaning of what was transmitted the result would be positively embarrassing. Figures like the mermaids may indeed have been the wonder of the forefathers, but in Shaftesbury's time Thomas Sprat in his History of the Royal Society called them fancies and Shaftesbury himself referred to modern miracle accounts as old wives' and children's tales.[1] As tales of fancy they were no stories of reality.

---

[1] Shaftesbury, Characteristics, II, p. 87.

Furthermore, there was not only the question of correspondence with reality but also that of coherence amongst different figures. Investigations into the credentials of a crest may have hown, for example, that the combination of a mermaid and a bear were equally well attested in its parts. Since the credentials of both were so impeccable the crest had become authoritative when in real life there may be a bear but certainly no mermaid. If we now extrapolate the problem with which Shaftesbury was faced, and follow it to its logical conclusion we shall find the following: There were many objects in the past and in the present which were very well attested and which did not fall into the category of mermaids. Since most of these things never appeared on crests the question of their coherence became even more urgent. We may even go further and say that even if the principle of correctness included the moral judgment that whatever was not good in the sources could not be historical, even then the question of coherence remained to be answered. Things such as customs, manners, constitutions may all be very well attested, but the question of coherence and meaning still remained. Shaftesbury mentioned in passing:

> . . . the real fine gentlemen, the lovers of art and ingenuity, such as have seen the world, and informed themselves of the manners and customs of the several nations of Europe; searched into their antiquities and records; considered their police, laws, and constitutions; observed the situation, strength and ornaments of their cities, their principal arts, studies and amusements; their architecture, sculpture, painting, music, and their taste in poetry, learning, language and conversation.[1]

The urbanity of those gentlemen sounded quite unlike the dusty antiquarianism of the College of Heralds, but neither here nor there was a principle of coherence and correspondence clearly in evidence. The principle of correctness and disinterestedness could establish reports of all manner of things

---

[1]Shaftesbury, Characteristics, II, pp. 262-263.

(e.g., fancy) and of all kinds of manners. What we have tried to explain
in the case of the mermaids was only an explication of the issues that we
already found earlier in the discussion of the miracles. Only now is it
possible to see more clearly the issues which were involved in Shaftesbury's
curious vacillation in his view of skepticism: the establishment of the
legitimacy of the present occurred at the expense of the reality of the
present. There was a status quo, but no reality. The present needed more
than a principle of legitimacy. It needed a principle of reality. It
could not only exist, it also had to be. For this purpose it must have a
vision of unity which was not only artificially externally "joined in one."
The present was a legitimate form, but it was a husk without the kernel
and even the husk was not all of one piece. Since history had been reduced
by Shaftesbury from a material to a formal and conforming significance,
since in fact history had become tradition and since events had disappeared
in favor of a disinterested verification procedure that was mediated primarily literarily, Shaftesbury must now shop around for another model of
reality which would help to retrieve vitality, coherence, and immediacy and
which did not embroil in cumbersome verification procedures of a historical
or philosophic kind.

Shaftesbury did not minimize or reject the legitimacy argument,
because for him it delineated the situation in place and time of England
in the late seventeenth and early eighteenth centuries. Dry as this argument from pedigree looked, it may have carried conviction with the third
Earl of Shaftesbury, but it was also true that such a present based solely
on legitimacy could not live from its own assertion of being, a being that
would consist mainly in a critique of the contradictions of the Christian
tradition. Shaftesbury's use of heraldry manifested a means to deal with

those contradictions. Shaftesbury passed on from criticism to construc-

tion[1] in trying to find a justification of the present in which he lived.

Fine gentleman wrote on customs and constitutions, manners, and morals,

but it was also necessary to determine what morals were. Shaftesbury's

search along these lines was predetermined in its outcome by his view of

classical antiquity: the "moral truth" by means of which he established

the disinterestedness and correctness of historical documents was super-

seded by "plastic truth." He quoted Aristotle in support of his view that

"the best poems [are] preferable to the best of histories," for the mere

historian, copies what he sees, and minutely traces every feature and odd

mark."[2]

Shaftesbury shared with Humanism the conviction that the present

can only be known through the past and that the older the past the greater

the truth. The crux of this argument was its ambiguity, for antiquity was

used in different contexts which determined what kinds of history if any

at all were to be of value. Shaftesbury in fact abandoned history through

antiquity. As we have seen, Shaftesbury did not see the antiquity of church

history in terms of the truth it revealed but in light of the partisanship

which it exhibited. Furthermore, the history of Israel only showed to him

the story of a quite particular and a "naturally very cloudy people,"[3] but

---

[1]Shaftesbury, Characteristics, I, p. 238. "On the other side, the
men of wit and Raillery, whose pleasantest entertainment is in the exposing
the weak sides of religion, are so desperately afraid of being drawn into
any serious thoughts of it, that they look upon a man as guilty of foul play
who assumes the air of a free writer and at the same time preserves any
regard for the principles of natural religion."

[2]Ibid., p. 96.

[3]Ibid., p. 22; see also II, pp. 189ff, 227. Both Shaftesbury and
Edwards shared a common anti-Jewish Occidental tradition. Shaftesbury
expressed the final authority of this tradition by translating it in terms
of natural characteristics. Edwards belonged to a way of thinking that
opened up that tradition toward a common future history.

no universal history that played such a role in Isaac Newton. The "language of the wisest and most learned of nations" that "is acknowledged to contain the principal and essential part of our holy revelation"[1] was therefore not that of Israel, but of Greece. Before Shaftesbury, for example, Ralph Cudworth had already at length argued in his extensive argument for the trinity that despite little differences the older genuine Platonists supported the position of the Orthodox fathers.[2] This support of church history from classical antiquity reappeared in Shaftesbury. Of the three parts of universal history -- church history, New Testament, Old Testament -- which had all served as models of antiquity in the past, Shaftesbury found only the New Testament helpful. Its characteristics of Hellenization pointed the way to classical antiquity which in turn had no philosophic regard for history and which gave the humanist Shaftesbury who, unlike Cudworth, had no metaphysical aspirations an option for aesthetics. Shaftesbury approved a stance which at the same time "was not of that kind which depends on genealogies or traditions, and ministers questions and vain jangling."[3] Instead of the usual references to Scripture and reason or to the reason of things and instead of the criterion of Scripture and history, Shaftesbury expressed himself to the effect that "our common religion and Christianity was founded on classical letters and Scripture." The potentially ahistoric character of the identification of truth and antiquity[4]

---

[1] Shaftesbury, Characteristics, I, p. 307.

[2] Cudworth, Intellectual System, I, pp. 788-789.

[3] Shaftesbury, op. cit., p. 193.

[4] C. S. Lewis, English Literature in the Sixteenth Century Excluding Drama (Oxford: Clarendon Press, 1954), pp. 20-28, 31; P. Meinhold, Geschichte der Kirchlichen Historiographie, I, 340, 363.

came to the surface once the Scriptural models lost their force of
conviction.

In the related area of poetry, Thomas Sprat mentioned several areas
from which imagery could be drawn. For his time he excluded from the list
"the wit of the Fables and Religions of the Ancient World," because they
were "well-nigh consum'd."[1] While Shaftesbury's aesthetic conception of
"plastic truth" reached back to antiquity, its metaphoric concretization
was expressed in terms of the notion of "plastic nature" as he found it in
the Cambridge Platonists. For Ralph Cudworth plastic nature was the middle
between a beginning and an end. In Shaftesbury both beginning and end were
absent and the middle became the center. Universal history which had comprised past, present, and future shrank to the present and the present and
nature through his view of antiquity were linked in such a way that the
present reached out for something eternally present in nature.

We have seen how the past impinged on the present as legal fiction.

When he talked about nature he did so in terms of "poetical fictions."
In either case, history as an event had disappeared and the medium of
divine communication was no longer either tradition or history, but nature.
The full extent of this dehistoricization is evident, if we take a closer
look at his interpretation of miracles as well as at his delineation of
nature as the two main landmarks on the opposite sides of the boundary
which he had insisted on drawing between the first and the subsequent act
of faith.

Shaftesbury's admission of miracles in the past and their dismissal
in the present presupposed the arrival of a simplified view of the

---

[1]Cf. Basil Willey, The Seventeenth Century Background, p. 194.

relationship between miracles and prophecy. Cudworth, for example, could
mention in the same paragraph and on the same level phenomena like "apparitions, witchcraft, miracles, prophecies and possessions" as proofs which
"evince that spirits, angels or demons, though invisible to us, are no
fancies, but real and substantial inhabitants of the world." At the same
time he also differentiated within this spiritual dimension between
miracles and prophecies.

> Both of which scripture prophecies, or Christ in the Old Testament,
> and from him in the new, are of equal if not greater force to us in
> the present ages, for the confirmation of our faith, than the miracles
> themselves recorded in the scriptures, we now having certain knowledge
> ourselves of many of these events, and being no way able to suspect
> but that the prophecies were written long before.[1]

The element of the charismatic was common to both miracles and prophecy,
but they represented different aspects of it. At one point in the historiographical controversies of the Great Awakening, Edwards on his part
therefore used the broader biblical phrase of "miraculous gifts."[2] These
gifts included word as well as event and the common assertion that miracles
had ceased upon the completion of the canon of Scripture could have therefore two different and even contradictory meanings according to where the
emphasis was being put. Thus, for example, in the New Testament story of
the resurrection of Lazarus the time between the word and the event was so
brief that interpretative attention could easily be absorbed into the
miraculous event itself and the analysis of its component parts of nature
and supernature. The event itself became an immediate and presentist phenomenon that happened in the past and that like other similar deeds could

[1] Cudworth, Intellectual System, II, pp. 132-133.

[2] The Great Awakening, p. 281.

no longer be repeated, for only the prophets, Jesus and the Apostles could perform them. On the other hand, in the case of the miraculous gifts of prediction recorded in Scripture, the word itself pointed beyond the completion of the canon to events in history and the present, even though the gift of prophecy itself had in fact ceased. The problem for the former view arose over an evaluation of contemporary miraculous events. Since Scripture gave no warrant for their repetition they could only constitute a breach of the order established by the canon. Scripture was a book of heraldry in which only so many permissible crests of arms were codified with no further additions allowed. Nevertheless, Shaftesbury's assertion that the bare events in the past authenticated a claim and established the legitimacy of a tradition had to provoke the question why something like this should be impossible in the present. "The attestation of men dead and gone, in behalf of miracles past and at an end, can never be of equal force with miracles present." Therefore it was maintained that in order to close the gap "the present must answer for the credibility of the past."[1] Shaftesbury and his opponents agreed that a miraculous event, whether past or present, was to be judged as if it were an experience open to immediate empirical observation. Cudworth, on the other hand, used the term miracle in order to refer to the past and the concept of prophecy in order to link the past with present events. The function of the similarity of and the differentiations between miracle and prophecy therefore corresponded to what we today would define in terms of a historical event. It was simply not enough to inquire into the facticity of past events and deny or assert the possibility of present miraculous events, but it was also

---

[1] Shaftesbury, Characteristics, II, p. 90.

necessary to be concerned with the purpose of such powerful events.
Cudworth defined faith as those things which do not fall under sight
"because they are either invisible or future."[1] Miraculous events certainly did prove a point, but the word or prophecy in addition asked and
answered the question as to the significance of events. Without the latter
events would be pointless and unrelated to other points and could become
arbitrary and harmful.

The universality of this line of argument is illustrated by
Memorial Providences, Relating to Witchcraft and Possession by Shaftesbury's
contemporary, Cotton Mather. The question which Mather here pursued was not
how the spiritual affected the present and how it acted in it, but whether
or not it did affect the present at all. The very word "providences"
assumed a different accent in this case. In the historiographical tradition of the Jeremiads, providences had meant the judgments and mercies to
individuals and to groups of individuals. They were not solely aimed at
evincing the reality of God apologetically, but their function was to convince of that reality effectually. The shift of emphasis from providences
to evidences in this work of Mather on witchcraft was signalled by the
absence of sin and repentance which had played a central role in the
Jeremiadic tradition.[2]

Cotton Mather reflected but a widespread trend around that time when
intellectuals like Henry More[3] and

---

[1] The Cambridge Platonists, p. 229.

[2] G. T. Miller, The Rise of Evangelical Calvinism, p. 92.

[3] Henry More (1614-1687) studied at Christ College, Cambridge (B.A.
1635, M.A. 1639), where he stayed on as fellow despite numerous offers of
higher preferment. He was a proliferous writer as poet, theologian, philosopher, and exegete. Originally from a Calvinist background, he became

Joseph Glanville[1] had gone so far as to join forces with popular religion in an effort to collect stories that were to support the continuing influence of supernatural spirits as a means to combat the atheism which they saw arising as a result of the emerging view of the universe as a machine. This quest obscured and even divorced in the concept of miracles the relationship between the power and the purpose of an event for the sake of proving only its power. Such a dissolution of the historical event into a battle between naturalism and supernaturalism had as its consequence that providences deteriorated into a "prodigious fallacy."[2]

Shaftesbury mentioned no names, but it was this background of confusion and insecurity over the constituent elements of the historical event which provided the background for his relentless attacks. Through the former experiences of a young convert Shaftesbury in his dialogue The

---

a strong influence within and beyond the group of Cambridge Platonists. In his criticism of Descartes he contributed to the theory of absolute space. His great intellectual powers as well as his interest in and defense of prodigies was contained in his book An Antidote Against Atheism, 1653 (DNB XIII, 868-870; Randall, The Career of Philosophy, I, 482ff).

[1] Joseph Glanville (1636-1680) studied at Exeter College, Oxford (B.A. 1655, M.A. 1658). He was chaplain to Francis Rous, one of Cromwell's lords. He was a friend of Henry More and an admirer of Richard Baxter. Upon publication of his Vanity of Dogmatizing (1664), he was elected fellow of the Royal Society. His posthumously published Sadducismus Triumphatus, or Full and Plain Evidence concerning Witches and Apparitions (1681) contained facts and experiments in favor of witchcraft (DNB VII, 1287-1290; Randall, Career of Philosophy, I, 500-507.

[2] "Prodigious fallacy mistakes sensation for significance. It is the erroneous idea that the historian's task is to describe portents and prodigies, and events marvellous, stupendous, fantastic, extraordinary, wonderful, superlative, astonishing, and monstrous -- and further, that the more marvelous, stupendous, etc. an event is, the more historic and eventful it becomes." David H. Fischer did not draw his examples for a characterization of this attitude from the latter half of the seventeenth century. He pointed to a craving for novelty that has become institutionalized in the coverage of "catastrophies and curiosities" by the modern "mass media." (Historians Fallacies, pp. 70-71.)

<u>Moralists</u> described the situation in the course of a brief but heated

exchange on the subject of miracles:

> . . . What an adventurer he had been of that kind, and on how many
> parties he had been engaged, with a sort of prople who were always on
> the hot scent of some new prodigy or apparition, some upstart revela-
> tion or prophecy. This, he thought, was true fanaticism errant. He
> had enough of this visionary chase, and would ramble no more in blind
> corners of the world, as he had been formerly accustomed, in ghostly
> company of spirit hunters, witch-finders, and layers-out for hellish
> stories and diabolical transactions. There was no need he thought, of
> such intelligences from hell to prove the power of heaven and being of
> a God. And now at last he began to see the ridicule of laying a stress
> on these matters, as if a providence depended on them and religion were
> at stake when any of these wild feats were questioned. He was sensible
> that there were many good Christians who made themselves strong parti-
> sans in this cause, though he could not avoid wondering at it, how he
> began to consider and look back.[1]

Good Christians may have been part of this hunt for prodigies, but this

could divert the attention from the fact that the interest in everything

extraordinary had led to the absurdity of proving the "power of heaven and

the being of a God" with "intelligences from hell." Shaftesbury charged

also that such "ghastly stories" of miracles catered to the inborn desire

of children and old people for novelty.[2] The sensationalism of the accounts

gave no "respite"[3] to collect one's thoughts. They swamped the present to

the extent that any sense for time disappeared. Discrimination gave way to

statistics as a criterion of truth, for "some modern zealots appear to have

no better knowledge of truth, no better manner of counting it, than by count-

ing noses."[4] The news that were forthcoming dwelt too much in the area of

the "churchyard and monuments"[5] and Shaftesbury finally ridiculed the sets

of "Lancashire noodles and remote provincial headpieces" that were being

---

[1]Shaftesbury, <u>Characteristics</u>, II, pp. 89-90.

[2]<u>Ibid.</u>, p. 87. [3]<u>Ibid.</u>, p. 91.

[4]<u>Ibid.</u>, I, p. 98. [5]<u>Ibid.</u>, II, p. 85.

offered as evidence.[1] In each of these cases the new, death, time, truth, and discrimination of judgment appeared in caricature as so many perverted elements of a view of history. Shaftesbury drew the conclusion that it may not be possible at all to make out the distinction between good and bad spirits in a given event.[2] He was therefore relieved to be able to point to the received opinion of the coincidence of the end of miracles and the completion of the canon of Scripture as a safeguard for tradition which at least signified some order whereas all the other elements bespoke nothing but disorder. The bad name that historical events thus received was still visible in Jonathan Edwards' apologetic distinction that while geographicall speaking Northampton lay "in the corner of the country,"[3] there was no occultism of any sort involved in the revival, for "these things ben't done in a corner."[4]

Shaftesbury's critique of sensationalism was perceptive, but nega-tive, for a constructive criticism of the notion of a historical event had been excluded by his own attitude towards Scripture. His view of tradition was convincing as long as it was considered over against the negative back-ground of political strifes of the past and the popular pursuits of the present, but taken on its own tradition for him was a legal fiction. Shaftesbury left behind both the fables of the past and the superstitions of the present, but even while he elected nature as the central metaphor of aesthetics the discussion over history obtruded again in the hymnic part of

---

[1] Shaftesbury, Characteristics, II, p. 98.

[2] Ibid., I, p. 32.

[3] The Great Awakening, p. 113.

[4] Ibid., p. 261.

the ongoing dialogue between the main participants in The Moralists who

bore the telling names of Theocles and Philocles.

Theocles set out to sing of "Nature unconfined by words and in loose

numbers." In the course of this praise Cudworth's theoretical construct

of "plastic nature" reappeared in a poetic rendering:

> O mighty Genius! Sole animating and inspiring power! Author and
> subject of these thoughts! Thy influence is universal, and in all
> things thou art inmost. From thee depend their secret spring of action.
> Thou movest them with an irresistible unwearied force . . . the vital
> principle is widely shared and infinitely varied, dispensed throughout,
> nowhere extinct.
>
> Nor can we judge less favorably of that consummate art exhibited
> through all the works of Nature, since our weak eyes, helped by mechanic
> art, discover in these works a hidden scene of wonders, worlds within
> worlds of infinite minuteness, though as to art still equal to the
> greatest, and pregnant with more wonders than the most discerning sense,
> joined with the greatest art or the acutest reason, can penetrate or
> unfold.[1]

When Theocles moved to the greater world, from the microscope to the tele-

scope, as it were, and as soon as he began to enter upon metaphysical ground,

Philocles insisted repeatedly that he abandon such lofty flights of specu-

lation and retreat "from the borders of our world" and "stick closer to

nature."[2] Theocles acceded to that demand in principle only, for when he

resumed his hymnic praise he pressed again quickly from "this our element

of earth" to the ultimate question of a first principle. He reflected on

the notion that the variety of Nature moves back to the One. In the peri-

odical conflagrations which secured the intervals between creations, all

would then be Deity. Of such a divinity that was "involved" before crea-

tion and that was "unfolded" in the "various map of Nature and this far

---

[1]Shaftesbury, Characteristics, II, pp. 110, 111.

[2]Ibid., p. 112.

visible world" Philocles preferred the latter over the former and urged

Theocles to concentrate on nature in his chant.[1] In response to this

request Theocles now took off on an "imaginary voyage" of the globe.[2] He

called it a wandering through different climates. In the course of it he

touched upon Asia[3] and Africa in a kind of geographic symbolism that turned

out to be ambiguous. This becomes clearest in the way in which he dealt

with the river Nile and the mountain Atlas in Africa. The river Nile for

him was the image of great productivity and bounty, but it was also a "sad

emblem" of superstition. In his description of the ascent of Atlas the

perspective changed three times: From below the rocks of Atlas prop the

very arch of heaven. As soon as the mountaineer could look down upon these

rocks he became aware of the "precipice" along which he walked. "Poor

mankind" was now shocked out of its thoughtless state when they

> see, as in one instant, the revolutions of the past ages, the fleet-
> ing forms of things, and the decay even of this our globe, whose youth
> and first formation they consider, whilst the apparent spoil and
> irreparable breaches of the wasted mountains show them the world itself
> only as a noble ruin, and make them think of its approaching period....'

After the traveller had climbed beyond the "midway" point, he found woods

which by their darkness, silence, and mysterious echoes struck him with a

horror different from the one which the slight of the wasted rocks had con-

veyed. According to Theocles it was in these woods that the ancients had

located religion. After this review of history, cosmology, religion, and

---

[1]Shaftesbury, Characteristics, II, pp. 118-119.

[2]See M. Nicolson, Mountain Gloom and Mountain Glory, pp. 290-291,
on the literary genre.

[3]Shaftesbury, op. cit., p. 120.

[4]Ibid., p. 123.

superstition the guide on this tour concluded his chant on the "sublime" with the observation that "Even we ourselves, who in plain characters may read divinity from so many bright parts of the earth, choose rather these obscurer parts to spell out that mysterious being which to our eyes appears at best under a veil of clouds...."[1] The perspicuity of the book of nature contrasted conspicuously with the complexity of the book of Scripture. For the sake of such clearer hermeneutics, Shaftesbury did no longer read the book of words and the book of works alternately or in succession as had been the custom,[2] but he endorsed the latter over against the former. In Scripture he had found a confusion of the literal and figurative senses, but at the same time he had not wanted to prejudge the case and had turned over the arbitration of the difficulties and their administration as mysteries to the experts. The book of nature, on the other hand, was self-evident and self-convincing reading material. Here he explicitly separated and eliminated difficulties and mysteries, and it was the function of the "imaginary voyage" within the dialogue to achieve this purpose. Theocles finally agreed with Philocles and reprimanded those who would forego the "plain characters" in favor of the obscurer parts of nature as "repositories of divinity." The exclusion of difficulties prevented among other things the inquiry into such questions as the way in which nature itself had changed in the course of history and what truth there was in a cyclical view of history. Instead Shaftesbury portrayed nature positively as an unceasing process in which the unpredictable was excluded. "A heap of sand or stones"

---

[1] Shaftesbury, Characteristics, II, pp. 123-124.

[2] Ernst Robert Curtius, European Literature and the Latin Middle Ages (1948; ppb. New York: Harper Torchbook, 1963), pp. 319-326.

or a "mist or cloud driven by the wind"[1] represented a side of nature and
reality for Shaftesbury which included change and thus had a place in his
thought only as a negative image. The end of the voyage was therefore the
affirmation of the beautiful rather than the sublime.[2] It was not an
advance but a return and retreat to

> our more conversable woods and temperate climate. Here no fierce
> heats nor colds annoy us, no precipices and cataracts amaze us, nor
> need we be afraid of our own voices while we hear the notes of such a
> cheerful choir [Theocles and Philocles are outdoors in the early morn-
> ing], and find the echoes rather agreeable and inviting us to talk.[3]

Another instance where we find a transition away from both a view of
history and research into history was the case of John Ray.[4] He belonged
to Boyle's generation and both remained uneasy about the Restoration
Settlement of Charles II. Ray indicated his position through exegesis as
well as through explicit statement. Ray, for example, quoted from Psalm
111:2 that "the works of the Lord are great, sought out of all them that
have pleasure therein." He concluded that "tho' it be principally spoken of
the works of providence, yet may as well be verify'd of the works of creation."[5] This interpretation was a deliberate shift of emphasis, for the
psalm itself dealt with the creation and history of the nation of Israel
and not with nature: "He showed his people what his strength could do,

---

[1]Shaftesbury, Characteristics, II, p. 124.

[2]E. Cassirer, The Philosophy of the Enlightenment (1932; E. T.
Princeton: Princeton University Press, 1951), p. 312.

[3]Shaftesbury, op. cit.

4John Ray (1627-1705), naturalist, was a fellow at Trinity College,
Cambridge. He was ordained deacon and priest in 1660, but he resigned in
1662. He was a friend of John Wilkins and belonged to the founding
generation of the Royal Society. (DNB XVI, 782-787.)

[4]John Ray, The Wisdom of God in Creation (1691; London:
1743), p. 38.

bestowing on them the lands of other nations." In a similar way Ray para-
phrased the words of I Corinthians 6:20: "Glorify God in Your Body, or
with your body, and in your spirit, which are God's; and not by redemption
only, of which the apostle there speaks, but by creation also."[1] On the
collective as well as on the individual level the natural elements were
asserted over those of history.

Ray's doctrine of the eternal sabbath reflected this shift in exegesis. The employment in eternity would not be "only in an uninterrupted and
endless act of love" upon the dissolution of the world, but it would also
include for individuals who departed to heaven the promise of a solution
of the world's problems, for "then shall we clearly see, to our great satisfaction and admiration, the ends and uses of these things, which were either
too subtle for us to penetrate and discover, or too remote or inaccessible
for us to come to any distinct view of."[2] The intensity and the extent of
the vision which would be attained did not refer to the course of history,
but to an understanding of the workings of nature. Nature was permeated
by a spiritual force and what was indistinct for the individual observer
would now become clear to him in his after life. God was not so much in
history as he was in nature. In order to state his doctrine of the eternal
sabbath more convincingly Ray employed the typological argument. The sabbath had been instituted originally as a day on which to commemorate the
works of creation from which God rested. Since the sabbath is a type of
the eternal sabbath a contemplation of nature will be part of its "business"
of rest also. Investigation of nature will lead to the knowledge of things,

[1]Ray, The Wisdom of God in Creation, pp. 386-387.
[2]Ibid., pp. 170-171.

while the attention only to historical research was associated with mere words: "No knowledge can be more pleasant than this, none that doth so satisfy and feed the soul; in comparison whereto that of Words and Phrases seem to me insipid and jejune."[1] While Ray's attitude proved to be a definite improvement over Bacon who had collected his data primarily from literary sources, this approach tended to make historical research in general an affair of the past:

> Nothing is universally blessed. Literary excellence, the study of languages and antiquities, Criticism, Grammar, carried by our immediate Predecessors to a midday zenith, seem in our day to have passed their peak and to be sinking into a decline. Rarely indeed appears among us a Casaubon, a Scaliger, a Selden, a Bochardt, a Vossius -- those lights and ornaments of former Days. Apparently the Learned of to-day are concerned to study things, but care less about words.[2]

The distinction which emerged here in Ray's thinking has been put very well by John Wilkins in his sermon on Providence. The text for the sermon was taken from Ecclesiastes 3:11: "He hath made every thing beautiful in his time: also he hath set the world in their heart, yet no man can find out the work that God maketh from beginning to end."[3] Wilkins observed that "by world here is not meant this material world, but saeculum. The succession and course of things, as the original does properly import."[4] The intention behind Wilkins' interpretation is clearer if we compare it to the use

---

[1] Ray, The Wisdom of God in Creation, pp. 169-170.

[2] Charles E. Raven, John Ray, Naturalist, His Life and Works (Cambridge: Cambridge University Press, 1942), p. 41. Isaac Casaubon (1559-1614), known for his scholarship in classical philology. Joseph Justus Scaliger (1540-1609) established chronology on a scholarly basis. John Selden (1584-1654), jurist and Orientalist. Samuel Bochard (1599-1667), naturalist, theologian, and Orientalist. Gerardus Joannis Vossius (1577-1642), theologian and philologist.

[3] John Wilkins, A Discourse Concerning the Beauty of Providence, p. 1.

[4] Ibid., p. 4.

Francis Bacon made of the same verse in a fragment which preceded The Advancement of Learning.[1] Bacon here understood "world" in such a way that man beheld and investigated both "the variety of things and the vicissitude of times,"[2] even though he could not find out everything. Wilkins for his part excluded a cosmological understanding of world in this text. On the other hand, when he addressed himself to his congregation on the subject of the vicissitude of times, he admonished them that "whatever comes to pass shall be beautiful, and therefore should be welcome."[3] It was only consistent with the scope of his text when he said that "the issue and event of things" are God's work and therefore what is "not under our power, should not be under our care."[4] The exegetical exclusion of world as cosmos and the dismissal of world as history appears in its true perspective when we realize that Wilkins was a supporter of and a participant in the emerging investigation of the cosmos which had to be exempted from restrictions similar to those imposed on questions after the course of history where it was especially difficult to find meaning and value at a time when the English Civil War was barely over. For Wilkins the world of history was not known, but the world of nature could be known.

---

[1] The full title of this posthumously published [1734] piece is Valerius Terminus of the Interpretation of Nature with the annotations of Hermes Stella, Bacon, Works, VI, pp. 10-24 (Preface and Note of the Editor); pp. 28-37 (Chapter I).

[2] Ibid., p. 32.

[3] Wilkins, A Discourse, p. 72.

[4] Ibid., p. 67.

Summary

Edwards in his outline for the History of the Work of Redemption
had defined Scripture as history and prophecy which included Old Testament,
Church History, and New Testament. For Shaftesbury none of these parts
functioned in such a way as to yield a general view of the historical world.
For him the Old Testament was neither the model of historical thinking nor
a prototype of literature, but the particularistic record of a "naturally
very cloudy people." Moreover, the Protestant Reformation had introduced a
high regard for Church History into religious thought, but the consequent
new awareness of the historical dimension had led to bitter controversies
and to bloody conflicts. Church historians like Gilbert Burnet used the
Baconian distinction between fact and interpretation and their differentiation between a necessary partiality and a detrimental partisanship was calcu-
lated as a means to avoid methodological bias and to reduce actual suffering.
For Shaftesbury, on the other hand, primary and secondary sources were
equally biased and not unlike William Chillingworth and John Hales he turned
agnostic with regard to church history. The New Testament finally possessed
credibility for him only insofar as its Greek medium of communication
alluded to the "disinterested" criterion of the literature of classical
antiquity. The argument from antiquity here revealed itself to be an argument against history and Shaftesbury's use of the contemporary metaphor of
plastic nature became a private aesthetic replacement for a view of history.

Shaftesbury's treatment of the style and of the miracles of Scripture
demonstrated this transition by means of a twofold dissociation. First, the
identification of genre and art turned Scripture into an inadmissibly mixed
and revolutionary genre which was defensible only in an antiquarian way as

learning, but which was not convincing aesthetically as literature. Shaftesbury's understanding of miracles, furthermore, introduced a dissociation between meaning and legitimacy, for the question was no longer what the miracles intended, but whether the record of their occurrence had been transmitted correctly. This emphasis on learning and legitimacy in turn defined Shaftesbury's attitude to tradition, for which he introduced the apt illustration of the then flourishing science of heraldry: a veneration of tradition and a belief in its social expediency and conservative trend coexisted with a skepticism as to its intelligibility.

He rejected the contemporary revival of interest in spectacular supernatural events. His criticism revealed that essential elements for a view of history such as the new, death, time, and discrimination of judgment were only caricatured in this quest. Unlike Edwards and Cudworth, Shaftesbury could not resolve such a distortion through a restoration of the differentiation between miracle and prophecy, or through the discrimination between the aspects of the powerful and the purposeful within the same general concept of "miraculous gifts" or glory, because for him Scripture was no longer a sufficient or an efficacious paradigm. In order therefore to find an alternative both to skepticism and to sensationalism, Shaftesbury employed the paradigm of plastic nature as a means to recover the teleological dimension in causality. From his description of an imaginary voyage it became clear that for Shaftesbury nature included the powerful as well as the purposeful while it excluded all unpredictable and discontinuous change: he eliminated cyclical as well as linear views of history and he avoided Europe and America as the representatives of the present and of the future.[1]

---

[1] Shaftesbury, Characteristics, II, p. 124.

Shaftesbury differed from John Ray in his way of expression but not in the general thrust of the underlying conviction. The former replaced a general view of history with a generic stance in aesthetics. The latter viewed his devotion to the scientific investigation of nature against the obsolete character of philological-historical research. These observations bring the argument of this study full circle, for they have drawn out a different line of development which was also indicated in the statement of our thesis for this dissertation in Chapter IV.[1] We have thus traced how Plastic Nature contributed both to the rise and the decline of a view of history depending on what role Scripture played as a paradigm in the thought of Edwards on the one hand and in that of Shaftesbury and John Ray on the other hand.

---

[1]See p. 140.

BIBLIOGRAPHY

Primary Sources

Bacon, Francis. Works. 14 vols. Ed. James Spedding, et al.
    Boston: Taggard and Thompson, 1863.

Boyle, Robert. The Theological Works. Ed. Richard Boulton. London:
    W. Taylor, 1715.

Bradford, William. Of Plymouth Plantation 1620-1647. Ed. Samuel E.
    Morison. New York: Knopf, 1970.

Calvin, John. Commentary on a Harmony of the Evangelists Matthew, Mark
    and Luke. Trans. William Pringle. Grand Rapids, Mich.: Eerdmans, 1949.

Calvin, John. Commentaries on the Epistles of Paul the Apostle to the
    Philippians, Colossians, and Thessalonians. Trans. John Pringle.
    Grand Rapids, Mich.: Eerdmans, 1948.

The Cambridge Platonists. Ed. Gerald R. Cragg. A Library of Protestant
    Thought. New York: Oxford University Press, 1968.

Chauncy, Charles. Seasonable Thoughts on the State of Religion in New
    England. Boston: Rogers and Fowle for Samuel Eliot 1743.

Colman, Benjamin. Practical Discourses on the Parable of the Ten Virgins.
    1713; Boston: Rogers and Fowle, 1747.

Cotton, John. A Brief Exposition of the Whole Book of Canticles; On Song
    of Solomon. Edinburgh: James Nichol, 1868.

_____. An Exposition Upon the Thirteenth Chapter of the Revelation.
    London: By M.S. for Chapman, 1655.

Cudworth, Ralph. The True Intellectual System of the Universe. 1678;
    Andover: Gould and Newman, 1837.

Davenport, John. The Knowledge of Christ. London: For L. Chapman, 1653.

Die Dogmatik der Evangelisch - Reformierten Kirche dargestellt und aus
    den Quellen belegt Von H. Heppe. Rev. Ed. Ernst Bizer. Neukirchen:
    Neukirchener Verlag, 1958.

Edwards, Jonathan. The Chief End for which God Created the World.
                                       The Works of President
    Edwards, I, rpt. New York: Burt Franklin, 1968. Pp. 441-535.

_____. The Distinguishing Marks. Boston: Kneeland, 1741. The Great
Awakening, ed. C. C. Goen. New Haven: Yale University Press, 1792.
Pp. 215-288.
_____. A Faithful Narrative. Boston: Kneeland, 1738. The Great
Awakening, ed. C. C. Goen. New Haven: Yale University Press, 1972.
Pp. 130-211.
_____. Freedom of the Will. Boston: Kneeland, 1754. Ed. P. Ramsay.
New Haven: Yale University Press, 1957.

_____. The Great Awakening, ed. C. C. Goen. New Haven: Yale
University Press, 1972.

_____. The History of the Work of Redemption.
The Works of President Edwards, V, rpt. New York: Burt Franklin,
1968. Pp. 7-320.

_____. Images and Shadows of Divine Things, ed. Perry Miller. New
Haven: Yale University Press, 1948.

_____. The Nature of True Virtue.
The Works of President Edwards, II, rpt. New York: Burt Franklin,
1968. Pp. 7-78.

_____. The Philosophy of Jonathan Edwards from His Private Notebooks,
ed, Harvey G. Townsend. Eugene: University of Oregon Press, 1953.

_____. Religion Affections. Boston: Kneeland, 1746. Ed. John E.
Smith, 1959.

_____. Representative Selections, ed. Clarence H. Faust and Thomas
H. Johnson. Rev. Ed.; New York: Hill and Wang, 1969.

_____. Some Thoughts Concerning the Revival. Boston: Kneeland, 1742.
The Great Awakening, ed. C. C. Goen. New Haven: Yale University Press,
1972. Pp. 291-530.

_____. An Unpublished Essay on the Trinity, ed. G. P. Fisher. New
York: Scribner's, 1903.

_____. The Works of President Edwards. Rpt. 10 vols. New York:
Burt Franklin, 1968.

Eliot, John. The Harmony of the Gospels in the Holy History of the
    Humiliation and Sufferings of Jesus Christ from His Incarnation to
    His Death and Burial. Boston: John Foster, 1678.

Johnson, Edward. Wonder Working Providence of Sions Savior. Ed. J.
    Franklin Jameson. Original Narratives of Early American History.
    New York: Scribner's, 1910.

Hubbard, William. A Funeral Meditation, from those words of the prophet Isaiah, Chapter 3:1,2,3 occasioned by the interment of Major Daniel Denison on September 22, 1982. Boston: S. Green, 1684

_____, A General History of New England. Cambridge: Hilliard and Metcalf, 1815

Locke, John. "Some Thoughts Concerning Reading and Study." Works, III. London: for W. Otridge, 1812.

[Mastricht, Petrus van]. Theoretico-Practica Theologia, qua, per singula capita Theologica, pars exegetica, dogmatica, elenchtica and practicia, perpena successione conjugantur. EDITIO NOVA, priori multo emendatior, and plus quam tertia parte auctior. ACCEDUNT: Historical Ecclesiastica, Plena Quidem; Sed Compendiosa: Idea Theologiae Moralis: Hypotyposis Theologiae Asceticae and Prion opus quasi novum auctore Petro van Mastricht, Trajecti, ad Rhenum: Ex Officina Thomae Appels, 1714.

Mather, Cotton. Diary. 2 vols. New York: Frederick Ungar Publishing Co., 1911.

_____. India Christiana. Boston: B. Green, 1723.

_____. Magnalia Christi Americana. 2 vols. Hartford: Silas Andrus and Son, 1855.

_____. Manuductio ad Ministerium, Directions for a Candidate of the Ministry. Boston: printed for Thomas Hancock, 1726.

_____. A New Offer to the Lovers of Religion and Learning. Boston: Bartholomew Green, 1710.

Mather, Increase. Doctrine of Divine Providence. Boston: By R. Pierce for J. Brunning, 1684.

_____. An Essay for the Recording of Illustrious Providences. London: G. Calvert, 1684.

_____. Mystery of Israel's Salvation Explained and Applyed. London: N.P., 1669.

Mather, Samuel. The Figures and the Types of the Old Testament. Dublin: N.P., 1683.

Morton, Nathaniel. New England's Memoriall. Cambridge, Mass.: S. Green for A. Johnson, 1669.

Newton, Isaac. Observations Upon the Prophecies of Daniel and the Apocalypse. London: J. Darby and T. Browne, 1733.

Oakes, Urian. New England Pleaded With. Cambridge, Mass.: S. Green, 1673.

Perkins, Williams. The Works of, ed. Ian Breward. Courtenay Library of Reformation Classics, 3. Appleford, Abingdon, Berkshire, England, 1970.

Prince, Thomas. A Chronological History of New England. Boston: Antiquarian Book Store, 1852.

Ray, John. The Wisdom of God Manifested in the Works of Creation. Eleventh Corrected edition. London: W. Innys, 1743.

Reformed Dogmatics, Set Out and Illustrated from the Sources, By Heinrich Heppe. Rev. Ed., Ernst Bizer; E. T. London: Allen and Unwin, 1950.

Shaftesbury, Anthony, Earl of. Characteristics of Men, Manners, Opinions, Times, ed. John M. Robertson, 1711; ppb. Indianapolis: Bobbs-Merrill, 1964.

Shepard, Thomas. Works. 3 vols. Boston: Doctrinal Tract and Book Society, 1853.

Sherlock, Thomas. The Use and Intent of Prophecy, in the Several Ages of the World. London: Printed for John Whiston, at Mr. Boyle's head in Fleetstreet, 1749.

Voltaire, Francois. Philosophical Dictionary. Trans. Peter Gay. New York: Harcourt, Brace and World, 1962.

Wesley, John. Works, XXIII. Bristol: William Pine, 1773.

Willard, Samuel. A Compleat Body of Divinity in Two Hundred and Fifty Expository Lectures on the Assembly's Shorter Catechism. Boston: Printed by B. Green and S. Kneeland for B. Eliot and D. Henchman, 1726.

Winthrop, John. The History of New England from 1630-1649, ed. James Savage. Boston: Phelps and Farnham, 1825-1826.

Wheare, Degory. The Method and Order of Reading Both Civil and Ecclesiastical Histories. E. T. London: 1685.

Secondary Sources

Abrams, M. H. Natural Supernaturalism, Tradition and Revolution in Romantic Literature. New York: Norton, 1971.

Althaus, Paul. Die Prinzipien der Deutsch Reformierten Dogmatik im Zeitalter der Aristotelischen Scholastik. Leipzig: A Deichtersche Verlagshandlung, 1914.

Ames, William. The Marrow of Theology, ed. John D. Eusden. Boston: Pilgrim Press, 1968.

Bailyn, Bernard. The New England Merchants in the Seventeenth Century. New York: Harper, 1955; ppb. Harper Torchbooks, 1964.

Baker, John Tull. "An Historical Examination of English Space and Time Theories from Henry More to Bishop Berkeley." Dissertation, Columbia University, 1930.

Bancroft, George. History of the United States from the Discovery. III. Boston: Charles C. Little, 1842.

Beardslee, John W. III. Reformed Dogmatics. A Library of Protestant Thought. New York: Oxford University Press, 1965.

Beaver, R. Pierce. Church, State, and the American Indians, Two and a Half Century of Partnership in Missions Between Protestant Churches and Government. St. Louis: Concordia Publishing House, 1966.

Beck, Lewis W. Early German Philosophy, Kant and His Predecessors. Cambridge, Mass.: The Belknap Press, 1969.

Benrath, Gustav Adolf. Reformierte Kirchengeschichtsschreibung an der Universität Heidelberg im 16. und 17. Jahrhundert. Band IX. Veröffentlichungen des Vereins für Pfälzische Kirchengeschichte, Speyer am Rhein, 1963.

Benz, Ernst. Ecclesia Spiritualis, Kirchenidee und Geschichtstheologie der Franziskanischen Reformation. Stuttgart: W. Kohlhammer, 1934.

Bercovitch, Sacvan. "The Historiography of Johnson's Wonder-Working Providence." Essex Institute Historical Collections, 104 (1968), 138-157.

_____. Horologicals and Chronometricals: The Rhetoric of the Jeremiads. Literary Monographs, 3. Madison: University of Wisconsin Press, 1970.

_____, ed. Typology and Early American Literature. Amherst: University of Massachusetts Press, 1972.

Berger, H. Calvins Geschichtsauffassung. Studien zur Dogmenschichte und Systematischen Theologie, vol. 6. Zürich: Zwingli Verlag, 1955.

Brumm, Ursula. "Edward Johnson's Wonder-Working Providence and the Puritan Conception of History." Jahrbuch fuer Amerika-Studien, 14-15, 1969-70.

Burr, Nelson R., ed. A Critical Bibliography of Religion in America. 2 vols. Princeton: Princeton University Press, 1961.

Caskey, James Stillman. "Jonathan Edwards' Catalogue." B. D. Thesis, Chicago Theological Seminary, 1931.

370

Cassirer, Ernst. The Philosophy of the Enlightenment. E. T. Princeton:
Princeton University Press, 1951.

Childs, Brevard S. Biblical Theology in Crisis. Philadelphia:
Westminster Press, 1970.

Cohn, Norman. The Pursuit of the Millennium: Revolutionary Millennarians
and Mystical Anarchists of the Middle Ages. Rev. and expanded edition.
New York: Oxford University Press, 1970.

Collingwood, R. G. The Idea of History. Oxford: Clarendon Press, 1946.

Conzelmann, Hans. An Outline of the Theology of the New Testament. 1968,
E.T.; New York: Harper, 1969.

Cragg, G. R. From Puritanism to the Age of Reason. Rpt. Cambridge:
Cambridge University Press, 1966.

Cremin, Lawrence A. American Education: The Colonial Experience 1607-1783.
New York: Harper & Row, 1970.

Curtius, Ernst Robert. European Literature and the Latin Middle Ages.
1948; ppb. New York: Harper Torchbook, 1963.

Daiches, David. Critical Approaches to Literature. London: Longmans, 1956.

Dexter, Franklin B. Biographical Sketches of the Graduates of Yale College,
October 1701-May 1745. New York: Holt and Company, 1885.

Diestel, Ludwig. Geschichte des Alten Testamentes in der Christlichen
Kirche. Jena: Mauke's Verlag, 1867.

Douglas, D. C. English Scholars 1660-1730. London, 1951.

Ebeling, Gerhard. Evangelische Evangelienauslegung, Eine Untersuchung zu
Luthers Hermeneutik. 1942; Rpt. Darmstadt: Wissenschaftliche
Buchgesellschaft 1962.

_____. Kirchengechichte als Geschichte der Auslegung der Heiligen
Schrift: Sammlung Gemeinverständlicher Vorträge aus dem Gebiet der
Theologie-und Religionsgeschichte, 189. Tübingen: Mohr-Siebeck, 1947.

Eames, Wilberforce. Early New England Catechisms, A Bibliographical Account
of Some Catechisms published before the Year 1800. Worcester, Mass.:
Charles Hamilton, 311 Main Street, 1898.

Fain, Haskell. Between Philosophy and History: The Resurrection of
Speculative Philosophy of History within the Analytic Tradition.
Princeton: Princeton University Press, 1970.

Farrar, F. W. History of Interpretation. 1886; rpt. Grand Rapids, Mich.:
Baker Book House, 1961.

Fischer, David Hackett. Historians' Fallacies. New York: Harper Torchbook, 1970.

Freudenthal, J. "Spinoza und die Scholastik." Philosophische Aufsätze, Eduard Zeller zu seinem Fünfzigjährigen Doctor-Jubiläum Gewidmet. Leipzig: 1887, pp. 85-138.

Fueter, Edward. Geschichte der Neueren Historiographie, Handbuch der Mittelalterlichen und Neueren Geschichte. Ed. Dietrich Gerhard. 3rd and enlarged ed. München: Oldenburg, 1936.

Fussner, F. Smith. The Historical Revolution, English Historical Writing and Thought 1580-1640. London: Routledge, 1962.

Gardner, Helen. The Limits of Criticism: Reflections on the Interpretation of Poetry and Scripture. Oxford: Oxford University Press, 1957.

Gassmann, Benno. Ecclesia Reformata, Die Kirche in den Reformierten Bekenntnisschriften. Freiburg: Herder, 1968.

Gay, Peter. The Enlightenment: An Interpretation, The Science of Freedom. New York: Knopf, 1969.

_____. The Loss of Mastery, Puritan Historians in Colonial America. 1966; ppb. New York: Vintage Books, 1968.

Gaustad, E. S. The Great Awakening in New England. 1957; ppb. Chicago: Quadrangle Books, 1968.

Gilsdorf, Aletha, J.B. "The Puritan Apocalypse: New England Eschatology in the Seventeenth Century." Dissertation, Yale, 1965.

Gummere, Richard M. The American Colonial Mind and the Classical Tradition. Cambridge: Harvard University Press, 1963.

Hall, Basil. "Biblical Scholarship: Editions and Commentaries." Cambridge History of the Bible, The West from the Reformation to the Present Day, ed. S. S. Greenslade, 3. Cambridge: Cambridge University Press, 1963. Pp. 38-93.

Hall, David D. The Faithful Shepard, A History of the New England Ministry in the Seventeenth Century. Chapel Hill: University of North Carolina Press, 1972.

Haller, William. Foxe's Book of Martyrs and the Elect Nation. London: J. Cape, 1963.

Handy, Robert T. A Christian America, Protestant Hopes and Historical Realities. New York: Oxford University Press, 1971.

_____. The Protestant Quest for a Christian America 1830-1930. Philadelphia: Fortress Press, 1967.

Hattoway M. "Paradoxes of Solomon: Learning in the English Renaissance." Journal of the History of Ideas, XXIX (1968), 499-630.

Hazard, Paul. The European Mind 1860-1715. 1935; ppb. New York: Meridian Books, 1968.

Headley, J. M. Luther's View of Church History. New Haven: Yale Universit Press, 1963.

Higham, John, et al. History, The Development of Historical Studies in the United States. Englewood Cliffs, N. J.: Prentice-Hall, Inc., 1965

_____. Writing American History, Essays on Modern Scholarship. Bloomington: Indiana University Press, 1970.

Hill, Christopher. Intellectual Origins of the English Revolution. Oxford At the Clarendon Press, 1965.

_____. The World Turned Upside Down, Radical Ideas During the English Revolution. New York: The Viking Press, 1972.

Hoffmann, G. Seinsharmonie und Heilsgeschichte bei Jonathan Edwards. Dissertation, Göttingen, 1956.

Hopkins, Samuel. "Memoirs of the Life, Experience and Character of the Late Rev. Jonathan Edwards." The Works of President Edwards. Rpt. New York: Burt Franklin, 1968. I, 1-119.

Howard, Alan B. "Art and History in Bradford's of Plymouth Plantation." William and Mary Quarterly, 28 (April 1971), 237-266.

_____. "The Web in the Loom: An Introduction to the Puritan Historians of New England." Dissertation, Stanford, 1968.

Iwand, Hans Joachim. Nachgelassene Schriften, ed. Helmut Gollwitzer. München: Kaiser, 1962.

Jantz, Harold. The First Century of New England Verse. 1944; rpt. New York: Russell and Russell, 1962.

Johnson, Thomas H. "Jonathan Edwards' Background of Reading," Publications the Colonial Society of Massachusetts, 28 December 1931, 193-222.

Kaegie, Werner. "Voltaire und der Zerfall des Christlichen Geschichtsbilde Historische Meditationen, I. Zürich: Fretz & Wasmuthy, 1942. Pp. 22 248.

Kamlah, Wilhelm. Apokalypse und Geschichtstheologie, die Mittelalterliche Auslegung der Apokalypse vor Joachin Von Fiore. Historische Studien, 285. Berlin: Verlag Dr. Emil Ebering, 1935.

Keuck, K. "Historia, Geschichte des Wortes und seine Bedeutung." Dissertation, Münster, 1934.

Kittel, Gerhard, Ed. Theological Dictionary of the New Testament. II. Grand Rapids, Mich.: Eerdmans, 1964.

Kraus, Hans Joachim. Geschichte der Historisch-Kritischen Erforschung des Alten Testamentes. Neukirchen: Verlag des Evangelischen Erzienungs- vereins, 1956.

_____. Psalmen. I. Neukirchen: Neukirchener Verlag, 1960.

Kuhn, Thomas S. The Structure of Scientific Revolutions. 2nd ed. International Encyclopaedia of Unified Science, 2. Chicago: University of Chicago Press, 1970.

Levin, David. In Defense of Historical Literature: Essays on American History, Autobiography, Drama, and Fiction. New York: Hill and Wang, 1967.

Levy, F. J. Tudor Historical Thought. San Marino, Calif.: The Huntington Library, 1967.

Lewis, C. S. English Literature in the Sixteenth Century Excluding Drama. Oxford: Clarendon Press, 1954.

Lewis, Charlton and Charles Short. A Latin Dictionary. Oxford: Oxford University Press, 1966.

Lloyd-Jukes, H. A. "Degory Wheare's Contribution to the Study and Teaching of Ecclesiastical History in England in the Seventeenth Century." Studies in Church History, ed. G. J. Cumming. 5. Leiden: E. J. Brill, 1969, 193-203.

Lovejoy, Arthur O. The Great Chain of Being, A Study of the History of an Idea. 1936; ppb. Cambridge: Harvard University Press, 1971.

Manuel, Frank E. Isaac Newton, Historian. Cambridge: Belknap Press, 1963.

Marsden, George M. "Perry Miller's Rehabilitation of the Puritans." Church History, 39 (1970), 91-105.

Martin, James P. The Last Judgment in Protestant Theology from Orthodoxy to Ritschl. Grand Rapids, Mich.: Eerdmans, 1963.

Meinhold, Peter. Geschichte der Kirchlichen Historiographie. I. Freiburg: Verlag Alber, 1967.

Menke-Glückert, Emil. Die Geschichtschreibung der Reformation und Gegenreformation: Bodin und die Begründung der Geschichtsmethodologie durch Bartholomäus Keckermann. Leipzig: J. C. Hinrichs'sche Buchhandlung, 1912.

Miller, Glenn T. "The Rise of Evangelical Calvinism: A Study in Jonathan Edwards and the Puritan Tradition." Dissertation, Union Theological Seminary, New York, 1971.

374

Miller, Perry. Jonathan Edwards. Cleveland: Meridian Books, 1965.

_____. The New England Mind, The Seventeenth Century. 1939, rpt.
Cambridge: Harvard University Press, 1954.

Moltmann, Jürgen. Christoph Pezel (1539-1604) und der Calvinismus in
Bremen. Bremen: 1958.

_____. "Jacob Brocard als Vorläufer der Reich-Gottes-Theologie und
der symbolisch-prophetischen Schriftauslegung des Johann Coccejus."
Zeitschrift für Kirchengeschichte, 71 (1960), No. 1 and 2, 110-129.

_____. Prädestination und Perseveranz, Geschichte und Bedeutung der
reformierten Lehre 'de perseverantia sanctorum.' Neukirchen:
Neukirchener Verlag, 1961.

_____. Theologie der Hoffnung, Untersuchungen zur Begründung und zu
den Konsequenzen einer Christlichen Eschatologie. 6th improved ed.
Munich: Chr. Kaiser, 1965.

Morison, Samuel Eliot. The Founding of Harvard College. Cambridge:
Harvard University Press, 1935.

_____. Harvard College in the Seventeenth Century. 2 vols.
Cambridge: Harvard University Press, 1936.

_____. The Intellectual Life of Colonial New England. 1936; rpt.
Ithaca: Great Seal Books, 1956.

Murdock, Kenneth B. "William Hubbard and the Providential Interpretation
of History." Proceedings of the American Antiquarian Society, 52
(1952), 15-37.

Nicolson, Marjorie Hope. Mountain Gloom and Mountain Glory, The Development
of the Aesthetics of the Infinite. 1959; ppb. New York: The Norton
Library, 1963.

Niebuhr, H. Richard. The Kingdom of God in America. 1937; ppb. New York:
Harper, 1959.

_____. The Social Sources of Denominationalism. 1929; ppb.
Cleveland: Meridian Books, 1957.

Nigg, Walter. Die Kirchengeschichtsschreibung: Grundzüge ihrer historischer
Entwicklung. München: C. H. Beck'sche Verlagsbuchhandlung, 1934.

O'Dea, Thomas F. The Sociology of Religion. Englewood Cliffs: Prentice-
Hall, Inc., 1966.

Ohly, Friedrich. Hohelied - Studien, Grundzüge einer Geschichte der
Hoheliedauslegung des Abendlandes bis um 1200. Wiesbaden: Fritz
Steiner Verlag, 1958.

Oxford English Dictionary, The Compact Edition of the. Oxford: Oxford
    University Press, 1971.

Ozment, Steven E. Mysticism and Dissent, Religious Ideology and Social
    Protest in the Sixteenth Century. New Haven: Yale University
    Press, 1971.

Parker, T.H.L. Calvin's New Testament Commentaries. London: SCM Press,
    1971.

Patrides, C. A. The Phoenix and the Ladder: The Rise and Decline of the
    Christian View of History. Berkeley: University of California
    Press, 1964.

Pettit, Norman. The Heart Prepared, Grace and Conversion in Puritan
    Spiritual Life. New Haven: Yale University Press, 1966.

Pfisterer, Rudolf. Von A bis Z, Quellen zu Fragen um Juden und Christen.
    Gladbeck: Schriftenmissionsverlag, 1971.

Piercy, Josephine K. Studies in Literary Types in Seventeenth Century
    America, 1607-1710. Studies in English, CI. New Haven: Yale
    University Press, 1939.

Preston, Joseph H. "English Ecclesiastical Historians and the Problem of
    Bias." Journal of the History of Ideas, 37 (1971), 203-220.

Preus, Robert. The Inspiration of Scripture, A Study of the Theology of
    the Seventeenth Century Lutheran Dogmaticians. Edinburgh: Oliver
    and Boyd, 1955.

Quistorp, Heinrich. Calvin's Doctrine of the Last Things. E.T. London:
    Lutterworth Press, 1955.

Rad, Gerhard von. Theologie Des Alten Testamentes. II. Munich: Chr.
    Kaiser, 1968.

Randall, John Herman, Jr. The Career of Philosophy. 2 vols. New York:
    Columbia University Press, 1962-1965.

Ratschow, Carl Heinz. "Das Heilshandeln und das Welthandeln Gottes:
    Gedanken zur Lehrgestaltung des Providentia-Glaubens in der evangelischen
    Dogmatik." Neue Zeitschrift fur Systematische Theologie, 1-2 (1959-
    1960), 25-80.

Raven, Charles E. Natural Religion and Christian Theology. I. Cambridge:
    Cambridge University Press, 1953.

_____. John Ray Naturalist, His Life and Works. Cambridge:
    Cambridge University Press, 1942.

Richardson, Cyril C. The Doctrine of the Trinity, A Clarification of What
    It Attempts to Express. Nashville: Abingdon Press, 1958.

Richardson, Cyril C. "The Ontological Trinity, Father and Son."
Religion in Life, 29 (1959-1960), 7-15.

Ritschl, Otto. Dogmengeschichte des Protestantismus. I. Leipzig:
Hinrich, 1908.

_____. "System und Systematische Methode in der Geschichte des
wissenschaftlichen Sprachgebrauches und der Philosophischen
Methodologie." Programm zur Feier des Gedächtnisses des Stifters der
Universität, König Friedrich Wilhelms III am 6. August 1906.
Herausgegeben vom Rektor und Senat der Rheinischen Friedrich-
Wilhelms-Universität. Bonn: Carl Georgi, 1906.

Sailor, Danton B. "Moses and Atomism." Journal of the History of Ideas,
XXV (1964), 3-16.

Schafer, Thomas A. "The Concept of Being in the Thought of Jonathan
Edwards." Dissertation, Duke University, 1951.

Scheible, Heinz. Die Entstehung der Magdeburger Zenturien, Ein Beitrag zur
Geschichte der historiographischen Methode. Schriften des Vereins für
Reformationsgeschichte, No. 183, vol. 72. Gütersloh: Verlagshaus Gerd
Mohn, 1966.

Scholder, Klaus. Ursprünge und Probleme der Bibelkritik im Siebzehnten
Jahrhundert. München: Chr. Kaiser, 1966.

Schöffler, Herbert. Neue Wege zur Englischen Literatur des Ochtzehnten
Jahrhunderts. 2nd ed. Göttingen: Vandenhoeck, 1958.

Schrenk, Gottlob. Gottesreich und Bund im Älteren Protestantismus vornehmlich bei Johannes Coccejus. 1923; rpt. Darmstadt: Wissenschaftliche
Buchgesellschaft, 1967.

Schweitzer, Albert. Geschichte der Leben-Jesu-Forschung. 1913; rpt.
Tübingen: Mohr-Siebeck, 1951.

Schweizer, Alexander. Die Glaubenslehre der Evangelisch-Reformierten
Kirche. I. Zürich: Orell, Füssli und Comp., 1844.

Shea, Daniel B., Jr. Spiritual Autobiography in Early America. Princeton:
Princeton University Press, 1968.

Shipton, Clifford K. New England Life in the Eighteenth Century.
Cambridge: Belknap Press, 1963.

_____. "Thomas Prince." Sibley's Harvard Graduates, V, 1701-1712.
Boston: Massachusetts Historical Society, 1937, 341-368.

Smith, H. Shelton, Robert T. Handy, and Lefferts A. Loetscher. American
Christianity: An Historical Interpretation with Representative
Documents. 2 vols. New York: Scribner's, 1960-1963.

Staedtke, Joachim. _Die Theologie des jungen Bullinger_. Zürich: Zwingli Verlag, 1962.

Sypher, G. Wylie. "Similarities between the Scientific and the Historical Revolutions at the End of the Renaissance." _Journal of the History of Ideas_, 26 (1965), 353-368.

Tholuck, A. _Das akademische Leben des Siebzehnten Jahrhunderts mit besonderer Beziehung auf die protestantisch-theologischen Fakultäten Deutschlands_. Halle: Eduard Anton, 1853.

Thomas, Keith. _Religion and the Decline of Magic_. New York: Scribner's, 1971.

Thompson, James Westfall. _A History of Historical Writing_. 2 vols. New York: Macmillan, 1942.

Tichi, Cecelia. "The Art of the Lord's Remembrancers: A Study of New England Puritan History." Dissertation, University of California (Davis), 1971.

_____. "Spiritual Biography and the Lord's Remembrancers." _William and Mary Quarterly_, 28 (1971), 64-85.

Tillich, Paul. _Perspectives on Nineteenth and Twentieth Century Protestant Theology_, ed. Carl Braaten. New York: Harper, 1967.

Toon, Peter, ed. _Puritans, the Millennium, and the Future of Israel: Puritan Eschatology 1600-1660_. Cambridge: James Clarke & Co., 1970.

Trinterud, L. J. _The Forming of an American Tradition, A Re-Examination of Colonial Presbyterianism_. Philadelphia: Westminster Press, 1949.

Tassel, David D. van. _Recording America's Past, An Interpretation of the Development of Historical Studies in America, 1607-1887_. Chicago: University of Chicago Press, 1960.

Wallace, Anthony F.C. _Religion: An Anthropological View_. New York: Random House, 1966.

Weber, Max. _The Protestant Ethic and the Rise of Capitalism_. E. T. New York: Scribner's, 1958.

_____. _Sociology of Religion_. Boston: Beacon Press, 1964.

Weber, Otto. _Grundlagen der Dogmatik_. II. Neukirchen: Erziehungsverein, 1959.

Weiser, Artur. _The Psalms, A Commentary_. Philadelphia: Westminster Press, 1962.

Westermann, Claus. _Beginning and End in the Bible_, ed. John Reumann. Facet Books, Biblical Series, 31. Philadelphia: Fortress Press, 1972.

Westermann, Claus. "Creation and History in the Old Testament." The Gospel and Human Destiny, ed. Vilmos Vajta. Minneapolis: Augsburg Publishing House, 1971. Pp. 11-38.

Willey, Basil. The Seventeenth Century Background. 1934; ppb. London: Penguin Books, 1962.

Williams, George Huntston. "Translated Study: The Puritans' Conception of Their First University in New England, 1636." Archiv fuer Reformationsgeschichte, 57 (1966), 152-180.

Williams, Glanmor. Reformation View of Church History. Ecumenical Studies in History. II. Richmond, Va.: Knox Press, 1970.

Wolff, H. H. "Die Einheit des Bundes; das Verhältnis von Altem und Neuem Testament bei Calvin." Dissertation, Halle, 1942.

Wolfson, Harry Austryn. The Philosophy of the Church Fathers. Vol. 1. 3rd ed., rev. Cambridge: Harvard University Press, 1970.

Wormald, B.H.G. Clarendon: Politics, History and Religion 1640-1660. Cambridge: At the University Press, 1951.

Zimmerli, Walther. "Verheissung und Erfüllung." Evangelische Theologie, 12 (1952-53), 34-59.

ABSTRACT

THE PRISM OF SCRIPTURES: STUDIES ON HISTORY AND HISTORICITY

IN THE WORK OF JONATHAN EDWARDS

K. Dieterich Pfisterer

This dissertation explores Edwards' understanding of history as a subject in its own right. In a series of studies we shall describe the background of this understanding of history, demonstrate and define the thesis of the argument for this dissertation, and move from there to a proof of the thesis. In conclusion we shall demonstrate the importance of the thesis e contrario through the explication of an argument in which it plays only a minor role.

Chapter I will, through an interpretation of Francis Bacon, delineate the wide spectrum of historiographical possibilities which were available in the general climate of the seventeenth century. Chapter II will then narrow down the focus of this survey to a description of New England as Edwards' most immediate background and to the presentation of illustrative case studies of the Massachusetts historians William Hubbard and Edward Johnson. In Bacon's classification of the variety of historical facts and the ways of their interpretation, Scripture appears as one historiographical mode and is defined in terms of a concept of prophecy which is said to pay attention to the unity of history as well as to those unique exegetical details which are necessary facts for the shaping of such a view of unity. Hubbard and Johnson as practicing historians help to exemplify the poly-historic, providential, and prophetic trends of the historiography of the time. We shall see that in Johnson the providential interpretation of history receives a consistent prophetic orientation which makes possible a better appreciation of the shades and subtleties of providence itself and which leads us to a formulation and pursuit of this comprehensive historiographical tradition in terms of the interpretative thesis of Scripture and exegesis.

Scripture is the identifiable focus for a significant and flexible tradition in historiography. For this dissertation, Scripture and exegesis will be as important as the configuration of ideas which A. O. Lovejoy comprehended under the term "chain of being" and which he has traced through the history of the mind of the West. Both interpretative theses, the chain of being and Scripture, serve as frames of reference within which the problematic relation between the one and the many, between unity and variety is reviewed and resolved. Scripture in particular claims to be both the one and the many, not only in terms of a simple juxtaposition, but in terms of a synthesis in which the vision and variety of history were fused while each retained its own focus. Scripture is, as it were, a prism, for Scripture as a literary document and the prism as a technological apparatus display a structure which makes possible a substantial coexistence of simplicity and variety. According to Jonathan Edwards, holiness in Scripture is often compared to light and comprehends the moral virtues. In nature itself "there is a variety of light. One and the same white light, though it seems to be an exceeding simple thing, yet contains a very great variety of rays, all of so many different lovely appearance."

This particular function of Scripture has been overlooked for the crucial time of transition and modernization in the seventeenth century because of a scholarly neglect and ignorance of the hermeneutics of the exegetical process. The analysis of Thomas Shepard's interpretation of

Scripture in Chapter III is designed to illustrate the importance of a detailed exegesis for a comprehensive view of history. Edwards himself used the idea if not the term *prism*. In one of his early experiments he demonstrated that if a piece of glass was held against the sun at a particular angle, then its light would be refracted into the many diverse colors of the rainbow. Chapter IV will utilize Thomas S. Kuhn's concept of the paradigm in order to define the chronology of Scripture and the coherence of Scripture in Edwards in such a way that Scripture appears at that angle where through its prismatic structure the coherence of vision and variety becomes perceptible in a view of history. Chapter V will focus on Edwards as the historian of the revival and prove how on the historiographical level Scripture as a prism integrates the uses of the past and suggests a historical model of community. Chapter VI will concentrate on Edwards' prolegomena to a historical system of theology and prove that on the metaphysical level Scripture as a prism leads to a theory of communication which conceptualizes the vision and variety of history ontologically as well as historically. Chapter VII will show in an interpretation

f Shaftesbury's Characteristics that the elimination of Scripture leads to estriction of vision and variety which in turn results in an abandonment rld of history.